Intuition
in Judgment and Decision Making

Intuition
in Judgment and Decision Making

Edited by

Henning Plessner
Cornelia Betsch • Tilmann Betsch

LEA Lawrence Erlbaum Associates
Taylor & Francis Group

New York London

Lawrence Erlbaum Associates
Taylor & Francis Group
270 Madison Avenue
New York, NY 10016

Lawrence Erlbaum Associates
Taylor & Francis Group
2 Park Square
Milton Park, Abingdon
Oxon OX14 4RN

© 2008 by Taylor & Francis Group, LLC
Lawrence Erlbaum Associates is an imprint of Taylor & Francis Group, an Informa business

Printed in the United States of America on acid-free paper
10 9 8 7 6 5 4 3 2 1

International Standard Book Number-13: 978-0-8058-5741-2 (Hardcover)

No part of this book may be reprinted, reproduced, transmitted, or utilized in any form by any electronic, mechanical, or other means, now known or hereafter invented, including photocopying, microfilming, and recording, or in any information storage or retrieval system, without written permission from the publishers.

Trademark Notice: Product or corporate names may be trademarks or registered trademarks, and are used only for identification and explanation without intent to infringe.

Library of Congress Cataloging-in-Publication Data

Intuition in judgment and decision making / edited by Henning Plessner, Cornelia Betsch, Tilmann Betsch.
   p. cm.
  Includes bibliographical references and index.
  ISBN-13: 798-0-8058-5741-2 (cloth : alk. paper)
  1. Intuition. 2. Judgment. 3. Decision making. I. Plessner, Henning. II. Betsch, Cornelia. III. Betsch, Tilmann.

BF315.5.I46 2007
153.4'4--dc22
                                  2006033206

Visit the Taylor & Francis Web site at
http://www.taylorandfrancis.com

and the LEA and Routledge Web site at
http://www.routledge.com

Contents

Preface   vii
List of Contributors   xvii

I THE NATURE OF INTUITION

1 The Nature of Intuition and Its Neglect in Research on Judgment and Decision Making   3
Tilmann Betsch

2 Intuition from the Perspective of Cognitive-Experiential Self-Theory   23
Seymour Epstein

3 Variants of Judgment and Decision Making: The Perspective of the Reflective-Impulsive Model   39
Roland Deutsch and Fritz Strack

4 Cue by Hypothesis Interactions in Descriptive Modeling of Unconscious Use of Multiple Intuitive Judgment Strategies   55
Robert M. Hamm

5 Can Neuroscience Tell a Story About Intuition?   71
Kirsten G. Volz and D. Yves von Cramon

II LEARNING AND INTUITION

6 On the Learning of Intuition   91
Robin M. Hogarth

7 Automatic Online Formation of Implicit Attitudes Toward Politicians as a Basis for Intuitive Voting Behavior   107
Henning Plessner, Tilmann Betsch, Elke Schallies, and Christiane Schwieren

8 Implicit Learning as a Means to Intuitive Decision Making in Sports   119
Markus Raab and Joseph G. Johnson

9	Base Rates: How to Make the Intuitive Mind Appreciate or Neglect Them	135
	Ido Erev, Dvorit Shimonowitch, Amos Schurr, and Ralph Hertwig	
10	Implications and Ramifications of a Sample-Size Approach to Intuition	149
	Klaus Fiedler and Yaakov Kareev	

III EMOTION AND INTUITION

11	Emotion, Motivation, and Decision Making: A Feeling-Is-for-Doing Approach	173
	Marcel Zeelenberg, Rob Nelissen, and Rik Pieters	
12	From Intuition to Analysis: Making Decisions with Your Head, Your Heart, or by the Book	191
	Elke U. Weber and Patricia G. Lindemann	
13	In the Forest of Value: Why Moral Intuitions Are Different from Other Kinds	209
	Jonathan Haidt and Selin Kesebir	
14	Chronic Preferences for Intuition and Deliberation in Decision Making: Lessons Learned About Intuition from an Individual Differences Approach	231
	Cornelia Betsch	

IV THE ASSETS AND DEFICITS OF INTUITION

15	The Benefits of Intuition	251
	Henning Plessner and Sabine Czenna	
16	Intuitive and Deliberate Strategies in Frequency Estimation	267
	Susanne Haberstroh	
17	The Sampling Trap of Intuitive Judgments	283
	Christian Unkelbach and Henning Plessner	
18	The Use and Disruption of Familiarity in Intuitive Judgments	295
	Steve Catty and Jamin Halberstadt	
19	Does Intuition Beat Fast and Frugal Heuristics? A Systematic Empirical Analysis	309
	Andreas Glöckner	

Index	327

Preface

An obvious experience of everyday life is that people frequently make judgments and decisions without explicit use of all the relevant information that is available from the environment and from their memory. Moreover, even if people are aware of all the particular details, they do not necessarily analyze every piece of information on a deeper level and weigh it in an explicit way before making decisions. On the contrary, people often go with the very first response that enters their mind, which is usually an immediate feeling, a spontaneous idea, or a sudden appearance of "I know what to do" or "this is the best choice." This typically happens without any apparent effort, and if asked, people cannot say why they came up with a certain response. Nevertheless, people tend to trust their intuitions so frequently simply because they are quite successful with them, and the intuitions seem to "satisfice" their needs in many situations (Simon, 1955). In addition, there is plenty of evidence that people's intuitions can outperform deliberate thinking processes under specific conditions (e.g., Wilson, 2002).

Gladwell (2005) described many corresponding examples of intuition in his bestselling popular science book *Blink: The Power of Thinking Without Thinking*. The great attention that this book received, not only in the general public and the media but also in the social and behavioral sciences, could lead to the impression that the observation of surprising human performances in the absence of complex deliberation is something that has been overlooked by psychologists for a long time. However, this impression would clearly be wrong. The study of human intuition is as least as old as psychology is an empirical science. For example, Gestalt psychologists of the early 20th century were already extensively studying the phenomenon of (sudden) insight in problem solving that shares many properties with the concept of intuition. This research gave many impulses for the understanding of related phenomena, and its influence on the study of intuition still continues today (e.g., Bastick, 1982; Bowers, Regehr, Balthazard, & Parker, 1990).

In fact, there is an almost endless list of fascinating phenomena and concepts that psychologists have brought into relation with a general concept of intuition as a distinct mental device. Among others, the list includes unconscious perceptions, "blindsight," pattern recognition, instinct, automatic processing, experiential knowing, tacit knowledge, religious experiences, emotional intelligence, nonverbal communication, clinical diagnoses, "thin slices of behavior," spontaneous trait inferences, the "mere exposure" effect, the primacy of affect, "thinking too much," priming, feelings as information, implicit attitudes, expertise, creativity, and the "sixth sense."

One can find excellent overviews of these topics in terms of intuition or the unconscious by Bastick (1982), Davis-Floyd and Arvidson (1992) Hogarth (2001), Myers (2002), and Wilson (2002), respectively. However, conceptualizing intuition on the basis of such a wide array of different phenomena leads to a certain fuzziness in the use of the term intuition. Accordingly, psychological definitions of intuition are typically clearer about what intuition "is not" and which features of intuition are absent rather than about what intuition "is." For example, Hogarth (2001) defined intuitions as responses that "are reached with little apparent effort and typically without conscious awareness. They involve little or no conscious deliberation" (p. 14). Of course, definitions like Hogarth's leave room for many different and contradictory assumptions about the nature of intuitive processes. Alternatively, feature lists have been proposed that include attributes such as associative, holistic, automatic, fast, and undemanding of cognitive capacities (e.g., Epstein, 1973; Hammond, Hamm, Grassia, & Pearson, 1987). However, these approaches typically leave open how many attributes must be present, necessary, and sufficient to recognize intuitive processes. The literature on human judgment and decision making, which is the domain of this book, have circumvented this problem for a long time by linking intuition almost exclusively to some well-defined, simplifying judgment heuristics.

INTUITION AS HEURISTIC PROCESSING

The view of intuition in judgment and decision making has been shaped markedly by the seminal heuristics and biases approach of Tversky and Kahneman (for overviews, see Gilovich, Griffin, & Kahneman, 2002; Kahneman, Slovic, & Tversky, 1982). According to this approach, when dealing with uncertainty, people rely on heuristics that typically yield accurate judgments but also give rise to systematic errors. The most prominent are the all purpose heuristics availability, representativeness, and anchoring and adjustment. Typically, they can be described as the use of indirect methods to predict the criterion to be judged. For example, the ease by which instances come to mind may be used as a proxy variable to arrive at judgments about quantity. As such, heuristic-based intuitions are constructed on the spot and thus are prone to reflect the properties of the judgment context, which can lead in the wrong direction under certain circumstances.

Kahneman (2003) clearly identified the application of judgmental heuristics with a mental system that shares properties of the concept intuition (System 1; Stanovich & West, 2000) as opposed to a deliberately controlled system (System 2). Heuristic/intuitive judgments were seen in Tversky and Kahneman's (Kahneman, 2003) view as occupying a position between automatic operations of perception and deliberate operations or reasoning. In principle, this view of intuitions as the products of heuristic processing is shared by alternative approaches to the use of mental shortcuts in judgment and decision making such as the "adaptive or heuristic toolbox program" (Gigerenzer & Selten, 2001; Gigerenzer, Todd, & the ABC Research Group, 1999) and the "adaptive decision-making approach" (Payne, Bettman, & Johnson, 1993).

THE LEARNING PERSPECTIVE ON INTUITION

In recent years, another view has been gaining influence in the field of judgment and decision making. We refer to this view as the "learning perspective" (e.g., Hogarth, 2001). The learning perspective builds on work that is primarily hosted in the literature on animal cognition, conditioning, and neuropsychology. According to the learning perspective, intuition relies on mental representations that reflect the entire stream of prior experiences (e.g., Betsch, Plessner, & Schallies, 2004). As such, intuition is holistic and can reveal a remarkable degree of accuracy if the learning context has provided representative and valid feedback. Based on direct experience, organisms establish mental representations of time, space, number, and value. Intuition capitalizes on these stored representations and often provides direct access to the criterion to be judged. It is not the result of inference processes or other constructive methods, but instead, intuition is reproductive; it primarily reflects experience rather than properties of the judgment context. Accordingly, this view heavily emphasizes the significance of prior experiences and knowledge for the understanding of human decision making and behavior (e.g., Betsch & Haberstroh, 2005; Epstein, 1991; Klein, 1999).

This view of intuition beyond heuristic processing has been accompanied by an increasing acknowledgment of the role of affect and emotions in judgment and decision making. Although the notion of the importance of feelings for human thinking processes can be traced back, for example, to one of the founders of psychology as an empirical enterprise, Wundt (1907), it is only recently that affect and emotions have been firmly incorporated into psychological models of judgment and decision making (e.g., Loewenstein, Weber, Hsee, & Welch, 2001; Slovic, Finucane, Peters, & McGregor, 2002; Zeelenberg & Pieters, 2006). At least since this development took place, the assumption that intuition is closely related to affect and emotion (Epstein, 1991, 1994) appears to be self-evident. Accordingly, the learning perspective on intuition in judgment and decision making aims at a strong link to the research on the interplay of cognition and emotion.

THE PURPOSE OF THIS BOOK

A main goal of our edited book is to bring the learning perspective into the discussion about intuition in judgment and decision making. In this book, we gather recent work on intuitive decision making that goes beyond the current dominant heuristic processing perspective. However, that does not mean that the authors in the book strictly oppose this perspective. On the contrary, we hope that the unique perspective of our book will help to tie together these different conceptualizations of intuition and develop an integrative approach to the psychological understanding of intuition in judgment and decision making. Accordingly, some of the chapters reflect prior research from the heuristic processing perspective in the new light of the learning perspective. In sum, the authors in the book provide a representative overview of what is currently known about intuition in judgment and decision making. The authors provide the latest theoretical developments, integrative frameworks, and state-of-the art reviews of research in the laboratory and in the field. Moreover, the authors of some chapters deal with applied topics. Therefore, this book is aimed not only at the interest of students and researchers from psychology but also at scholars from neighboring social and behavioral sciences such as economy, sociology, political sciences, and neurosciences.

OVERVIEW OF THE CHAPTERS

The volume consists of four parts. In the first part, the authors give an overview of theoretical frameworks and models of judgment and decision making that differentiate between an intuitive and an analytic thinking mode. The authors show how these models can explain and predict various aspects of intuitive decision making and also address some problems that occur with this distinction. In the second part of the volume, the authors focus on various aspects of learning as a basis for intuitive judgment and decision making. Among others, they aim at the determination of learning environments that support the development of "good" intuitions. In Part 3, the authors explore the role of affect and emotions in intuitive judgments and decisions. Finally, in the fourth part, the authors provide some answers to the questions of how accurate intuitive judgments and decisions are and under which circumstances they can outperform deliberate thinking processes.

Part I: The Nature of Intuition

T. Betsch (chap. 1, this volume) provides an extended introduction to the topic of this volume. Accordingly, he presents an overview of the study of intuition in the research of judgment and decision making. Moreover, he defines the concept of intuition as a thinking process of which the input is mostly provided by knowledge that has been acquired automatically, and the output is a feeling that can serve as a basis for judgments and decisions. T. Betsch presents empirical evidence from classical and recent work in this area that substantiates the basic claims of this approach.

Epstein (chap. 2, this volume) provides an up-to-date outline of his cognitive-experiential self-theory (CEST) on the background of the concept intuition. This theory postulated two information-processing systems long before it became usual to do so, for example, in social psychology. CEST differentiates between the "experiential system," which is an automatic learning system, and the "rational system," which is an inferential logical system. According to Epstein, intuition can be considered as the operation of the experiential system.

Deutsch and Strack (chap. 3, this volume) discuss their reflective impulsive model of social behavior in relation to the concept of intuition. They suggest that heuristic judgments are cut from the same cognitive cloth as systematic ones in that they both rely on syllogistic inferences and are, therefore, generated by the reflective system. Intuitive judgments, on the other hand, are shortcuts that use noetic, experiential, or behavioral information that is provided by mechanisms of the impulsive system.

Hamm (chap. 4, this volume) points to theoretical and methodological problems that arise with the assumption of multiple intuitive processes that can vary from person to person, from developmental stage to developmental stage, or from instance to instance. He offers a solution that uses a familiar but slightly modified regression analysis concept that allows for the observation of whether a judgment was made with one or another judgment strategy.

Volz and von Cramon (chap. 5, this volume) review literature on the investigation of neural correlates of intuitive processes. Among others, they report that empirical evidence for a functional distinction between intuitive and deliberate processes has still been weak and contradictory in previous imaging studies. Volz and von Cramon conclude that neurobiological-oriented research on intuition is just at the beginning and discuss possible future directions.

Part II: Learning and Intuition

A basic proposal in this book is that intuition is based on a learning mechanism. Hogarth (chap. 6, this volume) provides an overview of the influence of learning on various tasks of intuitive judgment and decision making. Among others, he discusses the rules by which people acquire their "cultural capital" or the inventory of intuitions that guide behavior. On the basis of this learning approach, Hogarth describes how the structure of the environment affects intuitions and draws implications for understanding what people can do to improve the quality of their intuitive judgments.

Plessner, Betsch, Schallies, and Schwieren (chap. 7, this volume) provide a corresponding empirical example of how intuitive preferences can be acquired in an automatic fashion. In two experiments, they demonstrate that people unintentionally acquire knowledge about (fictitious) politicians that can serve as a well-informed basis for intuitive voting behavior.

Raab and Johnson (chap. 8, this volume) focus on implicit learning as a central means to intuitive decision making in sports, which is a central thinking mode in fast-paced sports such as ball games. Implicit learning results in knowledge of situation–action relations that cannot be verbalized. Raab and Johnson discuss the benefits of intuitive versus deliberative decision making in sports by means of implicit or explicit learning strategies.

Erev, Shimonowitch, Schurr, and Hertwig (chap. 9, this volume) provide an explanation for contradictory findings concerning the sensitivity to base rates in classical work on statistical intuitions (base rate neglect) and in research on visual cognition (high sensitivity to base rates). They suggest that this apparent inconsistency can be understood by an analysis of the social environment in which people act. For example, the mere presentation of response categories can lead to an erroneous use of them. Erev et al. report three studies that support their assumptions.

Fiedler and Kareev (chap. 10, this volume) present a distinct learning approach to intuition whereby intuition is defined on the basis of sample size; that is, judgments and decisions are defined as intuitive to the extent that they rest on small samples. This approach is elaborated on in the theoretical context of a three-dimensional learning environment. With this approach, Fiedler and Kareev are able to describe several antecedents, consequences, and concomitants of intuition depending on the valence of information (positive vs. negative), the distance of decision outcomes (distant vs. proximal), and the decision criterion (lenient vs. conservative).

Part III: Emotion and Intuition

In this book, the authors' concept of intuition is, as outlined before, strongly associated with the role of feelings and emotions in judgment and decision making. Zeelenberg, Nelissen, and Pieters (chap. 11, this volume) present an overview of emotional processes that play a role during decision processes and delineate how emotions may operate in an intuitive manner. According to Zeelenberg et al.'s motivational feeling-is-for-doing approach, emotions can be understood as programs for intuitive decision making, imposing on the decision maker inclinations for action that most adequately serve current strivings.

Weber and Lindemann (chap. 12, this volume) explore the relation between qualitatively different decision modes that have been identified by behavioral decision researchers and affect-based versus calculation-based decision making. Weber and Lindemann present our studies that suggest that people are well aware of possessing a repertoire of decision modes ranging from quick intuitive responses to the effortful calculation of relative costs and benefits. Weber and Lindemann's studies also claim that situational characteristics and the needs and motives of the decision maker combine to determine the implicit choice of one or more of these modes.

Haidt and Kesebir (chap. 13, this volume) argue that moral judgments are mostly based on affect-based intuitive responses. Moreover, they suggest that moral intuitions result from a kind of social-perceptual system that allows people to see and feel a class of anthropocentric facts. Haidt and Kesebir discuss several consequences that follow from this unconventional approach.

C. Betsch (chap. 14, this volume) introduces a newly developed measure, the Preference for Intuition and Deliberation Scale (C. Betsch, 2004), that assesses individual preferences to base decisions on gut feelings or affect and also assesses preferences for thoughtful, reflective decisions. C. Betsch gives several empirical examples that demonstrate how the consideration of individual preferences can contribute to people's understanding of the role of intuition in judgment and decision making.

Part IV: The Assets and Deficits of Intuition

A great deal of interest in the concept of intuition in judgment and decision makings stems from the observation that intuitions can be surprisingly accurate. Plessner and Czenna (chap. 15, this volume) review empirical work that directly contrasts judgments and decisions that were made in an intuitive mode with those that were made in a deliberate fashion. However, there is no consistent finding of a superiority of one mode over the other. In the background of this review, Plessner and Czenna develop a theoretical model that allows for the determination of situations in which intuitions can outperform deliberate thinking. They present some recent results that support this model.

Haberstroh (chap. 16, this volume) investigates the accuracy of intuitions in the domain of frequency estimations. She suggests that spontaneous judgments are based on an automatic counting of instances that lead to relative accuracy. On the other hand, when people think carefully about their judgment, they consider additional information, for example, the availability of exemplars that can lead to biased judgments.

Unkelbach and Plessner (chap. 17, this volume) explore a deficit of intuitive judgments and decisions, that is, people's apparent insensitivity to sampling constraints. According to this perspective, intuitive judgments are impressively accurate in relation to the sample of information on which they are based. However, people are unaware of the constraints that are inherent in samples of everyday observations. This leads to a direct transfer of sampling biases into erroneous judgments and decisions. Unkelbach and Plessner discuss some ideas about how to deal with the apparent lack of awareness of sampling constraints in intuitive judgments.

Catty and Halberstadt (chap. 18, this volume) argue that reasoning before making a decision can disrupt the use of subjective feeling states such as the familiarity of an object. This can then lead to an overemphasis on seemingly important but ultimately irrelevant or ineffectual information. Catty and Halberstadt present two studies that together provide both a basis of intuitive reasoning and subjective familiarity as a mechanism by which intuition, as the antithesis of reasoning analysis, could be effective.

Glöckner (chap. 19) directly addresses the question of whether people apply simple heuristics or more complex processes based on the automatic information integration of multiple sources of information under conditions that promote intuitive judgment strategies. He reviews six studies that provide evidence for people's preferred use of a so-called consistency maximizing strategy, which is based on processes of parallel constraint satisfaction. This strategy allows for the immediate integration of multiple relevant cues and thus can be partly responsible for the many findings of surprising human performances under conditions of intuitive judgment and decision making.

ACKNOWLEDGMENTS

The book is partly based on the contributions to a conference on "Intuition in Judgment and Decision Making" held at the University of Heidelberg, Germany, in 2004. The conference was supported by a grant to Henning Plessner, Cornelia Betsch, and Tilmann Betsch from the German Science Foundation (Deutsche Forschungsgemeinschaft) via the Sonderforschungsbereich 504 (TP A10). We thank Barbara Kump for her help with preparing the book manuscript.

REFERENCES

Bastick, T. (1982). *Intuition: How we think and act*. New York: Wiley.
Betsch, C. (2004). Präferenz für Intuition und Deliberation. Inventar zur Erfassung von affekt- und kognitionsbasiertem Entscheiden [Preference for Intuition and Deliberation (PID): An Inventory for Assessing Affect- and Cognition-Based Decision-Making]. *Zeitschrift für Differentielle und Diagnostische Psychologie*, 25, 179–197.
Betsch, T., & Haberstroh, S. (Eds.). (2005). *The routines of decision making*. Mahwah, NJ: Lawrence Erlbaum Associates, Inc.
Betsch, T., Plessner, H., & Schallies, E. (2004). The value-account model of attitude formation. In G. R. Maio & G. Haddock (Eds.), *Contemporary perspectives on the psychology of attitudes* (pp. 252–273). Hove, England: Psychology Press.
Bowers, K. S., Regehr, G., Balthazard, C., & Parker, K. (1990). Intuition in the context of discovery. *Cognitive Psychology*, 22, 72–110.
Davis-Floyd, R., & Arvidson, P. S. (Eds.) (1997) *Intuition: The inside story*. New York: Routledge.
Epstein, S. (1973). The self-concept revisited or a theory of a theory. *American Psychologist*, 28, 404–416.
Epstein, S. (1991). Cognitive-experiental self-theory: An integrative theory of personality. In R. Curtis (Ed.), *The relational self: Convergences in psychoanalysis and social psychology* (pp. 111–137). New York: Guilford.
Epstein, S. (1994). Integration of the cognitive and the psychodynamic unconscious. *American Psychologist*, 49, 709–724.
Gigerenzer, G., & Selten, R. (Eds.). (2001). *Bounded rationality: The adaptive toolbox*. Cambridge, MA: MIT Press.
Gigerenzer, G., Todd, P. M., & the ABC Research Group. (Eds.). (1999). *Simple heuristics that make us smart*. New York: Oxford University Press.
Gilovich, T., Griffin, D., & Kahneman, D. (Eds.). (2002). *Heuristics and biases: The psychology of intuitive judgment*. New York: Cambridge University Press.
Gladwell, M. (2005). *Blink: The power of thinking without thinking*. New York: Little Brown.
Hammond, K. R., Hamm, R. M., Grassia, J., & Pearson, T. (1987). Direct comparison of the efficacy of intuitive and analytical cognition in expert judgment. *IEEE Transactions on Systems, Man, and Cybernetics*, 17, 753–770.
Hogarth, R. (2001). *Educating intuition*. Chicago: The University of Chicago Press.
Kahneman, D. (2003). Maps of bounded rationality: Psychology for behavioral economics. *American Economic Review*, 93, 1449–1475.
Kahneman, D., Slovic, P., & Tversky, A. (Eds.). (1982). *Judgment under uncertainty: Heuristics and biases*. Cambridge, England: Cambridge University Press.
Klein, G. (1999). *Sources of power. How people make decisions*. Cambridge, MA: MIT press.
Loewenstein, G., Weber, E., Hsee, C. K., & Welch, E. (2001). Risk as feelings. *Psychological Bulletin*, 127, 267–286.
Myers, D. G. (2002). *Intuition—its powers and perils*. New Haven, CT: Yale University Press.
Payne, J. W., Bettman, J. R., & Johnson, E. J. (1993). *The adaptive decision maker*. Cambridge, England: Cambridge University Press.
Simon, H. A. (1955). A behavioral model of rational choice. *Quarterly Journal of Economics*, 69, 99–118.
Slovic, P., Finucane, M., Peters, E., & McGregor, D. G. (2002). The affect heuristic. In T. Gilovich, D. Griffin, & D. Kahneman (Eds.), *Heuristics and biases: The psychology of intuitive judgment* (pp. 397–420). New York: Cambridge University Press.

Stanovich, K. E., & West, R. F. (2000). Individual differences in reasoning: Implications for the rationality debate. *Behavioral and Brain Sciences, 23*, 645–665.

Wilson, T. D. (2002). *Strangers to ourselves: Discovering the adaptive unconscious.* Cambridge, MA: Harvard University Press.

Wundt, W. (1907). *Outlines of psychology.* Leipzig, Germany: Wilhelm Engelmann.

Zeelenberg, M., & Pieters, R. (2006). Feeling is for doing: A pragmatic approach to the study of emotions in economic behavior. In D. De Cremer, M. Zeelenberg, & K. Murnighan (Eds.), *Social psychology and economics* (pp. 117–137). Mahwah, NJ: Lawrence Erlbaum Associates, Inc.

List of Contributors

Cornelia Betsch
Psychological Institute
University of Heidelberg
Heidelberg, Germany

Tilmann Betsch
Department of Psychology
University of Erfurt
Erfurt, Germany

Steve Catty
Department of Psychology
University of Otago
Dunedin, New Zealand

D. Yves von Cramon
Max Planck Institute for Human
  Cognitive and Brain Sciences
Leipzig, Germany

Sabine Czenna
Psychological Institute
University of Heidelberg
Heidelberg, Germany

Roland Deutsch
Lehrstuhl für Psychologie II
University of Würzburg
Würzburg, Germany

Seymour Epstein
Professor Emeritus
Psychology Department
University of Massachusetts
Amherst, MA, USA

Ido Erev
Max Wertheimer Minerva Center for
  Cognitive Processes
Faculty of Industrial Engineering
  and Management
Israel Institute of Technology
Haifa, Israel

Klaus Fiedler
Psychological Institute
University of Heidelberg
Heidelberg, Germany

Andreas Gloeckner
Max Planck Institute for Research
  on Collective Goods
Bonn, Germany

Susanne Haberstroh
Institute for Psychology
University of Osnabrück
Osnabrück, Germany

Jonathan Haidt
Department of Psychology
University of Virginia
Charlottesville, VA, USA

Jamin Halberstadt
Department of Psychology
University of Otago
Dunedin, New Zealand

Robert M. Hamm
Clinical Decision Making Program
Department of Family and Preventive
  Medicine
University of Oklahoma Health
  Sciences Center
Oklahoma City, OK, USA

Ralph Hertwig
Institute for Psychology
University of Basel
Basel, Switzerland

Robin M. Hogarth
Department of Economics and
  Business
University Pompeu Fabra
Barcelona, Spain

Joseph G. Johnson
Department of Psychology
Division of Brain and Cognitive
  Science
Miami University
Oxford, OH, USA

Yaakov Kareev
School of Education, Center of
  Rationality
The Hebrew University of Jerusalem
Giv'at Ram
Jerusalem, Israel

Selin Kesebir
Department of Psychology
University of Virginia
Charlottesville, VA, USA

Patricia G. Lindemann
Department of Psychology
Columbia University
New York, NY, USA

Rob Nelissen
Faculty of Social and Behavioural
  Sciences
Tilburg University
Tilburg, The Netherlands

Rik Pieters
Faculty of Economics and Business
  Administration
Tilburg University
Tilburg, The Netherlands

Henning Plessner
Psychological Institute
University of Heidelberg
Heidelberg, Germany

Markus Raab
Institute for Movement Sciences
  and Sport
University of Flensburg
Flensburg, Germany

Elke Schallies
Department of Psychiatry
University of Heidelberg
Heidelberg, Germany

Amos Schurr
Max Wertheimer Minerva Center for
  Cognitive Processes
Faculty of Industrial Engineering
  and Management
Israel Institute of Technology
Haifa, Israel

Christiane Schwieren
Department of Economics and
  Business
University Pompeu Fabra
Barcelona, Spain

Dvorit Shimonowitch
Max Wertheimer Minerva Center for
 Cognitive Processes
Faculty of Industrial Engineering and
 Management
Israel Institute of Technology
Haifa, Israel

Fritz Strack
Lehrstuhl für Psychologie II
University of Würzburg
Würzburg, Germany

Kirsten G. Volz
Max Planck Institute for Human
 Cognitive and Brain Sciences
Leipzig, Germany

Christian Unkelbach
Psychological Institute
University of Heidelberg
Heidelberg, Germany

Elke U. Weber
Graduate School of Business
Columbia University
New York, NY, USA

Marcel Zeelenberg
Faculty of Social and Behavioural
 Sciences
Tilburg University
Tilburg, The Netherlands

The Nature of Intuition

1

The Nature of Intuition and Its Neglect in Research on Judgment and Decision Making

TILMANN BETSCH

University of Erfurt

INTRODUCTION

There are as many meanings for the term *intuition* as there are people using it. Philosophers often conceive of intuition as a competence. Adopting the philosophical approach, the Encyclopædia Britannica (15th Edition, 1989) defines intuition as "the power of obtaining knowledge that cannot be acquired either by inference or observation, by reason or experience" (p. 000). This definition evokes some mystical connotations: If such a power really existed independent from experience and reason, where would it originate? Browsing the World Wide Web, one readily spots the answer: Intuition is the red telephone connecting us to above. Although there is considerable variety among the conceptions of the telephone and the distant entity, many inspired followers of New Age patchwork religions would agree that intuition is informed by a supernatural power. Indeed, this is an old view deeply rooted in the tradition of religious thinking. Feuchtwanger (1937) provided a nice illustration of this mystic power in his novel "Der falsche Nero" (The False Nero).[1] After Nero's death, Titus rules the Roman Empire. However, a former senator in the Roman provinces "revives" Nero to instigate a coup d'état against Titus. Terentius Maximus, the spitting image of the late Nero, is trained to copy the behavior of his idol in all respects. Taking over his new role perfectly, the impostor even learns to reevoke the daimonium of the emperor —the capability of the gifted to sense the will of the gods—to reach and justify political decisions.

---

[1] The English edition of the novel is entitled *The Pretender* (Feuchtwanger, 1937).

Psychologists are a bit more down to earth when studying intuition. Nevertheless, conceptual confusion remains. *The American Psychological Association Monitor on Psychology* (Vol. 36, No. 3, 2005) recently devoted a special feature to this issue. Winerman (APA Monitor on Psychology, 36, No. 3, 50–52, 2005) interviewed some distinguished researchers asking them to explain their views on the topic. The quotes Winerman (2005) provides in her articles reveal a variety of different views and approaches to the phenomenon. Some scholars focus on intuition as a *source* of knowledge. Accordingly, intuition is what we know without knowing how we learned it. Others suggest a *process* view by equating intuition with automatic or implicit processes of thinking. Finally, one spots proponents of a *system* view claiming that intuition is a distinct faculty of the human mind. The diversity of approaches notwithstanding, I dare to start with a definition of intuition:

> Intuition is a process of thinking. The input to this process is mostly provided by knowledge stored in long-term memory that has been primarily acquired via associative learning. The input is processed automatically and without conscious awareness. The output of the process is a feeling that can serve as a basis for judgments and decisions.

The definition is informed by major theoretical approaches to intuition. Adopting a process view on the subject, it captures the key attributes of Epstein's (1991, 1994; chap. 2, this volume) cognitive-experiential self-theory; Hogarth's (2001; chap. 6, this volume) distinction between tacit and deliberate processing; and Hammond, Hamm, Grassia, and Pearson's (1987; see also Hamm, chap. 4, this volume) model of intuitive and analytical cognition. All these models differentiate between two modes of thinking: a conscious and a subconscious one. The processes operating in the former are described as rational, deliberate, analytic, inferential, or reflective. The latter, the intuitive mode, is assumed to obey quite different processing principles. Epstein (1991; chap. 2, this volume) labels this mode "experiential" and provides a comprehensive list of features covering most of the properties that are commonly attributed to intuitive processing by the other models. Accordingly, the experiential mode processes information in an automatic, associative, holistic, nonverbal, and rapid fashion. These operations usually cannot be accessed by introspection and therefore cannot be verbalized. Intuitive processing resembles Greenwald and Banaji's (1995) concept of implicit cognition and Bargh's (1996) notion of automaticity.

The definition specifies the input to intuitive processing: knowledge acquired through experience and stored in long-term memory. As such, intuition primarily capitalizes on prior knowledge acquired via a slow learning system rather than on recently encountered information kept in short-term memory. The slow learning system is guided by the principles of associative learning that have been studied by using, for instance, Pavlovian, evaluative, and operant conditioning procedures. The intimate relation between prior experience and intuition is highlighted by most of the theories on intuition including those I cited previously.

According to my definition, the output of intuition is a feeling, for instance, the feeling of liking an entity or a feeling of risk. Feelings are a powerful means of communication, not only between individuals (e.g., via facial expressions) but also within the organism. Feelings arise involuntarily and immediately break into consciousness (Wundt, 1907; Zajonc, 1968, 1980). Thus, they can serve as an interruption device changing subsequent motivations (H. A. Simon, 1967; Weber & Lindemann, chap. 12, this volume; Zeelenberg, Nelissen, & Pieters, chap. 11, this volume). Feelings inform conscious thought (associated with prefrontal brain activity) about the work of the unconscious (associated with activity of the older regions of the human brain, e.g., the limbic system; for a more detailed approach to the neuroanatomy of intuition, see Volz & von Cramon, chap. 5, this volume). When the connections between the prefrontal cortices and the limbic system are impaired (e.g., due injury or illness), patients lack access to the affective component when evaluating options and forming decisions (Bechara, Damasio, Damasio, & Anderson, 1994). Not all kinds of feelings, however, map on the affective dimension. There are feelings that inform the organism about other properties of experience such as time, space, and number. Other examples of nonemotional feelings are feelings about cognitive processes, such as the feeling of knowing (Hart, 1965), which can be used in metacognitive evaluations and decisions. As a common denominator, all these feelings share the following properties: They are immediate, nonsymbolic, nonverbal; they evolve from experience, demanding only a minimal amount of cognitive resources and can serve as a basis for judgment and decision (see also Perrig, 2000). The role of feelings in intuition is most lucidly described by cognitive experiential self-theory (Epstein, 1994; chap. 2, this volume). It underlies a number of models of judgment and decision making including Hogarth's (2001; chap. 6, this volume) model of intuition and the heuristics and biases approach (Gilovich, Griffin, & Kahneman, 2002; Kahneman, Slovic & Tversky, 1982; Slovic, Finucane, Peters, & MacGregor, 2002).

DISTINGUISHING INTUITION FROM OTHER PROCESSES

The preceding definition has quite a narrow scope. It excludes a number of fast processes and reactions resembling intuition. All kinds of innate processes, such as reflexes and instinctive patterns of behavior, are not considered intuitive because they are not informed by prior knowledge stored in long-term memory. By the same logic, not every kind of elicitation of feelings can be attributed to intuition. The sting of a wasp immediately causes feelings of pain. These reactions, however, are not based on prior knowledge but are exclusively driven by the current situation.

On the other hand, the processing of prior knowledge is not a sufficient condition to identify a mental activity as intuitive. For example, attempting to recall the names of your friends in grammar school has nothing to do with intuition; although it is accompanied by feelings (e.g., the difficulty of recall), it involves a search in long-term memory and it rests on a process that cannot be accessed by introspection. The crucial difference between rehearsal and intuition is that the output of the former is a mental representation of an entity, whereas the latter is a feeling toward it. Assume you run into a man at the 20th anniversary party of your high school class graduation. You immediately sense a feeling of dislike.

To avoid getting into a conversation, you signal and shout some words to a couple of old friends sitting at a distant table. While you are walking toward them, you try to remember the man's name, which pops into your mind after some time; and suddenly, you also remember that it was he who always did nasty things to you such as taking your secret letters and showing them to the rest of the class. You applaud the product of your intuition (the immediate feeling) that has helped you to make the right decision (avoiding interaction). Recall of prior experiences was not necessary to make this decision. The decision was solely based on a feeling, which reflected prior knowledge without awareness.

The key feature of intuition is that it operates automatically on a subconscious level. As such, it differs from deliberate processes of thinking. Higher order processes of thinking are bounded by constraints of attention and memory capacity. People cannot place their attention on all relevant pieces of information at the same time. Rather, they have to focus on one piece after another. In other words, deliberative thinking involves sequential processing. Most of the decision strategies that have been described in the literature are sequential strategies and thus have been studied with the help of tools tracking the sequential acquisition of information (e.g., the mouselab procedure; see following). In contrast, automatic processes consider multiple pieces of information simultaneously. For example, the taste of a sip of wine depends on a huge number of variables simultaneously impacting multiple sensory organs. By virtue of parallel processing, a person immediately arrives at an overall evaluation of the wine integrating the interactions of the concert of factors. With extensive training, one can attempt to break an attitude down into some of its sources. This requires people to engage in sequential consideration of factors such as the fragrance, the degree of sourness or sweetness, and the tone of tastes resembling others known from experience. However, people are grateful that they do not have to rely on sequential processing to assess the degree of pleasure caused by having a glass of good wine.

Due to parallel processing, intuition is capable of handling a huge amount of information. Experience provides the organisms with a rich database on which intuition can unfold its power. As I show following, intuition is capable of reflecting the entire history of experiences made with an entity. Therefore, intuition can yield highly accurate judgments and decisions if the prior sample of experiences is representative for the current task (for limitations, see Unkelbach & Plessner, chap. 17, this volume).

Experiences can be stored in long-term memory. However, not every kind of experience is immediately stored in long-term memory. Regularly, repetition or elaboration are necessary preconditions for learning. One-trial learning is the exception rather than the rule. As such, long-term memory contains a substantial amount of overlearned or well-consolidated information. Most of people's behaviors are routines that have been frequently performed in the past. Because they are so overlearned, these routines can be selected and executed in an automatic fashion. Consolidation of knowledge and automatic processing relate to each other in a symbiotic fashion. Consolidation (e.g., via frequent repetition) enhances the likelihood that automatic processes come into play. In a similar vein, automatic processes are likely to capitalize on well-consolidated knowledge (James, 1890).

In a nutshell, intuition is assumed to exploit the capability of one's mind to process information in parallel. Parallel processes can handle a huge amount of information. In judgment and decision making, long-term memory provides the main database for this process. Therefore, intuition in judgment and decision making rests to a great extent on knowledge that is well consolidated and deeply ingrained in memory.

Several approaches to intuitive judgment and decision making converge in assuming that automatic and deliberate processes can (and mostly do) operate simultaneously and thus jointly shape thought and action (e.g., Betsch, 2005a; C. Betsch, chap. 14, this volume; Epstein, chap. 2, this volume; Glöckner, chap. 19, this volume; Hammond et al., 1987; Hogarth, 2001; Holyoak & Simon, 1999; D. Simon, Krawczyk, & Holyoak, 2004; Thagard & Millgram, 1995). Presumably, the ideal case of pure intuition or pure deliberation does not exist in reality. Accordingly, when distinguishing different strategies of thinking on the empirical level, one should seek to specify the relative contribution of the two processes. If automatic processes dominate, one should expect that the judgments or decisions are reached very quickly by virtue of parallel processing. At the same time, judgments and decisions should reflect a strong sensitivity for entire samples of prior experiences even if the sample is huge because parallel processes can handle a large amount of information. Moreover, intuitive judgments and decisions should be prone to undervalue the weight of new evidence because they strongly rely on consolidated knowledge. Figure 1.1 shows a coordinate system containing styles of processing, amount of information, and its degree of consolidation as dimensions.

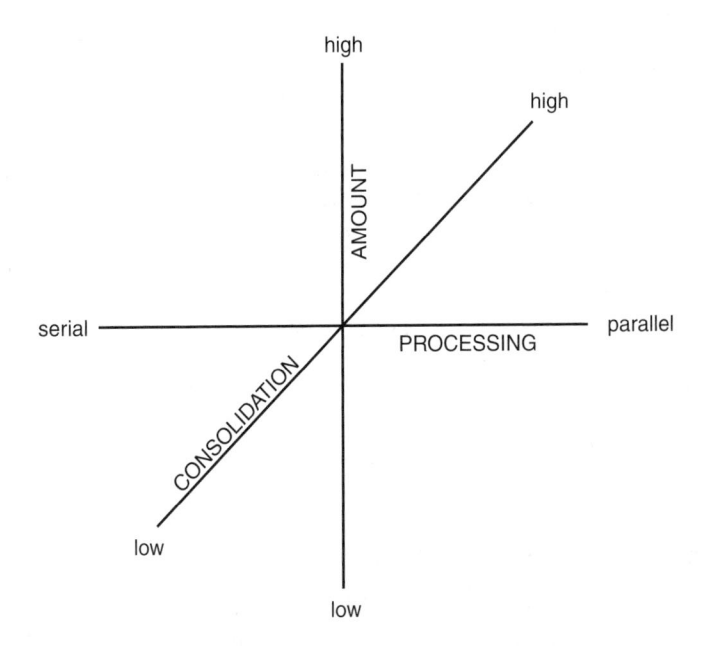

FIGURE 1.1 Characteristics of processing strategies in judgment and decision making. Intuitive strategies fall into the upper right quadrant.

Judgment and decision strategies dominated by intuition fit into the upper right quadrant. Conversely, deliberate strategies typically fall in the lower left quadrant. The amount of information that can be handled by deliberate strategies is comparatively low because deliberation involves focused and serial processing. It is bounded by the limited capacity of short-term memory. Deliberation is characterized by a focus of attention on particular pieces of information. Attention is primarily a function of the current situation. Hence, deliberative processing is less dominated by prior knowledge than intuition. The degree of consolidation of information can be very low, and herein lies one asset of deliberation: It is open to new evidence enabling the individual to contextualize and to rapidly adapt to changing situations. In contrast, intuition is more likely to produce conservatism in judgment and decisions because it is primarily driven by consolidated knowledge (see following).

THE NEGLECT OF INTUITION IN RESEARCH ON JUDGMENT AND DECISION MAKING

H. A. Simon (1955, 1982) was among the first to have broken the illusion that a person's deliberative mind would function in accordance with normative principles of rationality. The reason is simple. Most of these principles require individuals to consider and integrate a huge amount of information. Due to capacity limitations, individuals are simply not capable of deliberatively performing the operations required by normative rules. Note, however, that the notion of bounded rationality was developed with respect to conscious reasoning. The power of the automatic system was largely neglected. This neglect prevailed in subsequent research on intuitive judgment and decision making. Research on intuition is strongly associated with the pioneering work of the heuristics and biases program (Kahneman et al., 1982). This approach starts from the assumption that due to capacity constraints, humans have evolved a set of shortcut strategies for judgment and decision making. These strategies are called *heuristics*. Intuition has been equated with heuristic processing (Gilovich et al., 2002; Kahneman et al., 1982). As I show following, however, heuristics, to a substantial extent, rest on deliberative processes. As such, they can be considered shortcuts to deliberation rather than being intuitive strategies. The focus on deliberate activities of the human mind also dominates in other approaches to heuristic processing in decision research such as the adaptive decision-making approach (Payne, Bettman, & Johnson, 1993) and the research program on the heuristic toolbox (Gigerenzer, Todd, and the ABC Research Group, 1999). I consider three types of heuristics to illustrate my claim that intuition (characterized by automatic, parallel processing) has been largely neglected by research in the field of judgment and decision making.

Decison Making: Lexicographic Strategies

Rational decision makers are required to consider all relevant pieces of information about alternatives and to integrate them according to a weighted additive rule. Research has shown that decision makers are reluctant to consider all relevant information (Gigerenzer, 2004; Payne, Bettman, & Johnson, 1988; but see Bröder, 2000, 2003, for different results). Rather, they tend to base their decisions on the most important information. A couple of strategies have been suggested to model selective information acquisition in decision making (Payne et al., 1993). Many of them can be sorted into the class of lexicographic strategies. Lexicographic strategies start with comparing alternatives (e.g., consumer goods) by the most important attribute or evaluative dimension (e.g., price). If the alternatives have different values on the target dimension, the one with the most positive value can be chosen. Outcomes of the alternatives on all other dimensions are ignored. The take-the-best (ignore-the-rest) heuristics, suggested by Gigerenzer and Goldstein (1999), ideally follows this principle by using cue validity as a criterion to determine the importance of classes of information. Lexicographic strategies all have in common that information is processed in a serial fashion. Moreover, the decision is based on a small subset of the available information. In the majority of attempts to identify the use of these strategies, researchers have provided their participants with new evidence (e.g., Bröder, 2003; Payne et al., 1988). Prior knowledge is rarely considered in these studies. As such, lexicographic strategies for decision making are typical examples of nonintuitive heuristics. They are shortcuts to deliberation and, thus, fall into the lower left quadrant of Figure 1.1.

Judgments of Valence: The Peak-and-End Heuristic

Did you enjoy watching the football championship? How much do you like or dislike your colleagues? How well did the President perform during the first 100 days of his term? Addressing questions of this type requires judges to form summary evaluations or attitudes. Attitude objects often produce multiple outcomes that have to be integrated to form a summary evaluation. Similar to decision theory, models of attitude formation often suggest that information integration follows a linear aggregation rule. Different variants of linear rules have been put forward. The Fishbein and Ajzen (1974) model, for example, posits that attitudes reflect the sum of weighted evaluations, whereas information integration theory (Anderson, 1981) suggests that integration obeys an averaging principle. Based on the averaging principle, Fredrickson and Kahneman (1993); Kahneman, Fredrickson, Schreiber, and Redelmeier (1993); and Redelmeier and Kahneman (1996) have put forward a shortcut version for forming summary evaluations. Again, the core idea behind this approach is that individuals can only process a limited amount of information because their processing and memory capacities are constrained. Accordingly, summary evaluations mainly reflect those experiences with the attitude object that can be easily remembered such as recent or outstanding events. Specifically, application of the peak-and-end heuristic produces evaluative judgments reflecting the average of the peak and the end of a sequence of values. The heuristic rests on evaluation of a small sample of concrete events that can be kept in short-term memory. It is again an example of a deliberative heuristic.

Judgments of Probability and Frequency: The Availability Heuristic

Tversky and Kahneman (1973) proposed that most of people's judgments of frequency and probability are made with the help of a limited number of heuristics. The availability heuristic is an important one among these and has inspired a considerable amount of research activity (see Betsch & Pohl, 2002, for an overview). Within the heuristics and biases program (Kahneman et al., 1982), estimation by availability is considered a prototypical example of intuitive judgment. To check whether this notion accords with my concept of intuition, one must have a closer look at Tversky and Kahneman's specification of the availability heuristic. The following quote is taken from Tversky and Kahneman's (1973) seminal article on availability:

> A person is said to employ the availability heuristic whenever he estimates frequency or probability by the ease with which instances or associations could be brought to mind. To assess availability it is not necessary to perform the actual operations of retrieval or construction. It suffices to assess the ease with which these operations could be performed, much as the difficulty of a puzzle or mathematical problem can be assessed without considering specific solutions. (p. 208)

This theoretical statement specifies two alternatives as to how the availability heuristic can be applied. The first requires the individual to recall concrete instances, whereas the second does not rest on recall. Assume one asks a participant in a survey to estimate how often he went to the movies last year. Applying the recall-based version of the availability heuristic, she will start the judgment process by attempting to recall some concrete instances, in this case, movies she has watched in the cinema. In the simplest case, it suffices to recall a single instance because the estimate is said to be based not on the quantity of recalled instances but rather on the feeling of how easy or difficult it was to bring instances to mind. The more easily the survey participant can recall one or several examples, the higher will be her estimate of how often she went to the movies.

At first glance, this version of the availability heuristic seems to accord to my definition of intuition. The input to the process stems from experience and is stored in long-term memory. The heuristic capitalizes on associative learning. The stronger the associations between events (a certain movie) and the corresponding category (movies one has watched in the cinema), the easier it is to bring instances to mind. Thus, the degree of consolidation of knowledge matters. Moreover, the output of the process is a feeling that is used as a base for subsequent judgment. However, the recall process evoking these feelings rests on a reduced sample of concrete instances relevant for the judgment. Thus, only a few pieces of relevant information are considered by the availability heuristic, and the power of the automatic system is one partially used (although the application of the heuristic itself may not be under voluntary control and therefore might be considered as automatic; cf. Frederick, 2002).

The second version of the availability heuristic involves an assessment of the ease of recall without performing the recall process. The functioning of this process is not precisely specified by Tversky and Kahneman (1973), but their reference to puzzles or mathematical problems (see previous quote) suggests that metacognitive inference processes might be involved in the application of the recall-free version of the heuristic. Assume the female participant in the survey is a workaholic scientist who rarely goes out but rather spends the evenings planning research and writing articles. Given her self-representation ("I am an ambitious and hardworking scientist"), she might consider it difficult to come up with concrete examples and therefore might judge the frequency of her going to the movies as very low. Obviously, the underlying process of thinking has nothing to do with intuition. It rather provides a typical example of inference or reasoning. The recall-free version of the availability heuristic works in a serial fashion: It rests on a few pieces of symbolically represented knowledge, and it is metacognitively controlled.

At a bottom line, the availability heuristic is close to the other examples of heuristics I discussed previously. Although it may involve an assessment of feelings, it is not based on holistic processing and exploits only a narrow subset of relevant knowledge. Again, it mirrors the basic assumption underlying the heuristics and biases program that individuals are not capable of exploiting the richness of their experiences but instead have to rely on shortcut strategies that reduce the given problems to simpler ones (Tversky & Kahneman, 1973, p. 207; see also Kahneman & Tversky, 1996, p. 582).

THE POWER OF INTUITION: EMPIRICAL EVIDENCE

The strategies I discussed in the previous section are representative examples of the heuristics approach that is dominating the field of judgment and decision making. As I have shown, these heuristics are shortcut strategies to conscious thinking and reasoning. They process only small portions of relevant knowledge and only occasionally exploit the potentials of the automatic processing system. Hence, if one equates intuition with heuristic processing, one would neglect the nature and the power of intuition. However, does this presupposed power really exist? Is it really possible that judgments and decisions can reflect holistic processing capitalizing on the richness of prior experiences? In this part, I present some finding from recent experimental work evidencing the power of intuition. I arranged the review in accordance with the three parts of the previous section. Specifically, I consider decision making, judgments of valence, and judgments of probability and frequency.

Decision Making

The mouselab technology, originally developed by Johnson, Payne, Schkade, and Bettman (1986) for multiattribute decision problems, has become an indispensable tool for researchers to study the processes underlying decision making. Alternatives, attributes, and outcomes are arranged in a matrix that is shown to the participant on the computer screen (see Fig. 2.2). By clicking on a box with the computer mouse, a piece of information pops up representing the outcome produced by an alternative on a particular attribute dimension. The program protocols the

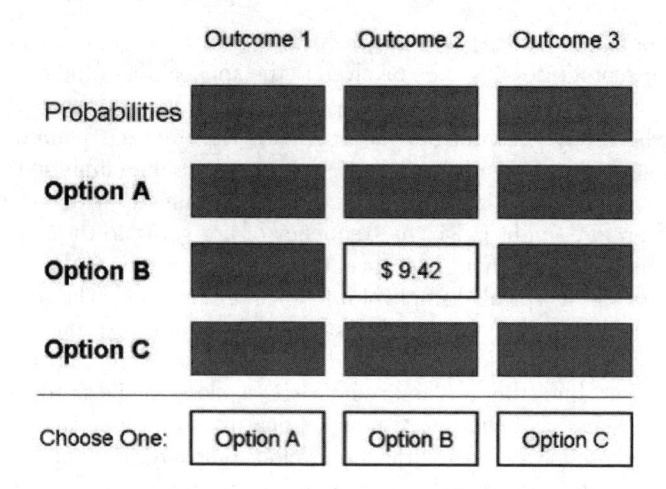

FIGURE 1.2 A typical mouselab.

participant's movements in the matrix. The pattern of information acquisition behavior is analyzed with the help of various methods to identify the type of decision strategy used by the individual. Most of the existence proofs of lexicographic strategies evidence stem from mouselab studies (e.g., Payne et al., 1988, 1993).

The mouselab hides outcome information to trace information searching. The use of a particular strategy is inferred from the individual's movements in the matrix measured by the number and sequence of opened boxes. Thus, information searching becomes costly in terms of time and motor effort required to open the boxes. In a series of experiments, Glöckner and Betsch (2006) and Glöckner, Betsch, and Schindler (2006) have presented participants with uncovered information ordered in a matrix similar to the classic mouselab tool. Astoundingly, Glöckner and Betsch (2006) and Glöckner et al. have found that spontaneous decisions by the majority of the participants reflected the entire sample of information presented in the matrix even under substantial time pressure. Only a few participants relied on lexicographic strategies when forming their decisions. These results indicate that the predominance of lexicographic strategies that have been found by laboratory studies may have been at least partly due to the research methodology forcing the individual to engage in step-by-step processing of information. Due to the fact that information search in the mouselab takes time and effort, participants have to focus on a few pieces of information when making quick decisions. It is not overly surprising that they also tend to focus on the most important attribute. Notwithstanding the artifical nature of this methodology, the findings have been generalized and interpreted as evidence for a causal relation between processing constraints and the use of the lexicographic strategies. Such conclusions seem to be plausible given H. A. Simon's (1982) notion of bounded rationality that has provided the background model for most of the research in human decision making. The studies I have cited demonstrate that decision makers are capable of simultaneously handling multiple pieces of information even under severe constraints. To account for the findings, Glöckner & Betsch (2006) have used a connectionist model that employs a parallel-processing algorithm. The parallel-processing account explains more variance than the heuristics approach assuming that individuals tend to rely on one-reason decision strategies (see Glöckner, 2006; chap. 19, this volume; Glöckner & Betsch, 2005; Glöckner et al., 2006).

The findings highlight the role of automatic processes in decision making. However, decisions were based purely on new evidence because all relevant information was given by the experimenter at the time a decision had to be made. In contrast, most of the choices people make in everyday life are memory-based decisions reflecting past experiences. Hence, to demonstrate the power of intuition, one has to consider situations allowing participants to rely on prior knowledge. Glöckner (2006; chap. 19, this volume) has replicated his findings in memory-based decision tasks. Specifically, Glöckner (2006; chap. 19, this volume) has demonstrated that memory-based decisions under time pressure reflected the total amount of information participants have learned prior to the decision task. The response latencies from these participants significantly differed from controls that were forced to deliberately consider a similar amount of information. These findings make a strong case for the advocated notion of intuition, which claims that it rests on parallel processing and a holistic consideration of prior experiences.

Judgments of Valence

Do you like the former President of the United States Bill Clinton? Kahneman et al. (1993) proposed that judgments of valence rely on a small subset of outstanding memories. Accordingly, you might start to recall facts, instances, or events associated with the former president. You may remember his affair with Monica Lewinsky or the fact that he left the Bush administration with a balanced budget at the end of his term. Your judgment may eventually reflect the average of the valences evoked by the few recalled instances. It is not always necessary, however, to scan memory before making judgments of valence. Familiar entities immediately evoke feelings of like or dislike (Wundt, 1907; Zajonc, 1968). In a series of experiments, my colleagues and I (Betsch, Hoffmann, Hoffrage & Plessner, 2003; Betsch, Kaufmann, Lindow, Plessner & Hoffmann, 2006 Betsch, Plessner, Schwieren, & Gütig, 2001) have shown that these immediate feelings can reflect the sum of experiences made with an attitude object.

In the majority of these experiments, Betsch et al. (2001, 2003, 2006) have used fictitious shares in the stock market as attitude objects. Participants have received information about the return values[2] produced by shares over several trading days. We have presented shares on a running caption at the bottom of a monitor. Simultaneously, participants have watched videotaped advertisements appearing in the background (Fig. 1.3). The format resembled the simultaneous presentation

---

[2] Participants were informed that a return value does not represent the absolute value of the share but the gain compared to the previous trading date. For example, "ELSKAR + 6" meant that the share ELSKAR had gained 6 Euros (or formerly Deutsche Mark) on a particular trading date on the Frankfurt stock exchange.

FIGURE 1.3 A screenshot from the stimulus presentation of the experiments on implicit attitude formation by Betsch, Plessner, et al. (2001).

of information in news channels on television. In this dual task situation, participants believed that watching the advertisements was the primary task, whereas reading the return values was announced as the "distracter" task. They expected to be probed for memory about the advertisements after the presentation. As another means to constrain deliberative attitude formation about the shares, we have exposed participants to extreme information overload. Specifically, we had them watch between 20 and 40 different advertisements while simultaneously encoding between 70 and 140 return values produced by four to eight shares shown at a high pace on the running caption. As an independent variable, we have varied the properties of the return distribution of the shares (e.g., sum of values, average, frequency, peaks). After the presentation and a memory test about the advertisements, participants have been unexpectedly asked to spontaneously judge how much they liked each of the shares. Their attitude judgments revealed a remarkable degree of sensitivity to the sum of values that each share had actually produced. Specifically, we found a perfect rank order correlation between mean evaluation of the shares and their actual sum of returns. Most notably, participants lacked any concrete memories about the return distributions. Moreover, they were unable to remember the sum or the average of return values. Postexperimental interviews revealed that participants did not intend to form attitudes during encoding and had no insight or awareness about their ability to differentiate the shares with respect to their performance. Most of them said they relied on their "gut reaction" or "intuitive feeling" when judging the shares.

Similar results have been found in other domains of judgment (see Betsch, Plessner, & Schallies, 2004, for an overview). Plessner, Betsch, Schallies, and Schwieren (chap. 7, this volume) report research conducted in the domain of political judgment. Again, participants' spontaneous judgment reflected the sum of prior experiences with the politicians, although they had no access to concrete memories at the time of judgment. The findings provide another piece of evidence showing that intuitions of valence can reveal a remarkable degree of sensitivity for the entire set of prior experiences. These results run counter to the heuristics approach assuming that intuitive judgments reflect only a subsample of recalled information such as proposed by the peak-and-end heuristic. The fact that the participants did not intend to form attitudes toward the targets and furthermore were lacking any insight into the process of attitude formation led (Plessner et al., chap. 7, this volume) to conclude that attitudes were formed automatically or implicitly. Input (prior experiences), functioning (automatic), and output (feeling) of this process converge with the concept of intuition I have advocated in this chapter.

Judgments of Probability and Frequency

Most people are bad statisticians. Lecturers teaching probability theory and statistics to undergraduates might subscribe to that statement, and in fact, the pessimistic assessment of people's thinking abilities seems to be supported by empirical evidence. The neglect of base rates is one of the numerous fallacies committed by both lay people and professionals, indicating their flawed understanding of the principles of probability theory (Eddy, 1982; Kahneman & Tversky, 1973). These deficits were demonstrated within a particular research paradigm that uses descriptions as stimuli. Accordingly, the experimenter provides the individual with a written problem resembling those everyone suffered from in school exams. Consider, for example, the well-known mammography problem. The individual's task is to estimate the conditional probability that a woman has breast cancer given that she received a positive result in a mammography screening. The base rate, the hit and false alarm rates of the diagnostic instrument, are stated in numerical format.[3] Participants usually have difficulties in solving such tasks. They often ignore base rates and mainly focus on new evidence (e.g., the hit rate of the diagnostic instrument) when forming their judgments. This commonly results in a tremendous overestimation of the conditional probability to be judged (given that base rates are low). Even if the task is made easier (e.g., by providing frequencies instead of probabilities), base-rate neglect remains in up to 50% of the participants (Gigerenzer & Hoffrage, 1995). Such findings have led judgment and decision researchers to

---

[3] Here is an example of the mammography problem: "The probability of breast cancer is 1% for a woman at age forty who participates in routine screening. If a woman has breast cancer, the probability is 80% that she will get a positive mammogram. If a woman does not have breast cancer, the probability is 9.6 % that she will also get a positive mammogram. A woman in this age group has a positive mammogram in a routine screening. What is the probability that she actually has breast cancer?" (Gigerenzer & Hoffrage, 1995, p. 685)

conclude that humans are bad intuitive statisticians (see also Erev, Shimonowitch, Schurr, & Hertwig, chap. 9, this volume).

Because many description-based tasks used in judgment research resemble arithmetic problems, they are likely to evoke deliberative rather than intuitive strategies of thinking (see, e.g., the thinking protocol analyses by Gigerenzer & Hoffrage, 1995). At best, the results obtained in the description paradigm indicate that individuals have problems in reasoning in accordance with normative rules. What happens, however, if one gives individuals the opportunity to really rely on their intuition? To do this, one has to provide them with the appropriate input. Following my concept of intuition, one has to ensure that participants do have access to knowledge stored in long-term memory, which in turn reflects their own experience.

Results obtained from the use of a learning paradigm dramatically change the picture. If participants are allowed to learn the distributions of variables by their own sampling, they become remarkably sensitive to base rates (Betsch, Biel, Eddelbüttel, & Mock, 1998). Fiedler, Brinkmann, Betsch, and Wild (2000) compared individual estimates with the expected conditional probabilities obtained from application of Bayes's theorem to the information participants sampled during the learning task. Both measures almost perfectly converged. At a bottom line, evidence obtained from experience-based judgments of probability challenge the notion that humans generally neglect base rates.

A pronounced sensitivity to base rates has also been documented in studies on routine decision making (for overviews, see Betsch & Haberstroh, 2005). Data from think-aloud studies has indicated that routine decision makers judge counterevidence to their routine less reliable than its prior success rate (Haberstroh, Betsch, Glöckner, Haar, & Stiller, 2005). The larger the sample of prior experiences, the higher the tendency that individuals become conservative in their judgments and decisions and underweigh new evidence. Conservatism manifests itself in a tendency to maintain the routine even when it obviously produces detrimental outcomes (e.g., Betsch, Haberstroh, Glöckner, Haar, & Fiedler, 2001).

The ability to process probabilities requires as a prerequisite that organisms are capable of sensitizing and storing the frequency of events. Similar to probabilistic reasoning, the heuristics approach has focused on the deficits in human frequency processing. One of the first demonstrations of the availability heuristic (Tversky and Kahneman, 1973) suggested that frequency judgments can be systematically biased. In their famous-names experiment, Tversky and Kahneman demonstrated that the estimation of category size can be biased by recall. Due to differential familiarity, exemplars of one category could be more easily recalled than exemplars from the other. Although the former category was smaller in size than the latter, it was judged to be larger by the participants. Tversky and Kahneman attributed these results to the application of the availability heuristic that infers frequency from the ease by which instances can be activated from memory. Because the availability heuristic was considered a tool for intuition, intuitive frequency processing became associated with errors and biases, prominently in the judgment and decision literature (e.g., Gilovich et al., 2002). Such a view, however, is not justified granting the overwhelming evidence accumulated in other fields of psychology such as memory research (e.g., Hasher & Zacks, 1984) and animal cognition (e.g., Gallistel, 1989). Recent reviews of the evidence reached the conclusion that human and nonhuman animals are remarkably good at registering the relative frequency of events (Sedlmeier & Betsch, 2002).

How is it, though, that biases in frequency judgments occur? One cause stems from the fact that most of the studies on frequency judgment have not controlled for the judgment mode. Hence, individuals are free to think as much as they wish before making their estimates. Moreover, measures of recall have sometimes been administered before the judgment measures were taken (e.g., Manis, Shedler, Jonides, & Nelson, 1993). Thus, the experimental procedure might additionally encourage individuals to employ deliberative strategies relying on concrete memories available in the recall protocol.

Haberstroh, Betsch, and Aarts (2006; see also Haberstroh, chap. 16, this volume) had participants perform different kinds of behaviors for a varying number of times and subsequently asked them to estimate behavior frequencies. Most important, Haberstroh et al. (2006) manipulated judgment mode as an independent variable. One half of the participants were asked to give spontaneous judgments, whereas the other half were instructed to think carefully before making judgments. In the deliberation condition, frequency judgments were systematically biased by recall. In convergence with the results of Tversky and Kahneman (1973), participants were unable to reproduce the actual relative frequencies in their judgments. The opposite happened in the spontaneous judgment condition. Individual estimates of this group perfectly mirrored the actual rank order of frequencies and did not correlate with recall measures. The studies by Haberstroh et al. (2006) indicated that judgments relying on intuition can be highly sensitive to the frequency of events actually experienced by the individual. The findings converge with those reported on probability estimation. In sum, one can conclude that people really have a power of intuitive understanding of quantity information.[4] Because of the experimental procedures commonly employed in judgment and decision research (stimulus input is description based, procedure fosters the application of deliberative strategies), intuition often cannot unfold its power.

CONCLUSION

In the previous sections, I have presented some findings from recent work on preferential decision making and on judgments of valence and quantity. The research paradigm that has been employed in most of these studies has shared the following properties: First, participants were given the opportunity to learn the pertinent information. In subsequent judgments and decisions, they could rely on prior knowledge acquired through their own experience. Second, they were confronted with multiple cue environments. Consequently, judgments and decisions could capitalize on a rich knowledge base. Third, participants were encouraged to make

---

[4] Nevertheless, they still lack the metacognitive insight in statistical problems. They do not understand at all, for example, the implications of constraints on the sampling process (cf. Fiedler, 2000; Unkelbach & Plessner, chap. 17, this volume).

decisions and judgments with low processing effort. They were exposed to, for example, time limit manipulations or were asked to make their judgments spontaneously. The conditions that have been set up by the authors of these studies are in line with my notion of intuition. Specifically, the experimental procedures allowed participants to rely on consolidated knowledge (i.e., knowledge stored in long-term memory). Participants were given the opportunity to utilize a huge amount of information. Moreover, manipulations of judgment mode enhanced the likelihood that parallel processes could direct judgments and decisions. These conditions mirror the key aspects of intuition shown in Figure 1.1 (parallel processing, consolidation, and a high amount of input information).

Most important, the results that have been produced by the cited studies converge in showing that spontaneous judgments and decisions can indeed reflect the total of prior experiences rather than a subset of information. It seems that intuition is almost unconstrained by capacity limits. A number of theories have assumed that this is possible because information is processed in parallel (e.g., connectionist models; for an overview, see Read, Vanman, & Miller, 1997; Smith, 1996). Unfortunately, a great deal of research on intuition has neglected these capacities of the automatic system that provide the origins of the power of intuition. In the field of judgment and decision research, parallel processes have rarely been considered. Often, researchers rely on experimental paradigms that even hinder participants' abilities to make judgments and decisions in an intuitive fashion. The dominant paradigm in this field of research—the so-called gambling paradigm—presents participants with unfamiliar situations, uses descriptions that sometimes appear to be rather artificial, and invites individuals to employ serial strategies of thinking (see Betsch, 2005b, and Hertwig, Barron, Weber, & Erev, 2004, for discussions). In convergence with the corresponding research methodology, theoretical approaches overemphasize the importance of deliberative processes. Most of the heuristics and decision strategies that have been documented in the literature are shortcuts to deliberation. The reasoning behind this can be traced back to H. A. Simon's (1982) notion of bounded rationality. Accordingly, thinking is constrained by working memory capacity, and so are the strategies people employ to cope with these boundaries. Hence, the heuristic approach to intuition advocates that individuals commonly process only subsets of information, rely on proxy variables for estimation, and strive to make things less complex than they are in the real world. These reduced strategies of thinking are labeled intuitive to distinguish them from formal rules of thinking and inference. One group of researchers focused on the deficits produced by the application of such heuristics (Kahneman et al., 1982). Another group focused on the assets and the adaptive value of these strategies (Gigerenzer et al., 1999). Both, however, have touched only the surface of intuition. Ironically, it was the godfather of these approaches himself, H. A. Simon (1955), who anticipated the power of intuition:

> My first empirical proposition is that there is a complete lack of evidence that, in actual choice situations of any complexity, these [expected utility] computations can be, or are in fact, performed ... but we cannot, of course, rule out the possibility that the unconscious is a better decision maker than the conscious. (p. 104)

REFERENCES

Anderson, N. H. (1981). Integration theory applied to cognitive responses and attitudes. In R. E. Petty, T. M. Ostrom, & T. C. Brock (Eds.), *Cognitive responses in persuasion* (pp. 361–397). Hillsdale, NJ: Lawrence Erlbaum Associates, Inc.

Bargh, J. A. (1996). Principles of automaticity. In E. T. Higgins & A. Kruglanski (Eds.), *Social psychology: Handbook of basic principles* (pp. 169–183). New York: Guilford.

Bechara, A., Damasio, A. R., Damasio, H., & Anderson, S. W. (1994). Insensitivity to future consequences following damage to human prefrontal cortex. *Cognition, 50,* 7–15.

Betsch, T. (2005a). Preference theory: An affect-based approach to recurrent decision making. In T. Betsch & S. Haberstroh (Eds.), *The routines of decision making* (pp. 39–65). Mahwah, NJ: Lawrence Erlbaum Associates, Inc.

Betsch, T. (2005b). Wie beeinflussen Routinen das Entscheidungsverhalten? [How do routines impact decision making?]. *Psychologische Rundschau. 56,* 261–270.

Betsch, T., Biel, G.-M., Eddelbüttel, C., & Mock, A. (1998). Natural sampling and base-rate neglect. *European Journal of Social Psychology, 28,* 269–273.

Betsch, T., & Haberstroh, S. (2005). (Eds.). *The routines of decision making.* Mahwah, NJ: Lawrence Erlbaum Associates, Inc.

Betsch, T., Haberstroh, S., Glöckner, A., Haar, T., & Fiedler, K. (2001). The effects of routine strength on adaptation and information search in recurrent decision making. *Organizational Behavior and Human Decision Processes, 84,* 23–53.

Betsch, T., Hoffmann, K., Hoffrage, U., & Plessner, H. (2003). Intuition beyond recognition: When less familiar events are liked more. *Experimental Psychology, 50,* 49–54.

Betsch, T., Kaufmann, M., Lindow, F., Plessner, H., & Hoffmann, K. (2006). Different principles of information integration in implicit and explicit attitude formation. *European Journal of Social Psychology, 36,* 887–905.

Betsch, T., Plessner, H., & Schallies, E. (2004). The value-account model of attitude formation. In G. R. Maio & G. Haddock (Eds.), *Contemporary perspectives on the psychology of attitudes* (pp. 000–000). Philadelphia: Psychology Press.

Betsch, T., Plessner, H., Schwieren, C., & Gütig, R. (2001). I like it but I don't know why: A value-account approach to implicit attitude formation. *Personality and Social Psychology Bulletin, 27,* 242–253.

Betsch, T., & Pohl, D. (2002). The availability heuristic: A critical examination. In P. Sedlmeier & T. Betsch (Eds.), *Etc.—Frequency processing and cognition* (pp. 109–119). Oxford, England: Oxford University Press.

Bröder, A. (2000). Assessing the empirical validity of the "take-the-best" heuristic as a model of human probabilistic inference. *Journal of Experimental Psychology: Learning, Memory, and Cognition, 26,* 1332–1346.

Bröder, A. (2003). Decision making with the "adaptive toolbox": Influence of environmental structure, intelligence, and working memory load. *Journal of Experimental Psychology: Learning, Memory, and Cognition, 29,* 611–625.

Eddy, D. M. (1982). Probabilistic reasoning in clinical medicine: Problems and opportunities. In D. Kahneman, P. Slovic, & A. Tversky (Eds.), *Judgment under uncertainty: Heuristics and biases* (pp. 249–267). Cambridge, England: Cambridge University Press.

Epstein, S. (1991). Cognitive-experiential self-theory: An integrative theory of personality. In R. Curtis (Ed.), *The relational self: Convergences in psychoanalysis and social psychology* (pp. 111–137). New York: Guilford.

Epstein, S. (1994). Integration of the cognitive and the psychodynamic unconscious. *American Psychologist, 49,* 709–724.

Feuchtwanger, L. (1937). *The pretender* (W. Muir & E. Muir, Trans.). New York: Viking.
Fiedler, K. (2000). Beware of samples! A cognitive-ecological sampling approach to judgment biases. *Psychological Review, 107*, 659–676.
Fiedler, K., Brinkmann, B., Betsch, T., & Wild, B. (2000). A sampling approach to biases in conditional probability judgments: Beyond base-rate neglect and statistical format. *Journal of Experimental Psychology: General, 129*, 399–418.
Fishbein, M., & Ajzen, I. (1974). Attitudes towards objects as predictors of single and multiple behavioral criteria. *Psychological Review, 81*, 59–74.
Frederick, S. (2002). Automated choice heuristics. In T. Gilovich, D. Griffin, & D. Kahneman (Eds.), *Heuristics and biases: The psychology of intuitive judgment*. (pp. 548–558). Cambridge, England: Cambridge University Press.
Fredrickson, B. L., & Kahneman, D. (1993). Duration neglect in retrospective evaluations of affective episodes. *Journal of Personality and Social Psychology, 65*, 45–55.
Gallistel, C. R. (1989). Animal cognition; Representation of space, time and number. *Annual Review of Psychology, 40*, 155–189.
Gigerenzer, G. (2004). Fast and frugal heuristics: The tools of bounded rationality. In D. Koehler & N. Harvey (Eds.), *Handbook of judgment and decision making* (pp. 62–88). Oxford, England: Blackwell.
Gigerenzer, G., & Goldstein, D. G. (1999). Betting on one good reason: The take the best heuristic. In G. Gigerenzer, P. M. Todd, and the ABC Research Group (Eds.), *Simple heuristics that make us smart* (pp. 75–95). Oxford, England: Oxford University Press.
Gigerenzer, G., & Hoffrage, U. (1995). How to improve Bayesian reasoning without instruction: Frequency formats. *Psychological Review, 102*, 684–704.
Gigerenzer, G., Todd, P. M., and the ABC Research Group. (1999). *Simple heuristics that make us smart*. Oxford, England: Oxford University Press.
Gilovich, T., Griffin, D., & Kahneman, D. (2002). (Eds.). *Heuristics and biases: The psychology of intuitive judgment*. Cambridge, England: Cambridge University Press.
Glöckner, A. (2006). *Strategy selection in memory-based decisions*. Manuscript submitted for publication.
Glöckner, A., & Betsch, T. (2006). *Evidence for automatic processes in decision making*. Manuscript submitted for publication.
Glöckner, A., & Betsch, T. (2005, August). *Empirical evidence for constructive and automatic processes in decision making*. Paper presented at the 20th Biennial Conference on Subjective Probability, Utility and Decision Making, Stockholm, Sweden.
Glöckner, A., Betsch, T., & Schindler, N. (2006). *Construction of probabilistic inferences by constraint satisfaction*. Manuscript submitted for publication.
Greenwald, A. G., & Banaji, M. R. (1995). Implicit social cognition: Attitudes, self-esteem, and stereotypes. *Psychological Review, 102*, 4–27.
Haberstroh, S., Betsch, T., & Aarts, H. (2006). *When guessing is better than thinking: Multiple bases for frequency judgments*. Manuscript submitted for publication.
Haberstroh, S., Betsch, T., Glöckner, A., Haar, T., & Stiller, A. (2005). The impact of routines on deliberate decisions: The microworld-simulation COMMERCE. In T. Betsch & S. Haberstroh (Eds.), *The routines of decision making*. Mahwah, NJ: Lawrence Erlbaum Associates, Inc.
Hammond, K. R., Hamm, R. M., Grassia, J., & Pearson, T. (1987). Direct comparison of the efficacy of intuitive judgment and analytical cognition in expert judgment. *IEEE Transactions on Systems, Man, and Cybernetics, SMC–17*, 753–770.
Hart, J. T. (1965). Memory and the feeling-of-knowing experience. *Journal of Educational Psychology, 56*, 208–216.

Hasher, L., & Zacks, R. T. (1984). Automatic processing of fundamental information: The case of frequency of occurrence. *American Psychologist, 12,* 1372–1388.
Hertwig, R., Barron, G., Weber, E. U., & Erev, I. (2004). Decisions from experience and the effects of rare events in risky choice. *Psychological Science, 15,* 534–539.
Hogarth, R. M. (2001). *Educating intuition.* Chicago: University of Chicago Press.
Holyoak, K. J., & Simon, D. (1999). Bidirectional reasoning in decision making by constraint satisfaction. *Journal of Experimental Psychology: General, 128,* 3–31.
James, W. (1890). *The principles of psychology* (Vol. 1). New York: Dover.
Johnson, E. J., Payne, J. W., Schkade, D. A., & Bettman, J. R. (1986). *Monitoring information processing and decisions: The mouselab system.* Unpublished manuscript, Center for Decision Studies, Fuqua School of Business, Duke University, Durham, NC.
Kahneman, D., Fredrickson, B. L., Schreiber, C. A., & Redelmeier, D. A. (1993). When more pain is preferred to less: Adding a better end. *Psychological Science, 4,* 401–405.
Kahneman, D., Slovic, P., & Tversky, A. (Eds.). (1982). *Judgment under uncertainty: Heuristics and biases.* Cambridge, England: Cambridge University Press.
Kahneman, D., & Tversky, A. (1973). On the psychology of prediction. *Psychological Review, 80,* 237–251.
Kahneman, D., & Tversky, A. (1996). On the reality of cognitive illusions: A reply to Gigerenzer's critique. *Psychological Review, 103,* 582–591.
Manis, M., Shedler, J., Jonides, J., & Nelson, T. E. (1993). Availability heuristic in judgments of set-size and frequency of occurrence. *Journal of Personality and Social Psychology, 65,* 448–457.
Payne, J. W., Bettman, J. R., & Johnson, E. J. (1988). Adaptive strategy selection in decision making. *Journal of Experimental Psychology: Learning, Memory and Cognition, 14,* 534–552.
Payne, J. W., Bettman, J. R., & Johnson, E. J. (1993). *The adaptive decision maker.* Cambridge, England: Cambridge University Press.
Perrig, W. J. (2000). Intuition and levels of control: The non-rational way of reacting, adapting and creating. In W. J. Perrig & A. Grob (Eds.), *Control of human behavior, mental processes and consciousness—Essays in honor of the 60th birthday of August Flammer* (pp. 103–122). Mahwah, NJ: Lawrence Erlbaum Associates, Inc.
Read, S. J., Vanman, E. J., & Miller, L. C. (1997). Connectionism, parallel constraint satisfaction processes, and Gestalt principles: (Re)introducing cognitive dynamics to social psychology. *Personality and Social Psychology Review, 1,* 26–53.
Redelmeier, D. A., & Kahneman, D. (1996). Patient's memories of painful medical treatments: Real-time and retrospective evaluations of two minimally invasive procedures. *Pain, 66,* 3–8.
Sedlmeier, P., & Betsch, T. (2002). *Etc.: Frequency processing and cognition.* Oxford, England: Oxford University Press.
Simon, D., Krawczyk, D. C., & Holyoak, K. J. (2004). Construction of preferences by constraint satisfaction. *Psychological Science, 15,* 331–336.
Simon, H. A. (1955). A behavioral model of rational choice. *Quarterly Journal of Economics, 69,* 99–118.
Simon, H. A. (1967). Motivational and emotional controls of cognition. *Psychological Review, 74,* 29–39.
Simon, H. A. (1982). *Models of bounded rationality.* Cambridge, MA: MIT Press.
Slovic, P., Finucane, M., Peters, E., & MacGregor, D. G. (2002). The affect heuristic. In T. Gilovich, D. Griffin, & D. Kahneman (Eds.), *Intuitive judgment: Heuristics and biases* (pp. 397–420). Cambridge, England: Cambridge University Press.
Smith, E. R. (1996). What do connectionism and social psychology offer each other? *Journal of Personality and Social Psychology, 70,* 893–912.

Thagard, P., & Millgram, E. (1995). Inference to the best plan: A coherence theory of decision. In A. Ram & D. B. Leake (Eds.), *Goal driven learning* (pp. 439–454). Cambridge, MA: MIT Press.

Tversky, A., & Kahneman, D. (1973). Availability: A heuristic for judging frequency and probability. *Cognitive Psychology, 5,* 207–232.

Wundt, W. (1907). *Outlines of psychology.* Leipzig, Germany: Wilhelm Engelmann.

Zajonc, R. B. (1968). Attitudinal effects of mere exposure. *Journal of Personality and Social Psychology, 9.*

Zajonc, R. B. (1980). Feeling and thinking: Preferences need no inferences. *American Psychologist, 35,* 151–175.

2

Intuition From the Perspective of Cognitive-Experiential Self-Theory

SEYMOUR EPSTEIN
University of Massachusetts at Amherst

INTRODUCTION

*I*ntuition has been given so many different meanings, some opposite to others, that it makes one wonder whether the term has any meaning at all. Perhaps there is no single concept that coherently encompasses the various views of intuition. Certainly that is one possibility. However, another possibility is that there is a meaningful construct that can assimilate all the valid features that have been ascribed to intuition within a single adaptive information-processing system. I make the case in this chapter that almost everything that has been attributed to intuition can be explained by the operation of a system that automatically learns from experience, which I refer to as the "experiential system." As a result of the operation of this system, people acquire a great reservoir of unconscious information.

I begin by presenting the attributes of intuition reported in a survey by Abernathy and Hamm (1995). The survey examined the use of the term *intuition* in medicine, education, and psychology among other sources (reported in Hammond, 1996, p. 63). I next present the most relevant aspects of a global theory of personality, cognitive-experiential self-theory (CEST), which I believe can importantly contribute to an understanding of intuition. I then apply the theory to an examination of the proposed attributes of intuition and note how they can be explained by CEST or indicate why the few that can not be explained are not valid aspects of intuition.

The attributes of intuition in the Abernathy and Hamm (1995) list (reported in Hammond, 1996) are presented in Table 2.1.

TABLE 2.1 Attribute List of Intuition by Abernathy and Hamm (1995) as Reported in Hammond (1996)

Intuition is different from other thinking
  Intuition is thought without analysis.
  Intuition produces different results than analytic thinking.
  Intuition is different from everyday thinking.
  Intuition is infallible.
  Intuition is a sense of a solution not yet fully developed.
  Intuition has a feeling of certainty.

Intuition uses special information
  Intuition is visual insight.
  Intuition requires attention to one's own internal feelings.
  Intuition is characteristic of people's performance of familiar tasks.
  Intuition is fast and easy.
  Intuition is pattern recognition.
  Intuition arises from complex systems of symbolic rules.
  Intuition is nonsymbolic thought, as in a neural network.
  Intuition involves functional reasoning.

Intuition is an option: If one can choose to do it, one can choose not to do it
  Intuition is just lazy thinking.
  Intuition is an unavoidable necessity.
  Intuitive cognition can outperform analysis
  Intuition is the prudent voice in some situations
  Intuition is the use of fallible heuristic strategies

Intuition involves judgment of importance

A THEORY OF PERSONALITY THAT CAN EXPLAIN INTUITION

As I demonstrate, CEST can account for and elucidate the attributes of intuition in the Abernathy and Hamm (1995) list. Equally important, it can indicate why the ones it can not account for are not valid attributes.

A fundamental assumption in CEST is that people operate by two cognitive systems: an "experiential system", which is a nonverbal automatic learning system, and a "rational system," which is a verbal reasoning system. The experiential system operates in a manner that is preconscious, automatic, nonverbal, imagistic, associative, rapid, effortless, concrete, holistic, intimately associated with affect, highly compelling, and minimally demanding of cognitive resources. It operates according to the hedonic principle, which corresponds to the reinforcement principle in learning theory and the pleasure principle of psychoanalysis, and essentially involves pursuing what is pleasurable and avoiding what is unpleasurable. Its schemas are primarily generalizations from emotionally significant intense or repetitive experience. It is the same system with which nonhuman animals have successfully negotiated their environments over millions of years of evolution.

The experiential system automatically establishes associations through classical conditioning, instrumental conditioning, and observational learning, all of which involve relations of stimuli and/or responses with outcomes. The associative connections are determined by similarity, contiguity, and emotional reinforcement. Although the experiential system encodes experience in the form of nonverbal concrete representations (e.g., images, feelings, physical sensations, metaphors, and scenarios), and its associations tend to be context specific, it is capable of generalization. It generalizes in the form of individual generalization gradients as well as from the confluence of two or more generalization gradients. The magnitude and breadth of its generalization gradients are a direct function of the emotional intensity of the events that are the sources of the generalizations. The three kinds of learning are regarded as subsystems within a more general system, as they serve a common function of automatically learning from experience, directly or by observation. In this respect, the experiential system is no different from any other system that includes subsystems such as a transportation system that includes air, sea, and ground transportation.

In contrast to the automatic learning of the experiential system, the rational system is a reasoning system that operates in a manner that is conscious, verbal, abstract, analytical, affect free, effortful, and highly demanding of cognitive resources. It acquires its beliefs by conscious learning from books, lectures and other explicit sources of information, and from logical inference; and it has a very brief evolutionary history. Thus, like the experiential system, it learns from experience, but it does so not through automatically establishing associations but by logical inference. Table 2.2 presents a comparison of the operating characteristics of the two systems.

The two systems are assumed to operate in parallel and to be bidirectionally interactive. All behavior according to CEST is influenced by a combination of both systems. However, for convenience, I often refer to behaviors as experientially or rationally determined if they are primarily determined by one system or the other. Their relative influence is assumed to vary along a dimension of pure experientiality at one end and pure rationality at the other (see Hammond, 1996, for a similar view). This assumption has been supported by research that has demonstrated various levels of compromises between the two systems (e.g., Denes-Raj & Epstein, 1994; Kirkpatrick & Epstein, 1992; Morling & Epstein, 1997; Yanko & Epstein, 1999). As all behavior is considered to be influenced by both systems; the poles of the dimension only exist as theoretical end points. The relative contribution of the systems is considered to be a function of the situation and the person. Lest it be unconvincing that all behavior in humans is influenced by both systems, consider the following thought experiments. First, imagine a situation in which a person is working on a mathematics problem. Although it might seem that this is a purely rational endeavor, it, like all other behavior, is influenced by the totality of a person's relevant past experience. For example, a person's previous experience with mathematics will necessarily automatically influence the person's attitude toward mathematics. If the attitude is favorable, it will facilitate performance; and if it is unfavorable, it will interfere with performance.

TABLE 2.2 The Two Systems of the Cognitive-experiential Self-theory

COMPARISON OF THE EXPERIENTIAL AND RATIONAL SYSTEMS

EXPERIENTIAL SYSTEM (An automatic learning system)	RATIONAL SYSTEM (A conscious reasoning system)
1. Preconscious	1. Conscious
2. Automatic	2. Deliberative
3. Concrete: Encodes reality in images, metaphors, and narratives	3. Abstract: Encodes reality in symbols, words, and numbers
4. Holistic	4. Analytic
5. Associative: Connections by similarity and contiguity	5. Cause-and-effect relations
6. Intimately associated with affect	6. Affect-free
7. Operates by hedonic principle (what feels good)	7. Operates by reality principle (what is logical and supported by evidence)
8. Acquires its schemas by learning from experience	8. Acquires its beliefs by conscious learning and logical inference
9. Outcome oriented	9. More process oriented
10. Behavior mediated by "vibes" from past experience	10. Behavior mediated by conscious appraisal of events
11. Rapid processing: Oriented toward immediate action	11. Slower processing: Capable of long delayed action
12. Resistant to change: Changes with repetitive or intense experience	12. Less resistant to change: Can change with speed of thought
13. Crudely differentiated: Broad generalization gradient; categorical thinking	13. More highly differentiated nuanced thinking
14. Crudely integrated: Situationally specific; organized in part by cognitive-affective modules	14. More highly integrated: Organized in part by cross-situational principles
15. Experienced passively and preconsciously: We are seized by our emotions	15. Experienced actively and consciously: We believe we are in control of our thoughts
16. Self-evidently valid: "Experiencing is believing"	16. Requires justification via logic and evidence

Next, consider a situation that might appear to be completely within the province of the experiential system: dreaming. Yet dreams are organized into a story, which indicates that they have some minimal logical organization (for a more detailed discussion of dreams from the perspective of CEST, see Epstein, 1999).

Neither system according to CEST is superior to the other. Each has its strengths and limitations. The rational system is capable of solving abstract problems, of planning, of applying principles broadly across situations, and of taking long-term considerations into account. The experiential system is able to effortlessly direct behavior in everyday life. It is a source of motivation and passion. Without it, the ability of people to engage in motivated behavior would be seriously compromised (e.g., Damasio, 1994). It can solve some problems that are beyond the capacity of the rational system because they require a holistic rather than analytic orientation, because they depend on lessons from lived experience, or because they require creativity via associative connections (see Hammond, 1996, for further discussion and research on this issue). As Norris and Epstein's (2007) research has indicated, the experiential system plays a particularly important role in creativity, humor, empathy, emotionality, and interpersonal relationships. Without an experiential system, people would be like robots with computers in their heads. They would be incapable of feeling. Although they would not experience destructive emotions such as road rage, it would be at the cost of being devoid of positive emotions such as love and empathy.

According to CEST, the two systems interact both simultaneously and sequentially. I first consider a sequential interaction. As the experiential system is the more rapidly reacting system, the initial reaction to a situation is experiential. If the initial response tendency is identified in the rational system as inappropriate, the rational system suppresses or adjusts the response tendency. If it is not identified as inappropriate, it is automatically expressed.

Now consider a sequence in which the experiential system reacts to the rational system. A response (including a thought) instigated by the rational system can produce associations in the experiential system, which can affect performance. Thus, responses in each system produce reactions in the other system as in a dance between the two systems. As previously noted, research has demonstrated the simultaneous influence of the systems on each other in the form of compromises between the two systems (e.g., Denes-Raj & Epstein, 1994; Yanko & Epstein, 1999).

Each system has a major advantage and disadvantage in influencing the other system. The rational system can understand the experiential system, whereas the experiential system cannot understand the rational system. On its part, the experiential system can influence the rational system without the rational system being aware that it is being influenced.

In the absence of awareness, the experiential system is free to influence conscious thinking and behavior. This need not be a serious problem in everyday living if people's experiential reactions are appropriate to begin with. However, it can be a source of serious problems when this is not the case. Awareness of the operation of the experiential system puts the rational system in a position in which it may be able to exercise control. Although it often succeeds, there are circumstances, as in irrational fears, in which despite a person's awareness of their irrationality, the person is unable to control the irrational thoughts.

An interesting question with obvious implications for intuition is whether the experiential system can reason. The answer depends on one's definition of reasoning. If its meaning is restricted to the application of rules of logic with the use of verbal symbols, the experiential system as a nonverbal system obviously cannot reason. However, if a broader definition is accepted, such as that reasoning is solving problems through the use of any form of mental activity in the absence of overt behavior, then the experiential system can reason. It can do so by the use of imagery in association with feelings. Although learning by overt trial and error does not qualify as reasoning, if the trial and error is carried out by visualization, it does qualify by this definition. Such reasoning has significant implications for intuition because it indicates how people's experiential system can include a reasoning component that operates in a different manner from that of the rational system.

The manner in which it operates, according to CEST, is that when people imagine alternatives, the alternatives are accompanied by "vibes" if not by more definitive emotions. *Vibes* are defined in CEST as vague feelings such as disquietude and agitation. The vibes or emotions then influence the subsequent behavior. Reasoning with images may be a useful procedure for humans to obtain new insights that they are unable to obtain from verbal reasoning.

An extensive research program has provided support for almost all of the major assumptions in CEST including the operating characteristics of the experiential system listed in Table 2.2. The interested reader can find summaries of this research in several publications (e.g., Epstein, 1998, 2003; Epstein & Pacini, 1999). Research results from two self-report instruments that measure different aspects of individual differences in experiential processing are of special interest with respect to intuition. One of the measures, the Rational-Experiential Inventory (REI; e.g., Epstein & Pacini, 1999; Epstein, Pacini, Denes-Raj, & Heier, 1996), provides information on the extent to which people operate according to experiential and rational thinking styles. The other measure, the Constructive Thinking Inventory (CTI; Epstein, 2001) assesses individual differences in the "intelligence" or efficacy of the experiential system. It does so by obtaining information on the constructiveness of the form and content of people's everyday automatic thoughts and interpretation of events.

It has been found in research with the REI that a rational thinking style is positively associated with measures of favorable adjustment including self-esteem, conscientiousness, extraversion, openness, ego strength, and favorable beliefs about the self and the world. It is negatively associated with various measures of maladjustment including anxiety, depression, and neuroticism and also with naïve optimism, categorical thinking, distrust, intolerance, fundamentalist religious beliefs, and extreme rightist political beliefs. An experiential thinking style is positively associated with esoteric beliefs, superstitious thinking, openness, positive thinking, naïve optimism, favorable interpersonal relationships, extraversion, agreeableness, favorable beliefs about the self and the world, sense of humor, creativity, social popularity, emotionality, empathy, and esthetic judgment. It is negatively associated with categorical thinking and distrust (for research that has supported these conclusions, see Epstein & Pacini, 2001; Epstein et al., 1996; Norris & Epstein, 2007; Pacini & Epstein, 1999; Pacini, Muir, & Epstein, 1998). Of particular interest, the two thinking styles make independent, supplementary contributions to a variety of predictions.

Scores on the CTI have been found to be independent of intellectual intelligence and more strongly positively correlated than measures of intelligence with a variety of measures of success in living including social success, work success, mental adjustment, and physical well-being (e.g., Epstein, 1992a, 1992b, 2001; Epstein & Katz, 1992; Epstein & Meier, 1989; Katz & Epstein, 1991; Scheuer & Epstein, 1997). So far, the only criterion variables with which intelligence-test scores produced stronger correlations than CTI scores have been measures of academic performance.

According to CEST, everything I have said about the experiential system is relevant to intuition because intuition is regarded as a subset of experiential processing. Intuition can be defined, according to CEST, as the accumulated tacit information that a person has acquired by automatically learning from experience. To complete the definition, it is necessary to establish its boundary conditions. As intuition is automatically acquired from personal experience; it does not include other nonrationally derived beliefs that although primarily influenced by the experiential system, were acquired in ways other than by personal experience. Thus, intuition does not include religious beliefs, which are based on faith, or formal superstitions, which are institutionally available beliefs. People do not fear black cats crossing their path because of personal experience but because it is an institutionally established superstition. Intuition also does not include beliefs acquired from experience if people are able to articulate the source of the beliefs. Knowing the source of a nonrationally derived belief violates the requirement that an intuitive belief must be tacit. That is, a defining aspect of intuition is that it involves knowing without knowing how one knows, which gives intuition its aura of mystery. People do not regard as intuitive the distrust by a holocaust victim of any person in a uniform. The source of the fear is evident to that person as well as to others. In contrast, people do regard as intuitive, for example, a woman's distrust of someone who unconsciously reminds her of another person who once harmed her. Although she has a strong impression that the person is not to be trusted, she is unable to account for her impression.

HOW THE EXPERIENTIAL SYSTEM ACCOUNTS FOR THE ATTRIBUTES OF INTUITION

As I previously noted, CEST can account for almost all of the proposed attributes of intuition summarized by Abernathy and Hamm (1995). Equally important, it can explain why those that it can not account for are not valid attributes of intuition.

The first general category in the Abernathy and Hamm (1995) list is that intuition is different from other kinds of thinking. This statement is in obvious agreement with the assumption in CEST that intuitive thinking operates according to the rules of the experiential system, which are different from the rules of the rational system.

The first specific attribute listed under the category just mentioned is that intuition is thought without analysis. This is perhaps the most widely proposed defining attribute of intuition (see Hammond, 1996; Myers, 2002). It also coincides with the dictionary definition (Merriam-Webster's Collegiate Dictionary, 1996). However, it only tells one what intuition is not. To determine what intuition is, one must turn to other attributes.

According to the second item, intuition produces different results than analytic thinking. This again follows directly from the difference between experiential and rational processing. As the two processing modes operate by different rules (see Table 2.2), they produce different results. For instance, research has demonstrated that processing in the rational and experiential modes often produces different decisions (e.g., Denes-Raj & Epstein, 1994; Epstein & Pacini, 2001; Epstein, Lipson, Holstein, & Huh, 1992; Kirkpatrick & Epstein, 1992).

The next item is that intuition is different from everyday thinking. According to CEST, although the rules of experiential processing govern intuition and are the same rules that govern everyday thinking, there is an important difference between intuitive thinking and everyday thinking. The difference is that in everyday thinking, people can usually state the reasons for their beliefs; whereas in intuitive thinking, the information is tacit and therefore can not be identified. Thus, a person may intuitively have a feeling that someone is dangerous but be unable to explain why, as the connection with the original source is inaccessible.

The next attribute is that intuition is infallible. This view is in direct opposition to the position of CEST according to which the experiential system can be either adaptive or maladaptive, depending on the appropriateness of past learning for a present situation (see also Unkelbach & Plessner, chap. 17, this volume).

Intuition in the next item is said to involve a sense of solution not yet fully developed. As intuition is based on implicit information in the experiential system, it can be further developed by making it explicit in the rational system. The sequence of an implicit intuitive stage followed by a conscious analytical stage has been reported for several important scientific discoveries.

In the next item, intuition is said to have a feeling of certainty. As can be seen in Table 2.1, processing in the experiential mode is described as self-evidently valid and therefore compelling. One reason for this is that the experiential system is intimately associated with emotion. It has been shown in research (e.g., Denes-Raj & Epstein, 1994; Edwards & von Hippel, 1995; Epstein et al., 1992; Pacini et al., 1998) that people often have greater confidence in their affective than in their purely cognitive judgments. It has also been found that experiential processing can override people's conscious beliefs (Denes-Raj & Epstein, 1994).

The second major category is that intuition uses special information. This is consistent with the experiential system operating by a different set of rules than the rational system. As a result, it is responsive to different kinds of information. For example, the experiential system is more responsive to concrete, holistic, emotionally arousing, visual, context-specific, and associative information than is the rational system, which is more responsive to abstract, analytical, factual, verbal, context-general information as well as to logical argument.

The first item under the category that intuition uses special information is that intuition is visual insight. This is consistent with the experiential system as a nonverbal imagistic system as indicated in Table 2.1. As I noted previously, reasoning with images provides a different way of solving problems from reasoning with words. That this may have important implications for creativity was suggested by Einstein (Levenson, 2003), among other scientists, who reported that he was better able to solve certain problems in physics by visualization than by thinking in words.

The next item states that intuition requires attention to feelings. Although the experiential system is intimately associated with feelings, it is not necessary to consciously attend to their feelings for people to respond intuitively. Nonhuman animals, unable to attend consciously to their feelings, respond to subtle cues in a manner that would be regarded as intuitive if exhibited by a person. As an example, consider the behavior of an animal that senses that someone has ill intentions toward it by detecting cues that are reminders of past abuse. Although deliberate attention to feelings is not a necessary condition for intuition to occur, attention to feelings can be useful in making implicit intuitive information explicit (see also T. Betsch, chap. 1, this volume).

The statement that intuition is characteristic of people's performance of familiar tasks is consistent with the assumption in CEST that behavior in everyday life is primarily directed by the experiential system, which consists mainly of familiar reactions to familiar tasks. Moreover, as behavior is practiced and becomes increasingly familiar, a shift takes place in the balance of the influence between the experiential and rational systems, with the experiential system gaining increasing control (see Bargh, 1997, for a similar view that he relates to automaticity). To put it more succinctly, as behavior becomes habitualized, it becomes experientialized.

The view that intuition is fast and easy is consistent with the operation of the experiential system as an automatic, rapidly reacting system that makes minimal cognitive demands (see Table 2.1). The aphorism that a picture is worth a thousand words captures the greater ease and rapidity with which the experiential system operates in comparison to the rational system.

The view that intuition is pattern recognition follows from the experiential system processing information in a holistic manner. Pattern recognition is an important aspect of intuitive processing, but it is hardly a sufficiently defining attribute. The experiential system does not respond only to patterns. It also responds to concrete, specific objects and events. According to CEST, the defining attribute of intuition is the tacit information that is acquired by automatically learning from experience.

CEST is in disagreement with the statement that intuition arises from complex systems of symbolic rules. The rules that govern experiential processing and therefore intuition are the well-established, relatively simple laws of associative learning, which include similarity, contiguity, and reinforcement. There is nothing complicated about behavior that is followed by rewards having a tendency to be reproduced and behavior that is followed by punishment tending to be avoided. In fact, the view that intuitive processing is complex is itself an interesting illustration of the influence of experiential on rational processing. It is an example of associative thinking according to which strange phenomena, such as beliefs that can not be articulated, are assumed to require complex explanations.

The position that intuition is nonsymbolic thought as in a neural network is consistent with CEST in some ways and inconsistent in others. First, consider the part of the statement that refers to intuition as nonsymbolic thought. According to CEST, intuition may or may not involve symbolic thought depending on the nature of the symbolism. If the symbolism represents events in the form of verbal symbols, such as words and numbers, then it is in the realm of the rational system and therefore is not consistent with intuitive thought. However, if the symbolism is in the form of concrete visual representations based on associative connections, as in metaphors, then it is within the realm of intuitive processing.

As for the part of the statement that refers to neural networks, the idea of cognitive-affective neural networks that are the substrata of the organization of the schemas in the experiential system is completely in accord with CEST (Epstein, 2007). A particularly influential class of such networks, according to CEST, consists of networks that have at their core an imagistic representation and associated feelings of an intense emotional experience such as a trauma (Epstein, 2007). The concept of neural networks that exist at different hierarchical levels and that interact with each other in both directions (bottom up and top down) is another important concept in CEST (Epstein, 2007).

The next statement is that intuition involves functional reasoning. If functional reasoning refers to reasoning that serves an adaptive function, then the statement is consistent with the assumption in CEST that the experiential system is an adaptive learning system.

The statement that intuition is an option that people can choose to do or not to do is only partly true according to CEST. As research has demonstrated (e.g., Denes-Raj & Epstein, 1994), people are often able to choose between behaving according to their experiential or their rational processing. However, to choose between the two processes requires people to be aware that they have choices (Payne, Bettman, & Johnson, 1993). Some people have no such awareness because they consider their behavior all of a piece. These people regard their experientially determined processing as rational because their decisions feel right to them (see Table 2.2; Denes-Raj & Epstein, 1994). Another reason why people may not be able to choose between alternative possibilities is that the experiential processing is so emotionally intense that they are unable to suppress its influence, as in phobias, compulsions, and certain superstitions.

The statement that intuition is lazy thinking is incorrect according to CEST. Lazy thinking implies a reduced amount of thinking (e.g., short-cut rational processing), not a different kind of thinking (e.g., experiential processing). According to CEST, it is important to avoid the error exhibited in several influential, social-pychological, dual-process theories of equating reduced or degraded deliberative processing with a different form of processing (e.g., Chen & Chaiken, 1999; Petty & Wegener, 1999). Intuition, rather than consisting of reduced rational processing, consists of experiential processing.

The view that intuition is an unavoidable necessity is consistent with CEST, according to which experiential processing is involved to a greater or lesser extent in all information processing. No person can react to any situation independent of the person's past experience. Moreover, although people could exist with only an experiential system, as attested to by nonhuman animals, they could not exist with only a rational system. Without an experiential system, people's ability to make decisions and take effective action would be seriously compromised (Damasio, 1994). As I noted elsewhere (Epstein, 2003), it may be difficult to live with the experiential system, but it would be impossible to live without it.

The view that intuitive cognition can outperform analysis is consistent with CEST. According to CEST, either system can outperform the other depending on the nature of the problem at issue. Behaving according to what has been automatically learned from experience is more efficient in many situations than attempting to solve problems by reasoning. In laboratory research, it has been demonstrated that making aesthetic evaluations and other kinds of subjective judgments by relying on intuition often outperforms judgments made by analytical reasoning (e.g., Hammond, 1996; Hammond, Hamm, Grassia, & Pearson, 1987; Plessner & Czenna, chap. 15, this volume; Wilson & Schooler, 1991). In problems that are too complex or that are structured in a manner that makes it impossible to objectively analyze their components, holistic, experiential judgments may provide the only possible approach. Included among such tasks are the establishment of satisfactory interpersonal relationships, which has been demonstrated in research to be more strongly positively associated with individual differences in experiential than in rational processing (Epstein et al., 1996; Pacini & Epstein, 1999; Norris & Epstein, 2007).

The view that intuition is the prudent voice in some situations readily follows from the operation of the experiential system. People automatically learn from experience that certain situations or people are dangerous. Such learning can occur in the absence of awareness; a person may simply have an intuitive impression that someone is not to be trusted without being able to account for the feeling. In the interest of caution, it is reasonable to attend to such feelings and treat them as possibly valid until proven otherwise.

CEST is only in partial agreement with the statement that intuition is the use of fallible heuristic strategies. This is because heuristic processing is sometimes fallible and sometimes adaptive, depending often on whether it is judged by normative standards or by standards of efficacy in everyday life (e.g., Donovan & Epstein, 1997; Epstein, Denes-Raj, & Pacini, 1995; Gigerenzer, 1991; Hammond, 1996). Moreover, intuitive processing is not restricted only to heuristic processing but includes other phenomena such as automatically forming impressions about people and events.

The last item is that intuition involves judgment of importance. According to CEST, there is a direct relation between the importance of schemas in the experiential system and the intensity of the emotions aroused by the schemas being activated. For example, if a woman reacts more emotionally when her appearance is evaluated than when her intelligence is evaluated, it can be assumed, no matter what she says, that at the experiential level, her appearance is more important to her than her intelligence. It is because of this relation that emotions are regarded in CEST as the royal road to the schemas in the experiential system.

In summary, almost all of the attributes of intuition in the Abernathy and Hamm (1995) list can be accounted for by the operation of the experiential system. The experiential system can explain why intuition is thought without analysis, why it is different from analytic thinking, why it provides incomplete solutions that require articulation by the rational system, why intuition is inherently highly compelling, why it often corresponds to nonverbal visual insight, why it is associated with feelings, why it operates in familiar tasks, why it is fast and easy, why it often involves pattern recognition, why it encodes events in the form of concrete representations, why it involves functional reasoning, why it is an unavoidable necessity, why it is a source of prudence in some situations, and why heuristic processing is an aspect of intuitive thinking when it involves processing in the experiential system but not when it involves short-cut processing in the rational system. The rules of experiential processing can also explain why some of the proposed attributes of intuition are inappropriate including the view that intuition is infallible, that intuition requires attention to feelings, that intuition is based on a complex system of symbolic rules, and that intuition is lazy thinking.

THE ADVANTAGES OF REGARDING INTUITION AS A SUBSET OF EXPERIENTIAL PROCESSING

The assumption that intuition is a subset of the operation of the experiential system has several advantages. First, it provides a scientifically meaningful explanation of a phenomenon that some have considered mysterious and beyond scientific comprehension. Second, it provides an answer to the question of how people are able to know without knowing how they know. The answer is that intuition is based on the vast store of tacit information that people have acquired by automatically learning from experience. Third, the characteristics of experiential processing as summarized in Table 2.2 provide a clearly articulated position for determining the validity or invalidity of various proposed attributes of intuition. Fourth, the proposed characteristics of the experiential system have almost all received experimental support (see reviews in Epstein, 2003; Epstein & Pacini, 1999). Fifth, CEST anchors intuition within the framework of a global theory of personality, which elucidates its relation to, and interaction with, many other personality variables. This not only allows intuition to be understood within a broader context, including its position in evolutionary development, but it also provides a source of new ideas about intuition including how it influences and is influenced by the rational system in a coordinated dance. Consider, as a further example, the issue of whether there are different levels of intuitive sophistication and if so, how they can be accounted for. Hogarth (2001), following Reber (1993), proposed three levels of automatic processing, basic, primitive, and sophisticated. I am in essential agreement that automatic processing exists at different levels of complexity, but there is more to the picture than levels of processing within a single system. I previously noted that the experiential system plays an important role in a wide range of behavior including classical conditioning at the simplest level and artistic and scientific creativity at the most advanced level (e.g., Epstein, 1994). This raises the question of how a relatively crude automatic learning system that humans share with other animals can, by itself, produce the highly complex behavior that results in great accomplishments in art, mathematics, and science. The answer, according to CEST, is that it can not do so by itself, but it can in interaction with the rational system. Thus, the experiential system, including its intuitive component, can introduce an associative, imagistic, holistic component into people's thinking that allows them to process information in a more creative and productive manner than if they were to rely solely on the linear, analytical reasoning of their rational system. More generally, and consistent with research findings, there is a synergistic effect when the two systems operate together in a harmonious manner (e.g., Donovan & Epstein, 1997; Epstein et al., 1995).

SUMMARY AND CONCLUSION

Intuition can be understood by the operating principles and characteristics of the experiential system of CEST. The experiential system is an automatic, nonverbal learning system that humans share with other animals. In addition, humans adapt to their environment with a rational system, which is a verbal reasoning system. All human behavior is assumed to be influenced by a combination of both systems. I demonstrated that the characteristics of experiential processing can explain in a highly coherent fashion almost all of the 20 attributes of intuition in a survey of the literature by Abernathy and Hamm (1995) and can indicate why the others are invalid. In addition to accounting for everyday intuition, the experiential system in combination with the rational system can also account for more complex behavior such as creativity and wisdom.

REFERENCES

Abernathy, C. M., & Hamm, R. M. (1995). *Surgical intuition: What it is and how to get it.* Philadelphia: Hanley & Belfus.

Bargh, J. A. (1997). The automaticity of everyday life. In R. S. Wyer (Ed.), *Advances in social cognition* (Vol. 10, pp. 1–61). Mahwah, NJ: Lawrence Erlbaum Associates, Inc.

Chen, S., & Chaiken, S. (1999). The heuristic-systematic model in its broader context. In S. Chaiken & Y. Trobe (Eds.), *Dual-process theories in social psychology* (pp. 73–96). New York: Guilford.

Damasio, A. R. (1994). *Descartes error: Emotion, reason, and the human brain.* New York: Avon Books.

Denes-Raj, V., & Epstein, S. (1994). Conflict between experiential and rational processing: When people behave against their better judgment. *Journal of Personality and Social Psychology, 66,* 819–829.

Donovan, S., & Epstein, S. (1997). The difficulty of the Linda conjunction problem can be attributed to its simultaneous concrete and unnatural representation, and not to conversational implicature. *Journal of Experimental Social Psychology, 33,* 1–20.

Edwards, K., & von Hippel, W. (1995). Hearts and minds: The priority of affective versus cognitive factors in person perception. *Personality and Social Psychology Bulletin, 21,* 996–1011.

Epstein, S. (1992a). Constructive thinking and mental and physical well-being. In L. Montada, S. H. Filipp, & M. J. Lerner (Eds.), *Life crises and experiences of loss in adulthood* (pp. 385–409). Hillsdale, NJ: Lawrence Erlbaum Associates, Inc.

Epstein, S. (1992b). Coping ability, negative self-evaluation, and overgeneralization: Experiment and Theory. *Journal of Personality and Social Psychology, 62,* 826–836.

Epstein, S. (1994). Integration of the cognitive and the psychodynamic unconscious. *American Psychologist, 49,* 709–724.

Epstein, S. (1998). *Constructive thinking: The key to emotional intelligence.* Westport, CT: Greenwood.

Epstein, S. (1999). The interpretation of dreams from the perspective of cognitive-experiential self-theory. In J. A. Singer & P. Salovey (Eds.), *At play in the fields of consciousness: Essays in honor of Jerome L. Singer* (pp. 59–82). Mahwah, NJ: Lawrence Erlbaum Associates, Inc.

Epstein, S. (2001). *Manual for the Constructive Thinking Inventory.* Odessa, FL: Psychological Assessment Resources.

Epstein, S. (2003). Cognitive-experiential self-theory of personality. In T. Millon & M. J. Lerner (Eds.), *Handbook of psychology: Vol. 5. Personality and social psychology* (pp. 159–184). Hoboken, NJ: Wiley.

Epstein, S. (2007). *Cognitive-experiential self-theory: A unified theory of personality.* Manuscript in preparation.

Epstein, S., Denes-Raj, V., & Pacini, R. (1995). The Linda problem revisited from the perspective of cognitive-experiential self-theory. *Personality and Social Psychology Bulletin, 11,* 1124–1138.

Epstein, S., & Katz, L. (1992). Coping ability, stress, productive load, and symptoms. *Journal of Personality and Social Psychology, 62,* 813–825.

Epstein, S., Lipson, A., Holstein, C., & Huh, E. (1992). Irrational reactions to negative outcomes: Evidence for two conceptual systems. *Journal of Personality and Social Psychology, 62,* 328–339.

Epstein, S., & Meier, P. (1989). Constructive thinking: A broad coping variable with specific components. *Journal of Personality and Social Psychology, 57,* 332–349.

Epstein, S., & Pacini, R. (1999). Some basic issues regarding dual-process theories from the perspective of cognitive-experiential self-theory. In S. Chaiken & Y. Trope (Eds.), *Dual-process theories in social psychology* (pp. 462–482). New York: Guilford.

Epstein, S., & Pacini, R. (2001). The influence of visualization on intuitive and analytical information processing. *Imagination, Cognition, and Personality: Consciousness in Theory, Research, and Clinical Practice, 20,* 195–217.

Epstein, S., Pacini, R., Denes-Raj, V., & Heier, H. (1996). Individual differences in intuitive-experiential and analytical-rational thinking styles. *Journal of Personality and Social Psychology, 71,* 390–405.

Gigerenzer, G. (1991). How to make cognitive illusions disappear: Beyond "heuristics and biases." In W. Stroebe & M. Hewstone (Eds.), *European review of social psychology* (Vol. 2, pp. 83–115). New York: Wiley.

Hammond, K. R. (1996). *Human judgment and social policy: Incredible uncertainty, inevitable error, unavoidable justice.* New York: Oxford University Press.

Hammmond, K. R., Hamm, R. M., Grassia, J., & & Pearson, T. (1987). Direct comparison of the efficacy of intuitive and analytical cognition in expert judgment. *IEE Transactions on Systems, Man, and Cybernetics, 17,* 753–770.

Hogarth, R. M. (2001). *Educating intuition.* Chicago: University of Chicago Press.

Katz, L., & Epstein, S. (1991). Constructive thinking and coping with laboratory-induced stress. *Journal of Personality and Social Psychology, 61,* 789–800.

Kirkpatrick, L. A., & Epstein, S. (1992). Cognitive-experiential self-theory and subjective probability: Further evidence for two conceptual systems. *Journal of Personality and Social Psychology, 63,* 534–544.

Levenson, T. (2003). *Einstein in Berlin.* New York: Bantam Dell.

Merriam-Webster's collegiate dictionary (10th ed.). (1996). Springfield, MA: Merriam-Webster.

Morling, B., & Epstein, S. (1997). Compromises produced by the dialectic between self-verification and self-enhancement. *Journal of Personality and Social Psychology, 73,* 1268–1283.

Myers, D. G. (2002). *Intuition, its powers and perils.* New Haven, CT: Yale University Press.

Norris, P., & Epstein, S. (2007). *Intuition, imagination, and feelings: Components and correlates of experiential processing.* Manuscript submitted for publication.

Pacini, R., & Epstein, S. (1999). The relation of rational and experiential information processing styles to personality, basic beliefs, and the ratio-bias phenomenon. *Journal of Personality and Social Psychology, 76,* 972–987.

Pacini, R., Muir, F., & Epstein, S. (1998). Depressive realism from the perspective of cognitive-experiential self-theory. *Journal of Personality and Social Psychology, 74,* 1056–1068.

Payne, J. W., Bettman, J. R., & Johnson, E. J. (1993) *The adaptive decision maker.* Cambridge, England: Cambridge University Press.

Petty, R. E., & Wegener, D. T. (1999). The elaboration-likelihood model: Current status and controversies. In S. Chaiken & Y. Trobe (Eds.), *Dual-process theories in social psychology* (pp. 41–72). New York: Guilford.

Reber, A. S. (1993). *Implicit learning and tacit knowledge: An essay on the cognitive unconscious.* New York: Oxford University Press.

Scheuer, E., & Epstein, S. (1997). Coping ability, reactions to a laboratory stressor, and symptoms in everyday life. *Anxiety, Stress, and Coping, 10,* 269–303.

Wilson, T. D., & Schooler, J. W. (1991). Thinking too much: Introspection can reduce the quality of preferences and decisions. *Journal of Personality and Social Psychology, 60,* 181–192.

Yanko, J., & Epstein, S. (1999). [Compromises between experiential and rational processing as a function of age-level]. Unpublished raw data.

3

Variants of Judgment and Decision Making
The Perspective of the Reflective-Impulsive Model

ROLAND DEUTSCH and FRITZ STRACK
University of Würzburg

INTRODUCTION

To navigate successfully through their environment, organisms must constantly solve problems, make judgments, and come to decisions. Everyday experience as well as scientific research suggests that people accomplish these tasks very differently: Sometimes insights, judgments, and decisions follow from elaborate, effortful thinking. At other occasions, however, people seem to come up with an insight or decision with little thinking by relying on judgmental shortcuts and gut feelings instead of a comprehensive analysis of the situation to come to a judgment. Many psychological theories approach this variability of judgment and decision making by distinguishing between discrete types of thinking such as analytic or intuitive thinking.

Our purpose in this chapter is to analyze the variability of judgment and decision making from the perspective of dual-system models of cognition and behavior (for similar attempts, see Epstein, 1991; chap. 2, this volume; Hogarth, 2005; Kahneman & Frederick, 2002; Lieberman, 2000; Sloman, 1996). Particularly, we elaborate on how features usually attributed to intuition and heuristic judgments may relate to the operation of distinct mental systems.

Since the mid 1970s, research on dual processes became particularly common in numerous areas of cognitive and social psychology. Widespread dualities are, among others, the distinction between automatic and controlled processes (e.g., Schneider & Shiffrin, 1977), symbolic versus subsymbolic processes (Smolensky, 1988), heuristic versus systematic thinking (e.g., Chaiken, 1980), conscious versus unconscious cognition (Greenwald, 1992), or affect versus cognition. Dual-system theories aim at describing common mental structures that may underlie such dualities (for overviews, see Epstein, 1994; Sloman, 1996). A pioneering dual-system model in social and personality psychology has been Epstein's cognitive-experiential self-theory (CEST; e.g., Epstein, 1991, 1994), which proposes the existence of an automatic, associative experiential system, and a resource demanding, verbal reasoning system called the rational system (for a detailed description, see Epstein, chap. 2, this volume). Many later dual-system models share basic assumptions with CEST. Yet they refine and expand the dual-systems idea by integrating research on fundamental memory systems (Smith & DeCoster, 2000), cognitive neuroscience (Lieberman, 2000), connectionist modeling (Smith & DeCoster, 1999), or motivational science (Strack & Deutsch, 2004).

In this chapter, we do not focus on differences between existing dual-system models (for a systematic comparison, see Smith & DeCoster, 2000) but use the reflective-impulsive model (RIM; Strack & Deutsch, 2004) of social behavior as a prototype for dual-system models. We start out with a brief overview of the processing principles of the RIM. In a second step, we give a more detailed description of the psychological mechanisms underlying variants of judgment and decision making.

OVERVIEW OF THE RIM

The RIM explains social cognition and behavior as a function of two processing systems, which follow distinct principles (see Fig. 3.1). The impulsive system (IS) directs behavior by linking external cues to behavioral schemata (Schmidt, 1975)

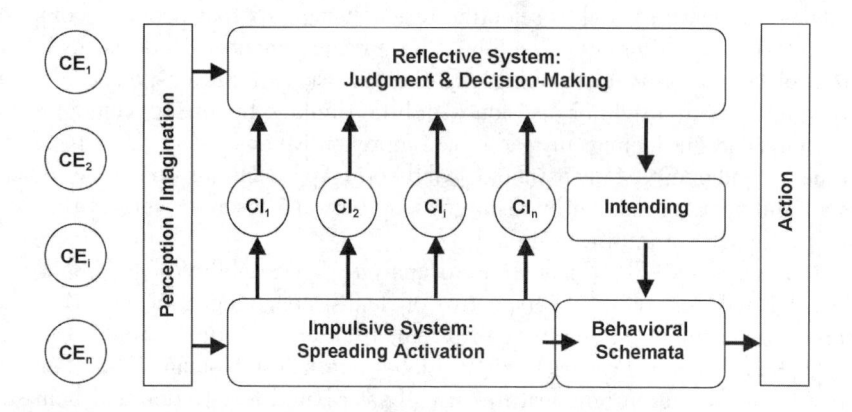

FIGURE 3.1 Schematic description of judgment and decision making in the reflective system. CE = environmental cues; CI = internal cues generated by the impulsive system (e.g., feelings, conceptual activation).

based on previously learned associations. This spread of activation occurs efficiently, independent of intentions, and in a parallel fashion, integrating a number of perceptual features present in a situation. The IS focuses on seeking pleasure and avoiding pain and is specifically tuned to ensure the satisfaction of fundamental needs such as nutrition, hydration, or sleep. To do this, the IS is endowed with three mechanisms: A multimodal associative memory including behavioral schemata, motivational orientation, and a device to mediate between memory activation and deprivation. During its operation, it generates various internal responses, the most important being the activation of concepts, affective and nonaffective feelings, and behavioral tendencies. These internal cues can be perceived by the reflective system (RS) and fed into judgment formation.

The RS has features complementary to the IS, serving different regulatory goals. It is specialized in generating a metarepresentation of what is activated in the IS and, if necessary, to fulfill executive functions such as overcoming habitual responses or putting together action plans in new situations or when habits fail (Lieberman, Gaunt, Gilbert, & Trope, 2002). Its functioning is directed by processing goals and depends on high cognitive resources and intermediate arousal. Its operations are slower than the operations of the IS and are based on a few, distinct, symbolic representations. It elicits actions as a consequence of decisions, which activate behavioral schemata through a process of intending (Gollwitzer, 1999). Intending automatically reactivates the behavioral schemata corresponding with the decision. The enhanced activation of these schemas increases attention to stimuli relevant for the behavioral implementation of the decision and increases the likelihood that an appropriate schema is triggered by a situation.

Two Judgmental Paths

Generally, the RIM assumes that all explicit judgments and decisions are exclusively generated in the RS. Yet environmental cues influence explicit judgments and decisions in two different ways (see Fig. 3.1). First, the RS may select environmental cues and directly integrate them into a judgment such as estimating a car's resale value based on the brand, its mileage, or relevant consumer reports. Second, perceiving environmental cues additionally leads to organismic responses (Bless & Forgas, 2000) generated by the IS. For instance, perceiving subtle facial cues of hostility may automatically elicit negative feelings, or seeing a member of a stereotyped group may push negative personality traits into one's consciousness (Devine, 1989). Just as environmental cues, these internal cues can feed into judgmental processes in the RS. One may judge a situation to be dangerous because it makes one feel anxious (Loewenstein, Weber, Hsee, & Welch, 2001), or one may regard a person as dishonest because the concept dishonest keeps popping into one's mind as long the person is present. Hence, environmental cues can either directly feed into judgments or indirectly, mediated by organismic responses. How does this distinction between direct and indirect cue effects relate to intuitive and heuristic judgments?

As Epstein (chap. 2, this volume) points out, the term *intuition* has been used in a multitude of meanings. Yet most characterizations emphasize two aspects:

Intuition is thought to be effortless and to occur with little process awareness (e.g., Bruner, 1960; Hammond, 1996; Hogarth, 2005; Kahneman & Frederick, 2002; Lieberman, 2000). Additional criteria are the acquisition through practice and personal experience (Epstein, chap. 2, this volume; Lieberman, 2000) and a dominance of affect and cognitive feelings (T. Betsch, chap. 1, this volume; Kahneman & Frederick, 2002; Loewenstein et al., 2001) or that intuition is based on holistic assessments of the situation (e.g., Hogarth, 2005). Others claimed that "intuition is nothing more and nothing less than recognition" (Simon, 1992, p. 155). Apparently, the term *intuition* has been used with varying connotation. This is also true for the term *heuristic processing*. As Kahneman and Frederick (2002) pointed out, the term sometimes refers to judgments and decisions based on automatic, feeling-arousing processes, which are not open to introspection. Other authors have used it in a more strategic sense and have referred to situations in which people knowingly focus on easy to process but imperfect cues to substitute effortful analysis.

At first sight, one may immediately associate intuition with judgments based on internal cues. As we argue more detailed later, however, only some of the typical features used to characterize intuition match with the concept of indirect cue effects in the RIM. On one hand, processing internal cues is assumed to be relatively effortless, and their generation results from holistic, parallel processing. Also, internal cues are conceptualized to be recognition based in that the IS relies on stored links between situational patterns and responses. On the other hand, the RIM foresees the possibility that people may gain insight into their impulsive processes. Also, internal cues are not limited to feelings but also include conceptual activation and behavioral tendencies. Moreover, impulsive responses may not only be driven by practiced or personally experienced associations. Instead, passively observed covariations or verbally conveyed information in absence of first-hand experiences (such as in racial stereotypes) may have powerful effects on impulsive responses. Likewise, the concept of heuristics as strategically used simple cues does not simply tie to one of the two systems because depending on the environment, simple cues may be available either outside or inside the organism.

Thus, although it may seem tempting to connect low-effort, low process awareness, holistic, and affect-based judgments to one specialized intuitive or heuristic process or system, the perspective provided by the RIM is different. Judgments based on internal cues can have some of these features, but they must not have all of them. From the vantage point of the RIM, intuition as defined by the preceding criteria is only a subset of a broader range of indirect cue effects, which we believe to be similarly important for understanding the variability of judgment and decision making. In the following sections, we describe these mechanisms in greater detail.

INPUTS INTO REFLECTION

In the RIM, all judgments follow from syllogistic reasoning, which infers the meaning of an internal or external cue for the judgment at hand (Kruglanski, Erb, Spiegel, & Pierro, 2003). A necessary prerequisite for this to happen is that the cue is categorized and interpreted in the light of general knowledge. For instance, to use the age of a person to judge whether she or he would enjoy a cruise vacation, a specific age must be attributed to the person. Then, the categorized cue must be transformed into judgments by rules (e.g., If a person is young, there is a low chance that she or he would be interested in a cruise). Such rules or naïve theories (Skurnik, Schwarz, & Winkielman, 2000) must be learned from personal experience, or they can be culturally transmitted.

Generally, cues vary in at least two ways. First, they vary in their objective validity. Second, they vary in the ease with which they can be processed: Some are simply available; others are accessible at varying costs. By available we mean that they are directly observable such as the skin color, sex, or behavior of a person; the brand or price of a product in the supermarket; or the length of a persuasive message. By accessible, we mean that the judge must engage in some activity to sample the information such as to observe a person's behavior in many situations, try out a product, read a consumer report about it, or read the arguments contained in a persuasive message. Hence, despite that judgments follow from a uniform process of reasoning, they vary considerably depending on the type and amount of information fed into the judgmental process and the complexity of the rule involved in the reasoning process. In what follows, we describe important external and internal cues.

External Cues

In most situations that call for a judgment or a decision, multiple relevant pieces of evidence are available or accessible in the environment. Generally, the type and number of relevant external cues for a judgmental task at hand is determined by the ecology surrounding an individual and cannot be predicted by our model. Research in social psychology, however, has identified a number of external cues, which are often used to generate social judgments and decisions. In persuasive settings, a number of features of messages (e.g., its length, the number of arguments) or the communicator (e.g., expertise, power, attractiveness) were identified to determine the outcome of persuasive attempts if the recipient is low in motivation and cognitive capacity (Petty & Wegener, 1999). If highly motivated and capable, the content of the message generally receives superior weight in judgment formation. When looking for explanations of other people's behaviors, less motivated and able participants often rely on a one-cue reasoning, which infers personality traits directly from categorized behaviors. With more cognitive capacity and motivation, additional cues, such as possible situational constraints of the other person's behavior, are attended to and integrated into the judgment (Lieberman et al., 2002). When forming impressions about other people, salient cues, signaling the membership in social groups, are sometimes used as single judgmental cues. When judging a person's social or professional skill, people may categorize a person according to her or his sex or ethnic group membership and then use category information as a basis for inferences. Under different conditions, people may draw on different, not so easy accessible cues such as individual information about the person to form a judgment (Brewer, 1988).

These lines of research suggest that people rely on simple external cues to reduce processing efforts but are willing and able to switch to more demanding strategies when appropriate. Also, the direct reflective processing of external cues is not holistic (but selective) in nature and per definition, excludes feelings aroused by the cue. Yet, depending on the specific cue, its processing may be either very efficient or very demanding. Processes based on demanding external cues are therefore most similar to what is often labeled *systematic* or *analytic thinking*. Processing based on less demanding external cues, on the other hand, resembles the strategic sense of heuristic processing outlined by Kahneman and Frederick (2002).

Internal Cues

In addition to being categorized and directly fed into judgmental processes, according to the RIM, external cues trigger automatic responses of the IS, which then may enter judgments. The RIM foresees three important classes of impulsive responses, which can serve as internal cues: conceptual activation, feelings, and spontaneous behavioral tendencies.

Conceptual activation. The memory functions of the IS provide an important input into judgments and decisions. Because the IS automatically associates frequently co-occurring features, it provides the organism with knowledge about the typical structure of the environment (Smith & DeCoster, 2000). Particularly, frequently co-occurring representations of perceptual features, valence, and behavioral programs form associative clusters (see J. L. McClelland, McNaughton, & O'Reilly, 1995). By a mechanism resembling pattern completion, perceiving or imagining a stimulus that is similar to parts of an associative cluster, the whole cluster will receive activation and will be more available to reflective processes (Higgins, 1996). Such memory activation serves as an important input to judgments. The most drastic example may be the emergence of automaticity in judgment and decision making (Logan, 1988). By repeatedly generating a judgment or decision (e.g., mentally multiplying 6×6), the result (36) will be stored in memory and associated with the representation of the original task. Consequently, merely perceiving the task automatically activates the correct response. By this means, the IS provides a powerful cue to judgments, which makes the original calculation obsolete.

Social cognition research has identified numerous examples of how the mere perception or imagination of stimuli immediately leads to memory activation, which then may enter further judgmental processes. For instance, seeing cues that signify membership in a social group can activate features stereotypically associated with that social group (e.g., Kawakami, Dion, & Dovidio, 1998). Also, stimuli previously associated with positive or negative events later can immediately reactivate this positivity or negativity, thereby influencing judgments of liking (Fazio & Olson, 2003). In addition to this direct input into judgments, activated concepts can shape the categorization of external cues. For instance, if a stimulus is processed (e.g., cues of hostility) that by stereotypic association may increase the activation of a social category (e.g., African American), this category is more likely to be used to categorize the target (e.g., Hugenberg & Bodenhausen, 2004). For this process to occur, the activation of the category can also result from a source different from the categorized target (e.g., Higgins, Rholes, & Jones, 1977).

Feelings. Through learning, moderated by genetic preparedness, concepts in the IS can contain affective representations. Numerous studies have suggested that merely perceiving such stimuli automatically arouses a state of core affect (e.g., Russell, 2003), resulting in positive or negative feelings. When experienced, the feelings can be categorized, attributed to an object, and the RS then may infer properties of the object based on the affect it aroused (Schwarz & Clore, 1988). Consistent with this notion, affective feelings and moods have been demonstrated to play an important role for judgments of utility (e.g., Bechara, Damasio, Tranel, & Damasio, 1997), liking (Payne, Chen, Govorun, & Stewart, 2005), life satisfaction (Schwarz & Clore, 1983), and risk (e.g., Loewenstein et al., 2001).

In addition to affective feelings, the IS generates feelings of ease or processing fluency accompanying the activation of contents in the IS. In numerous studies, a high feeling of ease while processing a target has been demonstrated to let people infer a high frequency or probability of the target (for a review, see Schwarz, 1998). By this route, feelings of ease influence judgments of one's own personality (e.g., Schwarz et al., 1991), of the fame of a person (e.g., Jacoby, Kelley, Brown, & Jasechko, 1989), judgments of liking (e.g., Wänke, Bohner, & Jurkowitsch, 1997), or personal risk assessments (Rothman & Schwarz, 1998).

Behavioral activation. Another informational basis for the generation of knowledge about others and about the self is observed behavior. Associative clusters in the IS not only contain perceptual and evaluative information but are also connected to motor representations. Therefore, activating a cluster with behavioral codes (e.g., by observing other people's behaviors or by thinking about actions) will preactivate these codes, possibly resulting in fragmentary or full behaviors.

Numerous studies have supported the assumption of strong associations between the conceptual and the motor representation of behavior (e.g., Niedenthal, Barsalou, Winkielman, Krauth-Gruber, & Ric, 2005). For instance, a functional magnetic resonance imaging study conducted by Roth et al. (1996) demonstrated that the brain regions activated during contraction of a muscle are also contracted during imagery of a movement involving the same muscle. The same happens even when actions by others are merely observed (Rizzolatti & Arbib, 1998); and as a consequence, humans tend to automatically imitate behaviors they observe (e.g., Chartrand & Bargh, 1999). Activating social stereotypes that contain behavioral aspects (e.g., the elderly being slow) modulates how behavior is executed (Dijksterhuis & Bargh, 2001), and thinking about interacting with others can automatically instigate facial expressions (e.g., Vanman, Paul, Ito, & Miller, 1997). These behavioral tendencies are perceivable and not caused by a conscious decision to act. Resembling self-perception theory (Bem, 1967), they can serve as internal cues to a variety of social judgments (see Niedenthal et al., 2005).

Internal cues, heuristics, and intuition. Different from external cues, the RIM predicts internal cues to be always relatively easy to process. The IS provides them in readily interpretable feelings, concepts that pop into one's mind, or as slight movements. Also, internal cues are based on an automatic and comprehensive assessment of many external cues at a time. Under some circumstances, internal cues may occur without any explicit knowledge about why one responds in such a way (Wilson, Lindsey, & Schooler, 2000). In these cases, judgments based on internal cues follow most of the common criteria for intuition. There are, however, cases in which a clear process knowledge is to be expected. One example is the automatization of previously reflectively solved tasks (e.g., Smith & Lerner, 1986). Other examples are situations in which appraisals or categorizations are a basis for emotional responses. Likewise, stereotypic associations may result mainly from socially shared knowledge and less so from direct, personal experience (Devine, 1989). In these cases, people may base their judgments on feelings or activated concepts, but they may be able to explain why these were activated. According to the common criteria, this would not qualify for intuition.

Cue Selection

How does the RS decide which cues to use in which situation? The RIM only gives a very general answer, which is similar to the answer provided by most dual process models (Chaiken & Trope, 1999): It depends on motivation and cognitive capacity. Generally, the RS is assumed to chose those cues which (a) serve best the current goal (such as accurate judgments or coming to a particular conclusion; cf. Kruglanski et al., 2003) and (b) are compatible with the available cognitive resources. There are only two a priori predictions derived from our theory regarding which cues will be most valid and which cues are easy to process.

First, because internal cues are generated automatically on the perception of external cues, they are always easy to process. External cues, however, are predicted to have much greater variability in ease of processing depending on their availability or accessibility in the environment. For instance, the length of a persuasive message is immediately perceivable, whereas a complex argument requires considerable cognitive work to be decoded. Second, the validity of external cues solely depends on the ecology the individual lives in; the validity of internal cues additionally depends on the operational principles of the IS. For instance, the IS is predicted to be insensitive to verbal negations and hence may yield false responses (see following). With extended experience, people will develop subjective theories about these two parameters and can exploit this knowledge for cue selection.

MODERATORS OF IMPULSES

How the IS responds to an array of stimuli primarily depends on the associations that were created through learning and on the momentary accessibility based on recent activation. In addition, however, more dynamic factors moderate the reactivity of the IS. Particularly, the accessibility of stored contents—perceptual, affective, and behavioral codes—varies as a function of motivational processes in the IS and RS. These moderators are of great importance for judgments and decisions because they influence the generation of internal cues. Here, we briefly describe three important factors and discuss their relevance for judgments and decisions.

Reflection

Because the RS has only a short-term memory, propositions have to be constantly construed and rehearsed during operation (J. L. McClelland et al., 1995), thereby activating concepts in the IS and changing its automatic reactivity. For instance, explicitly thinking whether an object has a particular attribute (e.g., if the Mississippi is longer or shorter than 2,850 miles) makes relevant knowledge more accessible (e.g., Strack & Mussweiler, 1997). Other examples for such influences stem from research on automatic stereotyping (Blair, 2002). For instance, deliberate mental imagery of counterstereotypes reduces the automatic activation of stereotypic contents (Blair, Ma, & Lenton, 2001).

Additionally, the RS directs activation to the IS as a result of behavioral decisions. Particularly, the process of intending constantly activates behavioral schemata that were part of the decision until the situation allows their translation into overt behavior. Empirical evidence suggests that goal pursuit indeed changes automatic response tendencies toward goal-relevant stimuli. Goal pursuit was demonstrated to increase the accessibility of goal-relevant stimuli (Förster, Liberman, & Higgins, 2005). Additionally, recent evidence suggests that goal pursuit makes positive aspects of goal-relevant objects particularly accessible (e.g., Ferguson & Bargh, 2004; Moors & De Houwer, 2001).

Deprivation

In addition to the moderating role of goal pursuit, the RIM postulates that the deprivation of basic needs directly changes the reactivity of the IS. In the RIM, this is achieved by a mechanism of incentive learning (Dickinson & Balleine, 2002). If a behavior is successful in ending a state of deprivation, the behavior, the situational condition, and the hedonic consequences become associated with the representation of this deprivation. Experiencing this deprivation automatically activates the previously appropriate behavioral schemata including the situational conditions of their functioning. Hence, it will increase the accessibility of object representations in the IS, which previously were relevant for ending the deprivation.

In support of these assumptions, experiments have demonstrated that deprivation influences the interpretation of ambiguous stimuli. For example, D. C. McClelland and Atkinson (1948) showed that hungry compared to satiated participants were more likely to identify ambiguous stimuli as food-related objects. In a related vein, thirsty participants were more efficient in recognizing drinking related words than nondeprived participants were (Aarts, Dijksterhuis, & De Vries, 2001). In addition, the associative mechanism we outlined previously predicts that the valence of objects or behaviors varies depending on deprivation. The associative cluster representing a need-relevant object (i.e., a slice of pie) contains representations of satisfaction (e.g., positive taste, joy of eating); the activation of this part of the cluster will be particularly enhanced through deprivation.

Therefore, the IS will respond with stronger positive affect to the object in a deprived than in a satiated state (e.g., Ferguson & Bargh, 2004; Seibt, Häfner, & Deutsch, 2007).

Motivational Orientation

The IS is endowed with a mechanism of global motivational orientation preparing the organism to decrease (approach) or to increase (avoidance) the distance toward an object (Cacioppo, Priester, & Berntson, 1993; Lang, 1995). Several conditions induce approach or avoidance orientations, the most important being processing of positive or negative information, experiencing positive or negative affect, or performing approach and avoidance behaviors (Neumann, Förster, & Strack, 2003).

Once induced, motivational orientations not only prepare the organism for approach and avoidance behavior but also have consequences for further stimulus processing. Particularly, numerous studies have demonstrated that people have a better memory for positive versus negative stimuli when encoded under approach motivation, whereas the opposite is the case for avoidance motivation (Förster & Strack, 1996). In addition, participants are quicker in making evaluative and lexical decisions about positive versus negative words in approach motivation, whereas the opposite holds for avoidance motivation (Neumann & Strack, 2000). These findings suggest that motivational orientations automatically facilitate processing of compatible stimuli, presumably by selectively lowering perceptual thresholds and/or increasing the accessibility of evaluatively compatible information.

ISSUES OF VALIDITY

What can be predicted about the validity of judgments formed on internal and external cues? Like other psychological models, the RIM has little to say about the validity of judgments based on external cues. Generally, the validity of such cues primarily depends on which features correlate with the judgmental criterion in the current environment. For instance, in some environments, the expert status of a communicator may be highly predictive of the validity of what they communicate, whereas this may not be the case in other environments. Hence, judges must gain knowledge about cue validities to make good judgments. Apparently, people are capable of learning even context-dependent contingencies to some degree (e.g., Fiedler, Walther, Freytag, & Stryczek, 2002) but are at the same time susceptible to a variety of sampling-related biases (Unkelbach & Plessner, chap. 17, this volume; Fiedler, 2000).

The RIM makes, however, predictions regarding the validity of internal cues. Their validity is not only depending on environmental factors but also to a large degree on characteristics of the IS. Because the IS processes many cues in parallel and automatically associates covarying features, it extracts regularities in the environment that cannot be easily detected by directly processing a selection of external cues (cf. Hogarth, 2005; Lieberman, 2000). This strength of the RS makes internal cues powerful predictors. Internal cues, however, can also fail because the operational characteristics of the IS prevent it from mastering several cognitive tasks. Probably most striking is the incapability of the IS to process logical negations unless they are highly schematic or practiced (Mayo, Schul, & Burnstein, 2004; Deutsch, Gawronski, & Strack, 2006). Experimental evidence suggests that the IS responds to negated stimuli (e.g., no sunshine) in the opposite way from what they imply logically. For instance, the IS would respond with positive affect and approach motivation to a negated positive. In a related vein, research has suggested that for learned associations the IS remain intact even after they were recognized as being wrong (see Gilbert, 1991).

Another possible source of invalid internal cues is the sensitivity of the IS to the presentation format of information. Particularly, perceptual similarity or feature overlap between the external cues and the associative clusters determine which associative clusters or parts of such clusters receive activation. Hence, perceiving the written word *bird* will result in a different activation than seeing a picture of an actual bird. Internal cues may reflect this variability and affect judgments in a sometimes undesirable manner.

Finally, the moderating factors we previously described can reduce the validity of judgments based on internal cues. For instance, current deprivation will intensify positive affective reactions toward food stimuli; avoidance motivation will increase attention toward fear stimuli and resulting negative affect. These influences rather reflect the actual instead of the long-term regulatory needs of the organism. Hence, when long-term judgments are based on internal cues, their validity will be reduced.

CONCLUSION

In summary, the RIM deviates from the notion that intuitive or heuristic judgments are generated by a distinct, intuitive system of information processing or are the result of unique cognitive operations. Instead, it assumes that intuitive and heuristic judgments are cut from the same cognitive cloth as their systematic counterparts. Although they are not distinct by the processes that generate them, intuitive and heuristic judgments differ in terms of their informational bases. Specifically, such judgments use cues that are less complex, which can be found either in the environment or can result from organismic responses to the environment such as affective and nonaffective feelings, conceptual activation, and behavioral responses.

Judgments based on such internal cues often have features usually ascribed to intuition such as being formed with little effort, low process awareness, being based on personal experience, or being based on feelings. As we have argued, however, some of these features can also be absent in judgments based on internal cues. Thus, according to the RIM, intuition as defined by common criteria represents a subset of a broader range of indirect cue effects mediated by responses of the IS.

Dual-system theories not only describe cognitive mechanisms underlying judgment and decision making. They also describe mechanisms by which the organism generates internal cues, which feed into judgments as substitutes for more complex, less available information (Kahneman & Frederick, 2002). These features, we believe, make them particularly fit to serve as a theoretical frame for studying variants of judgment and decision making.

ACKNOWLEDGMENTS

Preparation of this chapter was supported by a grant from the German Science Foundation (DFG) to Roland Deutsch (De 1150/1–1). We thank Cornelia Betsch, Tilmann Betsch, and Henning Plessner for their helpful comments on an earlier version of this chapter.

REFERENCES

Aarts, H., Dijksterhuis, A., & De Vries, P. (2001). On the psychology of drinking: Being thirsty and perceptually ready. *British Journal of Psychology, 92*, 631–642.

Bechara, A., Damasio, H., Tranel, D., & Damasio, A. R. (1997). Deciding advantageously before knowing the advantageous strategy. *Science, 275*, 1293–1295.

Bem, D. J. (1967). An alternative interpretation of cognitive dissonance phenomena. *Psychological Review, 73*, 185–200.

Blair, I. V. (2002). The malleability of automatic stereotypes and prejudice. *Personality and Social Psychology Review, 6*, 242–261.

Blair, I. V., Ma, J. E., & Lenton, A. P. (2001). Imagining stereotypes away: The moderation of implicit stereotypes through mental imagery. *Journal of Personality & Social Psychology, 81*, 828–841.

Bless, H., & Forgas, J. P. (Eds.). (2000). *The message within: The role of subjective experience in social cognition and behavior.* Philadelphia: Psychology Press.

Brewer, M. B. (1988). A dual process model of impression formation. In R. S. Wyer & T. K. Srull (Eds.), *Advances in social cognition* (Vol. 1, pp. 1–36). Hillsdale, NJ: Lawrence Erlbaum Associates, Inc.

Bruner, J. (1960). *The process of education.* Cambridge, MA: Harvard University Press.

Cacioppo, J. T., Priester, J. R., & Berntson, G. G. (1993). Rudimentary determinants of attitudes: II. Arm flexion and extension have differential effects on attitudes. *Journal of Personality and Social Psychology, 65*, 5–17.

Chaiken, S. (1980). Heuristic versus systematic information processing and the use of source versus message cues in persuasion. *Journal of Personality and Social Psychology, 39*, 752–766.

Chaiken, S., & Trope, Y. (Eds.). (1999). *Dual-process theories in social psychology.* New York: Guilford.

Chartrand, T. L., & Bargh, J. A. (1999). The chameleon effect: The perception behavior link in social perception. *Journal of Personality and Social Psychology, 76*, 893–910.

Deutsch, R., Gawronski, B., & Strack, F. (2006). At the boundaries of automaticity: Negation as reflective operation. *Journal of Personality and Social Psychology, 91*, 385–405.

Devine, P. G. (1989). Stereotypes and prejudice: Their automatic and controlled components. *Journal of Personality and Social Psychology, 56*, 5–18.

Dickinson, A., & Balleine, B. (2002). The role of learning in the operation of motivational systems. In H. Pashler & R. Gallistel (Eds.), *Steven's handbook of experimental psychology* (pp. 497–533). New York: Wiley.

Dijksterhuis, A., & Bargh, J. A. (2001). The perception-behavior expressway: Automatic effects of social perception on social behavior. In M. P. Zanna (Ed.), *Advances in experimental social psychology* (Vol. 33, pp. 1–40). San Diego: Academic.

Epstein, S. (1991). Cognitive-experiential self-theory: An integrative theory of personality. In R. Curtis (Ed.), *The relational self: Convergences in psychoanalysis and social psychology* (pp. 111–137). NY: Guilford.

Epstein, S. (1994). Integration of the cognitive and the psychodynamic unconscious. *American Psychologist, 49*, 709–724.

Fazio, R. H., & Olson, M. A. (2003). Implicit measures in social cognition research: Their meaning and use. *Annual Review of Psychology, 54*, 297–327.

Ferguson, M. J., & Bargh, J. A. (2004). Liking is for doing: The effects of goal pursuit on automatic evaluation. *Journal of Personality and Social Psychology, 87*, 557–572.

Fiedler, K. (2000). Beware of samples! A cognitive ecological sampling approach to judgment biases. *Psychological Review, 107*, 659–676.

Fiedler, K., Walther, E., Freytag, P., & Stryczek, E. (2002). Playing mating games in foreign cultures: A conceptual framework and an experimental paradigm for trivariate statistical inference. *Journal of Experimental Social Psychology, 38*, 14–30.

Förster, J., Liberman, N. & Higgins, E.T. (2005). Accessibility from active and fulfilled goals. *Journal of Experimental Social Psychology, 41*, 220–239.

Förster, J., & Strack, F. (1996). The influence of overt head movements on memory for valenced words: A case of conceptual-motor compatibility. *Journal of Personality and Social Psychology, 71*, 421–430.

Gilbert, D. T. (1991). How mental systems believe. *American Psychologist, 46*, 107–119.

Gollwitzer, P. M. (1999). Implementation intentions. Strong effects of simple plans. *American Psychologist, 54*, 493–503.

Greenwald, A. G. (1992). New Look 3: Reclaiming unconscious cognition. *American Psychologist, 47*, 766–779.

Hammond, K. R. (1996). *Human judgment and social policy: Irreducible uncertainty, inevitable error, unavoidable injustice.* New York: Oxford University Press.

Higgins, E. T., Rholes, W. S., & Jones, C. R. (1977). Category accessibility and impression formation. *Journal of Experimental Social Psychology, 13*, 141–154.

Higgins, E. T. (1996). Knowledge activation: Accessibility, applicability, and salience. In E. T. Higgins & A. W. Kruglanski (Eds.), *Social psychology: Handbook of basic principles* (pp. 133–168). New York: Guilford.

Hogarth, R. M. (2005). Deciding analytically or trusting your intuition? The advantages and disadvantages of analytic and intuitive thought. In T. Betsch & S. Haberstroh (Eds.), *The routines of decision making* (pp 67–82). Mahwah, NJ: Lawrence Erlbaum Associates, Inc.

Hugenberg, K., & Bodenhausen, G. V. (2004). Ambiguity in social categorization: The role of prejudice and facial affect in race categorization. *Psychological Science, 15*, 342–345.

Jacoby, L. L., Kelley, C., Brown, J., & Jasechko, J. (1989). Becoming famous overnight: Limits on the ability to avoid unconscious influences of the past. *Journal of Personality and Social Psychology, 56*, 326–338.

Kahneman, D., & Frederick, S. (2002). Representativeness revisited: Attribute substitution in intuitive judgment. In T. Gilovich, D. Griffin, & D. Kahneman (Eds.), *Heuristics and biases: The psychology of intuitive judgment* 49–81. New York: Cambridge University Press, 2002.

Kawakami, K., Dion, K. L., & Dovidio, J. F. (1998). Racial prejudice and stereotype activation. *Personality and Social Psychology Bulletin, 24*, 407–416.

Kruglanski, A. W., Erb, H.-P., Spiegel, S., & Pierro, A. (2003). The parametric unimodel of human judgment: A fanfare to the common thinker. In: L. G. Aspinwall & U. M. Staudinger (Eds.), *A psychology of human strengths: Perspectives on an emerging field* (pp. 197–210). Washington, DC: American Psychological Association.

Lang, P. J. (1995). The emotion probe—Studies of motivation and attention. *American Psychologist, 50*, 372–385.

Lieberman, M. D. (2000). Intuition: A social-cognitive neuroscience approach. *Psychological Bulletin, 126*, 109–137.

Lieberman, M. D., Gaunt, R., Gilbert, D. T., & Trope, Y. (2002). Reflection and reflexion: A social cognitive neuroscience approach to attributional inference. In M. Zanna (Ed.), *Advances in experimental social psychology* (Vol. 34, pp. 199–249). New York: Academic.

Loewenstein, G. F., Weber, E. U., Hsee, C. K., & Welch, N. (2001). Risk as feelings. *Psychological Bulletin, 122*, 267–286.

Logan, G. D. (1988). Toward an instance theory of automatization. *Psychological Review, 95*, 492–527.

Mayo, R., Schul, Y., & Burnstein, E. (2004). "I am not guilty" vs. "I am innocent": Successful negation may depend on the schema used for its encoding. *Journal of Experimental Social Psychology, 40*, 433–449.

McClelland, D. C., & Atkinson, J. W. (1948). The projective expression of needs: I. The effect of different intensities of the hunger drive on perception. *Journal of Psychology, 25*, 205–222.

McClelland, J. L., McNaughton, B. L., & O'Reilly, R. C. (1995). Why there are complementary learning systems in the hippocampus and neocortex: Insights from the successes and failures of connectionist models of learning and memory. *Psychological Review, 102*, 419–457.

Moors, A., & De Houwer, J. (2001). Automatic appraisal of motivational valence: Motivational affective priming and Simon effects. *Cognition and Emotion, 15*, 749–766.

Neumann, R., Förster, J., & Strack, F. (2003). Motor compatibility: The bidirectional link between behavior and evaluation. In J. Musch & K. C. Klauer (Eds.), *The psychology of evaluation: Affective processes in cognition and emotion* (pp. 371–391). Mahwah, NJ: Lawrence Erlbaum Associates, Inc.

Neumann, R., & Strack, F. (2000). Approach and avoidance: The influence of proprioceptive and exteroceptive cues on encoding of affective information. *Journal of Personality and Social Psychology, 79*, 39–48.

Niedenthal, P. M., Barsalou, L., Winkielman, P., Krauth-Gruber, S., & Ric, F. (2005). Embodiment in attitudes, social perception, and emotion. *Personality and Social Psychology Review, 9*, 184–211.

Payne, B. K., Cheng, C. M., Govorun, O., & Stewart, B. D. (2005). An inkblot for attitudes: Affect misattribution as implicit measurement. *Journal of Personality and Social Psychology, 89*, 277–293.

Petty, R. E., & Wegener, D. T. (1999). The elaboration likelihood model: Current status and controversies. In S. Chaiken & Y. Trope (Eds.), *Dual process theories in social psychology* (pp. 41–72). New York: Guilford.

Rizzolatti, G., & Arbib, M. A. (1998). Language within our grasp. *Trends in Neurosciences, 21*, 188–194.

Roth, M., Decety, J., Raybaudi, M., Massarelli, R., Delon-Martin, C., Segebarth, C., et al. (1996). Possible involvement of primary motor cortex in mentally simulated movement. A functional magnetic resonance imaging study. *Neuroreport, 7*, 1280–1284.

Rothman, A. J., & Schwarz, N. (1998). Constructing perceptions of vulnerability: Personal relevance and the use of experiential information in health judgments. *Personality and Social Psychology Bulletin, 24*, 1053–1064.

Russell, J. A. (2003). Core affect and the psychological construction of emotion. *Psychological Review, 110*, 145–172.

Schmidt, R. A. (1975). A schema theory of discrete motor skill learning. *Psychological Review, 82*, 225–260.

Schneider, W., & Shiffrin, R. M. (1977). Controlled and automatic human information processing: I. Detection, search, and attention. *Psychological Review, 84*, 1–66.

Schwarz, N. (1998). Accessible content and accessibility experiences: The interplay of declarative and experiential information in judgment. *Personality and Social Psychology Bulletin, 2*, 87–99.

Schwarz, N., Bless, H., Strack, F., Klumpp, G., Rittenauer-Schatka, H., & Simons, A. (1991). Ease of retrieval as information: Another look at the availability heuristic. *Journal of Personality and Social Psychology, 61*, 195–202.

Schwarz, N., & Clore, G. L. (1983). Mood, misattribution, and judgments of well-being: Informative and directive functions of affective states. *Journal of Personality and Social Psychology, 45*, 513–523.

Schwarz, N., & Clore, G. L. (1988). How do I feel about it? Informative functions of affective states. In K. Fiedler & J. P. Forgas (Eds.), *Affect, cognition, and social behavior* (pp. 44–62). Toronto, Ontario, Canada: Hogrefe International.

Seibt, B., Häfner, M., & Deutsch, R. (2007). Prepared to eat: How immediate affective and motivational responses to food cues are influenced by food deprivation. *European Journal of Social Psychology, 37*, 359–379.

Simon, H. (1992). What is an "explanation" of behavior? *Psychological Science, 3*, 150–161.

Skurnik, I., Schwarz, N., & Winkielman, P. (2000). Drawing inferences from feelings: The role of naive beliefs. In H. Bless & J. P. Forgas (Eds.), *The message within: The role of subjective experience in social cognition and behavior* (pp. 162–175). Philadelphia: Psychology Press.

Sloman, S. A. (1996). The empirical case for two systems of reasoning. *Psychological Bulletin, 119*, 3–22.

Smith, E. R., & DeCoster, J. (1999). Associative and rule-based processing: A connectionist interpretation of dual process models. In S. Chaiken & Y. Trope (Eds.), *Dual-process theories in social psychology* (323–336). New York: Guilford.

Smith, E. R., & DeCoster, J. (2000). Dual process models in social and cognitive psychology: Conceptual integration and links to underlying memory systems. *Personality and Social Psychology Review, 4*, 108–131.

Smith, E. R., & Lerner, M. (1986). Development of automatism of social judgments. *Journal of Personality & Social Psychology, 50*, 246–259.

Smolensky, P. (1988). On the proper treatment of connectionism. *Behavioral and Brain Sciences, 11*, 1–23.

Strack, F., & Deutsch, R. (2004). Reflective and impulsive determinants of social behavior. *Personality and Social Psychology Review, 8*, 220–247.

Strack, F., & Mussweiler, T. (1997). Explaining the enigmatic anchoring effect: Mechanisms of selective accessibility. *Journal of Personality and Social Psychology, 73*, 437–446.

Vanman, E. J., Paul, B. Y., Ito, T. A., & Miller, N. (1997). The modern face of prejudice and structural features that moderate the effect of cooperation on affect. *Journal of Personality and Social Psychology, 73*, 941–959.

Wänke, M., Bohner, G., & Jurkowitsch, A. (1997). There are many reasons to drive a BMW: Does imagined ease of argument generation influence attitudes? *Journal of Consumer Research, 24*, 170–177.

Wilson, T. D., Lindsey, S., & Schooler, T. Y. (2000). A model of dual attitudes. *Psychological Review, 107*, 101–126.

4

Cue by Hypothesis Interactions in Descriptive Modeling of Unconscious Use of Multiple Intuitive Judgment Strategies

ROBERT M. HAMM
University of Oklahoma

INTRODUCTION

*I*n this chapter, I address a methodological issue in the study of judgment, that is, the production of a response to a situation, on a continuous numerical scale. A key assumption of an important method for describing people's intuitive judgments cannot be verified. The method is the use of a statistical model, fit to a set of judgments, to describe the relation between the judgment response and the measured inputs to the judgment process. Such a statistical method requires multiple judgments in the same general situation, with varying situational elements or cues. Paramount among the features characterizing intuition is the person's lack of conscious awareness of the cognitive process (Hastie, 2001). If someone cannot report how his or her intuitive judgments are made, then it is impossible to verify the statistical description's assumption that all the judgments to which a model is fit are made with the same intuitive strategy.

If the individual makes judgments using two different strategies, then a statistical model of the total data set could be misleading. This point has often been made concerning the application of a single descriptive analysis to judgment data produced by more than one individual. It is also plausible, however, that multiple judgment strategies could be used by a single individual doing repeated judgments. Although it is easy to disaggregate the judgments made by different individuals, identifying which of a single individual's judgments were made by one strategy or another is more difficult.

Expert judgments on a numerical scale are considered intuitive because they have important features of intuition. Researchers studying intuition often define it using feature lists, as may be found in Epstein (1973, 2000; chap. 2, this volume), Hammond (1981, 1996; Hammond, Hamm, Grassia, & Pearson, 1987), and the summary of the review of two-system theories in Stanovich and West (2000, p. 659). Thus, expert judgment qualifies as intuition because it is fast, usually accurate, and in its details is out of the expert's conscious awareness (Abernathy & Hamm, 1994, 1995), features prominent in the defining lists. It may be argued that expert cognition is distinct from the intuition that is based on instinctual or emotional response tendencies or learning processes (T. Betsch, chap. 1, this volume; Epstein, 2000; chap. 2, this volume; Hogarth, chap. 6, this volume) because expertise is postulated to be based on explicit analytic processes that have become chunked and automatized (J. R. Anderson, 1993; Dreyfus, 1997; Ericsson & Kintsch, 1995). Are there two distinct types of intuition? Should the "analytic-intuitive" space be based on two dimensions rather than one? Resolution of these issues is beyond the scope of this chapter.

ASSUMPTIONS FOR THE APPLICATION OF STATISTICAL MODELING TO INTUITIVE JUDGMENTS

Fitting a statistical model of the cue–judgment relation to a set of repeated judgments can make a useful contribution to the study of intuition only if the set of judgments modeled has certain properties. First, the repeated judgments made in the research task must elicit the intuitive cognitive process that the researcher is interested in. Second, all the judgments in the set must be produced by the same intuitive process.

Some intuitive judgments are not stable if made repeatedly. Many investigations of heuristics and biases, for example, present people with novel word problems, for example, the response when asked "If the sum of the prices of a bat and a ball is $1.10, and the bat costs $1.00 more than the ball, what is the price of a ball?" (Kahneman & Frederick, 2002). With repeated exposure to the same situation (changing the superficial content and the particular numbers), people would likely soon change the way they see the problem. If the phenomenon being investigated depends on the judgment being the person's "first take," then doing the task repeatedly is not appropriate. This is why such studies ask many people the same single question and do not make statistical models of the judgment process. Generally, the statistical analysis of the relation of inputs to outputs in repeated judgments cannot be applied when a judgment process may change through learning, insight, or motivational changes (e.g., boredom or impatience) if the judgment is made repeatedly. Therefore, the only intuitive judgments that it is appropriate to study with statistical modeling of repeated judgments by the same person are those in which the judgment process can be expected to be stable. Examples would be familiar everyday judgments or expert judgments in the area of one's professional responsibility.

Even with a familiar intuitive judgment task, however, if the research task uses hypothetical situation descriptions rather than real experienced situations, the judgments it elicits may be different from the person's usual judgments. For the convenience of both the researcher and the research participant, studies that use repeated hypothetical judgment tasks often present information in an efficient, abstract form; allow little time for each response; and have no adverse consequences for a careless or uncharacteristic judgment. In effect, this is a different task from the intuitive judgment with which the participant is familiar, although the parts of the task have the same names and analogous structure. After several repetitions of such a hypothetical task, the research participant's judgment policy becomes different from what he or she usually does because he or she has experienced that the task has a different meaning than the familiar one. Telling the participant to act as if the task is real does not solve the problem.

Research that applies statistical models to intuitive judgments need not have these procedurally imposed disadvantages. With thoughtful planning and adequate researcher effort, the problems produced by artificial judgment tasks can be avoided. Suppose, for example, one wants to study the intuitive cognitive processes used by physicians judging how long a patient may stay in the intensive care unit. Ideally, the analysis would model multiple estimates by each individual physician to control for different individuals having different strategies. The data should be from physicians doing their usual task, as the environment presents them with the information and with the need to respond, rather than from physicians performing a novel, abstract, and inconsequential exercise.

The second property required if statistical models are to contribute to the understanding of intuitive judgment is that the person uses just one cognitive process in the set of judgments being modeled. It is plausible that this assumption does not hold in some important situations. Consider, for example, the emotionally aroused expert—an anxious emergency department physician, an excited Olympic figure skating judge, or an angry policeman. Imagine one has a set of judgments made by such an expert who does not report being consciously aware of the judgment process used on any of them. Thus, one does not know if these judgments were all made under the influence of emotional intuition, they were all expressions of the professional's intuitive expertise, or the set contains examples of each type of intuition.

If a set of intuitive judgments includes a mix of distinct cognitive strategies, this could compromise the accuracy of the statistical description. A descriptive model of the total set of judgments would be consistent with a variety of strategy accounts including (a) that one strategy was used exclusively (although with a bit of noise) and (b) that two (or more) strategies were used, each a particular proportion of the time, with some of the noise in the model coming from the different ways each strategy uses the cues. A statistical model can not indicate for certain whether the person is always applying a particular intuitive judgment strategy or is sometimes applying one strategy and sometimes another.

If the statistical description of the intuitive judgment policy one wishes to improve is inaccurate—for example, if the model assumes just one strategy, but actually there are two distinct strategies—then that statistical description does not provide the researcher with a reliable basis for improving an erroneous or biased intuitive strategy. An intervention that corrects one strategy may be irrelevant to the other. An intervention that tries to correct the average of two strategies may be ineffective in changing either one.

When there is the possibility of multiple distinct intuitive strategies, there are two options to assure that a statistical model accurately reflects the intuitive process. The researcher could modify the procedures used in observing the judgments so that the research participant uses only a single intuitive cognitive process, or the researcher could modify the statistical method to accommodate the distinct judgment strategies. The disadvantage of forcing the physician to use just one strategy so that the researcher may study it better with statistical modeling is that in doing so, the researcher could change the physician's judgment strategy even more than requiring repeated judgments does. The physician's use of multiple distinct intuitive strategies "in the world" is part of the intuitive phenomenon that one would want to understand, not to change. Also, an accurate description of an artificially stabilized judgment strategy would not allow an accurate assessment of the need to correct for error or bias in practical situations. This leaves only the path of modifying the statistical analysis method so that it can accommodate the existence of multiple strategies in the set of judgments. If there are multiple distinct intuitive strategies, the statistical method cannot help researchers understand intuition unless they can identify which judgments use which strategy.

DISCRIMINATION OF USE OF A SINGLE INTUITIVE JUDGMENT STRATEGY FROM USE OF A MIXTURE OF TWO OR MORE STRATEGIES

In this section, I demonstrate the problem that the possibility of multiple intuitive judgment strategies poses for the statistical modeling approach. Using simulated data, I show it's impossible to determine definitively whether a set of judgments was produced by a single, consistently used intuitive judgment strategy or by a pair of distinct strategies. However, if the researcher has a correct hypothesis about which judgments were made by different strategies, then a statistical modeling approach can confirm this hypothesis and describe the different strategies. Unfortunately, if the researcher lacks a basis to sort judgments into groups made by different strategies, it is unlikely to be feasible to use a systematic search procedure to induce hypotheses about which judgments were made by which strategy.

Statistical methods useful for descriptive modeling of the relations between stimulus features and judgment responses include multiple regression (e.g., Hammond, Hursch, & Todd, 1964; Stewart, 2001; Tucker, 1964; Wallace, 1923) and analysis of variance (ANOVA; e.g., N. H. Anderson, 1970) for judgments made on continuous or many-category scales, logistic regression for dichotomous judgments (Cooksey, 1996; Kee et al., 2003; Stewart, Hamm, and Tape, 2004), and conjoint analysis for choices between pairs of stimuli (Green & Wind, 1973). Production systems (Post, 1943; Simon, 1981) consisting of condition-action rules (Cooper, 2002) provide another method for modeling judgments (Johnson & Payne, 1985), although without techniques for fitting data by adjusting parameters to minimize error (see Bröder, 2000). The demonstration in this section uses multiple regression, but the analogous argument could be made for any of these modeling techniques.

Typically, multiple regression modeling of an individual's intuitive judgments assumes all the judgments are produced by a single rule that combines the cues, allowing for some inconsistency in the application of the rule:

$$Judgment = \beta_1 * Cue_1 + \beta_2 * Cue_2 + \beta_3 * Cue_3 + \beta_4 * Cue_4 + Err$$

Equation 1

To discover the judgment rule, the researcher measures the individual's judgments and the available cues (assuming the individual perceives them as measured) for a set of judged stimuli. The judgments are regressed onto the cues, producing a predictive formula:

$$\hat{Judgment} = \hat{\beta}_1 * Cue_1 + \hat{\beta}_2 * Cue_2 + \hat{\beta}_3 * Cue_3 + \hat{\beta}_4 * Cue_4$$

Equation 2

and a measure of the adequacy of the prediction, R^2, the proportion of the judgment's variance that this most predictive combination of the cues accounts for. The possibility of multiple strategies is represented by there being (at least) two distinct judgment producing rules, such as:

$$Judgment_a = \beta_{a1} * Cue_1 + \beta_{a2} * Cue_2 + \beta_{a3} * Cue_3 + \beta_{a4} * Cue_4 + Error_a$$
$$Judgment_b = \beta_{b1} * Cue_1 + \beta_{b2} * Cue_2 + \beta_{b3} * Cue_3 + \beta_{b4} * Cue_4 + Error_b$$

Equation 3

If one knows which judgments were made by each strategy, then finding the prediction rules is straightforward. Let the strategy choice be represented by the variable S, which takes values a and b, and fit different regression models contingent on which strategy was used:

If $S = a, \hat{Judgment} = \hat{\beta}_{a1} * Cue_1 + \hat{\beta}_{a2} * Cue_2 + \hat{\beta}_{a3} * Cue_3 + \hat{\beta}_{a4} * Cue_4$

If $S = b, \hat{Judgment} = \hat{\beta}_{b1} * Cue_1 + \hat{\beta}_{b2} * Cue_2 + \hat{\beta}_{b3} * Cue_3 + \hat{\beta}_{b4} * Cue_i$

Equation 4

The inadequacy of using a single regression model to describe a set of intuitive judgments that actually was produced by a mixture of two strategies would be evident in comparing the regression model's $\hat{\beta}_i$ (from Equation 2) with the β_{ai} and β_{bi} from the strategies in the strategy mixture that produced the judgments (Equation 3). The single regression model's $\hat{\beta}_i$ would likely be intermediate between β_{ai} and β_{bi} and thus would not accurately describe the role of Cue_i in either of the two intuitive judgment strategies that the person used. In contrast, if variable S accurately identifies the strategy used, then $\hat{\beta}_{ai}$ and $\hat{\beta}_{bi}$ (from Equation 4) would be close to β_{ai} and β_{bi}, respectively.

To fit judgment data guided by a mixture of two strategies, the following demonstration uses a dummy variable reflecting a hypothesis about which intuitive judgment strategy was used on each judgment. It constructs interaction terms by multiplying each of the cues by the dummy variable and uses these as predictors in the regression. If a "Dummy × Cue" interaction term contributes significantly in the regression analysis, it signals that the cue is used differently in the one set than in the other. Interaction terms have been used in judgment analysis to model judgment strategies in which the impact of one cue depends on the level of another (e.g., Poses et al., 1993). However, in this argument, the interacting factor is something outside of the stimulus itself. It is something in the judge, or in the situation, that either reflects or causes the use of different intuitive judgment strategies. For example, if the judge could report "I felt comfortable" versus "I felt uncomfortable" about a judgment, or if the judge's eyes were observed wandering left or wandering right, or if one part of the brain were activated or quiescent (Sanfey, Rilling, Aronson, Nystrom, & Cohen, 2003), this could be evidence reflecting the use of different intuitive judgment strategies. On the other hand, if it were observed that there was much or little noise in the room when a particular judgment was made, that a physician's previous patient had been stressful or relaxing, or that the judgment was made early versus late in the series of judgments, these could be signs of external factors that cause the judge to use different intuitive judgment strategies.

I constructed a set of data to simulate various possible mixes of judgment strategies, and then I fit different multiple linear regression models to those data. I generated the simulated judgments to represent judgment strategies that potentially use four available cues. The simulation is generic, but it could represent, for example, a physician who predicts how many days a critically ill patient will stay in the hospital with reference to four available cues but cannot explain how she or he makes those judgments. One does not know if she or he judges all cases using a single judgment strategy or uses different strategies on different cases. For the example, suppose that although the physician is unaware of it, she or he attends to different patient features when different nurse supervisors are on duty.

In the simulation, all cues and strategy-produced judgments are on the 0 to 1 scale. The four cues are uniform random variables. A fifth random variable is used in simulations of mixed judgment strategies to determine which of two strategies produces each particular judgment. (In this sort of mixture, different judgments in the set are produced by different strategies. Each judgment, however, is produced by just one strategy, not by a mixture of strategies.) If the goal is to use one strategy for $p\%$ and the other for $(1-p)\%$ of the judgments, then the strategy selection variable is set to one value if the uniform [0,1] random variable is p or less or else to the other value.

So that I may explore the effect of variation in the accuracy of strategy identification, this demonstration uses two strategy selection variables. One of them, $s5050$, is $+½$ for about half of the judgments (if the fifth random variable < 0.5), or else it is $-½$. The other, $s7525$, is $+½$ three-fourths of the time (when the random variable < 0.75), or else is –½. These alternative strategy selection variables are related because they are keyed off the same random variable; and hence, $s7525$'s mixture includes in its +½ category all the +½s and half the –½s of $s5050$'s mixture. This simulates a situation in which competing strategy mixture hypotheses might have partial overlap.

The data representing the simulated intuitive judgment strategies are produced by averaging the cue measures. Equal weights are used, and I added 20% additional random error. For example, a one-cue strategy that simply uses the first cue would be produced with the averaging formula "$= (4 * Cue_1 + Uniform\ Random\ Variable) / 5$," where the random variable covers the same range as the values of Cue 1. A strategy that uses two cues is produced by the formula "$= (2 * Cue_1 + 2 * Cue_2 + Uniform\ Random\ Variable) / 5$." A mixed strategy is produced by using one strategy if the strategy selection variable ($s5050$ or $s7525$) has the value +0.5 and the second strategy when it is –0.5.

The simulated judgment data set consists of 64 cases. Many past studies have required each participant to make 64 judgments. The more cases, the more burden for the participant and the more likely the strategy will change during the study, and yet the more likely it is that a well-specified statistical model will be significant.

The columns in Table 4.1 hold the regression model parameters for simulated judgment data generated by six different strategies or strategy mixtures. Strategy columns 1 through 3 represent strategies that use only Cues 1 and 2. Strategy column 1 was produced by the consistent application of a strategy that weights Cues 1 and 2 equally. The data modeled by strategy column 2 are a 50%/50% mixture

TABLE 4.1   Beta (standardized) coefficients for models predicting the judgment produced by each of 6 hypothetical data generating strategies. Dichotomous (–.5,+.5) variables s5050, s7525 and s50irr reflect which strategy is hypothesized to have produced each judgment. Boxed sections indicate the appropriate models for the strategy mixtures that generated the data.

Data generating strategy	1	2	3	4	5	6
Mixture percents	100%	50%/50%	75%/25%	100%	50%/50%	75%/25%
First strategy	Cue 1 & 2	Cue 1	Cue 1	Cue 1, 2, & 3	Cue 1 & 2	Cue 1 & 2
Second strategy		Cue 2	Cue 2		Cue 2 & 3	Cue 2 & 3
A. Regression model: main effects of cues						
Cue 1	.817	.426	.623	.506	.334	.543
Cue 2	.614	.537	.276	.627	.621	.637
Cue 3	–.013	–.182	–.188	.620	.308	.115
Cue 4	–.027	–.201	–.077	–.033	–.091	–.104
R^2	.925	.539	.484	.874	.519	.630

(continued)

TABLE 4.1. (CONTINUED)

Data generating strategy	1	2	3	4	5	6
Mixture percents	100%	50%/50%	75%/25%	100%	50%/50%	75%/25%
First strategy	Cue 1 & 2	Cue 1	Cue 1	Cue 1, 2, & 3	Cue 1 & 2	Cue 1 & 2
Second strategy		Cue 2	Cue 2		Cue 2 & 3	Cue 2 & 3

B. Regression model: cues and interactions with measure of hypothesis of 50%/50% strategy mixture

Cue 1	**.810**	**.520**	**.689**	**.500**	**.400**	**.569**
Cue 2	**.632**	**.473**	**.257**	**.629**	**.734**	**.675**
Cue 3	−.035	−.040	−.090	**.608**	**.315**	.114
Cue 4	−.043	−.027	.034	−.047	−.034	−.079
s5050 * Cue 1	−.030	**.892**	**.617**	−.032	**.865**	**.377**
s5050 * Cue 2	.102	**−.870**	**−.508**	.071	−.010	−.024
s5050 * Cue 3	−.098	−.022	.028	−.075	**−.731**	**−.380**
s5050 * Cue 4	.010	.063	−.059	.055	−.012	.070
R^2	.930	.948	.647	.877	.896	.717

C. Regression model: cues and interactions with measure of hypothesis of 75%/25% strategy mixture

Cue 1	**.813**	**.329**	**.524**	**.493**	.218	**.365**
Cue 2	**.630**	**.622**	**.466**	**.625**	**.705**	**.719**
Cue 3	.014	−.078	−.011	**.640**	**.474**	**.331**
Cue 4	−.053	−.129	−.024	−.033	−.079	−.062
s7525 * Cue 1	−.002	**.572**	**.874**	.065	**.553**	**.758**
s7525 * Cue 2	.011	**−.339**	**−.769**	−.004	−.195	−.158
s7525 * Cue 3	**−.155**	−.092	−.033	−.048	**−.494**	**−.690**
s7525 * Cue 4	.095	−.098	.045	.032	.136	.101
R^2	.935	.671	.943	.877	.689	.929

D. Regression model: cues and interactions with irrelevant strategy mixture hypothesis

Cue 1	**.837**	**.380**	**.598**	**.518**	**.370**	**.577**
Cue 2	**.630**	**.519**	**.291**	**.629**	**.675**	**.681**
Cue 3	−.021	−.145	**−.236**	**.597**	**.292**	.076
Cue 4	−.010	**−.262**	−.106	−.003	−.099	−.082
s50irr * Cue 1	−.023	−.102	.077	.143	−.300	−.029
s50irr * Cue 2	.084	−.088	−.222	.027	.027	.081
s50irr * Cue 3	−.032	.238	.280	−.116	.211	.067
s50irr * Cue 4	.058	−.208	−.083	.032	.184	.097
R^2	.932	.580	.520	.888	.572	.664

(contingent on variable s5050) between two single-cue strategies, one that uses only Cue 1 and the other that uses only Cue 2. The data in strategy column 3 were generated using variable s7525 and are an uneven 75%/25% mix between those two strategies. In parallel, the last three strategy columns in Table 4.1 represent strategies that make use of Cues 1 through 3. Strategy column 4 was produced by the consistent application of a strategy that weights the three cues equally. Strategy column 5 is a 50%/50% mix between two strategies, one that attends to Cues 1 and 2 and the other to Cues 2 and 3. Finally, strategy column 6 is a 75%/25% mix between those two strategies.

Within each column, the groups of rows of numbers represent four different multiple linear regression models. For each, the standardized regression coefficients, β's, and the proportion of variance explained, R^2, are shown. The statistically significant β weights are in bold font. Model A used only the four cues as predictors. Model B adds the interaction between each of the cues and s5050, the binary variable (−0.5, +0.5) representing the 50%/50% split between strategies. Because this is the strategy selection variable used in producing the data for strategy columns 2 and 5, Model B represents the performance of this analytic strategy with a perfectly accurate hypothesis when applied to those columns. Similarly, Model C adds four predictors that are the interaction between each of the cues and s7525 representing the 75%/25% split between strategies, and this is a perfect measure of the strategy mixture that produced the data for strategy columns 3 and 6. The regression parameters for the appropriate judgment set hypotheses are enclosed in boxes. Finally, Model D adds interaction terms with an uncorrelated strategy mixture variable, s50irrelevant [s50irr].

My simulation allows one to compare between columns to see how the regression analyses with the same predictors perform for data generated with different strategy mixtures. However, the naive researcher will most likely have just one data set and will not know how the data were generated and hence will be unable to make comparisons between columns of a single row. On the other hand, a researcher could easily apply several different interaction models to the same data set, thus comparing between rows in a single column of the table.

Consider first the regression models in Model A, which use the four cues as predictors. Given just one of the data sets (strategy columns), would inspection of the model features—β's, statistical significances, and total R^2—be sufficient to indicate whether a one-strategy model is correct or there is a mixture of strategies? Knowing how each data set was produced, one notices that in the left three strategy columns, where only Cues 1 and 2 were used in the judgment strategies, the regression analysis was sensitive to the cues, but in strategy column 2, it also falsely identified Cues 3 and 4. In strategy columns 4 to 6—where the simulated strategy used Cues 1, 2, and 3—the regression analyses missed Cue 3 in strategy column 6. Unless one knew the strategies used equal weights, one would not be suspicious that the small β's in strategy column 2 were false positives. A small β would not inform the naive researcher that the model has made a misidentification. Cue 2 in strategy column 3, for example, has a smaller weight because it was used in only one-quarter of the judgments; Cues 1 and 3 in strategy column 5 have smaller weights because they were used in half the judgments compared to Cue 2, which was used in every judgment. Although all strategies simulated here used equal weights, the researcher must also consider the possibility that in any strategy, the judge may allocate different weights to cues.

The feature of the Model A regressions that is closely associated with whether the simulated judgments were the product of one judgment strategy or two is the R^2 of the model. That a single-strategy regression model has a low R^2 does not, however, prove that two distinct judgment strategies were used. Typically, if R^2 is less than .90 or .70, the judgment researcher worries that the participant might be using a cue that has not been measured, or a cue combination not included in the model, or that the task is too hard, or the participant is not motivated to exercise control while doing the task (Stewart, 1988, 2001). Without stronger proof, the researcher would be taking a risk to conclude from a low R^2 that the data for strategy columns 2, 3, 5, or 6 were produced by the use of two distinct judgment strategies. The only form of stronger proof is to hypothesize that two subsets of the judgments were made with different strategies and then test to see if the regression identifies different strategies in the proposed sets.

The naive researcher analyzing just one data set has the option of trying different models to test the hypothesis that more than one intuitive judgment strategy might have been used in different subsets of an individual's judgments. The approach taken in this simulation is to hypothesize a division of the judgments into two sets, express this with the strategy subset variable, produce interaction terms between that and each cue, and let the regression analysis test if this substantially improves the R^2. The regression analysis also produces separate descriptions of the strategies used in each set. I demonstrate what happens with three hypothetical divisions that vary in their accuracy. As I noted previously, Model B is completely accurate for strategy columns 2 and 5 and partially accurate for strategy columns 3 and 6. Conversely, Model C is completely accurate for strategy columns 3 and 6 and partially for strategy columns 2 and 5. I could produce these models only because I knew how the data were generated. An uninformed researcher's hypothesis might be similar to Model D, a random division unrelated to how the data were generated.

If the researcher does not know which hypothesis is accurate, comparing the models applied to the same data set (strategy column) can provide useful information. For strategy columns 1 or 4, there is no gain in R^2 from including the interactions representing a hypothesized strategy mix other than the small gains expected from adding unrelated predictors to a regression equation. Thus, for strategy column 1, about 93% of the variance is accounted for in each of the four models and for strategy column 4, about 88%. However, it cannot be known whether the R^2 is unchanging within a strategy column because all the judgments were made by the same strategy or because two (or more) judgment strategies were used, but none of the hypothesized divisions of the judgments into two sets (Model B, C, or D) is correct. Given that the R^2 is fairly high in strategy columns 1 and 4, it would be reasonable to conclude there is just one strategy (or that if there are two strategies, they are so similar that it does not matter that one does not distinguish them). Had the R^2 been consistently lower, as if the researcher analyzing strategy column 2's data had tried Model A and several versions of Model D, it might have suggested there was a strategy mixture hypothesis not yet discovered. However, the researcher simply could not know this for sure.

For the data analyzed in strategy columns 2, 3, 5, and 6, the regression models had several levels of R^2, which suggests their hypotheses about how the data were grouped varied in accuracy. Model B's 50%/50% grouping variable $s5050$ exactly distinguishes the cases that were produced by each of the strategies in the strategy mixture that produced the data in strategy columns 2 and 5. In strategy column 2, where Cue 1 was used in the one strategy and Cue 2 in the other, the interaction terms involving $s5050$ and each of those cues (in Model B) were statistically significant, and the R^2 increased from .539 to .948. In strategy column 5, similarly, the R^2 increased from .519 to .896 when the appropriate interaction terms were added in Model B. Note that the interaction term with Cue 2 was not statistically significant because there was no difference in the involvement of Cue 2 between the two strategies in the mixture: one strategy used Cues 1 and 2, whereas the other used Cues 2 and 3. Analogous results may be seen with Model C in strategy columns 4 and 6 using the 75%/25% grouping variable $s7525$. The β's are larger for the cues that were used 75% of the time.

The uninformed researcher would not know that there was 20% noise in the simulation and that, for example, Model B uses the perfectly accurate strategy mixture variable for strategy column 2 in producing its interactions and hence could not know from inspecting the R^2 that the best solution had been found. No feature of the multiple regression model per se could indicate that there is no better Model E.

Using the statistically significant predictors, the descriptive model would be:

$$\hat{Judgment} = 0.520 * Cue_1 + 0.473 * Cue_2 + 0.892 * s5050 * Cue_1$$
$$- 0.870 * s5050 * Cue_2 \qquad \text{Equation 5}$$

Substituting each of the possible values of $s5050$, in turn, produces regression models describing the intuitive judgment models in each of the two (accurately) hypothesized subsets of the judgments:

If $s5050 = +½$,
$$\hat{Judgment} = (0.520 + 0.892 * 0.5) * Cue_1 + (0.473 - 0.870 * 0.5) * Cue_2$$
$$= 0.966 * Cue_1 + 0.038 * Cue_2 \qquad \text{Equation 6}$$

If $s5050 = +½$,
$$\hat{Judgment} = (0.520 - 0.892 * 0.5) * Cue_1 + (0.473 + 0.870 * 0.5) * Cue_2$$
$$= 0.074 * Cue_1 + 0.908 * Cue_2$$

This recaptures the data generating model of strategy column 2: in one set, essentially all weight is on Cue 1; in the other, it is on Cue 2. Thus, for the physician who uses patient cues differently in predicting how many days a patient will be in the intensive care unit when different nurse supervisors are on duty, if the researcher thought to group the physician's predictions according to which nurse is in charge, the researcher might know that with one nurse, the physician based her or his predictions on Cue 1 but on Cue 2 with the other nurse.

MECHANICAL SEARCH TO INDUCE HYPOTHESES ABOUT WHICH JUDGMENTS WERE MADE BY WHICH STRATEGIES

I have demonstrated that if the researcher has a good hypothesis about which judgments were made by different strategies, then by expressing the hypothesis as a strategy mixture variable, constructing interactions between this variable and each cue, and performing regression analysis, it is possible to test the hypothesized grouping and describe the judgment strategy used in each group. However, of course the problem with intuitive strategies is that neither the judge nor the researcher can confidently hypothesize which strategy is used to produce each judgment. Would it be reasonable to use a mechanical search procedure to discover how to divide the judgments into two groups? I consider whether such a search is feasible and whether one could defend its result as two distinct judgment strategies.

A brute force approach would search through all possible divisions of the n cases into two sets and identify the best division. For each division, the researcher could fit a regression model (with Group × Cue interaction terms as previously) and calculate the proportion of the total response variance it explains. The division with the greatest R^2 would be assumed to provide both (a) the most accurate statement of which judgments each strategy was used on and (b) the best descriptions of the two intuitive judgment strategies.

How many different ways are there to divide the n judgments into sets? I assume only two different strategies are used and call the sizes of the subsets r and $(n - r)$. This is an example of a combinatorial problem: How many ways are there to sample r objects from a population of size n? There are $_nC_r$ or $\binom{n}{r}$ or $\frac{n!}{r!(n-r)!}$ possible ways to divide the total set of judgments into two sets, where the size of the first set is r. When one considers all possible sizes of r, one must divide the total by 2 because each draw also produces its complement. (Alternatively, one could simply count only if $r < \frac{1}{2} n$ and halve $_nC_r$ when $r = \frac{1}{2} n$.)

In the preceding simulation, n was 64. A random variable determined whether each of the 64 judgments was produced by Strategy 1 or 2, so r could vary around its expectation of 32. If one had no basis on which to assign cases to same-strategy groups but one assumed there were exactly half the judgments in each group $[r = (n - r) = 32]$, there would be $\frac{64!}{32!(64-32)!} \Big/ 2$ or 9.16×10^{17} possible groupings.

If one was interested in groupings where both r and $(n - r)$ were at least 10, there would be 9.22×10^{18} possible groups. If one considers only groupings in which both r and $(n - r)$ were at least 30, there still would be 4.31×10^{18} possibilities.

Heuristic search algorithms can reduce the size of the search, with a high probability of finding the best division. One heuristic would start with a random initial allocation of judgments into sets, evaluate the impact of switching each judgment into the other set, choose the switch that produces the best gain in R^2, and repeat the process until no further gains are achieved. Although that algorithm could get stuck in a local maximum, smarter heuristics—for example, those that explore multiple random starting points or genetic algorithms that recombine parts of previous moderately successful solutions—can avoid problems of local maxima and will probably achieve good solutions in fewer steps. It remains to be determined whether a heuristic search could make it feasible to identify subsets of judgments that are describable with distinct cue-combination rules.

If automated search for sets of judgments with distinct prediction rules were feasible, should it be taken seriously? Consider two researchers. One of them hypothesized a division of judgments based on knowledge of factors that might cause, or signs that might reflect, the use of different intuitive strategies. When a variable reflecting this distinction was included in interactions in a regression model, it explained an additional 15% of the variance in the judgments over and above the null hypothesis that the individual uses just one judgment strategy. The second researcher applied a heuristic search algorithm that identified a division of the judgments that explained 20% more of the variance than the null hypothesis. Most researchers would take the division based on the search algorithm less seriously. The first researcher posed a hypothesis and confirmed it when the interaction regression analysis attained a particular score. The second researcher maximized that score, but no confirmation occurred. Perhaps a hybrid approach, where the researcher's initial hypothesis is "tuned" by a search algorithm, would be an acceptable compromise.

DISCUSSION

In this chapter, I have speculated about the existence of a problem that has not received much attention in the literature on the psychology of intuitive judgment and proposed a method to address it. The problem is that unobservable intuitive judgment might be accomplished using a mix of two or more distinct judgment strategies. This contrasts with the way intuitive judgment is usually viewed, which assumes an individual uses the same strategy on each repetition of a given task. It may in fact be very rare that an individual makes a set of intuitive judgments using two strategies, but because researchers have seldom looked for it (but see Simonsohn, 2007), they do not really know.

If an individual uses multiple intuitive judgment strategies, it violates the assumptions of any judgment policy description tool that fits statistical models relating the outputs of multiple judgments to their inputs. Multiple regression, ANOVA, and conjoint analysis assume there is just one dominant strategy plus noise due to lack of control, that is, the inability to consistently follow that one strategy. Where noise around a single strategy would hopefully not bias the conclusion about where its center lies, a mixture of two distinct judgment strategies might have an empty center, and hence, the statistical model's assumption that there is only one strategy could produce a very inaccurate conclusion.

The solution I offered in this chapter uses a familiar regression analysis concept (interaction terms) with the modification that the cues are interacted with a dichotomous dummy variable that reflects a hypothesis about whether each judgment was made with one or another judgment strategy. For this solution to be feasible, several conditions must be met. First, it must be possible to avoid a problem inherent in repeating an intuitive judgment many times—the possibility of changing the judgment task so it is no longer the intuitive task in which the researcher was originally interested. Second, the number of different strategies should probably be small. With three strategies, the number of possible divisions of the judgments into categories would be much larger than with two. In the regression analysis, each additional group would require an additional dummy variable. Further, it is implausible that an individual could stably use more than two intuitive judgment processes on a given task. Third, the researcher must be able to categorize, even if only partially accurately, which of the distinct intuitive judgment strategies was used on each instance. This may be done based on features of the situation hypothesized to cause the use of different intuitive judgment strategies or features of the individual's behavior hypothesized to reflect the use of different strategies. As I discussed previously, it is not likely that a heuristic search algorithm can identify sets of judgments that were made by validly distinct judgment strategies.

Assuming that the researcher can group judgments into sets hypothesized to have been created using the same judgment strategy, interaction terms are constructed by multiplying the strategy identity variable times each of the cue measures. Including these interaction terms in the regression analysis allows the researcher to discover if any cues are used differently in the two sets. If so, it would indicate that the hypothesized strategy identification has some validity, and the subgroup regression models would describe how the distinct judgment processes use the cues.

Subsequent to the Heidelberg conference in February of 2004, I have discovered just one example of multiple intuitive strategies: Simonsohn's (2007) demonstration that college admission officers evaluate individuals differently on cloudy and sunny days. With this proof that the phenomenon exists, the reader is encouraged to search for additional examples and to utilize the method described here to analyze the data.

REFERENCES

Abernathy, C. M., & Hamm, R. M. (1994). *Surgical scripts*. Philadelphia: Hanley and Belfus.
Abernathy, C. M., & Hamm, R. M. (1995). *Surgical intuition*. Philadelphia: Hanley and Belfus.
Anderson, J. R. (1993). *Rules of the mind*. Hillsdale, NJ: Lawrence Erlbaum Associates, Inc.
Anderson, N. H. (1970). Functional measurement and psychophysical judgment. *Psychological Review, 77*, 153–170.
Bröder, A. (2000). A methodological comment on behavioral decision research. *Psychologische Beitrage, 42*, 645–662.

Cooksey, R. W. (1996). *Judgment analysis: Theory, methods, and applications.* San Diego, CA: Academic.
Cooper, R. P. (2002). *Modelling high-level cognitive processes.* Mahwah, NJ: Lawrence Erlbaum Associates, Inc.
Dreyfus, H. L. (1997). Intuitive, deliberative, and calculative models of expert performance. In C. E. Zsambok & G. Klein (Eds.), Naturalistic decision making (pp. 17–28). Mahwah, NJ: Lawrence Erlbaum Associates Inc.
Epstein, S. (1973). The self-concept revisited or a theory of a theory. *American Psychologist, 28,* 404–416.
Epstein, S. (2000). The rationality debate from the perspective of cognitive-experiential self-theory. *Behavioral and Brain Sciences, 23,* 671.
Ericsson, K. A., & Kintsch, W. (1995). Long-term working memory. *Psychological Review, 102,* 211–245.
Green, P. E., & Wind, Y. (1973). *Multiattribute decisions in marketing: A measurement approach.* Hinsdale, IL: Dryden.
Hammond, K. R. (1981). *Principles of organization in intuitive and analytical cognition* (No. 231). Boulder, CO: Center for Research on Judgment and Policy, University of Colorado.
Hammond, K. R. (1996). *Human judgment and social policy: Irreducible uncertainty, inevitable error, unavoidable injustice.* New York: Oxford University Press.
Hammond, K. R., Hamm, R. M., Grassia, J. L., & Pearson, T. (1987). Direct comparison of the efficacy of intuitive and analytical cognition in expert judgment. *IEEE Transactions on Systems, Man, and Cybernetics, 17,* 753–770.
Hammond, K. R., Hursch, C.J., & Todd, F.J. (1964). Analyzing the components of clinical inference. *Psychological Review, 71,* 438–456.
Hastie, R. (2001). Problems for judgment and decision making. *Annual Review of Psychology, 52,* 563–583.
Johnson, E. J., & Payne, J. W. (1985). Effort and accuracy in choice. *Management Science, 31,* 395–414.
Kahneman, D., & Frederick, S. (2002). Representativeness revisited: Attribute substitution in intuitive judgment. In T. Gilovich, D. Griffin, & D. Kahneman (Eds.), *Heuristics and biases: The psychology of intuitive judgment* (pp. 49–81). Cambridge, MA: Cambridge University Press.
Kee, F., Jenkins, J., McIlwaine, S., Patterson, C., Harper, S., & Shields, M. (2003). Fast and frugal models of clinical judgment in novice and expert physicians. *Medical Decision Making, 23,* 293–300.
Poses, R. M., Wigton, R. S., Cebul, R. D., Centor, R. M., Collins, M., & Fleischli, G. J. (1993). Practice variation in the management of pharyngitis: The importance of variability in patients' clinical characteristics and in physicians' responses to them. *Medical Decision Making, 13,* 293–301.
Post, E. L. (1943). Formal reductions of the general combinatorial decision problem. *American Journal of Mathematics, 65,* 197–268.
Sanfey, A. G., Rilling, J. K., Aronson, J. A., Nystrom, L. E., & Cohen, J. D. (2003). The neural basis of economic decision-making in the Ultimatum Game. *Science, 300,* 1755–1758.
Simon, H. A. (1981). Otto Selz and information-processing psychology. In N. H. Frijda & A. deGroot (Eds.), *Otto Selz: His contribution to psychology* (pp. 147–163). The Hague, Netherlands: Mouton.
Simonsohn, U. (2007). Clouds make nerds look good: Field evidence of the impact of incidental factors on decision making. *Journal of Behavioral Decision Making, 20,* 143–152. The Wharton School, University of Pennsylvania, Philadelphia.

Stanovich, K. E., & West, R. F. (2000). Individual differences in reasoning: Implications for the rationality debate? *Behavioral and Brain Sciences, 23,* 645–726.

Stewart, T. R. (1988). Judgment analysis: Procedures. In B. Brehmer & C. R. B. Joyce (Eds.), *Human judgment: The SJT view* (pp. 41–74). Amsterdam: North-Holland.

Stewart, T. R. (2001). The lens model equation. In K. R. Hammond & T. R. Stewart (Eds.), *The Essential Brunswik: Beginnings, explications, applications* (pp. 357–362). New York: Oxford University Press.

Stewart, T. R., Hamm, R. M., & Tape, T. G. (2004). *A new formula and illustrative data for the logistic form of the lens model equation.* Paper presented at the 20th annual International Meeting of the Brunswik Society. From URL http://www.brunswik.org/newsletters/2004news.pdf on May 16, 2007.

Tucker, L. R. (1964). A suggested alternative formulation in the developments by Hursch, Hammond, and Hursch and by Hammond, Hursch, and Todd. *Psychological Review, 71,* 528–530.

Wallace, H. A. (1923). What is in the corn judge's mind? *Journal of the American Society of Agronomy, 15,* 300–304.

5

Can Neuroscience Tell a Story About Intuition?

KIRSTEN G. VOLZ and D. YVES VON CRAMON

Max Planck Institute for Human Cognitive and Brain Sciences

INTRODUCTION

According to the Oxford English Dictionary (http://www.oed.com), intuition is "the immediate apprehension of an object by the mind without the intervention of any reasoning process." In general parlance, knowing something without knowing how you know it. Most people would agree that intuitive insights appear as ideas or feelings that subsequently guide their thought and behavior. However, the specific cognitive processes underlying such intuitive decisions are not clear yet nor is the role of learning processes and their contribution to intuitive responses. One possibility to approach this issue is to incorporate neuroscientific results. Researchers whose primary interest is in cognition may wonder why they should actually care about neuroscientific findings. A short time ago, it was argued that knowing which parts of the brain light up during the processing of a specific task is not relevant for cognitive theory, nor does it expand theoretical concepts on cognition. However, knowing where in the brain processing takes place can tell researchers important potential correspondences between phenomenological different tasks, which might even be investigated in different parts of cognitive science. Likewise, imaging data can tell researchers whether small changes within one task can alter the strategy used by the participants on the basis of different areas activated. This circumstance is due to the fact that by now, brain areas can be characterized in terms of their role in implementing specific cognitive processes. Important to note is that this logic implies that the same brain area implements the same cognitive process regardless of the specific combination of processes realized in the actual task. Generally, the term *process* can be conceived of as referring to an operation or a set of operations that transforms an input into an output.

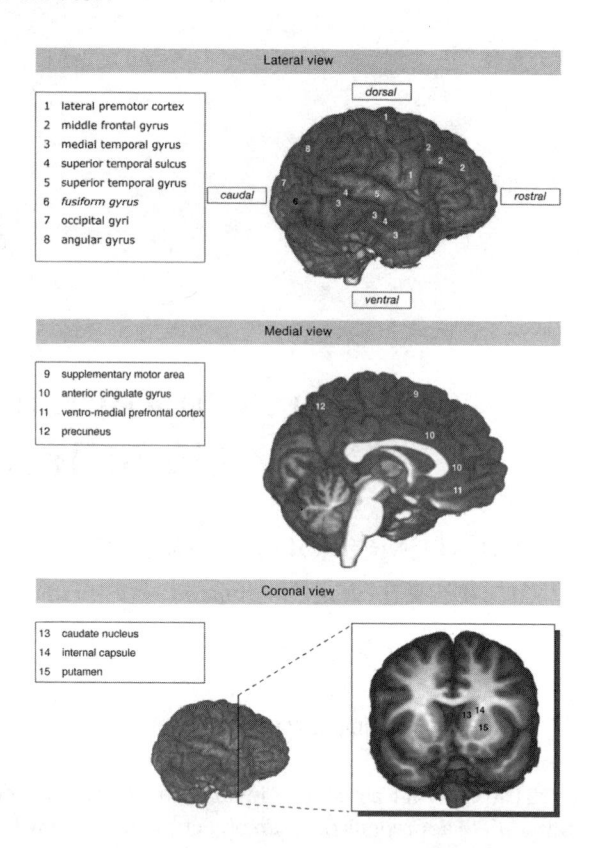

FIGURE 5.1 On the upper panel, the lateral surface of a right hemisphere including general direction readings is shown; on the middle panel, the medial view on a left hemisphere; and on the lower panel, a coronal view including a diagram where the slice is taken from. The fusiform gyrus (6) is not visible in the particular view but lies a bit farther in the gray substance.

The basic logic of inference in neuroscientific research is indicated as long as a particular process can be associated with a specific area. If there are no coherent findings with regard to the specificity of a particular brain region, one might approach this issue by determining the structural features of this area as well as its connectivity. Thus, by combining experimental psychology with neuroscience, additional information about the underlying mechanisms of a specific process can be revealed. Furthermore, one can learn more about the interaction between structure and process and how this might change with experience or age.[1]

---

[1] Certainly, when interpreting neuroimaging data, researchers have to be aware of its limits, that is, information is gained through a correlative method. Yet, the necessity of a particular brain area for a specific process can be shown by temporarily disrupting the area of interest by means of transcranial magnetic stimulation or by using the lesion method, that is, conducting patient studies.

Yet when trying to elucidate the cognitive architecture of intuitive decisions by means of consideration of neuroscientific results, one is faced with a dilemma: Until today, there has been a lack of imaging studies investigating the neural substrates of intuitive decisions, which is most probably due to the missing scientific definition of the concept of intuition. However, there are several studies that have examined the neural implementation of decisions that are reached without conscious reasoning such as studies on implicit memory, implicit learning, or feeling of knowing (FOK).[2] Unconscious processing has been considered as the prominent distinguishing feature of intuitive decisions (T. Betsch, chap. 1, this volume; Hogarth, 2001; Myers, 2002). The purpose of this article is hence to review those studies so as to determine a potential common network of unconscious processing. By then it will also become clear whether present studies on unconscious processing and reasoning may already have realized the concept of intuition but missed terming it accordingly.

So that the anatomy novice will be able to navigate through the brain, we give a schematic figure outlining the areas that we refer to in the text (see Fig. 5.1). However, before proceeding, we give a very brief insight in the basic logic of functional neuroimaging.

FUNCTIONAL NEUROIMAGING IN A NUTSHELL

Currently, the most often used functional neuroimaging technique is functional magnetic resonance imaging (fMRI).[3] This method measures local hemodynamic changes, that is, the dynamic regulation of the blood flow: Neurons, like all other cells, require energy to function. This energy is supplied in terms of glucose and oxygen whereby the oxygen is being carried in hemoglobin, which is the iron-containing, oxygen-transport metalloprotein in the red cells of the blood. The blood supply of the brain is dynamically regulated by providing more energy to momentary active assemblies of neurons, whereas inactive assemblies receive less energy. Oxygenated and deoxygenated blood hemoglobin differ in their magnetic properties, that is, the former is diamagnetic, whereas the latter is paramagnetic (Turner & Jezzard, 1994). As a result, the magnetic resonance signal of the blood is therefore slightly different contingent on the level of oxygenation, a phenomenon called the blood oxygenation level dependent (BOLD) signal. Higher BOLD signal intensities thus arise from an increased availability of oxygenated blood hemoglobin proportional to deoxygenated blood. It has long been known that the hemodynamic activity is closely linked to neural activity,[4] and more specifically, it was supposed that hemodynamic changes arise from the synaptic activity of active neural assemblies. Yet only now, it could be shown that the fMRI signal indeed "reflects the input and intracortical processing of a given area rather than its spiking output" (Logothetis, Pauls, Augath, Trinath, & Oeltermann, 2001, p. 150).

---

[2] We do not include studies on moral judgments, which were referred to as "affective intuitions" (Greene & Haidt, 2002), as this topic is explicated in detail in chapter 13 (this volume).

[3] Positron emission tomography (which also measures hemodynamic responses) is used less, as it applies radioactive tracers.

[4] Approximately 1 to 6 sec after a burst of neural activity, a hemodynamic response occurs.

Relating the indirectly measured brain activity to cognition is mostly done by the method of "subtraction" (Friston et al., 1996): During at least two separate cognitive tasks, brain activity is measured. The cognitive tasks are ideally designed so that they differ from one another only with respect to the specifically identifiable features of interest—such as a cognitive process, sensory modality, or type of information—but not with respect to sensory or motor requirements. Thus, the two cognitive tasks would differ by only a single feature. When the BOLD signal recorded during one of the two tasks, for example, the baseline task, is subtracted from the BOLD signal recorded during the other task, for example, the experimental task, the resulting pattern of brain activation is assumed to reflect the functional neuroanatomy of the specified cognitive difference between the two tasks. Regions in which the activity levels between the two tasks do not differ will not be included in the resulting pattern. Regions in which the activity is higher for the experimental task are said to show activation. Generally, the goal of imaging studies is to relate differences in brain activity between two conditions to the differences in the cognitive and mental processes that differentiate those two conditions.

A more sophisticated approach using a parametric design can reduce the problems of selecting the appropriate baseline. Assuming that the hemodynamic response varies with the amount of cortical processing engaged by an experimental task, parametric or correlational designs can provide information about the relationship between a stimulus parameter or behavioral response and the neurophysiological response elicited (Buchel, Holmes, Rees, & Friston, 1998). Accordingly, parametric designs are used to characterize and differentiate brain regions using their response profile in relation to the task parameters. In contrast to the method of subtraction, cognitive processes are not regarded as categorical invariants but rather considered as dimensions or attributes that can be expressed more or less.

IMPLICIT MEMORY

In general, the term *implicit memory* has been used to refer to the phenomenon that recent experience has an influence on behavior even though one does not recognize that memory is being used nor that one intentionally recollects prior experiences (e.g., Frensch, 1998; Schacter, 1987). The term *implicit memory* was at first used by Graf and Schacter (1985) to distinguish this type of memory from *explicit memory*, which has been defined as the conscious recollection of recently presented information, as expressed on traditional tests of free recall or recognition. A differentiation between explicit and implicit memory has been supported by two lines of evidence: First, amnesic patients with damage to the medial temporal lobe or to diencephalic structures show excellent performance in implicit tests on priming but catastrophically poor performance in explicit tests (Rugg, 1995). This dissociation gave rise to the conclusion that implicit memory tests can be carried out without medial temporal areas and diencephalic structures. Second, the differential malleability of performance, for example, by depth of processing or modality changes, also suggests a dissociation between implicit and explicit memory (Schacter, 1987).

The study of implicit memory has been dominated by a single paradigm: priming. The term *priming* refers to hypothetical processes underlying the priming effect, that is, the empirical finding that the identification of an object or the production of an item is facilitated by the individual's prior encounter with the same or a similar object or item. Generally, tests that have been used to measure priming effects can broadly be classified into perceptual and semantic (Habib, 2001). Perceptual priming tests are characterized by a perceptual relation—usually a visual one—between the retrieval cue and the target item. A typical perceptual priming test is stem completion: Participants study a list of words and later, at testing, they are presented with "stems" (initial three letters) of studied as well as nonstudied items and are asked to say the first word that comes to mind. Other perceptual priming tests most commonly used in priming research are lexical decision, word identification, and fragment completion. Priming effects are either indicated by a decrease in the latency to make a decision or by the increased tendency to complete stems or fragments with items previously studied.

In contrast, semantic[5] priming tests can be characterized by the fact that the relation between the retrieval cue and the target item refers to meaning rather than physical form. For example, in the category exemplar generation task, participants study a list of words (e.g., *eagle*), and later, at testing, they are required to generate instances of category names (e.g., *birds*). Priming is said to occur when more previously studied words are generated as exemplars than new instances.

One of the first imaging studies that investigated the neural correlates of perceptual priming was conducted by Squire et al. (1992). Squire et al. showed a decrease in activation within the right occipital cortex for the priming condition when contrasted with the baseline condition. This finding was suggested to indicate that processing of a stimulus requires less activity when encountered before. Subsequent experiments on perceptual priming have replicated the finding of decreased posterior cortical activation (i.e., within nonprimary visual cortices) for the primed condition when compared with the nonprimed condition (Badgaiyan, Schacter, & Alpert, 2003; Buckner et al., 1995; Thiel, Shanks, Henson, & Dolan, 2003). These data complement findings reported by Keane, Gabrieli, Mapstone, Johnson, and Corkin (1995) who showed a lack of perceptual priming in a patient with damage to the extrastriate cortex. Accordingly, brain imaging data converge on the conclusion that perceptually based priming is accompanied by a deactivation in extrastriate areas. Generally, the function of these regions has been associated with visual word and object processing (for an overview, see Schacter & Buckner, 1998).

In contrast, studies that have investigated the neural correlates of semantic priming have commonly found reduced activity in the prefrontal cortex (PFC), more specifically, a deactivation in the left inferior PFC (LIPFC; Buckner et al., 1998; Demb et al., 1995). Associated with a decrease in LIPFC activity was a concomitant decrease in reaction times for the primed items. The reasoning was that the primed items require less neural activity to be processed (a second time) than new items. Activation within LIPFC has not only been found for semantic priming

---

[5] Semantic priming is also denoted as conceptual priming.

effects but also during semantic (meaning-based) decisions or in semantic generation tasks but not during single-word reading (Gold, Balota, Kirchhoff, & Buckner, 2005; Kapur et al., 1994). Thus, the findings converged on the assumption that LIPFC activation reflects controlled semantic processes such as the strategic retrieval of meaning and/or the working with and evaluating of meaning.

The finding of reduced activation within LIPFC for semantic, that is, meaning-based priming and reduced activation in extrastriate areas for perceptual, that is, visual priming suggests priming effects to be reflected by modality-specific plasticity.

To test this assumption, Bergerbest, Ghahremani, and Gabrieli (2004) recently conducted a study on auditory repetition priming using environmental sounds. As predicted by Bergerbest et al., they found an activation decrease in the superior temporal gyrus and in the anterior and posterior superior temporal sulcus, that is, within the secondary auditory cortex. Moreover, the behavioral priming effect correlated significantly with the repetition-related activation reduction. These findings are taken to support the assumption that modality-specific priming is mediated by an activation reduction in the corresponding modality-specific brain region. Previous studies on auditory repetition priming using auditory word stem completion did not find any activation reduction in the auditory cortex (Badgaiyan, Schacter, & Alpert, 1999, 2001). An explanation may be that the implemented task rather involved lexical or phonological processing than purely acoustic or auditory processing, which in turn appeared to be the primary processing mode for environmental sounds (Bergerbest et al., 2004).

Together, neuroimaging findings on implicit memory, acquired by using the priming paradigm, have revealed priming effects to be mediated by an activation reduction in the very same brain regions that were responsible for the perceptual or conceptual processing of the stimuli. This finding suggests that priming effects are not a consequence of any one specialized implicit memory system but dependent on modality-specific processing. Starting from the concept of intuition as a modality-independent process, one would have expected to observe activation consistently within a specific network across different indirect memory tests. Obviously, this is not the case, at least not when using the priming paradigm.

IMPLICIT LEARNING

The term *implicit learning* was coined by Reber (1989) to refer to the process by which people acquire knowledge about rule-governed complexities of a stimulus environment independently of conscious attempts to do so. Reber (1993) and Berry and Dienes (1993) have showed that people exposed to various artificial structured situations, without being informed that there was any structure, were subsequently able to identify instances of the phenomenon or to predict the future occurrences. Accordingly, the study on implicit learning was considered to help in understanding those learning mechanisms that occur without consciousness, that is, not as a result of conscious hypothesis testing (Seger, 1997). Despite a burst of interest in this topic from about 1990 onward, there is still no generally accepted definition of the concept of implicit learning (for an overview, see the *Handbook of Implicit Learning* by

Stadler & Frensch, 1998). Mostly, implicit learning is subsumed as a form of implicit memory despite heavy objections from researchers on implicit learning. Yet, operationally the two concepts cannot be assessed separately, as the implicitness of learning is measured on the basis of the implicitness of memory retrieval (Shanks & St. John, 1994). A nonintrusive measure of the implicit character of learning itself, like neuroimaging data, can provide evidence for or against the suggested dissociation. Present imaging data point toward two distinguishable concepts.

The two paradigms primarily used in research on implicit learning are the serial reaction time (SRT) task (Nissen & Bullemer, 1987) and the artificial grammar learning (AGL) task (Reber, 1967). In SRT tasks, participants are presented with a series of visual stimuli, usually dots or asterisks, which are located at different screen locations. Participants are asked to respond to each stimulus' location by pressing a corresponding button. Unbeknownst to participants, the sequence of stimuli follows a predetermined pattern, which is iterated and intermixed with sequences of randomly determined locations. Implicit learning is said to occur when reaction times on sequence blocks are significantly shorter than those on random blocks. This task is considered implicit, as participants show learning without any explicit sequence knowledge, that is, they are unaware of the existence of any sequence. Participants report that they usually rely on their intuition or feelings to solve the task.

In AGL tasks, participants first study a list of nonword letter strings, which are generated from a finite set of complex rules that has been termed *artificial grammar*. In a following test phase, participants are told that the previously studied words followed an artificial grammar, which is not explained, and that their task is now to classify novel strings as grammatical or ungrammatical accordingly. The AGL task is categorized as implicit because participants show learning, measured by classification accuracy (usually performance levels above 60% to 70%), without any explicit rule knowledge and report to rely on their subjective feelings of what is grammatical and ungrammatical.

Based on the dissimilarity of the two dependent measures of implicit learning, that is, increasing speed in SRT tasks against increasing precision to classify items based on implicit knowledge in AGL tasks, Seger (1997, 1998) has proposed (at least) two forms of implicit learning: a motor-linked and a judgment-linked form. Beyond, the assumption that the SRT and AGL task may address the same implicit learning mechanism was challenged by the finding that patients with damage to the basal ganglia performed equally well as controls on AGL tasks but were severely impaired on SRT tasks. Likewise, imaging studies in normal populations that have used either the SRT or AGL task have reported different activation patterns. Hence, both conceptual considerations as well as empirical evidence suggest a differentiation of the implicit learning processes addressed by the two tasks.

A large body of research on implicit learning that has used the standard SRT task or slightly modified versions has observed activation within the striatum, a nuclear complex belonging to the basal ganglia, during implicit sequence learning, that is, when contrasting determined sequences with random sequences (e.g., Aizenstein et al., 2004; Daselaar, Rombouts, Veltman, Raaijmakers, & Jonker, 2003; Doyon, Owen, Petrides, Sziklas, & Evans, 1996; Hazeltine, Grafton, & Ivry,

1997; Rauch et al., 1997, 1998; Schendan, Searl, Melrose, & Stern, 2003; Werheid, Ziessler, Nattkemper, & Yves von Cramon, 2003). The term *striatum* is generic, as it subsumes the putamen and caudate nucleus.[6] Activation within the putamen was found to be significantly correlated with the learning effect measured by the magnitude of reaction time advantage (Rauch et al., 1997). Activation for implicit sequence learning has also been reported in components of the frontostriatal circuits including the dorsolateral PFC, parietal lobe, premotor cortex, anterior cingulate, and supplementary motor area (Hazeltine et al., 1997; Peigneux et al., 2000; Rauch et al., 1997, 1998; Schendan et al., 2003; Willingham, Salidis, & Gabrieli, 2002).

To test the basal ganglia's specificity with respect to the implicitness of sequence learning, it is worthwhile to consider lesion studies. The degenerative and heritable disorder of Huntington's disease (HD) is associated with atrophy in the striatum, especially within the caudate nucleus, and to a lesser extent in the cerebral cortex. Another degenerative disorder affecting the basal ganglia is Parkinson's disease (PD). This disorder is predominantly but not exclusively associated with lesions to the substantia nigra resulting in a loss of dopamine neurons projecting to the striatum. Results have revealed patients with PD and HD to be significantly impaired in SRT tasks (Knopman & Nissen, 1991; Laforce & Doyon, 2001; Smith & McDowall, 2004, 2006; Westwater, McDowall, Siegert, Mossman, & Abernethy, 1998) but not in AGL tasks (Peigneux, Meulemans, Van der Linden, Salmon, & Petit, 1999; Reber & Squire, 1999; Smith, Siegert, McDowall, & Abernethy, 2001; Witt, Nuhsman, & Deuschl, 2002). Yet there have also been a few studies that have shown that some forms of implicit learning are preserved in patients with PD (Smith & McDowall, 2004, 2006; Smith et al., 2001; Werheid et al., 2003). For instance, Smith et al. (2001) used a verbal version of the SRT task and found unimpaired implicit learning effects in patients with PD. Likewise, implicit learning effects were reported in a recent study in which Smith and McDowall (2006) used a version of the SRT that also reduced motor demands. Smith and McDowall (2006) investigated implicit learning of a spatial sequence, a stimulus-response sequence, and an integrated spatial and/or stimulus-response sequence. Results were suggested to show that patients with PD most likely experience difficulties in sequence learning tasks that require the integration of pattern information from multiple sources. This interpretation is supported by the findings by Werheid et al. (2003) who observed reduced learning effects on the standard version of the SRT task but unimpaired learning effects on a version in which the spatial component of the sequence has been removed. That is, stimulus presentation was central, therewith excluding linking between stimulus and response locations. Yet whether the specific function of the striatum may be related to the integration of sequential information across the sensory and motor domain remains for future studies.

However, evidence for this assumption derives from another line of research that has investigated the neuroanatomy of reward-related learning. Studies on this issue have consistently found activation within the (dorsal and ventral) striatum

---

[6] Both nuclei dispose of reciprocal connections with the substantia nigra, a structure containing dopamine.

during the learning of stochastic contingencies, usually realized in gambling paradigms with monetary incentives (e.g., Delgado, Miller, Inati, & Phelps, 2005; Delgado, Nystrom, Fissell, Noll, & Fiez, 2000; Haruno et al., 2004; Knutson, Westdorp, Kaiser, & Hommer, 2000; Volz, Schubotz, & von Cramon, 2003). Activation within the caudate nucleus has been shown to be correlated with the magnitude of behavioral change during learning such that activation is essential early in learning of action-outcome contingencies and decreases as learned associations become more and more predictable (Berns, Cohen, & Mintun, 1997; Delgado et al., 2005; Haruno et al., 2004). These findings led to the assumption that the striatum encodes errors in reward prediction, potentially mediated by dopamine signals (Schultz, 2000). The commonality between reward-related learning and implicit learning may be the successful establishment of representations of consistent associations between stimuli and responses allowing for anticipatory spatial orienting and therewith for efficient response planning processes. Together, it may be prolific to integrate the two lines of research to converge on a conclusion with respect to the specific function of the striatum.

To determine whether the striatum specifically reflects the unconscious component of the learning process (during the SRT task), one has to directly compare implicit with explicit sequence learning. In the study by Schendan et al. (2003), participants performed an implicit and an explicit version of the SRT task. In the latter, participants were asked to memorize the repeating sequence. Unexpectedly, Schendan et al. found learning-related activation for implicit as well as for explicit learning within the striatum. Hence, when contrasting implicit with explicit learning, no activation differences were observed. Similar results were found by Willingham et al. (2002) who reported significant overlap in activation between the implicit and explicit condition within striatal and frontal activation during both learning conditions. Likewise, Aizenstein et al. (2004) observed striatal activation during implicit and explicit learning. The primary difference between the two learning conditions was the direction of activation changes in extrastriate cortex: Whereas explicit learning elicited an increase in activation within the visual cortex, implicit learning was associated with lower activation in this area.

In the study by Rose, Haider, Weiller, and Buchel (2002), they investigated whether striatal activation may be involved during the learning of flexible relational contingencies without awareness. Rose et al. implemented a sophisticated design allowing for the separate assessment of explicit skill acquisition and implicit learning of abstract relations. Results showed a functional separation of the two learning processes: Whereas skill acquisition, which was based on practicing fixed stimulus-response associations, increasingly activated the basal ganglia, the implicit learning of abstract relations increasingly activated the medial temporal lobe (MTL). Although MTL activation has so far been linked to conscious recollection of memories (Eldridge, Knowlton, Furmanski, Bookheimer, & Engel, 2000), MTL activation in Rose et al.'s study was elicited by knowledge that was consciously not accessible.

Together, these results support the assumption that striatal activation may specifically reflect (a) the learning of stimulus-response associations that require the integration of patterned information from multiple sources, a process that may not need to be conscious, or (b) the processing and integrating of reward-related information. Both approaches emphasize the predictability of upcoming responses: The answer on the actual trial is triggered or predicted by the answer on the previous trial, or the actual answer is determined by the event's global probability of occurrence. The finding of striatal activation during explicit sequence learning does not support the assumption of this area to specifically reflect the unconscious component of learning processes.

Compared to research on implicit learning using the SRT task, there are only a few imaging studies using the AGL task; beyond, these findings are rather controversial. When they contrasted grammatical with ungrammatical items, Lieberman, Chang, Chiao, Bookheimer, and Knowlton (2004) reported significant activation within the basal ganglia, MTL, and inferior frontal cortex, whereas Skosnik et al. (2002) observed significant activation within superior occipital gyrus and fusiform gyrus. When successfully with unsuccessfully discriminated items were compared, significant activation was observed within superior occipital gyrus, angular gyrus, precuneus, and middle frontal gyrus (Skosnik et al., 2002). Based on these results, Skosnik et al. (2002) suggested the occipital and angular gyrus as prime candidates for AGL.

Recently, it has been suggested that high performance levels in AGL tasks might rather reflect explicit remembering of surface features than implicitly acquired rule knowledge. Grammatical test strings usually bear greater similarity to the studied strings in terms of frequency of specific bigrams and trigrams, which is denoted as chunk strength or fragment familiarity (Peigneux et al., 1999; Thiel et al., 2003). To control for this confound, Lieberman et al. (2004) generated grammatical and ungrammatical test strings that were matched for chunk strength. Thus, Lieberman et al. could disentangle brain areas sensitive to chunk strength from those sensitive to rule use. Results revealed activation within caudate nucleus for rule adherence and activation within MTL for chunk strength.

The dissociation between brain areas involved in explicit item learning and those involved in implicit rule learning was also aimed at in the study by Fletcher, Buchel, Josephs, Friston, and Dolan (1999). By using a sophisticated paradigm, activation associated with item learning (within-block learning) was observed in medial parietal and medial frontal areas, whereas activation associated with rule learning (across-block learning) was observed in the left PFC. The inconsistent findings of the two studies concerning brain areas sensitive to abstract rule learning may be accounted for by differential proceedings: In the Fletcher et al. study, participants received no training session but were explicitly asked from the first trial onward to find the underlying grammatical rule. Immediate feedback after each trial was given, indicating whether participants' responses were correct. In contrast, Lieberman et al. (2004) used the same proceeding as in former AGL studies, which do not provide any feedback and ask participants to rely on their "gut feeling" about grammaticality. Thus, it can be assumed that the different findings depend on the instruction given to participants.

Together, current evidence on implicit learning using the SRT task has consistently revealed the striatum as a putative neural correlate; yet, there is evidence questioning the striatum to specifically reflect the implicitness or unconscious component of the learning process. Evidence on the neural substrates of implicit learning addressed by the AGL task is comparatively little and beyond divers. Hence, it remains to future studies to determine the neural correlates of the unconscious component during a judgment-linked form of learning.

FOK

When presented with general knowledge questions that people are not able to answer immediately, they may nevertheless have a FOK that the "sought-after information is indeed available in store and worth searching for" (Koriat, 2000, p. 150). Generally, the term *FOK* is used to refer to people's prediction of a subsequent memory performance on previously nonrecalled items. Imaging studies on FOK have generally used two sorts of paradigms: Either participants were presented with general knowledge questions and had to indicate whether they knew the answer, did not know the answer, or had a FOK of the correct answer when presented among alternatives; or participants first engaged in a study phase and later in a test phase in which they were required to retrieve the previously studied items.

In the study by Maril, Simons, Mitchell, Schwartz, and Schacter (2003), the latter sort of paradigm was used: Participants were asked to encode word pairs, and later at testing, they were presented with one word and asked to retrieve the respective associated word. Retrieval-related activation was found within the left inferior frontal gyrus (IFG) such that trials in which the words were recalled elicited greater activation than FOK trials, which in turn were associated with greater responses than trials in which the words were not recalled. A very similar activation pattern was found within posterior parietal cortex. These findings were interpreted to mirror the phenomenology of graded recall success for the sought-after information. Accordingly, FOK is conceived of as an intermediate state of retrieval. This assumption has been supported by the findings that no brain region elicited FOK-specific activation when compared to know or don't know trials (Maril et al., 2003; Maril, Simons, Weaver, & Schacter, 2005).

To avoid shortcomings of cognitive subtraction, Kikyo, Ohki, and Miyashita (2002) used a parametric approach to systematically investigate the relationship between levels of FOK and the BOLD response. In Kikyo et al.'s study, participants had to judge their potential to recognize the correct answer among alternatives for items they failed to recall. By using FOK ratings as a parameter (including the don't know trials), Kikyo et al. identified inferior, dorsolateral, and medial prefrontal cortices as regions whose activity increased as FOK ratings became greater. These regions remained significant even when response latencies were controlled for by a second (reaction time) parameter. Based on the finding that IFG was not involved in successful recall processes, its specific role for FOK processes was suggested.

Yet, the specific involvement of IFG during FOK was challenged by findings from Schnyer et al. (2004) using a lesion method. Schnyer et al. (2004) specifically found patients with damage to the ventral medial PFC (VMPFC, which is a part of the orbitofrontal cortex) to show a clear FOK impairment. Thereupon,

Schnyer, Nicholls, and Verfaellie (2005) conducted an fMRI study within a normal population and used an episodic FOK paradigm. Results were taken to indicate a specific role of the VMPFC during accurate FOK judgments. The suggestion of VMPFC reflecting a subjective feeling of which decision to make coincides with results reported by Bechara, Tranel, and Damasio (2002). Based on a series of studies, Damasio (2002) and Damasio and his colleagues suggested the so-called somatic marker hypothesis, which claims that the VMPFC serves as a store of implicitly acquired linkages between factual knowledge and bioregulatory states including those that constitute feelings and emotion. Accordingly, somatic signals guide decisions advantageously and mostly in an unconscious fashion, yet in case of a damage to the VMPFC, decision making is selectively impaired as the somatic states, normally indicating the favorable course of action cannot be accessed.

Consider that there have been few imaging studies on FOK so far, it would be premature to reason on its neural correlates. It remains for future studies to determine the specific roles of the VMPFC and prefrontal areas with respect to decisions that are based on a gut feelings.

CONCLUDING REMARKS

Given the lack of imaging studies on the neural architecture of intuitive decisions, the aim of this synopsis was to determine the existence of a consistently reported neural network suggested to reflect unconscious processing. The summarized results considering imaging studies on implicit memory, implicit learning, and FOK seemed not to suggest a common neural network for unconscious processing. Hence, the approach to converge on the specific cognitive processes underlying intuitive decisions by means of neuroscientific results on unconscious information processing was not continuative.

In consideration of this fact, it is obvious that researchers are at the beginning of a neurobiologically oriented research on intuition (see also Volz & von Cramon, in press). At first, the most important issue will be to create an intuitive task that is adaptive for fMRI investigations. Only by then could neuroscience contribute to theory building with respect to intuitive decisional processes. In our view, AGL may constitute a promising approach to begin with. In this paradigm, individuals unintentionally acquire knowledge, which is later successfully applied to new situations without an understanding how this was achieved. In doing so, individuals (unconsciously) capitalize on stored mental representations, which reflect the entire stream of prior experiences that are associated with the critical event such as sensory, visceral, and experiential representations (for a corresponding definition of intuition, see also T. Betsch, chap. 1, this volume). Accordingly, we conceive of intuition as a synthetic psychological function in that it apprehends the totality of a given situation and synthesizes isolated bits of data and experiences related to the situational demands to reach a decision (Khatri & Ng, 2000).

If we were asked to speculate on the neural substrate subserving such an integrative function, we would suggest the (medial) orbitofrontal cortex (OFC) as a putative correlate. Based on its neuroanatomical connectivity, the OFC seems especially positioned to integrate sensory and visceral information to modulate behavior through both visceral and motor systems (Kringelbach, 2005). Particularly, the primate OFC receives input from all sensory modalities—that is, gustatory, olfactory, somatosensory, auditory, and visual input—and hence is probably the most polymodal region in the brain except for the rhinal area (Kringelbach & Rolls, 2004). For this reason, the OFC has often been suggested to play an important role in emotional processing (e.g., Davidson & Irwin, 1999; Nauta, 1971). By direct extensive projections from the hippocampal formation to the (median) OFC (Cavada, Compañy, Tejedor, Cruz-Rizzolo, & Reinoso-Suárez, 2000), the latter can also access and integrate experiential information. Furthermore, the (medial) OFC has direct access to information concerning the motivational significance of predictive cues through its connection with the amygdala complex (Schoenbaum, Setlow, Saddoris, & Gallagher, 2003).

Damage to this area in humans has been shown to be associated with personality changes and gross impairments in everyday life decision making (Bechara et al., 2002; Eslinger & Damasio, 1985). Specifically, patients with such damage have been described as deciding against their best interests and being unable to learn from previous mistakes despite intact intellectual abilities otherwise (Bechara et al., 2002). The disadvantageous choice behavior has been suggested to result from the patient's inability to integrate emotional and/or visceral signals into the decision-making process (Bechara et al., 2002; Damasio, 1996). The consideration of intuitive responses as being mainly guided by affective signals may strongly suggest the acquisition of autonomic responses during decision making and correlate those with the hemodynamic response.

In conclusion, it remains to be seen whether future studies implementing an original intuitive task will suggest the OFC as a putative correlate of intuitive decisions. In the worst case scenario, future research will not reveal a common neural network for intuitive decisions but different networks for different paradigms, which may indicate a revision of the concept of intuition.

REFERENCES

Aizenstein, H. J., Stenger, V. A., Cochran, J., Clark, K., Johnson, M., Nebes, R. D., et al. (2004). Regional brain activation during concurrent implicit and explicit sequence learning. *Cerebral Cortex, 14*, 199–208.

Badgaiyan, R. D., Schacter, D. L., & Alpert, N. M. (1999). Auditory priming within and across modalities: Evidence from positron emission tomography. *Journal of Cognitive Neuroscience, 11*, 337–348.

Badgaiyan, R. D., Schacter, D. L., & Alpert, N. M. (2001). Priming within and across modalities: Exploring the nature of rCBF increases and decreases. *Neuroimage, 13*, 272–282.

Badgaiyan, R. D., Schacter, D. L., & Alpert, N. M. (2003). Priming of new associations: A PET study. *Neuroreport, 14*, 2475–2479.

Bechara, A., Tranel, D., & Damasio, A. R. (2002). The somatic marker hypothesis and decision-making. In F. J. Boller & J. Grafman (Eds.), *Handbook of neuropsychology* (2nd ed., pp. 117–143). Amsterdam: Elsevier.

Bergerbest, D., Ghahremani, D. G., & Gabrieli, J. D. (2004). Neural correlates of auditory repetition priming: Reduced fMRI activation in the auditory cortex. *Journal of Cognitive Neuroscience, 16,* 966–977.

Berns, G. S., Cohen, J. D., & Mintun, M. A. (1997). Brain regions responsive to novelty in the absence of awareness. *Science, 276,* 1272–1275.

Berry, D. C., & Dienes, Z. (1993). *Implicit learning: Theoretical and empirical issues.* Hillsdale, NJ: Lawrence Erlbaum Associates, Inc.

Buchel, C., Holmes, A. P., Rees, G., & Friston, K. J. (1998). Characterizing stimulus-response functions using nonlinear regressors in parametric fMRI experiments. *Neuroimage, 8,* 140–148.

Buckner, R. L., Goodman, J., Burock, M., Rotte, M., Koutstaal, W., Schacter, D., et al. (1998). Functional-anatomic correlates of object priming in humans revealed by rapid presentation event-related fMRI. *Neuron, 20,* 285–296.

Buckner, R. L., Petersen, S. E., Ojemann, J. G., Miezin, F. M., Squire, L. R., & Raichle, M. E. (1995). Functional anatomical studies of explicit and implicit memory retrieval tasks. *Journal of Neuroscience, 15,* 12–29.

Cavada, C., Compañy, T., Tejedor, J., Cruz-Rizzolo, R. J., & Reinoso-Suárez, F. (2000). The anatomical connections of the macaque monkey orbitofrontal cortex: A review. *Cerebral Cortex, 10,* 220–242.

Damasio, A. R. (1996). The somatic marker hypothesis and the possible functions of the prefrontal cortex. *Philosophical Transactions of the Royal Society of London: Series B. Biological Sciences, 351,* 1413–1420.

Damasio, A. (2000). *The feeling of what happens: Body and emotion in the making of consciousness.* Orlando, FL: Harvest Books.

Daselaar, S. M., Rombouts, S. A., Veltman, D. J., Raaijmakers, J. G., & Jonker, C. (2003). Similar network activated by young and old adults during the acquisition of a motor sequence. *Neurobiology of Aging, 24,* 1013–1019.

Davidson, R. J., & Irwin, W. (1999). The functional neuroanatomy of emotion and affective style. *Trends in Cognitive Sciences, 3,* 11–21.

Delgado, M. R., Miller, M. M., Inati, S., & Phelps, E. A. (2005). An fMRI study of reward-related probability learning. *Neuroimage, 24,* 862–873.

Delgado, M. R., Nystrom, L. E., Fissell, C., Noll, D. C., & Fiez, J. A. (2000). Tracking the hemodynamic responses to reward and punishment in the striatum. *Journal of Neurophysiology, 84,* 3072–3077.

Demb, J. B., Desmond, J. E., Wagner, A. D., Vaidya, C. J., Glover, G. H., & Gabrieli, J. D. (1995). Semantic encoding and retrieval in the left inferior prefrontal cortex: A functional MRI study of task difficulty and process specificity. *Journal of Neuroscience, 15,* 5870–5878.

Doyon, J., Owen, A. M., Petrides, M., Sziklas, V., & Evans, A. C. (1996). Functional anatomy of visuomotor skill learning in human subjects examined with positron emission tomography. *European Journal of Neuroscience, 8,* 637–648.

Eldridge, L. L., Knowlton, B. J., Furmanski, C. S., Bookheimer, S. Y., & Engel, S. A. (2000). Remembering episodes: A selective role for the hippocampus during retrieval. *Nature Neuroscience, 3,* 1149–1152.

Eslinger, P. J., & Damasio, A. R.(1985). Severe disturbances of higher cognition after bilateral frontal lobe ablation: Patient EVR. *Neurology, 35,* 1731–1741.

Fletcher, P., Buchel, C., Josephs, O., Friston, K., & Dolan, R. (1999). Learning-related neuronal responses in prefrontal cortex studied with functional neuroimaging. *Cerebral Cortex, 9,* 168–178.

Frensch, P. A. (1998). One concept, multiple meanings: On how to define the concept of implicit learning. In M. A. Stadler & P. A. Frensch (Eds.), *Handbook of implicit learning* (pp. 47–104). London: Sage.

Friston, K. J., Price, C. J., Fletcher, P., Moore, C., Frackowiak, R. S. J., & Dolan, R. J. (1996). The trouble with cognitive subtraction. *NeuroImage, 4,* 97–104.

Gold, B. T., Balota, D. A., Kirchhoff, B. A., & Buckner, R. L. (2005). Common and dissociable activation patterns associated with controlled semantic and phonological processing: Evidence from fMRI adaptation. *Cerebral Cortex, 15,* 1438–1450.

Graf, P., & Schacter, D. L. (1985). Implicit and explicit memory for new associations in normal and amnesic subjects. *Journal of Experimental Psychology: Learning, Memory, and Cognition, 11,* 501–518.

Greene, J. & Haidt, J. (2002). How (and where) does moral judgment work? *Trends in Cognitive Sciences, 6,* 517–523.

Habib, R. (2001). On the relation between conceptual priming, neural priming, and novelty assessment. *Scandinavian Journal of Psychology, 42,* 187–195.

Haruno, M., Kuroda, T., Doya, K., Toyama, K., Kimura, M., Samejima, K., et al. (2004). A neural correlate of reward-based behavioral learning in caudate nucleus: A functional magnetic resonance imaging study of a stochastic decision task. *Journal of Neuroscience, 24,* 1660–1665.

Hazeltine, E., Grafton, S. T., & Ivry, R. (1997). Attention and stimulus characteristics determine the locus of motor-sequence encoding. A PET study. *Brain, 120,* 123–140.

Hogarth, R. M. (2001). *Educating intuition.* Chicago: The University of Chicago Press.

Kapur, S., Rose, R., Liddle, P. F., Zipursky, R. B., Brown, G. M., Stuss, D., et al. (1994). The role of the left prefrontal cortex in verbal processing: Semantic processing or willed action? *Neuroreport, 5,* 2193–2196.

Keane, M. M., Gabrieli, J. D., Mapstone, H. C., Johnson, K. A., & Corkin, S. (1995). Double dissociation of memory capacities after bilateral occipital-lobe or medial temporal-lobe lesions. *Brain, 118,* 1129–1148.

Khatri, N., & Ng, H. A. (2000). The role of intuition in strategic decision making. *Human Relations: Studies Towards the Integration of the Social Sciences, 53,* 57–86.

Kikyo, H., Ohki, K., & Miyashita, Y. (2002). Neural correlates for feeling-of-knowing: An fMRI parametric analysis. *Neuron, 36,* 177–186.

Knopman, D., & Nissen, M. J. (1991). Procedural learning is impaired in Huntington's disease: Evidence from the serial reaction time task. *Neuropsychologia, 29,* 245–254.

Knutson, B., Westdorp, A., Kaiser, E., & Hommer, D. (2000). FMRI visualization of brain activity during a monetary incentive delay task. *Neuroimage, 12,* 20–27.

Koriat, A. (2000). The feeling of knowing: Some metatheoretical implications for consciousness and control. *Consciousness and Cognition, 9,* 149–171.

Kringelbach, M. L. (2005). The human orbitofrontal cortex: Linking reward to hedonic experience. *Nature Reviews: Neuroscience, 6,* 691–702.

Kringelbach, M. L., & Rolls, E. T. (2004). The functional neuroanatomy of the human orbitofrontal cortex: Evidence from neuroimaging and neuropsychology. *Progress in Neurobiology, 72,* 341–72.

Laforce, R., Jr., & Doyon, J. (2001). Distinct contribution of the striatum and cerebellum to motor learning. *Brain and Cognition, 45,* 189–211.

Lieberman, M. D., Chang, G. Y., Chiao, J., Bookheimer, S. Y., & Knowlton, B. J. (2004). An event-related fMRI study of artificial grammar learning in a balanced chunk strength design. *Journal of Cognitive Neuroscience, 16,* 427–438.

Logothetis, N. K., Pauls, J., Augath, M., Trinath, T., & Oeltermann, A. (2001). Neurophysiological investigation of the basis of the fMRI signal. *Nature, 412,* 150–157.

Maril, A., Simons, J. S., Mitchell, J. P., Schwartz, B. L., & Schacter, D. L. (2003). Feeling-of-knowing in episodic memory: An event-related fMRI study. *Neuroimage, 18,* 827–836.

Maril, A., Simons, J. S., Weaver, J. J., & Schacter, D. L. (2005). Graded recall success: An event-related fMRI comparison of tip of the tongue and feeling of knowing. *Neuroimage, 24,* 1130–1138.

Myers, D. G. (2002). *Intuition. Its powers and perils.* New Haven, CT: Yale University Press.
Nauta, W. J. (1971). The problem of the frontal lobe: A reinterpretation. *Journal of Psychiatric Research, 8,* 167–187.
Nissen, M. J., & Bullemer, P. (1987). Attentional requirements of learning: Evidence from performance measures. *Cognitive Psychology, 19,* 1–32.
Peigneux, P., Maquet, P., Meulemans, T., Destrebecqz, A., Laureys, S., Degueldre, C., et al. (2000). Striatum forever, despite sequence learning variability: A random effect analysis of PET data. *Human Brain Mapping, 10,* 179–194.
Peigneux, P., Meulemans, T., Van der Linden, M., Salmon, E., & Petit, H. (1999). Exploration of implicit artificial grammar learning in Parkinson's disease. *Acta Neurologica Belgica, 99,* 107–117.
Rauch, S. L., Whalen, P. J., Savage, C. R., Curran, T., Kendrick, A., Brown, H. D., et al. (1997). Striatal recruitment during an implicit sequence learning task as measured by functional magnetic resonance imaging. *Human Brain Mapping, 5,* 124–132.
Rauch, S. L., Whalen, P. J., Curran, T., McInerney, S., Heckers, S., & Savage, C. R. (1998). Thalamic deactivation during early implicit sequence learning: A functional MRI study. *Neuroreport, 9,* 865–870.
Reber, A. S. (1967). Implicit learning of artificial grammars. *Journal of Experimental Psychology, 77,* 353–363.
Reber, A. S. (1989). Implicit learning and tacit knowledge. *Journal of Experimental Psychology: General, 118,* 219–235.
Reber, A. S. (1993). *Implicit learning and tacit knowledge: An essay in the cognitive unconscious.* Oxford, England: Oxford University Press.
Reber, P. J., & Squire, L. R. (1999). Intact learning of artificial grammars and intact category learning by patients with Parkinson's disease. *Behavioral Neuroscience, 113,* 235–242.
Rose, M., Haider, H., Weiller, C., & Buchel, C. (2002). The role of medial temporal lobe structures in implicit learning: An event-related FMRI study. *Neuron, 36,* 1221–1231.
Rugg, M. D. (1995). Memory and consciousness: A selective review of issues and data. *Neuropsychologia, 33,* 1131–1141.
Schacter, D. L. (1987). Implicit memory: History and current status. *Journal of Experimental Psychology: Learning, Memory, and Cognition, 13,* 501–518.
Schacter, D. L., & Buckner, R. L. (1998). On the relations among priming, conscious recollection, and intentional retrieval: Evidence from neuroimaging research. *Neurobiology of Learning and Memory, 70,* 284–303.
Schendan, H. E., Searl, M. M., Melrose, R. J., & Stern, C. E. (2003). An FMRI study of the role of the medial temporal lobe in implicit and explicit sequence learning. *Neuron, 37,* 1013–1025.
Schnyer, D. M., Nicholls, L., & Verfaellie, M. (2005). The role of VMPC in metamemorial judgments of content retrievability. *Journal of Cognitive Neuroscience, 17,* 832–846.
Schnyer, D. M., Verfaellie, M., Alexander, M. P., LaFleche, G., Nicholls, L., & Kaszniak, A. W. (2004). A role for right medial prefontal cortex in accurate feeling-of-knowing judgements: Evidence from patients with lesions to frontal cortex. *Neuropsychologia, 42,* 957–966.
Schoenbaum, G., Setlow, B., Saddoris, M. P., & Gallagher, M. (2003). Encoding predicted outcome and acquired value in orbitofrontal cortex during cue sampling depends upon input from basolateral amygdala. *Neuron, 39,* 855–867.
Schultz, W. (2000). Multiple reward signals in the brain. *Nature Reviews: Neuroscience, 1,* 199–207.

Seger, C. A. (1997). Two forms of sequential implicit learning. *Consciousness and Cognition, 6,* 108–131.
Seger, C. A. (1998). Multiple forms of implicit learning. In M. A. Stadler & P. A. Frensch (Eds.), *Handbook of implicit learning* (pp. 295–320). London: Sage.
Shanks, D. R., & St. John, M. F. (1994). Characteristics of dissociable human learning systems. *The Behavarioral and Brain Sciences, 17,* 367–447.
Skosnik, P. D., Mirza, F., Gitelman, D. R., Parrish, T. B., Mesulam, M. M., & Reber, P. J. (2002). Neural correlates of artificial grammar learning. *Neuroimage, 17,* 1306–1314.
Smith, J. G., & McDowall, J. (2004). Impaired higher order implicit sequence learning on the verbal version of the serial reaction time task in patients with Parkinson's disease. *Neuropsychology, 18,* 679–691.
Smith, J. G., & McDowall, J. (2006). The implicit sequence learning deficit in patients with Parkinson's disease: A matter of impaired sequence integration? *Neuropsychologia, 44,* 275–288.
Smith, J., Siegert, R. J., McDowall, J., & Abernethy, D. (2001). Preserved implicit learning on both the serial reaction time task and artificial grammar in patients with Parkinson's disease. *Brain and Cognition, 45,* 378–391.
Squire, L. R., Ojemann, J. G., Miezin, F. M., Petersen, S. E., Videen, T. O., & Raichle, M. E. (1992). Activation of the hippocampus in normal humans: A functional anatomical study of memory. *Proceedings of the National Academy of Sciences of the USA, 89,* 1837–1841.
Stadler, M. A., & Frensch, P. A. (1998). *Handbook of implicit learning.* London: Sage.
Thiel, C. M., Shanks, D. R., Henson, R. N., & Dolan, R. J. (2003). Neuronal correlates of familiarity-driven decisions in artificial grammar learning. *Neuroreport, 14,* 131–136.
Turner, R., & Jezzard, P. (1994). Magnetic resonance studies of brain functional activation using echo-planar imaging. In R. W. Thatcher, M. Hallett, T. A. Zeffiro, E. R. John, & M. Huerta (Eds.), *Functional neuroimaging: Technical foundations* (pp. 69–78). Orlando, FL: Academic Press.
Volz, K. G., Schubotz, R. I., & von Cramon, D. Y. (2003). Predicting events of varying probability: Uncertainty investigated by fMRI. *Neuroimage, 19,* 271–280.
Volz, K. G., & von Cramon, D. Y. (2006). What neuroscience can tell about intuitive processes in the context of perceptual discovery. *Journal of Cognitive Neuroscience, 18,* 2077–2087.
Werheid, K., Ziessler, M., Nattkemper, D., & von Cramon, D. Y. (2003). Sequence learning in Parkinson's disease: The effect of spatial stimulus-response compatibility. *Brain and Cognition, 52,* 239–249.
Westwater, H., McDowall, J., Siegert, R., Mossman, S., & Abernethy, D. (1998). Implicit learning in Parkinson's disease: Evidence from a verbal version of the serial reaction time task. *Journal of Clinical and Experimental Neuropsychology, 20,* 413–418.
Willingham, D. B., Salidis, J., & Gabrieli, J. D. (2002). Direct comparison of neural systems mediating conscious and unconscious skill learning. *Journal of Neurophysiology, 88,* 1451–1460.
Witt, K., Nuhsman, A., & Deuschl, G. (2002). Intact artificial grammar learning in patients with cerebellar degeneration and advanced Parkinson's disease. *Neuropsychologia, 40,* 1534–1540.

II

Learning and Intuition

6

On the Learning of Intuition

ROBIN M. HOGARTH
University Pompeu Fabra

INTRODUCTION

One approach to study the link between intuition and learning is to ask what distinguishes people who have acquired "good" or effective intuitions from "bad" ones. In other words, how do people acquire intuitions and can they learn to do this more effectively?

The purpose of this chapter is to explore these issues. To do so, I first outline what I mean by intuition. In short, I conceive of intuitive responses as being generated by the more primitive of two systems of thought known as "experiential" (Epstein, 1994; chap. 2, this volume), "System 1" (Stanovich & West, 1998), or "tacit" (Hogarth, 2001). Second, I discuss the rules by which people acquire their "cultural capital" or the inventory of intuitions that guide behavior. In particular, I sketch the boundary between responses that are instinctive as opposed to learned, and I highlight the challenge of explicating how people learn intuitions in the form of preferences. Third, I discuss how the structure of the environment affects intuitions and emphasize both its functional and dysfunctional consequences.

Finally, I draw implications for understanding what people can do to improve the quality of their intuitive judgments. More generally, I make the point that good and bad intuitions are acquired in automatic fashion. Moreover, by understanding this process, people can improve the proportion of good intuitions learned—and at little cost.

INTUITION: DEFINITION AND ROLES

In Hogarth (2001), I adopted the terms *tacit* and *deliberate* to distinguish two systems of thought. The former is distinguished by being triggered automatically. It is effortless, speedy, often confidence inducing, sensitive to context, lacking conscious awareness, producing "approximate" responses, and reactive. The latter is deliberate and requires effort. It is proactive and can be controlled, guided, and made explicit. It is abstract, rule governed, and precise. Broadly speaking, the tacit system is intuitive and the deliberate system is analytic. Indeed, in Hogarth (2001), I adopted a broad definition of intuition by stating that "the essence of intuition or intuitive responses is that *they are reached with little apparent effort, and typically without conscious awareness. They involve little or no conscious deliberation*" (p. 14).

Equating the outputs of intuition with the tacit system hides the fact that there are many types of outputs and that these can involve different systems. This has particular significance for learning. For example, it is important to distinguish between outputs of the tacit system that have an instinctive—as opposed to learned—origin. A puff of air to the eye, for instance, produces an instantaneous, involuntary closing of the eyelid, an innate reaction. On the other hand, based on past experience, one may or may not react on seeing a word flashed on a screen. Other intuitive responses can involve a mix of innate and learned behavior. Consider, for example, the expression of emotions.

The Roles of Intuition

Intuition plays different roles in mental life. Consider inferences. These can look forward and backward in time. Forward inferences are essentially predictions. One observes something and immediately makes an effortless inference as to what is expected next or related to what has just been seen. Bowers, Regehr, Balthazard, and Parker (1990) referred to this as intuition in the "context of justification." In justification, people provide responses to specific questions or stimuli, for example, how fast do you think that car is traveling? What are the chances that . . . ?

Inferences that look backward in time are diagnostic. The task here is to generate a hypothesis that explains an observation. Bowers et al. (1990) referred to this as intuition in the "context of discovery." This can be trivial (e.g., a crossword puzzle) or important (e.g., scientific reasoning). In both cases, intuition exhibits itself by the sudden emergence of possible solutions in consciousness that follows the trying out of various "ideas" at a subconscious level, a phenomenon that has been labeled *insight*.[1]

Many intuitions can also be classified as the expression of preferences. For example, one sees two items of clothing and can immediately—and effortlessly—tell which you prefer. If one accepts as a fact that this preference is not innate, then one must have learned it—but how?[2] Also, does the way you acquire intuitive preferences differ from how you acquire intuitive inferences?

It is important to emphasize that intuitions are rarely precise. On the contrary, the outcomes of intuitive processes are typically approximate and experienced in the form of feelings as opposed, say, to words or numbers. Hypotheses are not well

---

[1] For a fascinating account of how insightful solutions to problems involve different neural activity than noninsightful solutions, see Jung-Beeman et al. (2004).
[2] In the following, I discuss the fact that not all intuitive preferences are learned.

defined, and predictions may not even be falsifiable. This lack of precision does, of course, affect the ability to learn from experience in that it can make feedback ambiguous. On the other hand, the extent to which imprecision matters in hypotheses or predictions depends on characteristics of the situation considered. "Loose" predictions and hypotheses are often better than none.

Finally, it is clear that people have many intuitions at their disposition for resolving their daily problems—whether in the domain of inferences or preferences. I refer to such stocks or inventories of intuitions as "cultural capital." That is, over time, people build up ways of interpreting the world through a process of continual learning. Moreover, because it reflects experience, cultural capital has both common and distinctive elements—common with respect to experiences that people have shared and distinctive because all experiences are, at one level, unique.

HOW DO PEOPLE ACQUIRE THEIR CULTURAL CAPITAL?

Two principles underlie learning within the tacit system. One is the observation of frequencies of events or objects in the environment and the extent to which they covary. The second is the notion of reinforcement. The consequences (rewards or costs) of some connections attract more attention than others. Key questions, therefore, center on what people observe and their associated consequences.

Nature Versus Nurture

It is important to stress that even if they cannot be proven to be innate, infants possess adult-like learning processes. For example, Marcus, Vijayan, Bandi Rao, and Vishton (1999) showed that infants as young as 7 months have the ability to infer linguistic rules from speech as indicated by their ability to perceive patterns in nonsense syllables. After being exposed to patterns that take the form A-B-A, infants express surprise when confronted by a sequence in the form A-B-B. In addition, the initial knowledge that infants (as young as 3 months old) appear to possess covers notions such as distinctions between the animate and inanimate, what constitutes a whole object, and that objects affect each other only if there is contact between them (Spelke, 1994, 1998).

Spelke (1994) argued that many such cognitive abilities—that she labeled "initial knowledge"—are innate and subsequently become the foundation of many adult intuitions. As Spelke (1994) said

"Initial knowledge is central to commonsense reasoning through development. Intuitive knowledge of physical objects, people, sets, and places develops by enrichment around a constant core, such that knowledge guiding infants' reasoning stands at the center of the knowledge guiding the intuitive reasoning of older children and adults." (p. 439)

The extent to which particular cognitive skills are learned or innate is subject to dispute (Baillargeon, 1994, 2004). However, the fact remains that learning by infants, children, and adults seems to follow similarly constrained mechanisms.

In some cases, these are sensitive to content (e.g., having different expectations for the animate and inanimate). On the other hand, both children and adults exhibit the use of similar "general algorithms" for the important task of attributing cause (cf. Einhorn & Hogarth, 1986; Shultz, 1982).

In brief, the human system is endowed with and develops mechanisms for learning that can operate both with and without the use of conscious attention. For example, as has been demonstrated by Hasher and Zacks (1979, 1984), people have an amazing and automatic capacity to record in memory the frequency of a wide variety of naturally occurring events.[3] Moreover, this is done without the intention to do so and is not necessarily improved by training and feedback. In addition, the ability is remarkably stable across age groups and for people with different intellectual abilities. (See also Sedlmeier & Betsch, 2002.)

Implicit Learning

The picture that emerges is that humans possess effortless routines for classifying—categorizing and maintaining tallies of—many different aspects of their experience. This has also been studied under the generic label of *implicit learning* and has generated much interest (see, e.g., Frensch & Rünger, 2003; Seger, 1994). From this perspective, it is significant that many studies have demonstrated that when people interact with novel tasks, their ability to perform well typically precedes their ability to verbalize—or make explicit—their understanding of the tasks (see, e.g., Berry & Broadbent, 1984, for computer games representing economic situations and Reber, 1993, concerning the learning of artificial grammar). Moreover, explicit attempts to learn can sometimes lead to inferior understanding relative to implicit learning.

Implicit learning, however, is not limited to mechanical-like tasks. Lewicki, Hill, and Czyzewska (1992) examined implications in the social domain. Lewicki et al. (1992) stated "these processes are not limited to the housekeeping operations, such as retrieving information from memory or adjusting the level of arousal; they are directly involved in the development of interpretive categories, drawing inferences, determining emotional reactions, and other high-level operations traditionally associated with consciously controlled thinking." (p. 801)

Expertise

The fact that many activities are exercised in an intuitive manner does not, of course, mean that they were originally acquired in this way. This applies to many physical skills such as driving an automobile. Here the skills (e.g., changing gears) are so practiced and overlearned that the person can no longer explain how they are achieved. What started explicitly becomes automated—and thus intuitive—

---

[3] As an example, ask yourself how many times you have been to the cinema in the last 6 months. After an instant of thought, most people can provide rough answers to this question. Yet no one ever admits to having deliberately stored this information in memory in anticipation of being asked the question.

over time. This also applies to mental skills and bears on the issue of how people acquire expertise in specific domains.

Note first, however, that to the extent that intuition is the fruit of experience, differences in intuition between people reflect their different experiences, and intuition is thus domain specific. People with high levels of intuitive skills in one area (say art) should not be expected to have good intuitions in other areas (such as engineering). Indeed, domain specificity is one of the characteristics of expertise. Moreover, achieving expertise within a particular domain (say chess or physics) requires devoting much time to the activity (see, e.g., Simon & Chase, 1973). For example, high performers in music have typically followed demanding regimes of deliberate practice and benefited from the guidance of good teachers or coaches (Ericsson & Lehmann, 1996). Interestingly, this demonstrates that even experts can profit from coaching to refine their intuitive skills. Once skills have been overlearned, self-insight is difficult, and a third-party perspective becomes necessary.

Perhaps the most interesting dimension of intuitive expertise lies in the area of backward inference or diagnosis. Studies have revealed important differences between the strategies of experts and novices. The latter tend to be explicit in setting goals and then trying to work backward through the details of a problem to attain the goal. Experts, however, tend first to take in the details of the problem, then—through a process of recognizing similarities—to find a framework that fits the data and, finally to work forward from that framework to explore possible solutions (Ericsson & Charness, 1994). The key lies in recognizing patterns or similarities to patterns. Klein (1998) suggested that experts learn what patterns to expect in specific situations, and their diagnostic activity involves comparisons with expectations. Do the data match or is something missing? In terms of learning, expertise involves the encoding of intuitive patterns; the more expert a person, the more patterns available in memory (as in chess; Chase & Simon, 1973).

Preparedness

If all learning processes simply followed observations and reinforcement, the prediction of what people learn would be straightforward. However, this is not the case. For example, in a famous experiment, Watson and Rayner (1920; Watson is the noted early 20th-century psychologist) demonstrated that they could condition an 11-month-old boy ("little Albert") to become afraid of a white rat, a rabbit, and a dog when these were paired with a startling noise. On the other hand, a later study by Bregman (1934) that used the same procedure failed to induce learning when conventional, inanimate objects such as blocks of woods and cloth curtains were paired with the startling noise.[4]

Seligman (1970, 1971) has proposed that humans and animals are differentially "prepared" to see connections between different kinds of variables, that is, there is an interaction between content and rules in the process of learning. Moreover,

---

[4] There have been many inaccuracies in the telling of what happened to little Albert. See Harris (1979).

Seligman (1970, 1971) argued for a "continuum of preparedness;" people are prepared to associate or make connections between some events, "unprepared" to associate others, and "counterprepared" to associate still others. For example, even after just one trial, rats have been shown to learn to associate distinctive-tasting food and a gastrointestinal illness (induced by X rays) even though the illness does not occur close in time to the ingestion of the tainted food. On the other hand, rats appear to be counterprepared to associate taste with shocks administered to the feet (Garcia, 1981; Garcia, McGowan, Ervin, & Koelling, 1968). More recently, Öhman and Mineka (2001, 2003) have developed a theory of how certain fears are learned automatically. Specifically, Öhman and Mineka (2001, 2003) argued for the existence of specific brain modules (with dedicated neural circuitry centered on the amygdala) that allow rapid identification and fear reactions to quite specific stimuli such as serpents and other reptiles. Interestingly, the evidence Öhman and Mineka cited was not that humans and animals (specifically monkeys) are born with fear reactions to snakes but that mere observation that others fear snakes was sufficient to induce learning (they cite evidence involving monkeys that have and have not been bred in captivity).

That content affects learning considerably complicates people's ability to make statements about the underlying mechanisms. In particular, it suggests that these reflect humans' evolutionary heritage. Humans are more prepared to learn some types of connections than others, and such general or "content-free" mechanisms that people do have are constrained in particular ways. As an example, consider learning a new language. For children, this is largely automatic. For adults, it is a painful, deliberate process. The biological facility for language learning is constrained by maturational processes (Pinker, 1994).

Preferences

What can be said about the learning of preferences? Why do people differ in their tastes, and how much of this can be attributed to implicit or intuitive learning?[5]

Clearly, many preferences are biological in nature. People prefer to eat sweet rather than sour foods. People are more comfortable with intermediate rather than extreme temperatures. Preferences for different physical activities also vary across the life span. On the other hand, there are also large individual differences in preferences. People like different types of music, sports, literature, and so on. Moreover, it is not clear that people have intentions to form different preferences and that these are learned in an explicit way. Instead, the preferences that people exhibit are clear manifestations of tacit or intuitive learning. One fascinating example is the finding that popular culture (e.g., music) seems to have its greatest impact on people in their late teens to early 20s such that each generation is "marked" by different icons (e.g., fashions, songs, singers, and so on; Holbrook & Schindler, 1994).

Perhaps the best clue to the learning of preferences is the work of Zajonc (1968) on the "mere-exposure effect" (see also Betsch, Plessner, Schwieren, & Gütig, 2001;

---

[5] Whereas the learning of preferences that guide decision making is an important topic, it cannot be said that it has attracted the attention it deserves (Hogarth, 2007).

Bornstein, 1989). As is well known, this started with the observation that people have greater affect for more frequently occurring objects. Zajonc (1968) first examined words. Zajonc presented people pairs of antonyms such as *forward/backward*, *high/low*, or *on/off*. Zajonc then asked them to state which word in each pair had "the more favorable meaning, represented the more desirable object, event, state of affairs, characteristic, etc." (p. 5). Zajonc also determined the frequency with which each word was used in English. Zajonc's results showed a remarkable relation between preferences and relative frequencies. At least 97% of Zajonc's respondents preferred *forward* to *backward, high to low,* and *on* to *off*. In English, the first of each of these pairs of words appeared more frequently than the second (e.g., *forward* was approximately 5.4 times more frequent than *backward*). In further experiments, Zajonc demonstrated the effect with fake "Turkish" words, Chinese-like characters, and photographs of students (see Bornstein, 1989; Harrison, 1977).

Why is mere exposure effective? Perhaps the most plausible explanation is based on learning theory. Unless a stimulus is perceived negatively, repeated exposure is seen as positive and increases affect through repeated experience. Whether psychologists understand this principle or not, it is clear that the concept is well understood in other parts of society. Corporations, for example, spend enormous resources in making their names familiar to the public through repeated advertising. In many cases, no attempt is even made to provide information about products. The goal is simply to strengthen affective bonds with brand names. Think, for example, of Benetton®. Of course, the process is not as simple as I have suggested here because repeated exposure can, in some circumstances, lead to satiation and then induce negative affect. In addition, people seek variety.

A further example is provided by organizations that socialize (indoctrinate?) their members by controlling their environments. This occurs in schools, religious organizations, armies, corporations, professions, and families and is often explicitly managed. Socialized members learn not only to have the same beliefs about the world but also the same tastes.

In the final analysis, people's preferences express what they like and how much. Whereas a person may use deliberate thinking in trading off different attributes when evaluating choice alternatives (e.g., a product or a job candidate), the implied weights one gives to the different attributes are clearly heavily influenced by implicit learning. Possibly, the simplest expression of this is the so-called affect heuristic proposed by Slovic, Finucane, Peters, and MacGregor (2002). People just choose what they like. This may, of course, partially reflect inherent tendencies (e.g., for sweet as opposed to bitter food). Indeed arguments for why people have particular tastes can often be justified through evolutionary arguments (e.g., appreciation of beauty in members of the opposite sex; Buss, 1989). However, expressing preferences in modern life involves more than responding to biological drives, and much work remains to be done in unraveling the tacit processes by which preferences are learned (see also Betsch, 2005).

Parenthetically, the existence of external criteria (e.g., in prediction tasks) and normative models (such as Bayes's theorem) have been critical to studies of inferential learning—whether implicit or explicit. One can measure whether participants have learned and if so, how well. Preferential inference, however, lacks such criteria. How should people update their preferences? How does one know if people have acquired "appropriate" preferences? Without answers to these questions, understanding the learning of preferences is severely handicapped.

IMPORTANCE OF THE ENVIRONMENT: STRUCTURE AND FEEDBACK

The learning of intuitions takes place largely in the absence of explicit attention. It is also constrained by the characteristics of the environment. This "obvious" statement is important because it means that one can only learn intuitively from data that are seen. In many cases, this is not a problem. However, there are also cases in which drawing accurate inferences requires the observation of data that are not available.

The Illusion of Validity

Consider the paradigmatic case of personnel selection discussed by Einhorn and Hogarth (1978). A personnel manager believes he or she is a good judge of future employees. The manager gives each job candidate a test (based on an interview), selects those who score high, and rejects the others. Subsequently, the manager finds that those who score well on the test also do well in their jobs, and this reinforces the manager's belief in the validity of the test (his or her interviewing skills). The problem, however, is that the data that the manager sees is not sufficient to assess the manager's interviewing ability. To test this, the manager should also observe outcomes associated with rejected candidates. The actual data the manager encounters can support an intuition that might not be well founded.

More generally, Einhorn and Hogarth (1978) argued that taking action on the basis of a judgment often precludes the ability to observe outcomes associated with actions not taken, and this can seriously bias learning. A further difficulty arises if the person also engages in behavior that affects the final outcome (e.g., providing the new hire with special training). Einhorn and Hogarth (1978) referred to this as a "treatment effect." The first judgment made creates a chain of events that results in a self-fulfilling prophecy.

Thomas (1983) provided a stunning illustration in discussing the diagnostic activities of an early 20th-century physician in New York. Apparently, this distinguished physician—revered for his intuitive diagnostic ability—examined patients by first palpating their tongues and second, predicting illness. After such examinations, many patients did indeed fall ill. The physician "was a more effective carrier, using only his hands, than Typhoid Mary" (Thomas, 1983, p. 22).

A Conceptual Framework

Consideration of these phenomena led Einhorn (1980) to develop the concept of outcome irrelevant learning structures. These are environments in which the feedback people receive is irrelevant to the validity of their judgments.

In Hogarth (2001), I elaborated on this by also considering the consequences of errors that can vary from lenient to exacting. In addition, quality of feedback can vary from relevant to irrelevant, thus resulting in four categories of learning structures: relevant exacting, irrelevant exacting, relevant lenient, and irrelevant lenient. With speedy and accurate feedback, learning is facilitated.[6] However, and as I noted previously, when feedback is noisy, delayed, or biased, valid learning is unlikely.

In addition, there are many decisions for which feedback is not available such that it is not clear what an individual might infer from taking action. I speculate that in the absence of outcome feedback, people use surrogates that might be related to the context in which decisions are taken. For example: Is the decision accompanied by feelings of confidence? Is there something about the situation that recalls prior successful outcomes? Does the lack of a negative outcome result in similar feelings to a positive outcome and under what circumstances? and so on.

These are difficult but important issues about which little is known. In an attempt to study them, I (Hogarth, 2006) recently used the experiential sampling method (Csikszentmihalyi & Larson, 1987; Hurlburt, 1997) to attempt to measure the extent to which people receive feedback on their everyday decisions. I (Hogarth, 2006) sampled the decisions of both business executives and undergraduate students by sending text messages to their cell telephones at randomly chosen moments and asked them to complete a short questionnaire about the last decision they had taken (prior to receiving the text message). By decision was meant any action whether trivial or important (as might be expected, most were trivial). Of particular significance was the large number of decisions for which participants said they had or would not receive feedback (35% for executives and 48% for students). Moreover, for the executives, much of the expected feedback was quite delayed (in one third of the cases, the expected delay exceeded 1 week). Interestingly, both executives and students expressed much confidence that their decisions were "right" (even when they did not expect to receive feedback) as well as great confidence in the validity of the feedback that they would receive.

One could argue that these data only describe explicit decisions and thus nonintuitive processes. However, this is not obvious. Most of the decisions described involved trivial, everyday matters, and it is unclear how the structure of these differ from decisions taken intuitively.

Errors experienced during learning can differ depending on the environments in which they occur. In particular, how good intuitions learned need to be depends on what I call the exactingness of environments (Hogarth, Gibbs, McKenzie, & Marquis, 1991). In *lenient* environments, intuitive judgments do not have to be accurate. In walking down a corridor, for example, intuition need only indicate a general direction because corrective feedback, received in real time, is sufficient

---

[6] It is not, of course, always the case that immediate feedback is the most effective for learning. Sometimes, delays in feedback can be beneficial (Golec, 2005; Schooler & Anderson, 1990).

to mitigate errors (cf., Hogarth, 1981). In an *exacting* environment, on the other hand, the cost of minor errors can be huge. Consider, for example, the intuitive skills required of a brain surgeon or tightrope walker.

Implications for Learning Intuitions

When feedback is relevant, accurate learning is an automatic consequence of activity. Moreover, as tasks move from lenient to exacting, one would expect the accuracy of learning to increase (although performance during learning may not exhibit this pattern; Hogarth et al., 1991).

As I noted previously, however, when feedback is irrelevant, learning may not be appropriate. In lenient environments, this may not be important. Much superstitious behavior, for example, can be placed in the irrelevant-lenient quadrant (assuming "benign superstitions"). On the other hand, irrelevant-exacting environments can be quite dangerous as witnessed by the example of the early 20th-century physician.

To summarize, one can think of learning structures as being favorable or unfavorable to accurate learning. I use the expressions *kind* and *wicked*. The contention is that the validity of intuitions depend on the learning structures prevailing when these were acquired. "*Kind learning structures lead to good intuitions; wicked ones do not*" (Hogarth, 2001, p. 89).

In the preceding text, I have mainly used physical examples for illustration (e.g., walking down a corridor or the physician palpating tongues). However, intuitive learning also occurs in the social domain. Consider, for example, the way in which people intuit the feelings of others and how they read nonverbal cues in communication. These play an important role in everyday life, and yet people find it difficult to explain explicitly to what cues they attend. That such abilities can be effective was dramatically illustrated by Ambady and Rosenthal (1993) in their studies of how students can judge the effectiveness of teachers on the basis of small samples of behavior (so-called thin slices).

On the other hand, it also follows that experience—or intuitive learning—in the social domain necessarily leads to the acquisition of prejudices. Kanter (1993), for example, illustrated this in relation to automatic reactions to the statistical distributions of males and females in positions of authority in organizations. Similarly, Fiedler (2000) showed how biased sampling can induce erroneous beliefs (i.e., prejudices) about the abilities of others (see also Unkelbach & Plessner, chap. 17, this volume).

Gender Differences

It is illuminating to consider gender differences. Clearly, given the necessarily domain-specific nature of intuition, one would not expect women to have, on average, "better" intuition than men in male-dominated activities such as engineering or certain sports. On the other hand, both men and women deal with people, and so it is legitimate to ask whether they differ in these "soft" intuitive skills and how learning might be implicated.

Graham and Ickes (1997) distinguished between what they called the different "empathic abilities" of men and women. Graham and Ickes identified three categories: vicarious emotional responding, nonverbal decoding ability, and empathic accuracy (i.e., being able to infer the content of another person's thoughts or feelings). Graham and Ickes showed that women possess greater intuitive ability than men for the first two categories but not the third. (See also Edwards, 1998; Hall, 1984.)

Why do women exhibit greater skills than men? As Graham and Ickes (1997) noted, both evolutionary and environmental explanations can be advanced. As to the former, one could argue that as traditional caregivers, women would be differentially selected for their ability to read nonverbal cues within social situations; whereas for men, it would have been more physical tasks such as hunting in which other skills such as spatial orientation would have been more important. The environmental explanation, on the other hand, holds that girls and boys are socialized in different ways. In particular, girls learn to behave in ways that are more respectful of the feelings of others and are less dependent on physical power that plays such an important role in male socialization. Graham and Ickes pointed out that the two explanations are not exclusive. Even if women once had quite small genetic advantages over men, the way women are socialized could have magnified differences across time, thereby resulting in a kind of self-fulfilling prophecy at the societal level.

My own speculation is that from early childhood, females learn to observe behavior better than males. Thus, by the time they reach adulthood, women have just observed much more behavior than men. For example, consider the behavior of primary school children in a playground. Whereas boys typically engage in playing in an active way with other boys (e.g., different ball games), girls tend to congregate with other girls and talk about their experiences. The learning styles are quite different. Furthermore, as they grow older, girls learn that the world treats them as though they are a "minority" group, and hence, to be successful, they need to observe how others act before taking actions themselves. Boys, on the other hand, take actions but—in so doing—have less opportunities to develop observational skills (cf. Frabble, Blackstone, & Scherbaum, 1990).

IMPLICATIONS FOR ACQUIRING GOOD INTUITIONS

As a first remark, it is important to emphasize that people's intuitive learning systems are always operating—accumulating evidence about their beliefs and reinforcing actions taken—largely without their conscious awareness (e.g., Plessner, Betsch, Schallies, & Schwieren, chap. 7, this volume; Raab & Johnson, chap. 8, this volume). In many ways, people are constantly being shaped by the environments in which they live. The major implication, therefore, if people want to shape their intuitions, is to make conscious efforts to inhabit environments that expose them to the experiences and information that form the intuitions that they want.

This principle is, I believe, generally recognized by society. Corporations, for example, have job-rotation schemes whereby employees are exposed to different parts of a business to sensitize them to different perspectives. Many professions have long used apprenticeships for training and particularly for domains where knowledge is tacit. In addition, whereas the manifest function of the academic seminar or conference is to disseminate and refine knowledge, its latent function is to train scholars how to conduct research.[7]

Taking this principle to the next logical step, people should be proactive in seeking the environments that will provide them with the learning opportunities they need (cf. Hogarth, 2001). In other words, learning should be managed.

One important form is paying attention to feedback and particularly, understanding whether it is relevant. For example, in some professions (e.g., physicians employed in emergency rooms in large urban hospitals), feedback can be systematically delayed or missing. However, attempts could still be made to obtain feedback on a sample basis. In general, a conscious awareness of whether one's intuitions have been gained in kind or wicked environments can help assess how much to trust one's intuitions.

This latter point is important in dealing, for example, with intuitions in the form of emotions. At one level, one can think of emotions as being learned reactions to particular classes of stimuli. In many—if not most—cases, they are highly functional. Fear, for example, can be vital. On the other hand, emotions with less intensity might be elicited and suggest actions in other situations; for example, should you trust another person on a particular dimension because you like him or her? Rather than either ignoring or trusting one's emotions blindly, I believe it is better to treat "emotions as data" (Hogarth, 2001). In other words, people should be aware that the information transmitted by their emotions is just part of the data that should be considered.

A further point relates to making intuitive explicit methods for making judgments and decisions that are known to be effective. Previously, I (Hogarth, 2001) called this "making scientific method" intuitive. The key idea is that there are several good decision-making principles that people have a tendency to violate, for example, failing to ignore sunk costs. However, is it possible to educate people to recognize and respond intuitively with appropriate responses to situations in which these principles apply? In other words, can one replace "misleading" intuitions with "correct" ones? Based on the results of at least one program (Nisbett, Fong, Lehman, & Cheng, 1987), I believe this is possible. However, much remains to be done.

Finally, intuitive judgments and decisions play a major role in people's lives in cases in which the stakes are both big and small. Although people lack a complete picture, recent years have seen increasing understanding of these phenomena and the crucial role played by learning via automatic, tacit processes. Much, if not most of the time, these automatic processes operate in a person's favor. However, there is also evidence of significant dysfunctionalities (such as when experience

---

[7] If you ask a scholar attending a seminar presentation whether he or she learned anything, the typical answer is "not much." On the other hand, the sum of knowledge obtained from regularly attending such seminars is typically thought to be much greater than the sum of the individual parts, thereby explaining why scholars continue to attend specific seminars even if the expected gains from a single seminar are so small. Graduate students certainly learn much from attending series of seminars.

tacitly reinforces inappropriate responses). By providing an analysis of how this process occurs, in this chapter, I have suggested how people might harness the automatic nature of intuitive learning processes to operate even more powerfully in their favor.

ACKNOWLEDGMENTS

This research was financed partially by a grant from the Spanish Ministerio de Educación y Ciencia. I am also grateful for helpful comments received from the editors.

REFERENCES

Ambady, N., & Rosenthal, R. (1993). Half a minute: Predicting teacher evaluations from thin slices of nonverbal behavior and physical attractiveness. *Journal of Personality and Social Psychology, 64*, 431–441.
Baillargeon, R. (1994). How do infants learn about the physical world? *Current Directions In Psychological Science, 3*, 133–140.
Baillargeon, R. (2004). Infants' physical world. *Current Directions In Psychological Science, 13*, 89–94.
Berry, D. C., & Broadbent, D. E. (1984). On the relationship between task performance and associated verbalisable knowledge. *Quarterly Journal of Experimental Psychology, 36*, 209–231.
Betsch, T. (2005). Preference theory: An affect-based approach to recurrent decision making. In T. Betsch & S. Haberstroh (Eds.), *The routines of decision making* (pp. 39–65). Mahwah, NJ: Lawrence Erlbaum Associates, Inc.
Betsch, T., Plessner, H., Schwieren, C., & Gütig, R. (2001). I like it but I don't know why: A value-account approach to implicit attitude formation. *Personality and Social Psychology Bulletin, 27*, 242–253.
Bornstein, R. F. (1989). Exposure and affect: Overview and meta-analysis of research, 1968–1987. *Psychological Bulletin, 106*, 265–289.
Bowers, K. S., Regehr, G., Balthazard, C., & Parker, K. (1990). Intuition in the context of discovery. *Cognitive Psychology, 22*, 72–110.
Bregman, E. (1934). An attempt to modify the emotional attitude of infants by the conditioning response technique. *Journal of Genetic Psychology, 45*, 169–198.
Buss, D. M. (1989). Sex differences in human mate preferences: Evolutionary hypotheses tested in 37 cultures. *Behavioral & Brain Sciences, 12*, 1–49.
Chase, W. G., & Simon, H. A. (1973). Perception in chess. *Cognitive Psychology, 4*, 55–81.
Csikszentmihalyi, M., & Larson, R. (1987). Validity and reliability of the experience-sampling method. *Journal of Nervous and Mental Disease, 175*, 526–536.
Edwards, K. (1998). The face of time: Temporal cues in the facial expression of emotion. *Psychological Science, 9*, 270–276.
Einhorn, H. J. (1980). Learning from experience and suboptimal rules in decision making. In T. Wallsten (Ed.), *Cognitive processes in choice and decision behavior* (pp. 1–20). Hillsdale, NJ: Lawrence Erlbaum Associates, Inc.
Einhorn, H. J., & Hogarth, R. M. (1978). Confidence in judgment: Persistence of the illusion of validity. *Psychological Review, 85*, 395–416.
Einhorn, H. J., & Hogarth, R. M. (1986). Judging probable cause. *Psychological Bulletin, 99*, 3–19.

Epstein, S. (1994). Integration of the cognitive and the psychodynamic unconscious. *American Psychologist, 49,* 709–724.

Ericsson, K. A., & Charness, N. (1994). Expert performance: Its structure and acquisition. *American Psychologist, 49,* 725–747.

Ericsson, K. A., & Lehmann, A. C. (1996). Expert and exceptional performance: Evidence of maximal adaptation to task constraints. *Annual Review of Psychology, 47,* 273–305.

Fiedler, K. (2000). Beware of samples! A cognitive-ecological sampling approach to judgment biases. *Psychological Review, 107,* 659–676.

Frabble, D. E. S., Blackstone, T., & Scherbaum, C. (1990). Marginal and mindful: Deviants in social interactions. *Journal of Personality and Social Psychology, 59,* 140–149.

Frensch, P. A., & Rünger, D. (2003). Implicit learning. *Current Directions in Psychological Science, 12,* 13–18.

Garcia, J. (1981). Tilting at the paper mills of academe. *American Psychologist, 36,* 149–158.

Garcia, J., McGowan, B., Ervin, F. R., & Koelling, R. (1968). Cues: Their relative effectiveness as reinforcers. *Science, 160,* 794–795.

Golec, P. (2005). *Positive influence of delayed feedback on decision making—advocating a lost cause?* Unpublished PhD thesis, University Pompeu Fabra, Barcelona.

Graham, T., & Ickes, W. (1997). When women's intuition isn't greater than men's. In W. Ickes (Ed.), *Empathic accuracy* (pp. 117–143). New York: Guilford.

Hall, J. A. (1984). *Nonverbal sex differences: Communication accuracy and expressive style.* Baltimore: Johns Hopkins University Press.

Harris, B. (1979). Whatever happened to little Albert? *American Psychologist, 34,* 151–160.

Harrison, A. A. (1977). Mere exposure. In L. Berkowitz (Ed.), *Advances in experimental social psychology* (Vol. 10, pp 39–83). New York: Academic.

Hasher, L., & Zacks, R. T. (1979). Automatic and effortful processes in memory. *Journal of Experimental Psychology: General, 108,* 356–358.

Hasher, L., & Zacks, R. T. (1984). Automatic processing of fundamental information: The case of frequency of occurrence. *American Psychologist, 39,* 1372–1388.

Hogarth, R. M. (1981). Beyond discrete biases: Functional and dysfunctional aspects of judgmental heuristics. *Psychological Bulletin, 90,* 197–217.

Hogarth, R. M. (2001). *Educating intuition.* Chicago: The University of Chicago Press.

Hogarth, R. M. (2007). Behavioral decision making at 50: Achievements, prospects, and challenges. In S.H. Oda (Ed.), *Advances in experimental economics. Lecture notes in economics and mathematical systems, 590,* Springer.

Hogarth, R. M. (2006). Is confidence in decisions related to feedback? Evidence from random samples of real-world behavior. In K. Fiedler & P. Juslin (Eds.), *Information sampling and adaptive cognition* (pp. 456–484). Cambridge, England: Cambridge University Press.

Hogarth R. M., Gibbs, B. J., McKenzie, C. R. M., & Marquis, M. A. (1991). Learning from feedback: Exactingness and incentives. *Journal of Experimental Psychology: Learning, Memory, and Cognition, 17,* 734–752.

Holbrook, M. B., & Schindler, R. M. (1994). Age, sex, and attitude toward the past as predictors of consumers' aesthetic tastes for cultural products. *Journal of Marketing Research, 31,* 412–422.

Hurlburt, R. T. (1997). Randomly sampling thinking in the natural environment. *Journal of Consulting and Clinical Psychology, 67,* 941–949.

Jung-Beeman, M., Bowden, E. M., Haberman, J., Frymiare, J. L., Arambel-Liuu, S., Greenblatt, R., et al. (2004). Neural activity when people solve verbal problems with insight. *PLoS Biology, 2,* 0500–0510.

Kanter, R. M. (1993). *Men and women of the corporation* (2nd ed.). New York: Basic Books.

Klein, G. (1998). *Sources of power: How people make decisions.* Cambridge, MA: MIT Press.

Lewicki, P., Hill, T., & Czyzewska, M. (1992). Nonconscious acquisition of information. *American Psychologist, 47,* 796–801.

Marcus, G. F., Vijayan, S., Bandi Rao, S., & Vishton, P. M. (1999). Rule learning by seven-month-old infants. *Science, 283,* 77–80.

Nisbett, R. E., Fong, G. T., Lehman, D. R., & Cheng, P. W. (1987). Teaching reasoning. *Science, 238,* 625–631.

Öhman, A., & Mineka, S. (2001). Fear, phobias, and preparedness: Toward an evolved module of fear and fear learning. *Psychological Review, 108,* 483–522.

Öhman, A., & Mineka, S. (2003). The malicious serpent: Snakes as a prototypical stimulus for an evolved module of fear. *Current Directions in Psychological Science, 12,* 5–9.

Pinker, S. (1994). *The language instinct: How the mind creates language.* New York: HarperCollins.

Reber, A. S. (1993). *Implicit learning and tacit knowledge: An essay on the cognitive unconscious.* New York: Oxford University Press.

Schooler, L. J., & Anderson, J. R. (1990). The disruptive potential of immediate feedback. In M. Piattelli (Ed.), *Proceedings of the annual conference of the Cognitive Science Society* (pp. 702–708). Hillsdale, NJ: Lawrence Erlbaum Associates, Inc.

Sedlmeier, P., & Betsch, T. (Eds.). (2002). *Etc.: Frequency processing and cognition.* Oxford, England: Oxford University Press.

Seger, C. (1994). Implicit learning. *Psychological Bulletin, 115,* 163–196.

Seligman, M. E. P. (1970). On the generality of the laws of learning. *Psychological Review, 77,* 406–418.

Seligman, M. E. P. (1971). Phobias and preparedness. *Behavior Therapy, 2,* 307–320.

Shultz, T. R. (1982). Rules of causal attribution. *Monographs of the Society for Research in Child Development, 47,* 1–51.

Simon, H. A., & Chase, W. G. (1973). Skill in chess. *American Scientist, 61,* 394–403.

Slovic, P., Finucane, M., Peters, E., & MacGregor, D. G. (2002). The affect heuristic. In T. Gilovich, D. Griffin, & D. Kahneman (Eds.), *Heuristics and biases: The psychology of intuitive judgment* (pp. 397–420). New York: Cambridge University Press.

Spelke, E. (1994). Initial knowledge: Six suggestions. *Cognition, 50,* 431–445.

Spelke, E. (1998). Nativism, empiricism, and the origins of knowledge. *Infant Behavior and Development, 21,* 181–200.

Stanovich, K. E., & West, R. F. (1998). Individual differences in rational thought. *Journal of Experimental Psychology: General, 127,* 161–188.

Thomas, L. (1983). *The youngest science: Notes of a medicine watcher.* New York. Viking.

Watson, J. B., & Rayner, R. (1920). Conditioned emotional reactions. *Journal of Experimental Psychology, 3,* 1–14.

Zajonc, R. B. (1968). Attitudinal effects of mere exposure. *Journal of Personality and Social Psychology Monographs, 9*(2, Pt. 2), 1–27.

7

Automatic Online Formation of Implicit Attitudes Toward Politicians as a Basis for Intuitive Voting Behavior

HENNING PLESSNER, TILMANN BETSCH, and ELKE SCHALLIES
University of Heidelberg

CHRISTIANE SCHWIEREN
University Pompeu Fabra

INTRODUCTION

Every year, political parties spend billions of dollars on electoral campaigns. According to survey data, however, these efforts seem to be useless because voters are found to be generally ill informed about parties, candidates, and issues when asked on election day (e.g., Smith, 1989). In contrast, the results of recent studies on attitude formation in the political domain have given some good reasons to argue that the resources spent on campaigns are not wasted completely. Specifically, Lodge, Steenbergen, and Brau (1995) found people to be sensitive to campaign information in that overall evaluations of candidates are adjusted to their online evaluations of individual campaign messages and events. Although people forgot most of the campaign information they had been exposed to over time, their actual preferences and voting choices were found to be informed by their summary evaluations. These effects have been accounted for by an online model of information processing (cf. Hastie & Park, 1986). According to Lodge et al. (1995), people draw politically relevant conclusions from campaign information about politicians the very moment they process information. These immediate assessments are assumed to be integrated into a "running tally" that reflects the summary evaluation of a candidate at any given point in time. Moreover, the running tally is immediately updated and stored in long-term memory, whereas the original campaign information may be forgotten. Subsequent judgments, for example, preceding a vote, are assumed to be based on running tallies rather than on recollections of the original campaign information. This was named the "hot cognition" hypothesis of intuitive voting behavior (Lodge & Taber, 2005). However, one crucial assumption of the running tally model is that it works only if people's goal is to form an overall impression about a politician.

Betsch, Plessner, and Schallies (2004) asserted that the encoding of evaluative information can also trigger effects like those reported by Lodge et al. (1995) when people do not actively intend to form an impression about an attitude object, for example, by affecting people's implicit attitudes (Greenwald & Banaji, 1995). According to the value-account approach to implicit attitude formation (Betsch et al., 2004), the mere encoding of value-charged information automatically initiates the online formation of summary evaluations. In this chapter, we therefore argue that people's implicit attitudes toward politicians can reflect campaign information even if people did not intend to evaluate these politicians during the encoding of campaign messages. In the following section, we describe the value-account approach in more detail.

THE VALUE-ACCOUNT APPROACH TO IMPLICIT ATTITUDE FORMATION

In social psychology, an array of almost classical studies has found that attitudinal judgments can reflect specific aspects of past experiences even when people's concrete memories about these experiences are inadequate, biased, or have faded altogether (e.g., Anderson & Hubert, 1963; Greenwald, 1968; Kunst-Wilson & Zajonc, 1980; Staats & Staats, 1958; Wilson, Hodges, & LaFleur, 1995). The value-account approach to implicit attitude formation (Betsch et al., 2004) provides an explanation for such effects that is in line with a number of models that have been developed in the study of animal choice according to which organisms are able to automatically cumulate the intensities or values of outcomes in mental accounts (e.g., Davis, Staddon, Machado, & Palmer, 1993; Hull, 1943). The basic assumption of the model is that the mere encoding of value-charged stimuli is a sufficient condition to initiate online formation of summary evaluations. Further, the value-account approach posits that the mechanism by which the values of the stimuli are integrated is best described by a summation principle. To highlight the underlying accumulative process of information integration, Betsch et al. (2004) proposed the term *value account* for the aggregate memory structure. Finally, value accounts are assumed to be highly accessible. It follows from these assumptions that attitude judgments should be likely to reflect the sum of previous experiences even in the absence of any concrete memories about a target attitude object especially when cognitive capacities at the time of judgment are constrained. As one assumes that attitudes are formed in an implicit fashion (cf. Greenwald & Banaji, 1995), the summary evaluations represented in value accounts should also have an influence on implicit attitude measures such as, for example, the affective priming procedure (Fazio, Sanbonmatsu, Powell, & Kardes, 1986) or the Implicit Association Test (IAT; Greenwald, McGhee, & Schwartz, 1998).

Although the notion that attitude formation can occur without intent to form an impression has already been made in the literature on persuasion (e.g., Petty & Cacioppo, 1986), the value-account approach allows for unique predictions beyond standard approaches to attitude formation and change (cf. Betsch et al., 2004).

In a series of experiments, Betsch, Hoffmann, Hoffrage, and Plessner (2003); Betsch, Kaufmann, Lindow, Plessner, and Hoffmann (2006); and Betsch et al. (2001) have provided ample evidence for the basic assumptions of the value-account approach. The experimental paradigm that has been developed in these studies rests on an information presentation format familiar from contemporary news broadcasts. Specifically, participants had watched a series of (videotaped) commercials, and a running caption at the bottom of the screen had displayed the returns several shares had scored at different stock markets and at several points in time (Betsch et al., 2001). Instructions had portrayed the experiment as concerned with the human capacity to simultaneously process information stemming from multiple sources. Specifically, the study had allegedly addressed the efficiency of TV commercials when another kind of information had been presented simultaneously (e.g., return information about shares). Participants were instructed to concentrate on the commercials and learned that they would later have to answer some questions about the commercials. They were further requested to read the information appearing in the running captions aloud during stimulus presentation. This had been announced as a secondary task intended to constrain participants' information-processing capacities. After watching the video, participants were asked to evaluate each of the shares. Using this paradigm, it had been recurrently found that participants could not accurately differentiate between the presented shares when asked to estimate the sum and the average of returns. However, when they had been asked to judge their attitudes toward the shares on a good–bad scale, judgments reflected a high degree of sensitivity to the differences of the shares in the actual sum of returns. One limitation of these findings was that gains had been exclusively varied in the return distribution and not losses.

In the first place, shares had been chosen as attitude objects in these studies (Betsch et al., 2001, 2003, 2006) because shares are mainly associated with one goal (i.e., profit). It was, therefore, reasonable to have assumed that increasing objective scale values would have led to an increase in participants' subjective values, thus making it possible to quantify precisely the values conveyed by the stimuli. In this fashion, it was possible to differentiate between the principle of averaging in information integration (e.g., Anderson, 1981) and the principle of summation that has been proposed by the value-account approach (Betsch et al., 2001, 2006). In the evaluation of politicians, however, multiple goals are involved (e.g., environment protection, social welfare, etc.). Therefore, it is not possible to control the values that people assign to campaign information in the same manner as it was with returns of shares as value-charged stimuli. However, the general process of automatic attitude formation that is proposed by the value-account approach should apply to the political domain as well. That is, we expected the mere encoding of campaign messages, either with an assigned positive or negative value, to trigger the formation of implicit attitudes toward politicians. We conducted two experiments to test this assumption.

EXPERIMENT 1

In the first experiment, we tested the hypotheses that (a) people automatically form summary evaluations of candidates on the basis of campaign messages that they encounter even in the absence of the intention to form an impression about the respective politicians; and (b) later on, they are able to use their summary evaluation in attitudes judgments even if they have forgotten most of the campaign messages.

We recruited a total of 40 students (from various faculties of the University of Heidelberg) for participation in an experiment on "grammar in political speech." We assigned half of them to an "impression formation" condition, and we assigned the other half to a "grammar check" condition.

We exposed all participants to 12 single-sentence statements of each of five fictitious politicians that appeared in a mixed order on a computer screen (e.g., "Politician C said: People with larger incomes should pay higher taxes"). The five politicians were represented by a letter and by a pictogram of a man in a suit. It differed between the five politicians in the bearing and the suit color.

In a pretest, 20 students judged a total of 100 political statements with respect to valence on a rating scale ranging from −5 (*very bad*) to +5 (*very good*). On the basis of these ratings, we selected the 12 statements for each politician such that the five politicians differed markedly in the judged summary evaluation of their statements (see columns 2 and 3 of Table 7.1). For example, the 12 statements attached to politician D had been evaluated very negatively on average, whereas the statements of politician E had been judged rather positively on average.

Instructions informed participants that the experiment was concerned with political statements. We told half the participants that their task was to form an impression about each of five politicians on the basis of a sample of their political

TABLE 7.1 Attitude Judgments in Experiment 1

	Pretest		Task			
			Impression		Grammar	
Politician	M	SD	M	SD	M	SD
D (very negative)	−2.67	1.08	−2.05	2.82	−1.14	2.14
A (negative)	−0.82	0.80	−0.34	2.61	−0.49	1.96
B (neutral)	0.50	1.32	0.24	1.87	0.35	2.45
E (positive)	1.56	0.78	0.98	1.61	0.88	1.82
C (very positive)	2.26	1.18	0.87	2.35	0.11	1.47

statements (impression formation). We therefore asked them to read each statement carefully and to judge its valence immediately after its presentation by means of a vertical scroll bar with the endpoints labeled as "very good" at the top and "very bad" at the bottom. We told the remaining participants that the experiment investigated how good people are in detecting whether a political statement is articulated in an active or a passive voice (grammar check). We also asked the participants in this condition to read each statement carefully. Instead of judging its valence, we asked them to decide whether a statement was in a passive or an active voice immediately after its presentation. Before the presentation started, participants practiced the use of the computer program that was later used to measure the dependent variables.

Each of the 60 political statements appeared on the computer screen for 5 sec. Pretests with these materials had shown that this was just enough time for participants to encode the semantic content of the statements. Immediately after presentation of the statements and the respective judgments, we administered the dependent measures. First, we requested participants to evaluate each of the five politicians. We provided ratings for each politician on a separate screen, and we asked participants to give spontaneous answers to the question "How do you like this politician?" using a scroll bar with the endpoints "very good" and "very bad." The politicians were represented by both, the letters A to E, and the respective pictogram. Afterwards, we asked participants to assign each of the 60 political statements to the five politicians in a cued recall task. Each statement appeared on a screen followed by a multiple-choice table with the options "politician A" to "politician E." At the end of the session, we probed participants for suspicion, debriefed them, and paid them.

As expected, the attitudes toward the two politicians reflected the sum of the (pretested) values of previously encoded positive and negative political statements (see Table 7.1). The analysis of variance (ANOVA) for the attitude judgments revealed a highly significant main effect for the factor politician, $F(4, 152) = 7.60$, $p < .01$. No other effects were obtained (all $Fs < 1$). This effect occurred even though participants were not able to assign the statements accurately to the politicians in a cued recall task. We analyzed the frequency of choice for all statements using chi-square tests. No differences occurred for most of the statements in both between-subject conditions. In those eight cases in which a politician had been chosen more frequently as the source of a statement than one would expect by chance, it was the wrong one. These findings held in the impression formation and also in the grammar check condition. Therefore, the data supported our assumption that the mere encoding of value-charged stimuli automatically triggers the formation of value accounts in memory. Moreover, we found that these value accounts can reflect all previous experiences people had with an attitude object, that is, positive as well as negative events.

Although it is very unlikely that the results in the grammar condition stem from explicit memories, this alternative interpretation cannot completely be excluded on the basis of these data because we asked participants for explicit attitude ratings that could still be constructed from explicit memories that we were not able to assess with the cued recall task. Therefore, we introduced an implicit attitude measure in our second experiment.

EXPERIMENT 2

Current theories in attitude research have differentiated between automatic or implicit attitudes on one hand and explicit attitudes on the other (e.g., Fazio, 1990; Greenwald et al., 2002; Wilson, Lindsey, & Schooler, 2000). Whereas the study of explicit attitudes has a long tradition in social psychology, research on implicit attitudes is a rather novel issue that has been triggered by cognitive psychologists' recent debate about unconscious memories and corresponding developments in the measurement of automatic evaluations (cf. Banaji, 2001). A few years ago, Greenwald et al. (1998) presented the IAT, a new method to measure the differential evaluative association of two target concepts. It has been asserted that the IAT allows for the assessment of implicit attitudes by comparing response times in two combined discrimination tasks. In one task, for example, participants are asked to sort names to two target concepts (Japanese vs. Korean), whereas in the second task, they have to classify valenced words as either positive or negative. If participants were faster in providing responses when the concepts Japanese and positive evaluation share the same response key than when these concepts require different responses, they are assumed to hold more positive implicit attitudes toward Japanese than toward Koreans. Although there have been some critical remarks on this method (e.g., Fiedler, Messner, & Bluemke, 2006; Plessner & Banse, 2001) regarding primarily its value as a diagnostic instrument, its usefulness as a dependent measure is without doubt.

The IAT procedure has already been found to be a helpful tool in the assessment of implicit attitudes toward politicians (e.g., Maison, 1999). The aim of this experiment was to replicate the findings of Experiment 1 using participants' responses in an adapted IAT version as dependent variable and therefore to test the assumption that the mere encoding of value-charged stimuli alters implicit attitudes.

A total of 80 students of different majors at the University of Heidelberg volunteered for an experiment called "grammar in political speech." We randomly assigned them to the four experimental conditions resulting from a 2 × 2 factorial design with the between-subject factors information (statements vs. no statements) and order of combined classification tasks in the IAT (see following).

Participants in the statements conditions listened to 12 statements of each of four politicians that had been audiotaped by the same speaker, thus avoiding differences between politicians with regard to the pleasantness of their voices. We chose the statements from the same pretested sample as in Experiment 1. This time, we assigned statements to politicians as follows: We rated the statements of a politician named Holder as negative on average, whereas we rated the statements of a politician named Kevan as positive. Finally, we rated statements assigned to two politicians named Diederik and Selbeck as neutral. The inclusion of two neutral politicians was intended to increase cognitive load during encoding, thus making it unlikely that participants would form exemplar memories. Each audiotaped statement was introduced by the name of the respective politician (e.g., "Mr. Kevan said: ...") to ensure the associative encoding of each statement with the politician who gave it.

To assess participants' implicit attitudes toward the two target politicians Kevan (positive statements on average) and Holder (negative statements on average), we used an adapted IAT version that we constructed in agreement with the steps taken in the original version described in Greenwald et al. (1998).

Depending on the between-subject factor information, participants either completed the IAT procedure first (no statements), or we asked them to listen to the audiotape via headphone before taking the IAT (statements). In the latter case, we used the same cover story and instructions as in the grammar condition of Experiment 1. To obtain a complete encoding of individual statements, we asked participants to pause the audiotape after each of the 48 statements and to mark whether a statement was in passive or active voice on a questionnaire.

The IAT program was an adapted version of the program used by Kühnen et al. (2001). After a short warm-up task, the relevant blocks for this study began. In the first block, either the name Holder or the name Kevan appeared around the center of the screen, and names had to be categorized as instances of the category "politician Holder" or "politician Kevan" (40 trials). To ensure that participants actually paid attention to this primitive task, the names appeared on various positions around the center of the PC screen. In the next block, the participants' task was to classify 40 adjectives according to their valence as instances of the category "positive" or "negative." We asked half the participants to use the left key for positive adjectives (task Order A), and we asked the other half to use the right key for identifying positive words (task Order B). The third block constituted the first combined classification task. We presented both politicians and adjectives during this block. Depending on which key positive and negative adjectives had been assigned to during the second block, participants either had to press the same response key to identify politician Kevan and positive adjectives (and, consequently, the other key to identify politician Holder and negative adjectives) or politician Kevan and negative adjectives. In the fourth block, we only presented adjectives, and we reversed the assignment of positive and negative adjectives to the two response keys. The last block again consisted of a combined classification task, that is, we presented both politicians and adjectives. As the assignment of positive versus negative adjectives to response keys had been reversed, however, the combined assignment was opposite to the one used during the first combined task. We randomized the order in which we presented the stimuli within blocks for each participant. After participants had completed the last block, we debriefed them.

We handled IAT data in accordance with a standard procedure (Greenwald & Nosek, 2001). That is, we dropped the first 2 trials of each of the combined blocks, we recoded latencies less than 300 ms to 300 ms and latencies greater than 3,000 ms to 3,000 ms, and we log transformed the resulting values prior to averaging. The untransformed mean latencies are depicted in Table 7.2.

We subjected the data of the combined trials to a 2 × 2 × 2 (Information × Task Order × Response Assignment) ANOVA with repeated measurement on the last factor. Only a significant interaction between information and response assignment emerged, $F(1, 76) = 4.21$, $p < .05$ but no other effects (all $Fs < 2$). Therefore, we collapsed data over the factor task order (see Figure 7.1). Simple effect analyses support the assumption that there was an IAT effect ($M = 50.3$ ms, $SD = 95.8$) when

TABLE 7.2 Mean Latency Results in the Combined Tasks of the IAT by Response Assignment, Information, and Task Order in Experiment 2

	Response Assignment			
	Holder/Positive Kevan/Negative		Kevan/Positive Holder/Negative	
Information	M	SD	M	SD
No Statements				
Task Order A	878	145	882	144
Task Order B	879	148	880	141
Statements				
Task Order A	886	175	835	132
Task Order B	938	134	888	153

participants had listened to politicians' statements prior to the IAT procedure and no effect when they had not ($M = -2.9$ ms, $SD = 124.9$), $t(78) = 2.19$, $p < .05$.

More precisely, participants of the statements condition were faster when responses to politician Kevan (positive statements on average) and positive adjectives on one hand and responses to politician Holder (negative statements on average) and negative adjectives on the other hand shared a response key than when they did not. These differences have been commonly interpreted as differences in implicit attitudes (Greenwald & Nosek, 2001; but see also Fiedler et al., 2006); that is, participants had a more positive implicit attitude toward politician Kevan than toward politician Holder. No such differences occurred, as expected, in the no statement condition in which people had no prior experiences with the politicians Kevan and Holder.

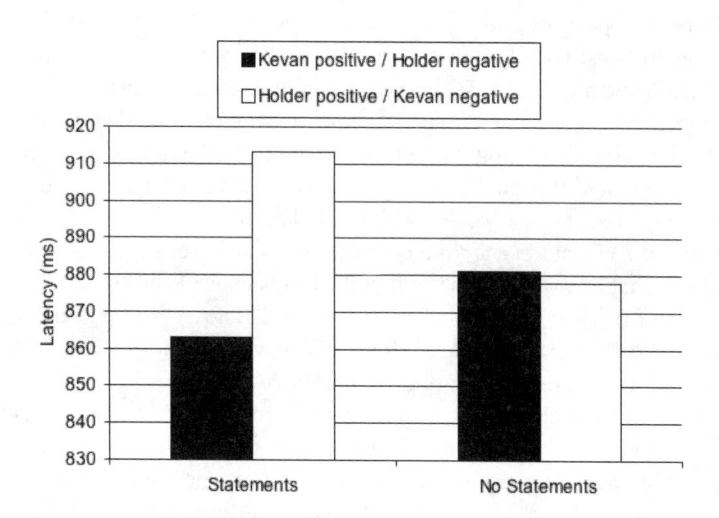

FIGURE 7.1 Mean latency results in the combined tasks of the Implicit Association Test by response assignment and information in Experiment 2.

These results replicate the findings of Experiment 1 and support our assumption that the mere encoding of political statements triggers the automatic formation of implicit attitudes toward the respective politicians.

CONCLUSIONS

In a study on attitude formation in the political domain, Lodge et al. (1995) found people who had the goal to form an impression about a politician to form summary evaluations of candidates on the basis of all campaign messages they had encountered. Later on, they were able to use their summary evaluation in judgments and choices even if they had forgotten most of the campaign messages. In two experiments, we found evidence that effects like these occur even in the absence of people's intention to form impressions about the respective politicians. In line with the assumptions made by the value-account approach to implicit attitude formation (Betsch et al., 2004), the mere encoding of political statements automatically initiated the formation of attitudes toward politicians. Additionally, these experiments provide evidence for two assumptions of the value-account approach that have not been tested before. First, we found summary evaluations reflected political statements for both statements with an assigned positive value and statements with an assigned negative value. Previous experiments had found supporting evidence for the value-account approach with gains in the domain of share returns (Betsch et al., 2001, 2003, 2006), but we did not vary losses in the same manner. Second, we found value accounts developed from the experiences with value-charged stimuli affected an explicit measure as well as an implicit attitude measure, that is, an IAT (Greenwald et al., 1998). The latter finding provides conclusive evidence for the assumption that the processes described in the value-account approach lead to the formation of implicit attitudes that need no conscious recollection of stored memories (Greenwald & Banaji, 1995). In the domain of political attitude formation, similar results have been obtained with an affective priming procedure (Lodge & Taber, 2005) and with the recoding of event-related potentials in the brain (Morris, Squires, Taber, & Lodge, 2003).

Our chapter started with the consideration that the billions of dollars that parties spend in electoral campaigns could be wasted because voters seem not to remember specific campaign messages. On the basis of our findings, one may argue that electoral campaigns have an effect nonetheless. Even if campaign messages' valence is encoded incidentally, that is, without the goal of evaluation, the evaluative contents have an influence on people's summary evaluation of politicians and are thus likely to affect their intuitive votes on election day (cf. Lodge et al., 1995).

ACKNOWLEDGMENTS

The studies were financially supported by a grant from the Deutsche Forschungsgemeinschaft (BE 2012/1–2). Many thanks to Peter Freytag for helpful comments on a draft version of this chapter.

REFERENCES

Anderson, N. H. (1981). *Foundations of information integration theory.* New York: Academic.
Anderson, N. H., & Hubert, S. (1963). Effects of concomitant verbal recall on order effects in personality impression formation. *Journal of Verbal Learning and Verbal Behavior,* 2, 379–391.
Banaji, M. R. (2001). Implicit attitudes can be measured. In H. L. Roediger, J. S. Nairne, I. Neath, & A. Surprenant (Eds.), *The nature of remembering: Essays in honor of Robert G. Crowder* (pp. 117–150). Washington, DC: American Psychological Association.
Betsch, T., Hoffmann, K., Hoffrage, U., & Plessner, H. (2003). Intuition beyond recognition: When less familiar events are liked better. *Experimental Psychology,* 50, 49–54.
Betsch, T., Kaufmann, M., Lindow, F., Plessner, H., & Hoffmann, K. (2006). Different mechanisms of information integration in implicit and explicit attitude formation. *European Journal of Social Psychology,* 36, 887–905.
Betsch, T., Plessner, H., & Schallies, E. (2004). The value-account model of attitude formation. In G. R. Maio & G. Haddock (Eds.), *Contemporary perspectives on the psychology of attitudes* (pp. 252–273). Hove, England: Psychology Press.
Betsch, T., Plessner, H., Schwieren, C., & Gütig, R. (2001). I like it but I don't know why: A value-account approach to implicit attitude formation. *Personality and Social Psychology Bulletin,* 27, 242–253.
Davis, D. G. S., Staddon, J. E. R., Machado, A., & Palmer, R. G. (1993). The process of recurrent choice. *Psychological Review,* 100, 320–341.
Fazio, R. H. (1990). Multiple processes by which attitudes guide behavior: The MODE model as an integrative framework. In M. P. Zanna (Ed.), *Advances in experimental social psychology* (Vol. 23, pp. 75–109). San Diego, CA: Academic.
Fazio, R. H., Sanbonmatsu, D. M., Powell, M. C., & Kardes, F. R. (1986). On the automatic activation of attitudes. *Journal of Personality and Social Psychology,* 50, 229–238.
Fiedler, K., Messner, C., & Bluemke, M. (2006). Unresolved problems with the "I," the "A," and the "T": A logical and psychometric critique of the Implicit Association Test (IAT). *European Review of Social Psychology,* 17, 74–147.
Greenwald, A. G. (1968). Cognitive learning, cognitive response to persuasion and attitude change. In A. G. Greenwald, T. C. Brock, & T. M. Ostrom (Eds.), *Psychological foundation of attitudes* (pp. 147–170). New York: Academic.
Greenwald, A. G., & Banaji, M. R. (1995). Implicit social cognition: Attitudes, self-esteem, and stereotypes. *Psychological Review,* 102, 4–27.
Greenwald, A. G., Banaji, M. R., Farnham, S. D.; Rudman, L. A., Nosek, B. A., & Mellot, D. S. (2002). A unified theory of implicit attitudes, stereotypes, self-concept, and self-esteem. *Psychological Review,* 109, 3–25.
Greenwald, A. G., McGhee, D. E., & Schwartz, J. L. K. (1998). Measuring individual differences in implicit cognition: The implicit association test. *Journal of Personality and Social Psychology,* 74, 1464–1480.
Greenwald, A. G., & Nosek, B. (2001). Health of the Implicit Association Test at age 3. *Zeitschrift für Experimentelle Psychologie,* 48, 85–93.
Hastie, R., & Park, B. (1986). The relationship between memory and judgment depends on whether the judgment task is memory-based or on-line. *Psychological Review,* 93, 258–268.
Hull, C. L. (1943). *Principles of behavior.* New York: Appleton-Century.
Kühnen, U., Schießl, M., Bauer, N., Paulig, N., Pöhlmann, C., & Schmidthals, K. (2001). How robust is the IAT? Measuring and manipulating implicit attitudes of East- and West-Germans. *Zeitschrift für Experimentelle Psychologie,* 48, 135–144.

Kunst-Wilson, W. R., & Zajonc, R. B. (1980). Affective discrimination of stimuli that cannot be recognized. *Science*, 207, 557–558.

Lodge, M., Steenbergen, M. R., & Brau, S. (1995). The responsive voter: Campaign information and the dynamics of candidate evaluation. *American Political Science Review*, 89, 309–326.

Lodge, M., & Taber, C. S. (2005). The automaticity of affect for political leaders, groups, and issues: An experimental test of the hot cognition hypothesis. *Political Psychology*, 26, 455–482.

Maison, D. (July, 1999). *The Implicit Attitude Test: A Polish application to national political attitudes*. Paper presented at the 12th General Meeting of the European Association of Experimental Social Psychology in Oxford, England.

Morris, J. P., Squires, N. K., Taber, C. S., & Lodge, M. (2003). Activation of political attitudes: A psychophysiological examination of the hot cognition hypothesis. *Political Psychology*, 24, 727–745.

Petty, R. E., & Cacioppo, J. T. (1986). *Communication and persuasion: Central and peripheral routes to attitude change*. New York: Springer.

Plessner, H., & Banse, R. (Eds.). (2001). Attitude measurement using the Implicit Association Test (IAT) [Special issue]. *Zeitschrift für Experimentelle Psychologie*, 48(2).

Smith, E. R. A. N. (1989). *The unchanging American voter*. Berkeley: University of California Press.

Staats, A. W., & Staats, C. K. (1958). Attitudes established by classical conditioning. *Journal of Abnormal and Social Psychology*, 57, 37–40.

Wilson, T. D., Hodges, S. D., & LaFleur, J. (1995). Effects of introspecting about reasons: Inferring attitudes from accessible thoughts. *Journal of Personality and Social Psychology*, 69, 16–28.

Wilson, T. D., Lindsey, S., & Schooler, T. Y. (2000). A model of dual attitudes. *Psychological Review*, 107, 101–126.

8

Implicit Learning as a Means to Intuitive Decision Making in Sports

MARKUS RAAB
University of Flensburg

JOSEPH G. JOHNSON
Miami University

INTRODUCTION

Distinctions and dichotomies abound in research on cognitive processes such as those between automatic and controlled processes (Shiffrin & Schneider, 1977), which are manifest in a number of domains. However, it is not necessarily useful to draw arbitrary distinctions merely for the sake of classification. As researchers, we should ask ourselves whether such distinctions serve a useful purpose in terms of the theories and models of human behavior that we develop. Supposition of "dual processes" seems to have run its course in some fields such as social psychology (Chaiken & Trope, 1999) in which researchers now have mixed opinions about the need for this a priori assumption (Strack, 1999). In other fields, there seems to be a longstanding, pervasive, and (most important) empirically supported tendency to endorse a discrete division—such as that between implicit and explicit learning styles (Stadler & Frensch, 1998).

Recently, there has been renewed interest in applying such a dichotomy to judgment and decision processes; primarily, this results in a distinction between intuitive and deliberate decision making (T. Betsch, chap. 1, this volume; Sloman, 2002). In this chapter, we seek to integrate the learning style and decision process distinctions in a common framework that allows us to explore their usefulness. Specifically, we analyze decisions in sports—a real-world domain for dynamic decision making under time pressure—with an emphasis on how learning style and decision process are related.

The remainder of the chapter is organized as follows. First, we describe what we refer to as a decision protocol (cf. Orasanu & Connolly, 1993) to see exactly what processes may be described as intuitive or deliberate and how learning impacts subsequent decision making. Second, we briefly review and summarize some relevant literature on the distinction between intuitive and deliberate decision making in sports and likewise for the distinction between implicit and explicit learning styles. Ultimately, we provide a synthesis of these four (previously independent) concepts in a new model.

A PROTOCOL FOR SPORTS DECISION MAKING

What exactly does making a decision entail? There are many phase models of decision making in the literature (Koehler & Harvey, 2004), but we borrow the decision protocol of Orasanu and Connolly (1993) because it includes the execution of decisions that is especially relevant when considering sports decisions. We apply what Orasanu and Connolly believed to be the seven key components of a decision specific to the domain of sports; this is useful for operational definition in the remaining sections. We note that not every decision situation will be comprised of all seven of these stages. However, these seven stages are particularly relevant for the sports domain that is the focus of this chapter. The sports domain offers a chance to explore real-world decisions, made by motivated and experienced agents, in rich environments under various conditions (e.g., uncertainty, time pressure). We take advantage of this natural opportunity to study decision making that occurs outside of the laboratory on the playing field.

The first step in a decision is the *presentation* of the problem. Although this may seem to be a trivial or obvious step, it has actually been the focus of a great deal of research in judgment and decision making—such as work on framing effects (e.g., Tversky & Kahneman, 1981). That is, the subsequent steps of a decision are not independent of the manner in which a decision is encountered or the way it is presented. The next step is the *identification* of the constraints, resources, and goals facing the decision maker. These properties can be specific, such as limited time or information available, or they can be abstract such as the goal of maximizing expected payoff. Third, the *generation* of possible solutions to the problem, or courses of action, occurs. This step in particular may not be relevant to many laboratory decision-making tasks in which participants are often presented explicitly with the options from which they must choose.

The fourth step of the decision-making protocol, *consideration* of possible solutions, is the one typically regarded as representing the whole of the decision-making process. By this, we imply that the first three stages are often taken for granted—if they are appreciated at all—in much decision-making research. Similarly, the next two stages are rarely dissociated from the output of the consideration phase. *Selection* of a course of action is generally seen as synonymous with identifying the "winner" of the consideration phase; and *initiation* of the selected action is almost always seen as a straightforward extension of a mentally selected option to a physically realized one. Finally, the last stage of a decision protocol is the *evaluation* of the decision made including the appraisal of feedback information if any exists.

We offer a brief sports example to illustrate each of these seven stages. Imagine a forward in soccer who is dribbling toward the goal and is approached by a defender. At this point, the decision problem has presented itself: what action to take in response to the approaching defender. The forward identifies the constraints on his behavior (e.g., he cannot pass offside) and prioritizes his goals (e.g., above all, retain possession; but score if possible). In light of these, he generates possible options that he may undertake such as shooting at the goal, passing to a wing player, or dribbling away from the defender. He considers these courses of action, perhaps by ranking them according to their likelihood of achieving his top goal (retaining possession). Then, he selects an action; this is likely to be the one with the highest rank. He initiates the action by physically performing so as to bring about the action he selected (e.g., physically dribbling the ball to the right). In doing so, he buys time for the wing player to streak toward the goal where he passes the ball and assists in a score—resulting in positive evaluation of his decision.

INTUITIVE AND DELIBERATE PROCESSING IN SPORTS

To begin our discussion of intuitive and deliberate processes, we are careful to employ a particular operational definition. Intuitive processes are generally assumed to be automatic activations of (semantic) networks (Anderson, 1983). We follow suit in defining *intuitive* (as opposed to deliberate) decisions as fast decisions that are based on a perceived pattern of information that is often linked automatically to a specific action or sets of actions (see Hogarth, 2001). However, we stress that routine behavior is not the same as intuitive processes. Rather, the latter may serve as a basis for the former, especially in the absence of creative or emotional aspects not in line with an automatic information-processing perspective (Schönpflug, 1994, but see Lieberman, 2000). Therefore, the link between intuitive processes when deciding and the preference to use these (as opposed to deliberative) processes is derived through tacit information accumulated over long-term experience (e.g., Epstein, chap. 2, this volume).

We prefer to view decision-making style as a continuum rather than as a dichotomy (cf. Hamm, chap. 4, this volume; Hammond, 1996). That is, rather than classifying behavior as intuitive or deliberate, it may be more fruitful to consider a spectrum of decision-making processes with these two extremes. Because decision-making processes cannot be directly observed, they are often operationalized by measures such as deliberation time or susceptibility to dual task interference (e.g., deliberate processes are slower and more susceptible; Kahneman & Frederik, 2002). In this context, we only have ordinal relations to claim one process is "more intuitive" than another, or we must introduce some threshold or criterion for determining, for example, how quickly a process must occur to be considered intuitive. With this continuous nature in mind, we now describe what "more deliberate" or more intuitive decision making suggests for the relevant stages of our protocol.

Intuitive and Deliberate Processes in the Decision Protocol

We can precisely localize the influence of intuitive versus deliberate processes by utilizing the seven-stage schematic we developed in the previous section. That is, we now see exactly where and how intuitive decisions may differ from deliberate ones. When one speaks of intuitive and deliberate decision making, it does not necessarily mean that the entire protocol is performed intuitively or deliberately. Rather, we should independently consider each phase of the decision protocol. For example, the presentation and identification of information for the aforementioned soccer player may foster intuitive processes only if a coach constructs situations of high time pressure. Indeed, we conceptualize the distinction between these two processes primarily in the third and fourth stages (generation and consideration)—the key internally active segments of the decision-making protocol. Traditionally, these two stages have not been considered together in decision-making research. There has been relatively little research on how options are generated—because they are often explicitly presented in experiments—and even less that have related option generation to subsequent consideration and selection (for notable exceptions, see Johnson & Raab, 2003; Klein, Wolf, Militello, & Zsambok, 1995). Nevertheless, we can employ concepts and results from previous research in determining which decision-making process may result.

Option generation can be performed deliberately in which rules may dictate how to develop viable solutions to a problem (Sloman, 2002). In contrast, option generation may be akin to spreading activation in a representation network, proceeding with little conscious effort or direction (Johnson & Raab, 2003). For example, suppose the first option generated by the soccer forward in the preceding example is a pass to the right wing player. Depending on the organization of the forward's internal corpus of options, spreading activation would suggest that options that are most similar to this first option would be generated next (Johnson & Raab, 2003; Klein et al., 1995). If similarity is based on the spatial attributes of options, then perhaps the next generations may be passing to the right fullback, dribbling to the right, shooting to the right of the goal, or lobbing to the right corner. In contrast, deliberate option generation suggests more formal rules for determining the order of generated options. Perhaps training has taught the forward to always generate passing options prior to shooting options, which would change the order of generated options (and the options themselves) in our example.

Consideration of the generated options occurs independently from the generation process—intuitively generated options may be considered deliberately, for example. A great deal of research has examined intuitive versus deliberate processes of consideration, to which we cannot devote a great deal of discussion here (see, for an overview, Glöeckner, chap. 19, this volume; Plessner & Czenna, chap. 15, this volume). Intuitive consideration may involve little or no actual consideration at all: favor what is most salient or most readily comes to mind; see if each option, in turn, is sufficient on all attributes; do what one did the last time; and so forth. A deliberate process may involve relatively simple rules or heuristics (e.g., Gigerenzer, Todd, & The ABC Research Group, 1999) or more cognitively intensive algorithms such as weighted summation.

Evidence for Intuitive and Deliberate Processes in Sports

In keeping with the focus of this chapter, we provide some examples of intuitive and deliberate processes from the sports domain in particular rather than an extended general review. It seems plausible that different types of decisions in sports may be conducive to differential processing. For example, a coach may use deliberate and careful analysis of countless statistics to decide which pitcher to use in late relief of a baseball game. In contrast, a streaking basketball player on a "fast break" may need to trust her or his intuitions on whether to pass or shoot. In sports, verification for suppositions such as these has just started to develop. This evidence is primarily the result of an effort to show that intuitive decision making can be at least as successful as more deliberate strategies.

The presentation of information to athletes and their subsequent identification of the situation are often varied by the amount and type of instruction or feedback a coach employs. For instance, setting up a tactical game-like situation or scrimmage without much instruction may result in generally intuitive processes compared to guided-discovery instruction of an if–then rule associated with specific attack training (Smeeton, Williams, Hodges, & Ward, 2005). In sports, such rule-based instructions are widespread and commonly used to produce deliberative processes when deciding. For instance, educational concepts such as "teaching games for understanding" (McMorris, 1998) provide learners with explicit knowledge and encourage deliberative thinking about tactics before training such skills.

A recent study (Johnson & Raab, 2003) on option generation and resulting choices provides evidence for the presence—and perhaps the superiority—of intuitive option generation in sports. Johnson and Raab (2003) demonstrated that intuitive option generation results in better choices than deliberate and prolonged option generation in experienced handball players. Johnson and Raab's "take-the-first" heuristic describes how people generate options in a given situation and choose among them. The heuristic consists of an information search rule (i.e., generation) and a decision rule (i.e., consideration). The search rule suggests that the stimuli trigger the first option generated, which then serves as a point from which option generation proceeds (see also Klein et al., 1995). Subsequent generation is characterized as spreading activation driven by the (dis)similarity between options (represented in a semantic network) as well as the strength of the option and the stimuli presented.

In the research reported by Johnson and Raab (2003), participants with different levels of handball expertise performed a video decision task in which they were shown an attack situation that was "frozen" when a particular attacker received the ball. Participants were asked to assume the role of this player and to (a) immediately speak the option that intuitively came first to mind; then (b) generate as many options they thought would be appropriate; and finally (c), pick the best option for this situation from all options that were generated. In support of the heuristic's proposed intuitive generation process, initial options were reported immediately on the onset of each trial, and subsequently generated options could be classified by their similarity to the initial option.

Johnson and Raab (2003) also provide support for intuitive processes in choosing (i.e., selection) among the generated options. Specifically, chosen options were often among the first generated, which suggests that participants trusted their instincts, electing to take the first rather than perform an algorithmic comparison among options. Furthermore, this quick process seemed to produce better decisions than longer, more deliberate consideration of the options. Further evidence for the benefits of intuitive consideration come from Halberstadt and Levine (1999), who used a framework of Wilson and Schooler (1991) that distinguishes between intuitive and "reflective" (deliberate) processes. Halberstadt and Levine asked self-described basketball experts before actual basketball games to predict the outcome. Half of the spectators were asked to analyze and list reasons for their predictions, whereas the other half were instructed not to analyze their reason but predict intuitively. The results indicate that deliberate reasoning results in fewer correct predictions (see also Plessner & Czenna, chap. 15, this volume).

Finally, evidence for intuitive and deliberative decision making is quite marginal in the last two stages of the protocol (initiation and evaluation). For instance, in ice hockey defensive tactics, both the initiation of eye fixations to important parts of the ice and the resulting defense movements are fast and intuitive by elite players but slower and more deliberative by non-elite players (Martell & Vickers, 2004). Furthermore, there is some evidence that giving batters in baseball minimal feedback for evaluation of their decisions enhances batting skills in transfer and retention; however, full feedback for decision evaluation enhances batting skills during acquisition (Vickers, Livingston, Umeris-Bohnert, & Holden, 1999).

Both intuitive and deliberate processes seem to be used to differing degrees in the various stages of the decision-making process in sports. It is important to consider what factors might determine whether any given situation will be processed more deliberately or more intuitively. We propose that the learning style of the decision maker is a key factor and therefore turn now to an introduction of learning styles in sports.

IMPLICIT AND EXPLICIT LEARNING STYLES

A very common distinction in learning is the level of how much explicit information is given to the learner (i.e., implicit vs. explicit learning dimension; see Stadler & Frensch, 1998, for an overview). The concepts of implicit and explicit learning may be best explained by looking at the learning situation itself. Situations in which actions are incidental in nature engender implicit learning, whereas situations in which actions are intentional in nature engender explicit learning.

Incidental learning (Perrig, 1996; Thorndike & Rock, 1934, p. 1) is learning in a situation without the intention to learn or without explicit knowledge about the underlying rule structure of the situation. For instance, in language comprehension and production, native speakers learn through immersion, naturally picking up cues and proper syntax, grammar, semantics, and so forth. In contrast, learning a language from foreign language textbooks or courses often results in more explicit study of linguistic structures, rules, and exceptions.

In sports, tactical decisions learned through playing "pick-up games" may result in good but nonverbalizable individual decisions. For example, the acquisition of if–then rules, whereby a learner performs in specific situations (if) with specific actions (then), relies mainly on implicit learning (McPherson & Thomas, 1989). Yet there also exists the possibility of explicit learning of rules and strategies. If a player is introduced to an attack situation by a coach using a blackboard demonstration and skill-like training, repeating the same movement in one context, then the player will likely produce verbalizable knowledge of these rules and rely more on explicit learning.

Implicit and explicit learning are generally still treated as dichotomous even though both can occur for any one decision. However, recently the adoption of a continuum and interactions between these learning styles has become more prominent (Rossetti & Revonsuo, 2000; Sun, Slusarz, & Terry, 2005). We, too, advocate the viewpoint that these two learning styles, much like intuitive and deliberative processing in the previous section, exist on a graded continuum. Therefore, as in the previous section, we examine ordinal relations (e.g., more implicit) within the framework of our decision protocol.

Implicit and Explicit Learning in the Decision Protocol

Implicit and explicit learning processes can be mapped to a continuum describing the nature of feedback (cf. Hogarth, chap. 6, this volume). For instance, complete lack of instruction about task goals, cue importance, cue utilization, and ideal performance would be characteristic of feedback fostering completely implicit learning. In contrast, extensive training in the desirable outcomes of a task as well as what cues to use and how to use them in achieving the outcome describe explicit learning. In reality, many situations may provide a moderate degree of feedback. This may be in the form of only some explicit instruction (e.g., which cues to use but not how to integrate them) or explicit feedback only some of the time (e.g., partial reinforcement). We explore exactly where these forms of feedback occur in—and how they subsequently influence—the decision protocol.

Distinctions between implicit and explicit learning play a key role in the first two stages of the decision protocol. First, a decision situation may be presented in a manner that highlights either an implicit or explicit goal or knowledge structure. Performance on objectively identical experimental tasks can vary greatly depending on the domain frame, the instructional set (Reber, 1967), or "cover story" (Ceci & Liker, 1986). For example, even if implicit, nonverbalizable rules are successful in one situation, such as handicapping horse races, these may not transfer to more abstract situations that rely on explicit application of the same rules (Barnett & Ceci, 2002).

Second, the type of learning in a task can affect the identification stage of subsequent encounters. We restrict ourselves here to just a couple illustrative examples of identification processes—goal identification and identification of relevant information. In determining the appropriate goal(s) in a situation, explicit learning provides specific, relatively stable goals in well-defined tasks. In contrast, purely implicit learning involves tasks that are more ill defined, without precise goals or performance metrics. Explicit learning, in many cases, includes detailed and specific tenets for information search and importance—for example, first determine if the defense is zone or man to man, then count the number of linebackers, and so on. Information handling is not precisely governed when implicit learning is involved, but rather a quarterback perhaps scans the downfield defense and notices something that "sticks out" such as single coverage on a star receiver.

The distinction of implicit and explicit generation and consideration of options is widely present in sports. For instance, in the last 20 or so years, a number of sports associations have developed handbooks to describe how to verbalize the kind of options that should be generated and considered in a specific situation. These so called situation-method references are still used in different sports such as golf, softball, tennis, badminton, and many more (Griffin, Mitchell, & Oslin, 1997). We believe that implicit or explicit selection and initiation is mainly influenced by the preceding stages, although relevant empirical evidence is quite scarce.

The role of learning is manifest most overtly in the seventh stage of the decision-making protocol. Specifically, learning involves evaluation of the decision outcome and incorporation of feedback for adapting future behavior. That is, learning describes how the evaluation of previous decisions affects (primarily) identification and consideration in subsequent decisions. Feedback itself can be characterized as more implicit or more explicit. If successful performance is clearly defined and/or rewarded, it is possible to distinguish the behavior giving rise to this performance in an explicit manner. If, on the other hand, performance is more difficult to assess, then reinforcement of the causal behaviors is more subtle or implicit.

Evidence for Implicit and Explicit Learning in Sports

Whereas the implicit versus explicit learning distinction is well known in cognitive psychology, this distinction has been rarely used in sports psychology (see Masters, 2000; McMorris, 1998; and Raab, 2003, for exceptions). Furthermore, the advantage of one learning style over the other in sports decision making (see Raab, 2003, for an overview) has rarely been empirically investigated. We briefly review research from sports psychology that supports our theoretical discussion of the influence of learning style including work that compares performance between learning styles.

The influence of implicit and explicit learning on the presentation and identification in sports tasks was discussed recently (Raab, 2007) in a review indicating that the amount and kind of instruction as well as the organization of training situations lead to different (re)presentations of tactical knowledge and amount of transferability between different situations. For instance, the instruction of the coach or the situational characteristics of training determine the learning style of if–then rules for mapping situational factors to choices. Furthermore, different instruction techniques influence the identification of constraints and goals, which in turn affect transfer of this tactical knowledge across sports or situations. Unfortunately, influences of learning styles on generation are not empirically investigated in sports to the best of our knowledge.

The consideration and selection processes are also impacted by learning style. In a series of experiments (Raab, 2003), novices were trained either implicitly (observational training) or explicitly (if–then rules) to learn tactical decisions in sports situations of varying complexity. Directly after training and 4 weeks later, they were required to make allocation decisions in a retention test. The results suggest that implicit learning of tactical situations results in nonverbalizable, intuitive decision making—when implicit learners were asked to recall or recognize the rules underlying the situations, they were unable to do so. When prompted or required to learn implicitly, gleaning situation structure and responding correctly are often naturally salient, and explicit information interferes with this automatic encoding. This conjecture is also supported by differences in performance, as measured by choice quality and decision time, based on learning condition.

In terms of performance, implicit learners outperformed explicit learners in low-complexity situations (manipulated by perceptual similarity or the number of if–then rules). However, in highly complex situations, explicit learners surpassed implicit learners and benefitted from instructions to focus on specific "information-rich" elements of the situation. This basic finding was replicated in different sports such as basketball, handball, and volleyball (Raab, 2003)—all sports in which allocation decisions had to be made quickly.

The initiation and evaluation processes of movements are influenced by implicit and explicit learning styles as well. For instance, initiation of movements are mainly implicit by default, and research of this initiation process has been reviewed in sports quite often (see Jackson & Farrow, 2005, for a recent overview). Self-evaluation based on explicit learning is present in sports concepts such as teaching games for understanding (Griffin et al., 1997) in which athletes are asked after their movements to evaluate and explain their choices. Contrary self-evaluation is also implicitly learned through active comparisons of the anticipated consequences and the real consequences of an intended movement. These comparisons can be learned implicitly and need not be verbalized by the athlete (Hoffmann, 1995).

Taken together, the results we have presented so far have strong implications for the relationship between (implicit–explicit) learning style and (intuitive–deliberate) processing. Specifically, the results of Raab's (2003) study suggest a disposition for more intuitive processing in implicitly learned situations as evidenced by dependent measures (e.g., response time) and self-report. Motivated by the state of current research, we turn now to a formal elaboration of the relationship between learning style and intuitive/deliberative processing. To anticipate our main hypothesis, we believe there is a strong coupling between implicit (explicit) learning, and intuitive (deliberate) decision-making processes.

SYNTHESIS OF LEARNING AND PROCESSING STYLES IN DECISION MAKING

In the previous two sections, we localized within the decision protocol of Orasanu and Connolly (1993) (a) the source of distinction between intuitive and deliberate decision making and (b) the differential effects of implicit and explicit learning. In this principal section, we tie these points together to make general propositions about the relation between learning and processing styles in decision making (Figure 8.1).

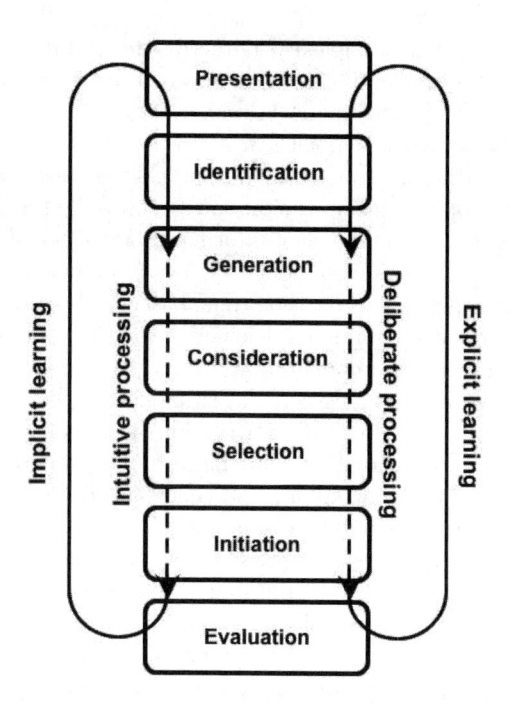

FIGURE 8.1 Simple model relating learning and processing styles within a general theoretical decision-making protocol. Learning styles are solid lines, and decision-making processes are dashed lines. Note that although intuitive (deliberative) processes are shown as strictly tied to implicit (explicit) learning, this is a modal tendency rather than a rule.

Figure 8.1 demonstrates the simple relationship between learning style (solid lines) and decision-making processes (dashed lines) within the protocol we introduced in this chapter. Note that Figure 8.1 has been simplified in that intuitive processes are tied to implicit learning and deliberative processes are tied to explicit learning. However, we are aware that intuition may not be only a result of implicit learning but can be also learned explicitly and by experience, becomes automatic. Furthermore, we reiterate that we adopt the viewpoint that both learning and processing style exist on continua rather than as discrete types (although Figure 8.1 is simplified in this respect as well). We detail the relationship between learning and processing style and across decision-making stages.

First, we propose that learning style exerts the strongest influence on the presentation and identification stages, as we discussed earlier; this is illustrated by the solid lines traversing these stages in Figure 8.1. For example, explicit learning is more likely to include direct instruction (presentation) and promote identification of particular goals or attributes. In contrast, implicit learning by definition does not include formal instruction and relies on the decision maker to identify appropriate task-relevant information, constraints, goals, and so forth.

Second, based on the presentation and identification characteristics in conjunction with the learning history, subsequent processing proceeds either more intuitively or more deliberately (dashed lines in Fig. 8.1). Assume that a decision agent is faced with a task on numerous occasions. Sometimes task features provide the means for executing explicit strategies, but otherwise behavior is more "trial and error." The former results in explicit learning of the appropriate associations (which options to consider and how to do so), whereas the latter results in subjective updating of which options are appropriate. That is, implicit learning (and its associated task features) is more likely to produce intuitive decisions, whereas explicit learning characteristics will tend to initiate deliberate decision making.

In cases in which a strategy is explicitly learned and validated through feedback evaluation, those options conforming to the explicit rule are deliberately retrieved (generated). Continued application of the prescribed rule dictates subsequent deliberate consideration. In contrast, when implicit learning is necessary, option generation is less precise because it is based on variable reinforcement strengthened only through successful experience. Then, there also exists no rule for formally considering the generated options, and intuition prevails (e.g., perhaps in the form of some inherently favored heuristic). The selection and initiation of options is then influenced by the processing of the previous stages.

Finally, feedback (evaluation) is the criterion primarily used to classify learning as implicit or explicit; this is shown by solid lines at the bottom of Figure 8.1. In other words, it is the nature of feedback that we use as an operational definition for learning style. This in turn determines the corresponding features of task presentation and identification that begin the decision protocol anew.

Consider the following concrete example of an attack situation in sports. In hopes that a coach's players will adopt a particular strategy, the coach uses a blackboard to diagram an upcoming play. The coach then describes the intended outcome of the play (e.g., an uncontested shot) and identifies which members of the opposing team should be taken most seriously. These support a subset of distinct strategies (e.g., sequences of ball movements) the coach approves, depending on the physical position of the key defenders. The players are told which options are better under which circumstances and what criteria to use in deciding whether to select an action (e.g., defender distances). During an ensuing time-out, the coach discusses with his players their performance to assist in future use of the same play.

In the preceding example, the coach was hoping for explicit learning of a deliberate decision schema, so the coach presented the problem formally on a blackboard. The coach identified the important information and the goal of the situation as well as how to use this information. The players, as a result, were afforded the ability to use deliberate processes during the play: first, to generate a specific subset of successful actions; then, to use a rule about defender distances in considering which action to perform; then, to select the appropriate option and to initiate it. The feedback from the coach during the time-out allows players to evaluate their performance and allows the coach to tailor instruction in future instances based on the players' errors (or lack thereof).

It is important that we stress a few qualifications about our model as shown in Figure 8.1. First, we maintain that processing occurs independently of learning style but suggest that there is a high degree of correlation between them. That is, although they are distinguished by line type, there are tendencies to see the cycles indicated that pair one type of processing and learning. However, we do not suggest that behavior proceeds deterministically according to our depiction. There are certainly cases in which more implicit learning can give rise to deliberate processes and vice versa. For example, over time, a strategy that is acquired through explicit learning—such as the coach's diagrammed play we discussed previously—may become automatic as a result of continued use that then elicits more intuitive processing; or behavior learned implicitly may be verbalizable as an explicit strategy by think-aloud protocols and therefore promotes deliberative processing. Keep in mind also that the concepts of deliberate and intuitive processing are poles of a continuum, not discrete operating modes.

Situational factors, although not shown in the model, are also of vital importance in decision making. The situation or environment influences the exogenous characteristics such as the presentation (e.g., instruction, format, etc.), identification (e.g., attention, importance weighting, etc.), and feedback (e.g., correct–incorrect) that affect the endogenous stages of generation and consideration. It remains to be seen the extent to which these situational factors correlate to each learning type. That is, as we discussed earlier, certain task features would certainly be more conducive to each learning style. This presents a challenge, however, in determining the unique (independent) effects of situational factors that are not mediated by the role of learning style.

CONCLUSIONS AND FUTURE DIRECTIONS

We merged two lines of research: one favoring the distinction between intuitive and deliberate decisions and the other contrasting implicit and explicit learning of decision making. The benefit of this simple framework is to formally define the coupling of implicit learning to intuitive decision making and of explicit learning to deliberate decision making. Furthermore, we have couched this model within specific stages of the decision-making process. Each of these key advances is open to future empirical investigation.

Note that we do not claim that either type of learning or processing is globally superior; rather, depending on the situation and/or the individual, one way of deciding or using experiences may result in better choices than another. Based on the findings cited herein, for example, it seems that implicit learning may help in less complex situations and explicit learning in more complex situations. Furthermore, intuitive decisions may result in good decisions in experts but not necessarily in novices because they lack representative sampling due to their relative paucity of experience. The wide variety of task/context effects and individual differences that interact with learning style and intuitive–deliberative processing to affect performance should benefit from future research; as we see it, many key questions remain. What are the situations and individual differences that determine whether intuitive or deliberative processing may be more successful? To what extent is implicit learning the basis of intuitive processing?

Finally, theoretical and practical implications can be derived from our framework. Theoretically, implicitly learned intuitive decisions reflect an opposition to rational models of decision making that claim that more information and careful deliberation reign supreme. However, we do not know exactly what mechanisms drive the implicit acquisition of structure from the environment that helps to discover principles and develop strategies for improving decision techniques. Practically, it is useful to develop decision training programs in sports as well as in other contexts that appreciate when intuitive versus deliberate thinking helps to make good decisions (Hogarth, chap. 6, this volume; Klein, 2003; Raab, 2003). A recent review of training programs revealed that these can be placed along the implicit–explicit learning continuum (Raab, 2007). Furthermore, some training programs widely used in school and club settings in Canada, France, Germany, the United Kingdom, and the United States of America promote a sport-specific perspective (i.e., becoming an expert in soccer requires only soccer training). Other approaches endorse a general perspective that a wide experience in different sports and training of abilities will transfer later to specific performance as well. We do not know yet how much the dimensions of learning style and specificity influence the effectiveness of intuitive and deliberative decision making in sports. However, current state of the art suggests that if most situations in the target sport reveal high need for fast decisions, then intuitive processes may provide the desired quickness and (especially through experience) accuracy.

REFERENCES

Anderson, J. R. (1983). *The architecture of cognition.* Cambridge, MA: Harvard University Press.

Barnett, S. M., & Ceci, S. J. (2002). When and where do we apply what we learn?: A taxonomy for far transfer. *Psychological Bulletin, 128,* 612–637.

Ceci, S. J., & Liker, J. K. (1986). A day at the races: A study of IQ, expertise, and cognitive complexity. *Journal of Experimental Psychology: General, 115,* 255–266.

Chaiken, S., & Trope, Y. (Eds.). (1999). *Dual-process theories in social psychology.* New York: Guilford.

Gigerenzer, G., Todd, P., & The ABC Research Group. (Eds.). (1999). *Simple heuristics that make us smart.* New York: Oxford University Press.

Griffin, L. A., Mitchell, S. A., & Oslin, J. L. (1997). *Teaching sport concepts and skills: A tactical game approach.* Champaign, IL: Human Kinetics.

Halberstadt, J. B., & Levine, G. M. (1999). Effects of reasons analysis on the accuracy of predicting basketball games. *Journal of Applied Social Psychology, 29,* 517–530.

Hammond, K. R. (1996). *Human judgment and social policy.* Oxford, England: Oxford University Press.

Hoffmann, J. (1995). Der implizite Erwerb von Handlungswissen [Implicit acquisition of action knowledge]. *Sportpsychologie, 2,* 56–66.

Hogarth, R. M. (2001). *Educating intuition.* Chicago: Chicago University Press.

Jackson, R. C., & Farrow, D. (2005). Implicit perceptual training: How, when, and why? *Human Movement Science, 24,* 308–325.

Johnson, J., & Raab, M. (2003). Take the first: Option generation and resulting choices. *Organizational Behavior and Human Decision Processes, 91,* 215–229.

Kahneman, D., & Frederick, S. (2002). Representativeness revisited: Attribute substitution in intuitive judgment. In T. Gilovich, D. Griffin, & D. Kahneman (Eds.), *Heuristics and biases. The psychology of intuitive judgment* (pp. 49–81). Cambridge, England: Cambridge University Press.

Klein, G. (2003). *Intuition at work: Why developing your gut instincts will make you better at what you do.* New York: Doubleday.

Klein, G., Wolf, S., Militello, L., & Zsambok, C. (1995). Characteristics of skilled option generation in chess. *Organizational Behavior and Human Decision Processes, 62*, 63–69.

Koehler, D.J. & Harvey, N. (Eds.). (2004). *Blackwell handbook of judgment and decision making.* Malden, MA: Blackwell.

Lieberman, M. D. (2000). Intuition: A social cognitive neuroscience approach. *Psychological Bulletin, 126,* 109–137.

Martell, S. G., & Vickers, J. N. (2004). Gaze characteristics of elite and near-elite athletes in ice hockey defensive tactics. *Human Movement Science, 22,* 689–712.

Masters, R. S. W. (2000). Theoretical aspects of implicit learning in sports. *International Journal of Sport Psychology, 31,* 530–541.

McMorris, T. (1998). Teaching games for understanding: Its contributions to the knowledge of skill acquisition from a motor learning perspective. *European Journal of Physical Education, 3,* 65–74.

McPherson, S. L., & Thomas, J. R. (1989). Relation of knowledge and performance in boys' tennis: Age and expertise. *Journal of Experimental Child Psychology, 48,* 190–211.

Orasanu, J., & Connolly, T. (1993). The reinvention of decision-making. In G. Klein, R. Orasanu, R. Calderwood, & C. Zsambok (Eds.), *Decision-making in action: Models and methods* (pp. 3–20). Norwood, NJ: Ablex.

Perrig, W. J. (1996). Implizites Lernen [Implicit learning]. In J. Hoffmann & W. Kintsch (Eds.), *Lernen* (pp. 203–234). Göttingen, Germany: Hogrefe.

Raab, M. (2003). Decision making in sports: Implicit and explicit learning is affected by complexity of situation. *International Journal of Sport and Exercise Psychology, 1,* 310–337.

Raab, M. (2007). Think SMART, not hard—A review of teaching decision making in sports from an ecological rationality perspective. *Journal of Physical Education and Sport Pedagogy, 12,* 1–18.

Reber, A. S. (1967). Implicit learning of artificial grammars. *Journal of Verbal Learning and Verbal Behavior, 6,* 855–863.

Rossetti, Y., & Revonsuo, A. (Eds.). (2000). *Beyond dissociation: Interaction between dissociated implicit and explicit processing.* Amsterdam: Benjamins.

Schönpflug, W. (1994). Intuition–Alltagsphänomen, Spitzenleistung oder Gottesgabe? [Intuition—Everyday phenomena, peak performance, or God's gift?]. *Psychologie und Sport, 8,* 67–77.

Shiffrin, R. M., & Schneider, W. (1977). Controlled and automatic human information processing: 1. Detection, search, and attention. *Psychological Review, 84,* 1–66.

Sloman, S. A. (2002). Two systems of reasoning. In T. Gilovich, D. Griffin, & D. Kahneman (Eds.), *Heuristics and biases: The psychology of intuitive judgment* (pp. 379–397). Cambridge, England: Cambridge University Press.

Smeeton, N. J., Williams, A. M., Hodges, N. J., & Ward, P. (2005). The relative effectiveness of various instructional approaches in developing anticipation skill. *Journal of Experimental Psychology: Applied, 11,* 98–110.

Stadler, M. A., & Frensch, P. A. (Eds.). (1998). *Handbook of implicit learning.* Thousand Oaks, CA: Sage.

Strack, F. (1999). Beyond dual-process models: Toward a flexible regulation system. *Psychological Inquiry, 10,* 166–169.

Sun, R., Slusarz, P., & Terry, C. (2005). The interaction of the explicit and the implicit in skill learning: A dual-process approach. *Psychological Review, 112,* 159–192.

Thorndike, E. L., & Rock, R. T., Jr. (1934). Learning without awareness of what is being learned or intent to learn it. *Journal of Experimental Psychology, 17,* 1–19.

Tversky, A., & Kahneman, D. (1981). The framing of decisions and the psychology of choice. *Science, 211,* 453–458.

Vickers, J. N., Livingston, L. F., Umeris-Bohnert, S., & Holden, D. (1999). Decision training: The effects of complex instruction, variable practice and reduced delayed feedback on the acquisition and transfer of a motor skill. *Journal of Sports Sciences, 17,* 357–367.

Wilson, T. D., & Schooler, J. W. (1991). Thinking too much: Introspection can reduce the quality of preferences and decisions. *Journal of Personality and Social Psychology, 60,* 181–192.

＃ 9

Base Rates
How to Make the Intuitive Mind Appreciate or Neglect Them

IDO EREV, DVORIT SHIMONOWITCH, and AMOS SCHURR
Israel Institute of Technology

RALPH HERTWIG
University of Basel

INTRODUCTION

*I*n his book *Bully for Brontosaurus: Reflections in Natural History*, the late Harvard paleontologist Gould (1992) concluded that "our minds are not built (for whatever reason) to work by the rules of probability" (p. 469). Coming from a scientist whose thinking was deeply rooted in evolutionary theorizing, this proclamation was, well, unexpected. It implies nothing less than that our cognitive machinery is somehow out of synchrony with the probabilistic structure of the world. Gould's epiphany was inspired by the findings of one of the most influential, recent research programs in cognitive psychology: the heuristics-and-biases program (e.g., Kahneman, Slovic, & Tversky, 1982). According to this program, when dealing with the twilight of uncertainty, people rely on a limited number of simplifying heuristics rather than more formal and computationally and informationally more extensive algorithmic processing. The heuristics are regarded as typically yielding accurate judgments but also giving rise to systematic errors. Recently, the heuristics, often regarded as "general purpose heuristics—availability, representativeness, and anchoring and adjustment" (Gilovich, Griffin, & Kahneman, 2002, p. xv), have been identified with a mental system akin to "intuition" (see Epstein, chap. 2, this volume; Epstein, 1994; Stanovich & West, 2000).

One key domain in which intuitive judgment—embodied in terms of simple, general-purpose heuristics—departs from what is taken to be good judgment is belief updating. When updating their beliefs, good judges should respect Bayes's theorem. It defines how one should integrate prior probability, summarizing what one knew about the problem, with independent specific evidence.[1] Because of their reliance on simple heuristics such as representativeness, people, according to Kahneman and Tversky (1973), fail to appreciate the relevance of prior probability in the presence of specific evidence. This failure, the so-called base-rate fallacy, is "perhaps one of the most significant departures of intuition from the normative theory of prediction" (Kahneman & Tversky, 1973, p. 242).

For many years, the "base-rate fallacy, with its distinctive name and arsenal of catchy and counterintuitive illustrations . . . had a celebrity status in the literature" (Koehler, 1996, p. 1); and one influential review confidently concluded, "The genuineness, the robustness, and the generality of the base-rate fallacy are matters of established fact" (Bar-Hillel, 1980, p. 215). In the 1990s, however, a controversial debate over whether people are able to reason in a Bayesian way (see Koehler, 1996) and on the robustness and interpretation of systematic errors in probabilistic reasoning more generally (e.g., Gigerenzer, 1996; Kahneman & Tversky, 1996) arose. Interestingly, this debate has taken little note of the fact that other faculties of the human mind, in particular, human perception and memory, are assumed to effectively approximate optimal statistical inference, thus correctly combining new data with a veridical probabilistic mental model of the environment (e.g., Anderson & Milson, 1989; Anderson & Schooler, 1991; Freeman, 1994; Knill & Richards, 1996; Körding & Wolpert, 2004; Simoncelli & Olshausen, 2001). Only recently, Griffiths and Tenenbaum (2006) highlighted this striking discrepancy: intuitive cognitive judgments under uncertainty that are being portrayed as the result of error-prone heuristics, insensitive to prior probabilities, versus the near optimality of other human capacities.

Our goal in this chapter is to help to reconcile these conflicting conclusions. We begin by providing an illustration of some representative yet conflicting findings from the psychology of intuitive judgment and of visual cognition. Then, we turn to a potential way of reconciling them.

INTUITIVE AND VISUAL COGNITION: CONCURRENT BASE-RATE NEGLECT AND BASE-RATE SENSITIVITY

Tversky and Kahneman (1974) reported a classic demonstration of neglect of base-rate information in a probabilistic reasoning task, the "engineer-lawyer problem." Participants were told that a panel of psychologists had written personality descriptions

---

[1] Bayes's theorem is a rule for revising a prior probability, or base rate (as it is often called) into a posterior probability after new data have been observed. According to the theorem, the posterior probability is: $p(H_1|D) = p(H_1)\, p(D|H_1)/p(D)$. In odds form, Bayes's theorem tells one how much confidence people should retain in the relative validity of two hypotheses once they learn outcome D has occurred.

of 30 engineers and 70 lawyers based on the results of personal interviews and personality tests. Then they learned that five descriptions had been chosen at random from this pool. After reading these descriptions, participants assessed the probability that each of the persons described was an engineer (low base-rate condition: 30% engineers). Other participants were given the same descriptions and task but with 70 engineers and 30 lawyers (high base-rate condition: 70% engineers).

People's sensitivity to these base rates, or the lack thereof, can best be illustrated with one of the personality descriptions that was constructed to be totally uninformative with regard to the person's profession. It read as follows:

> Dick is a 30-year-old man. He is married with no children. A man of high ability and motivation, he promises to be quite successful in his field. He is well liked by his colleagues.

With the provision of this worthless piece of evidence, Bayes's theorem predicts that the posterior probabilities in the low and high base-rate conditions should map onto the respective base rates. Instead, the base-rate information had a weak (although significant) effect on participants' judgments. The probability that Dick was a lawyer was estimated to be 50% and 55% for the low and high base-rate conditions, respectively. Kahneman and Tversky (1973) concluded "When worthless specific evidence is given, prior probabilities are ignored" (p. 242). Kahneman and Tversky (1973) termed this behavior *base-rate neglect*.[2]

In a study of visual cognition, Simons and Levin (1997) provided an ingenious demonstration that people behave as though they strongly relied on base-rate information. Simons and Levin's participants saw a video showing an experimenter who approaches a pedestrian to ask for directions. While the pedestrian is providing directions, two workers carrying a door rudely pass between the experimenter and the pedestrian. During this brief interruption, a different person replaces the original experimenter. Even though the two people look quite different and have distinctly different voices, about 50% of the participants, watching the video, failed to notice that the person asking the question has changed. One way to interpret this "blindness to change" is that many people place too much faith in the base rates, here the base rate of the interlocutor permanence (i.e., typically, a person with whom one is conversing is not suddenly replaced with another).[3]

---

[2] Subsequent studies have demonstrated that certain variables can decrease people's tendency to neglect base-rate information. For example, base rate is less likely to be ignored when it is perceived to be causally relevant (Ajzen, 1977; Tversky & Kahneman, 1982), when participants themselves performed and observed the random sampling of information (e.g., the personality description; Gigerenzer, Hell, & Blank, 1988; Nisbett & Ross, 1980), and when it is learned from experience (Betsch, Biel, Eddelbüttel, & Mock, 1998). Nevertheless, almost all studies that have focused on Dick-like problems appear to support the view of insufficient use of base-rate information in intuitive judgment. Indeed, some researchers (notably Cohen, 1981) have actually criticized this line of research and have said that it shows such trivial results that base rate should be neglected in these situations.

[3] Additional illustrations of the effect of base rates and prior probabilities in visual cognition can be found in Biederman, Mezzanotte, and Rabinowitz (1982); Eisenberg and Becker (1982); Foss (1969); Frost and Katz (1989); Grainger and Segui (1990); and Howes (1957).

THE IMPACT OF MERE PRESENTATION

To reconcile the conflicting results and conclusions drawn in research on probabilistic reasoning and visual cognition, respectively, we focus on one distinct property of the experimental settings that may cause these opposite behaviors, namely, the stipulation of possible responses. For illustration, we return to the engineer-lawyer problem. In that study (Tversky & Kahneman, 1974), participants were explicitly told that the 30-year-old Dick "was either a lawyer or an engineer." In the blindness-to-change study (Simons & Levin, 1997), in contrast, people were not told that the questioner may or may not have changed. Rather, people's awareness of the change or lack thereof was inferred from their answers to other questions. This difference matters. Erev, Leybman, and Hertwig (2005) suggested that the mere presentation of possible responses involving events or event categories increases the impact of a priori less likely categories.

The effect of mere presentation can be explained in terms of a dilemma that any person considering base rates faces. On which of the often-infinite possible categories and associated base should one focus? Take as an example the blindness-to-change study (Simons & Levin, 1997). At any given moment, the environment could change or be changed in an infinite number of ways. Keeping track of and monitoring these countless ways in which the world could change is impossible for any real person; real people navigate the world under the constraints of limited time, knowledge, and computational capacities (see Gigerenzer, Todd, & the ABC Research Group, 1999; Simon, 1991). Thus, real people cannot help but ignore the infinite potential for change and instead bet on a rather stable world or bet on changes that have a high a priori likelihood (or a high base rate of occurrence). There are occasions, however, when these defaults need to be revised. One cue that is likely to prompt revision is the explicit presentation of a priori unlikely events or event categories. In other words, unlikely categories—such as the change of the interlocutor during a conversation—are more likely to be considered when their possible occurrence is explicitly invoked. People may be even more inclined to take a priori unlikely events into account if the unlikely categories have been explicitly called on by a third party: a party who is assumed to obey a basic principle of communication, namely, cooperativeness, and subordinate maxims such as that of relevance (Grice, 1975; Hilton, 1995). Explicitly bringing into play a rare category—as the sender of a message (e.g., an experimenter)—is likely to prompt the receivers to treat this category as more probable than they would do otherwise.

In what follows, we describe three intentionally simple studies that demonstrate the impact of merely mentioning response categories on the appreciation or lack thereof of base rates.

THE EFFECT OF MERE PRESENTATION IN PERCEPTUAL IDENTIFICATION

The first demonstration (Study 1) involves a visual stimulus used in a classic visual cognition experiment. It involves a variant of the "B 13" example used by Bruner and Minturn (1955; and see Kahneman, 2003). Our question is the following: Will

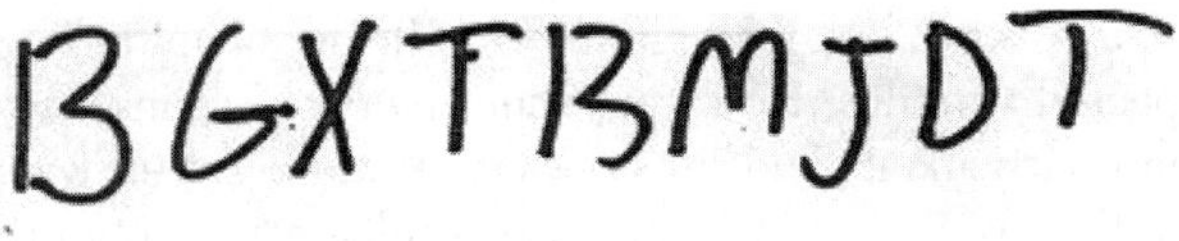

B GX T B M J D T

FIGURE 9.1 Stimulus used in Study 1.

the explicit presentation of two possible responses diminish the effect of prior knowledge (of relevant base rates)?

To find an answer, we employed a between-subject design with two experimental conditions. Participants in the memory and decision condition saw a series of stimuli, and we asked them to memorize it. We also asked them to decide whether the stimulus in the center of the series—see Figure 9.1—represented the letter "B" or the number "13." Subsequently, they reconstructed the series. Participants in the memory condition encountered the same series but were asked merely to memorize and then reconstruct it. For our purposes, we analyzed only the interpretation of the ambiguous symbol that could be read to be either a letter or a number. The memory condition enabled us to examine the interpretation of this symbol without the experimenter having invoked the number.

One class of 75 industrial engineering and economics students from the Technion, Israel, participated in the experiment. The average age was 25, and about 50% of the participants were males. We assigned students on the right side of the classroom ($n = 41$) to the memory condition, and we assigned students on the left side ($n = 34$) to the memory and decision condition. Students in the memory and decision condition read the following instructions:

> A list of stimuli is about to be presented in front of you for 10 seconds. During the presentation, your task is to learn the list by heart (and to decide whether the stimulus in the center is a "B" or a "13"). You will then be asked to remember the list from memory.

The instructions in the memory condition were identical, except for the omission of the decision instruction (the phrase enclosed in parentheses).

How did the suggestion of an unlikely event change people's judgment? Of the 41 students in the memory condition, only 4 remembered having seen a 13; 28 remembered having seen a B, and 9 did not remember it at all. In contrast, in the memory and decision condition, 14 of the 34 students reported that they saw a 13, 18 thought that the symbol represented a B, and 2 failed to remember it.

Excluding the students who did not remember the critical stimulus, the proportion who believed they had seen a 13 was significantly higher ($z = 2.78, p \ll .01$) in the memory and decision condition (14/32 = 44%) than in the memory condition (4/32 = 12%).

These findings support the mere-presentation thesis. The likelihood of perceiving a two-digit number rather than a letter (13 vs. B) increases when the presence of a numeral is explicitly invoked via the possible response categories. As in a typical visual cognition study, the implicit choice in the memory condition was driven by participants' reasonable expectations that the somewhat ambiguous stimulus in the center of a series of letters is a letter as well: Here only 12% of participants saw the unexpected stimulus. However, when the two responses were presented side by side and participants had to choose explicitly between B and 13, almost half decided in favor of the unlikely stimulus—unlikely in light of the context. In other words, the request to consider two possible interpretations of an ambiguous symbol suffices to boost the likelihood of the unlikely interpretation.

THE EFFECT OF MERE PRESENTATION IN A CLASSIC DEMONSTRATION OF THE BASE-RATE NEGLECT

We designed the next demonstration (Study 2) to examine the robustness of the results found in Study 1 in the context of category membership judgments—the very context in which classic studies of base-rate neglect such as the engineer-lawyer study (Tversky & Kahneman, 1974) were conducted.

To be able to create naturalistic stimuli (Koehler, 1996), we conducted a pilot study in which we asked 14 randomly chosen Technion students to complete a short questionnaire (Figure 9.2). Students' answers yielded 14 personality descriptions.

Respondents, students of industrial engineering and economics, saw photocopies of the completed (handwritten) questionnaires, excluding the first question (i.e., faculty), and we asked them to decide in which faculty each of the students described was studying. We compared two response mode conditions in a between-subject design. We asked participants in the open condition ($n = 41$) to write down the name of the faculty they considered to be the right one. In the list condition ($n = 43$),

Faculty [major] _____

Favorite leisure activity _____

Favorite food _____

Travel abroad _____

Workplace _____ # of hours per week _____

Hobbies _____

The prettiest building in the country _____

Important technological invention _____

Self-description _____

FIGURE 9.2 The self-description questionnaire used in Study 2.

TABLE 9.1 Study 2: The Objective Statistics and Main Results. The left-hand columns present the categories (Technion's faculties), the population statistics and the sample statistics. The right-hand columns present the choice proportion and estimated base rates in the two conditions (Open and List).

	Objective data				People's judgments			
	Population		Sample		Response prop.		Subj. base rate	
Faculty	Freq.	Prop.	Freq.	Prop.	Open	List	Open	List
Material eng.	152	0.02	0	0.00	0.01	0.02	0.02	0.02
Biology	218	0.02	1	0.07	0.02	0.03	0.03	0.04
Education	222	0.02	0	0.00	0.01	0.03	0.03	0.03
Mathematics	256	0.03	1	0.07	0.01	0.04	0.04	0.04
Food eng.	257	0.03	0	0.00	0.03	0.03	0.04	0.04
Chemistry	270	0.03	1	0.07	0.02	0.02	0.04	0.04
Agricultural eng.	289	0.03	1	0.07	0.03	0.04	0.04	0.04
Chemical eng.	341	0.04	0	0.00	0.02	0.04	0.04	0.04
Physics	354	0.04	0	0.00	0.04	0.04	0.04	0.04
Aerospace eng.	524	0.06	1	0.07	0.03	0.05	0.04	0.04
Medicine	534	0.06	0	0.00	0.01	0.05	0.07	0.06
Architecture	655	0.07	2	0.14	0.09	0.08	0.06	0.07
Computer science	733	0.08	0	0.00	0.16	0.11	0.10	0.10
Civil eng.	1008	0.11	2	0.14	0.07	0.07	0.08	0.07
Mechanical eng.	1081	0.11	1	0.07	0.16	0.13	0.10	0.09
Industrial eng.	1150	0.12	2	0.14	0.20	0.14	0.10	0.11
Electrical eng.	1406	0.15	2	0.14	0.10	0.09	0.13	0.12

we presented participants with a list of the Technion's 17 faculties, and we asked them to indicate their judgment by marking the faculty considered to be the right one.[4] We told participants that their goal was to maximize the number of accurate responses. To encourage accuracy, a bonus of 5 Shekels ($1.70) for each correct response was promised to a participant who would be chosen at random. After concluding their judgments, all 84 participants received the same sheet on which we asked them to record their estimates of the base rates (proportions) of the Technion's 17 faculties.

How did the mere-presentation effect play out in this context previously shown to be conducive to base-rate neglect? The first five columns in Table 9.1 present the Technion's 17 faculties, the number of students enrolled in each faculty (in the relevant year), the proportion of students in each faculty from the total student population, and the frequency and proportion of the sample (the 14 students who

---

[4] Notice that in this setting, the implications of the mere-presentation hypothesis is identical to the list effect documented in Fischhoff, Slovic, and Lichtenstein (1978).

completed the self-description questionnaire) in each faculty. The last four columns present the main results: the proportion of the different responses (over the 14 descriptions) under the two experimental conditions and the average subjective base rate, respectively.

To measure the effect of base rates on students' responses, we transformed each faculty membership judgment into a quantitative response by relating it to the respective size of the faculty. For example, the response "biology" was coded as 218, the number of students enrolled at the biology faculty. The average of these numbers over the 14 responses was defined as the base-rate sensitivity (BRS) score. For example, if 7 responses involve a faculty with 600 students, and the other 7 responses involve a faculty with 1,000 students, the BRS score is (7/14)(600) + (7/14)(1,000) = 800. Thus, large BRS scores imply a tendency to select large, high base-rate faculties. The average score was 859 in the open condition but merely 754 in the list condition. The difference between the two conditions was highly significant, $t(82) = 4.33$, $p \ll .0001$.

A participant whose sensitivity to base rates could be described by the "probability matching" rule (see Birnbaum, 1983) was expected to have a BRS score in the range of 791 to 811. Thus, the results demonstrate that the actual sensitivity to base rates in the open condition exceeded that assuming a probability-matching strategy, $t(41) = 3.17$, $p \ll .003$. In the list condition, in contrast, people's sensitivity to base rates was lower than one would expect under a probability-matching strategy, $t(43) = -2.4$, $p \ll .02$. People's higher sensitivity in the open condition paid off: They were more accurate than students in the list condition, albeit that the difference in the average frequencies of accurate responses—3.1 in the open condition and 2.6 in the list condition—was only marginally significant, $t(82) = 1.6$, $p = .11$.

To examine whether participants may have rested their judgments on subjective base rates, which may not correspond exactly to the objective ones, we computed two correlations for each person. The first is the correlation between the frequencies of choices of the different faculties with the objective base rates. The second is the correlation between the choice frequencies with the assessed subjective base rates (i.e., the responses elicited in the second part of the study). The choice frequencies of the majority of the participants in both conditions correlated more strongly with the objective base rates than with the subjective ones. Across the two conditions, the proportion of participants whose choice frequencies were better predicted by the objective base rates (52/84) was significantly greater than .5 (sign test, $p \ll .015$).

The results of Study 2 demonstrate that explicitly presenting possible response categories—Technion's faculties—affected the (implicit) use of base rates. That is, the mere-presentation effect is not restricted to the interpretation of ambiguous visual stimuli. In a context in which the response categories were not explicitly presented but respondents themselves generated the category (faculty) most likely in their view, judgments proved to be tuned to base rates. Indeed, the impact of base rate was stronger than would be expected if participants had resorted to a probability-matching response strategy. In contrast, the effect of base rates waned when all 17 response categories were laid out in front of people, and they had to judge which was the most likely one. With such imposition of the categories, the effect of base rates was even smaller than expected assuming a probability-matching criterion. Indeed, these data do not even rule out the possibility that under these circumstances, people arrived at their judgments by neglecting base rates altogether.

HOW THE MERE-PRESENTATION EFFECT FOSTERS BAYESIAN REASONING

One interpretation of the results we obtained in Studies 1 and 2 suggests that the presentation of possible responses (or response categories) has pernicious effects on people's inferences. On this view, base-rate information impacts open answers appropriately, whereas the mere-presentation effect in "constrained" answers compromises the role of base rates on people's reasoning. According to a second interpretation, however, the mere-presentation effect simply attenuates the impact of base-rate information. Thus, in a situation in which people tend to overweight base rates, the mere-presentation effect can also foster appropriate inferences. In the final study (Study 3), we demonstrated this potential of the mere-presentation effect. We made use of a traditional children's riddle, which reads as follows:

> Danny broke his leg. When he got to the hospital the surgeon said: "I cannot operate on him. He is my son, although I am not his father." How can that be possible?

To appreciate how this riddle relates to the weighting of base-rate information, note that the vast majority of surgeons (at least in Israel at the time the study was run) are male. This riddle was popular because many people failed to see that the obvious answer is "the surgeon is Danny's mother." Thus, the difficulty of this riddle results from what can be described as a tendency to overweight base rates.[5]

A between-subject design included three experimental conditions and involved 71 industrial engineering students from the Technion. In the not-father condition, we presented 25 participants with the riddle as we described previously. A total of 16 participants in the not-mother condition read a version in which the words "not his father" were replaced with the words "not his mother." By comparing both conditions, one can investigate whether the failure to solve the riddle is consistent with the phenomenon of overweighting base rates. If so, one would expect a higher rate of correct (reasonable) responses in the not-mother condition than in the not-father condition. Finally, we presented 31 participants in the p[probability] (mother) condition with the standard riddle puzzle (as in the not-father condition), but we modified the question. We replaced the original question, "How can that be possible?," with the request to "Please assess the probability that the surgeon is Danny's mother."

---

[5] It can also be described as an example of stereotypical thinking and/or the usage of the representativeness heuristic. In this context, these terms have similar implications. See Beyth-Marom and Fischhoff (1983); Locksley, Borgida, Brekke, and Hepburn (1980); Locksley, Hepburn, and Ortiz (1982); and McCauley (1994).

TABLE 9.2 Frequencies of the Correct and Incorrect Answers in Study 3.

Condition	Task	Number of participants	Correct answers	Incorrect answers
Control	Explain how it can be possible	24	7	17
Not mother	Explain how it can be possible	16	16	0
p(mother)	Estimate the probability that the surgeon is the boy's mother	31	25 (19 estimates of 100%, and 6 estimates between 75% and 99%)	6

How did the mere-presentation effect play out in this context that had previously been shown? The main findings are presented in Table 9.2. Each single participant (100%) in the not-mother condition arrived at the plausible explanation that the surgeon is the boy's father. In contrast, in the not-father condition, merely 29% (7 out of 24) of participants arrived at the explanation that the surgeon is the boy's mother. Other participants gave creative explanations such as "bad relationship between father and son," "stepfather," "adopted child," "close emotional feelings," and "sperm donation." The difference in the proportions of insightful answers in the not-mother and not-father conditions, respectively, was significant, $t(38) = 6.08, p \ll .001$.

In the p(mother) condition, 19 (61%) out of 31 participants assessed the probability that the surgeon was the boy's mother as 1; an additional 6 students assessed the probability as greater than 0.75. Only 4 (12%) assessed the probability to be below 0.5. In a conservative comparison of the not-father condition and the p(mother) condition, we focused on the proportion of "Mother with certainty" responses (i.e., p(mother) = 1). Again, the difference (between 61% to 29%) was significant, $t(53) = 2.45, p \ll .01$.

To conclude, this simple demonstration shows that the mere-presentation effect can foster good reasoning by channeling people's attention. When the most reasonable answer happens to be the low base-rate category, the mere presentation of this category (e.g., by asking participants to estimate its probability) suffices to move the large majority of the participants toward it.

CONCLUSIONS

We conducted three simple studies that demonstrated the impact of merely mentioning response categories on the appreciation or lack thereof of base rates. The mere-presentation effect can help to explain why research on intuitive judgments under uncertainty and research on visual cognition arrived at opposite conclusions: insensitivity to prior probabilities and near-optimal statistical inferences in human perception and memory. When we asked our participants—without bringing into play a rare category or event—what they remembered, saw, or thought they saw proved sensitive to base rates. This sensitivity, however, seemingly disappeared when the experimenter explicitly invoked unlikely categories by framing the response categories accordingly.

More on the Psychology of the Mere-Presentation Effect

Objects continue to exist even when they are no longer visible. Becoming aware of this empirical regularity has been hailed as one key step infants take in their cognitive development. Based on observing his own children, Piaget (1936) concluded that "object permanence" was typically achieved at 8 to 9 months of age during the sensorimotor stage of cognitive development. Infants before this age—who do not have a clear sense of objects persisting when out of sight—would not grope for a teddy bear when suddenly the light went out. Of course, assuming the permanence of objects is not always correct. Sometimes objects stop existing when they stop being visible. Object permanence, however, is an adaptive assumption that renders navigating the world much simpler. Last, but not least, object permanence can be seen as a manifestation of the infant's (growing) sensitivity to base rates.

Mortal humans who operate under the constraints of, for instance, limited time, information, energy, and computational capacity need to make myriad adaptive and simplifying assumptions about the world. For instance, in responding to a question or a problem, nobody can search and consider all possible options (e.g., response, response categories, or solutions), regardless of their a priori probability. In fact, there may not even be an optimal point at which search for further options ought to be stopped. If so, reasoners may decide to efficiently invest their resources by searching and evaluating predominantly those responses and response categories that are a priori likely. This reasonable assumption, however, can be suspended through a speaker's mere presentation of unlikely responses and response categories. To communicate is to claim someone's attention and hence to imply that the information communicated is relevant (Sperber & Wilson, 1986). Consequently, the hearer is likely to interpret the mere presentation of an unlikely category or event as a suggestion that the speaker considers it to be more relevant than may be expected on the basis of its prior probability. If the speaker is cooperative and aims to minimize the joint cognitive costs, he or she will not call on categories that are utterly unlikely and thus irrelevant.

The mere-presentation effect is the logical consequence of a cooperative venture called communication. Of course, the mere-presentation effect will not necessarily result in reasonable inference. When the mere presentation of the complete set of response categories is devoid of any information regarding their prior probabilities—Study 2 is an instance of such a scenario—the mere presentation can stand in the way of good performance. Finally, the magnitude of the mere-presentation effect is likely to be subject to factors such as experience. When people face the same choice problem over and over again, they may quickly learn that the presentation of response categories does not convey any extra and relevant information (see Betsch, Biel, Eddelbüttel, & Mock, 1998; Fielder, Brinkmann, Betsch, & Wild, 2000; Yechiam, Erev, & Barron, 2005).

Base-Rate Neglect, Conversational Maxims, and Intuition

According to Kahneman (2003), the research that Tversky and Kahneman (1974) conducted was "guided by the idea that intuitive judgments occupy a position—perhaps corresponding to evolutionary history—between the automatic operations of perception and the deliberate operations of reasoning" (Kahneman, 2003, p. 450). In the terminology that permeates many of today's discussions of how the mind reasons, Kahneman (2003) located flawed statistical intuitions and the cognitive machinery that drives them, that is, heuristics, in the first of two types of cognitive processes, which Stanovich and West (2000) labeled *System 1* and *System 2*. The operations of System 1 are typically characterized as fast, automatic, effortless, associative, and difficult to modify. In contrast, the operations of System 2 are depicted as slower, serial, effortful, and deliberately controlled. System 2 is involved in all voluntary actions—including overt expressions of the intuitive judgments that originated in System 1. Consequently, erroneous intuitive judgment such as base-rate neglect involves failures of both systems: System 1, which generated the misstep in the first place, and System 2, which failed to detect and correct it.

The utility of this and similar dichotomies has been hotly debated (e.g., Gigerenzer & Regier, 1996; Sloman, 1996). Our goal was not to rehash this debate. Rather, we believe that our few simple studies have produced a couple of interesting insights beyond the System 1 versus System 2 dichotomy. First, whether or not people take base rate into account is not merely the function of the cognitive system. It is also a function of the social environment: here, the provision of responses and response categories and the acceptance of specific social norms that guide communication. Second, what appears as inconsistent behavior—sensitivity to base rates in the open condition of Study 1 and little sensitivity in the list condition—can result from the same underlying cognitive process. The inconsistency is shaped by the combination of a response environment and a social environment that—unless told otherwise—is assumed to be cooperative. Third, it follows that investigations of intuitive statistical processes and their outcomes, may they be errors or correct responses, stand to benefit from an analysis of the social environment in which people act (see also Fiedler & Kareev, chap. 10, this volume). Last but not least, to the degree that statistical intuitions are guided by the interaction of heuristics and social environments, intuitions can be influenced by redesigning the latter (e.g., suspending maxims of conversation or changing the framing of a response).

REFERENCES

Ajzen, I. (1977). Intuitive theories of events and effects of base rate information on prediction. *Journal of Personality and Social Psychology, 35,* 303–314.

Anderson, J. R., & Milson, R. (1989). Human memory: An adaptive perspective. *Psychological Review, 96,* 703–719.

Anderson, J. R., & Schooler, L. J. (1991). Reflections of the environment in memory. *Psychological Science, 2,* 396–408.

Bar-Hillel, M. (1980). The base-rate fallacy in probability judgments. *Acta Psychologica, 44,* 211–233.

Betsch, T., Biel, G. M., Eddelbüttel, C., & Mock, A. (1998). Natural sampling and base-rate neglect. *European Journal of Social Psychology 28*, 269–273.
Beyth-Marom, R., & Fischhoff, B. (1983). Diagnosticity and pseudodiagnosticity. *Journal of Personality and Social Psychology, 45*, 1185–1195.
Biederman, I., Mezzanotte, R. J., & Rabinowitz, J. C. (1982). Scene perception: Detecting and judging objects undergoing relational violations. *Cognitive Psychology, 14*, 143–177.
Birnbaum, M. H. (1983). Base rates in Bayesian inference: Signal detection analysis of the cab problem. *American Journal of Psychology, 96*, 85–94.
Bruner, J. S., & Minturn, A. L. (1955). Perceptual identification and perceptual organization. *Journal of General Psychology, 53*, 21–28.
Cohen, L. J. (1981). Can human irrationality be experimentally demonstrated? *Behavioral and Brain Sciences, 4*, 317–370.
Eisenberg, P., & Becker, C. (1982). Semantic context effects in visual word recognition, sentence processing and reading: Evidence for semantic strategies. *Journal of Experimental Psychology: Human Perception and Performance, 8*, 739–756.
Epstein, S. (1994). Integration of the cognitive and the psychodynamic unconscious. *American Psychologist, 49*, 709–724.
Erev, I., Leybman, I., & Hertwig, R. (2005). *Context, mere presentation and the impact of rare events.* Working paper, Technion, Haifa, Israel.
Fiedler, K., Brinkmann, B., Betsch, T., & Wild, B. (2000). A sampling approach to biases in conditional probability judgments: Beyond base rate neglect and statistical format. *Journal of Experimental Psychology: General, 129*, 399–418.
Fischhoff, B., Slovic, P., & Lichtenstein, S. (1978). Fault trees: Sensitivity of estimated failure probabilities to problem representations. *Journal of Experimental Psychology: Human Perception and Performance, 4*, 330–344.
Foss, D. (1969). Decision processes during sentence comprehension: Effects of lexical item difficulty and position upon decision times. *Journal of Verbal Learning and Verbal Behavior, 8*, 457–462.
Freeman, W. T. (1994). The generic viewpoint assumption in a framework for visual perception. *Nature, 368*, 542–545.
Frost, R., & Katz, L. (1989). Orthographic depth and the interaction of visual and auditory processing in word recognition. *Memory and Cognition, 17*, 302–310.
Gigerenzer, G. (1996). On narrow norms and vague heuristics: A reply to Kahneman and Tversky. *Psychological Review, 103*, 592–596.
Gigerenzer, G., Hell, W., & Blank, H. (1988). Presentation and content: The use of base rates as a continuous variable. *Journal of Experimental Psychology: Human Perception and Performance, 14*, 513–525.
Gigerenzer, G., & Regier, T. (1996). How do we tell an association from a rule? Comment on Sloman (1996). *Psychological Bulletin, 119*, 23–26.
Gigerenzer, G., Todd, P. M., & the ABC Research Group. (1999). *Simple heuristics that make us smart.* New York: Oxford University Press.
Gilovich, T., Griffin, D., & Kahneman, D. (2002). *Heuristics and biases: The psychology of intuitive judgment.* Cambridge, England: Cambridge University Press.
Gould, S. J. (1992). *Bully for brontosaurus: Reflections in natural history.* New York: Norton.
Grainger, J., & Segui, J. (1990). Neighborhood frequency effects in visual word recognition: A comparison of lexical and masked identification latencies. *Perception and Psychophysics, 47*, 191–198.
Grice, H. P. (1975). Logic and conversation. In P. Cole & J. L. Morgan (Eds.), *Syntax and semantics: Vol. 3. Speech acts* (pp. 41–58). New York: Academic.
Griffiths, T. L., & Tenenbaum, J. B. (2006). Optimal predictions in everyday cognition. *Psychological Science, 17*(9), 767–773.

Hilton, D. J. (1995). The social context of reasoning: Conversational inference and rational judgment. *Psychological Bulletin, 118*, 248–271.

Howes, D. (1957). On the relation between the intelligibility and frequency of occurrence of English words. *Journal of the Acoustical Society of America, 29*, 296–305.

Kahneman, D. (2003). Maps of bounded rationality: Psychology for behavioral economics. *American Economic Review, 93*, 1449–1475.

Kahneman, D., Slovic, P., & Tversky, A. (Eds.). (1982). *Judgment under uncertainty: Heuristics and biases.* Cambridge, England: Cambridge University Press.

Kahneman, D., & Tversky, A. (1973). On the psychology of prediction. *Psychological Review, 80*, 237–251.

Kahneman, D., & Tversky, A. (1996). On the reality of cognitive illusions. *Psychological Review, 103*, 582–591.

Knill, D. C., & Richards, W. A. (1996). *Perception as Bayesian inference.* Cambridge, England: Cambridge University Press.

Koehler, J. J. (1996). The base rate fallacy reconsidered: Normative, descriptive and methodological challenges. *Behavioral and Brain Sciences, 19*, 1–53.

Körding, K., & Wolpert, D. M. (2004). Bayesian integration in sensorimotor learning. *Nature, 427*, 244–247.

Locksley, A., Borgida, E., Brekke, N., & Hepburn, C. (1980). Sex stereotypes and social judgment. *Journal of Personality and Social Psychology, 39*, 821–831.

Locksley, A., Hepburn, C., & Ortiz, V. (1982). Social stereotypes and judgments of individuals. *Journal of Experimental and Social Psychology, 18*, 23–42.

McCauley, C. (1994). Stereotypes as base rate predictions. Commentary on Koehler on base-rate. *Psycoloquy, 5*(05). Retrieved May 22, 2007, from http://www.cogsci.ecs.soton.ac.uk/cgi/psyc/newpsy?5.05

Nisbett, R. E., & Ross, L. (1980). *Human inference: Strategies and shortcomings of social judgment.* Englewood Cliffs, NJ: Prentice-Hall.

Piaget, J. (1936). *La naissance de l'intelligence chez l'enfant.* Geneva: Delachux et Niestlé.

Simon, H. A. (1991). Cognitive architectures and rational analysis: Comment. In K. van Lehn (Ed.), *Architectures for intelligence* (pp. 25–39). Hillsdale, NJ: Lawrence Erlbaum Associates, Inc.

Simoncelli, E. P., & Olshausen, B. (2001). Natural image statistics and neural representation. *Annual Review of Neuroscience, 24*, 1193–1216.

Simons, D. J., & Levin, D. T. (1997). Failure to detect changes to attended objects in motion pictures. *Psychonomic Bulletin & Review,* 4501–4506.

Sloman, S. A. (1996). The empirical case for two systems of reasoning. *Psychological Bulletin, 119*, 3–22.

Sperber, D., & Wilson, D. (1986). *Relevance: Communication and cognition.* Cambridge, MA: Harvard University Press.

Stanovich, K. E., & West, R. F. (2000). Individual differences in reasoning: Implications for the rationality debate. *Behavioral and Brain Sciences, 23*, 645–665.

Tversky, A., & Kahneman, D. (1974). Judgment under uncertainty: Heuristic & biases. *Science, 185*, 1124–1131.

Tversky, A., & Kahneman, D. (1982). Evidential impact of base rates. In D. Kahneman, P. Slovic, & A. Tversky (Eds.), *Judgment under uncertainty: Heuristic and biases* (pp. 153–160). Cambridge, England: Cambridge University Press.

Yechiam, E., Barron, G., & Erev, I. (2005). The role of personal experience in contributing to different patterns of response to rare terrorist attacks. *Journal of Conflict Resolution, 49*, 430–439.

10

Implications and Ramifications of a Sample-Size Approach to Intuition

KLAUS FIEDLER
University of Heidelberg

YAAKOV KAREEV
Hebrew University Jerusalem

INTRODUCTION

*T*here are several different meanings attached to intuition, which has become a prominent concept in research on judgment and decision making (T. Betsch, chap. 1, this volume; Epstein, chap. 2, this volume; Gilovich, Griffin, & Kahneman, 2001; Hogarth, 2001). In the context of dual-process theories (Chaiken & Trope, 1999), intuitive processing may be considered an opposite of systematic processing, or intuition appears as an affective processing style that is driven by feelings rather than arguments and reasons (C. Betsch, 2006; Haidt & Kesebir, chap. 13, this volume; Zeelenberg, Nelissen, & Pieters, chap. 11, this volume). In decision-making research, the notion of intuition would be applied to bounded rationality due to limited resources (H. A. Simon, 1956). In the area of metacognition, intuition could refer to the absence of monitoring and control processes. Some researchers have even come to consider intuition a personality trait (C. Betsch, 2004; chap. 14, this volume; Epstein, chap. 2, this volume; Epstein, Pacini, Denes-Raj, & Heier, 1996; Scott & Bruce, 1985).

In this chapter, we delineate a different approach, which is by no means inconsistent but largely overlaps with the aforementioned definitions. However, our approach is simpler and refrains from a number of rather strong assumptions to which other conceptions subscribe. Using a simple and straightforward criterion, we define *intuition* in terms of the size of the sample used in reaching a decision: Judgments and decisions are intuitive to the extent that they rest on small samples.

To be sure, there is no absolute numerical measure for a small sample. What is small, rather, depends on the task setting and the knowledge domain. However, on a domain-specific ordinal scale, the distinction of small and large samples would appear to be easy and natural. A personality scale with 10 items (such as the *Präferenz für Intuition und Deliberation* [Preference for Intuition and Deliberation] measuring intuitive dispositions; C. Betsch, 2004; chap. 14, this volume) constitutes a small sample compared to another scale comprising over 100 items. Hiring a candidate after a 5-min job interview, rather than an extensive assessment, would be said to rely on a small sample and so would judging somebody's intelligence or honesty after 10 s of acquaintance (Ambady & Rosenthal, 1992). Thus, using short versions of personality tests, making fast hiring decisions, or quick judgments at almost zero acquaintance would be classified as intuitive according to the previous definition.

We believe that such a simple operational approach to intuition has several advantages. First, of all the attributes supposed to characterize intuition—the gut feeling, its phenomenological experience, the wholistic strategy—sample size would appear to be the most objective and straightforward measure. Second, an operational definition in terms of small information samples is compatible with most other measures as we already mentioned. Third, with respect to the principle of parsimony, we avoid the problems associated with the strong assumption that intuition is a stable personality trait or the dual-process assumption that at any point in time, cognitive processes are either in a reflective or in an intuitive mode but never in both (Hamm, chap. 4, this volume).

Finally, and most important, sample size is a theoretically fertile variable, giving rise to a rich set of testable implications that can be derived from statistical decision models. These implications lead to a theory of intuitive decision making that goes beyond global statements such as "intuitive decisions are better than expected," "intuition is a key to satisfaction," or "less is more." Rather, the intuition = sample-size approach leads to clear-cut predictions about antecedent conditions of intuitive decisions, their benefits and costs, and the advantages and disadvantages of intuitive decisions.

PREVIEW

Having introduced our basic definition, we now provide a preview of this chapter. In the next section, we introduce an information-sampling approach that has been proven to elucidate the relationship between sample size and decision accuracy. We review the basic findings obtained within that framework, showing that paucity of information can help or hinder accurate decision making. We introduce a distinction between two kinds of accuracy, estimation accuracy and choice accuracy, and point out that whereas large samples lead to accurate estimates, small samples exhibit their superiority when it comes to making clear-cut choices.

In the following sections, we extend and elaborate on the basic sampling model in the theoretical context of a three-dimensional learning environment, encompassing three generic dimensions: the valence of information (positive vs. negative), the distance of decision outcomes (distant vs. proximal), and the decision criterion (lenient vs. conservative). Several antecedents, consequences, and concomitants of intuition can be described within this three-dimensional space. To anticipate, we show that natural learning environments facilitate intuitive decisions in negative domains based on small samples and lenient decision thresholds. In signal-detection terms, such lenient decision thresholds tend to produce many false alarms but few false negatives. In contrast, in positive domains, information samples tend to be large, imposing a stricter decision criterion with more false negatives than false alarms. We also show that distant decisions are characterized by smaller samples than proximal decisions, with corresponding differences in terms of false alarms and false negatives. Finally, the analogous influence on intuition (i.e., decisions informed by small samples) of (positive vs. negative) valence and (large vs. small) distance reflects the fact that these two dimensions are not independent. A negative attitude toward an object, or an avoidance tendency, is naturally represented as a large or increasing distance. As in multidimensional scaling, distance expresses dissimilarity between the attitude holder and the attitude object. In contrast, a positive attitude or approach tendency is evident in small distance or increasing closeness, proximity, or intimacy. Proximity means similarity. Thus, the moderators of intuitive processing can be reasonably understood within a three-dimensional theory space spanned by the variables of valence, distance, and sample size.

SAMPLE SIZE: A FRUITFUL THEORETICAL CONCEPT

Consider a simple binary consumer choice problem: A consumer wants to purchase a car, with the decision problem reduced to a binary choice between two different brand Models, A and B. Assume there is objective evidence for assets (denoted +) and deficits (denoted −) of both models but that the manufacturers do not reveal the entire universe of all + and − data that define the objective quality. Suppose that in (latent) reality, the rate of all + experiences with Model A is higher (80%) than that of Model B (40%). The consumer does not have access to this objective population parameter but only to a sample of data, the acquisition of which is restricted, time consuming, and expensive. However, information acquisition is unbiased, that is, every bit of information, whether + or −, is equally likely to be sampled from the objective database. Within this simple environmental task setting, consumer decision making amounts to drawing an n-item sample of observations (describing + or − aspects associated with Option A or B) and making a choice in favor of the option with the higher proportion of + data in the sample. Thus, if p^* (+/A), the proportion of positive outcomes for A, is higher than p^* (+/B)—let us call this a positive contingency between alternatives and outcomes—then a correct choice will be made. If the observed contingency p^* (+/A) − p^* (+/B) is negative, the decision will be wrong. (An asterisk indicates an estimated sample proportion.)

To be sure, the accuracy of this strategy (i.e., the likelihood to choose the better alternative, A) relies heavily on the faithfulness of the samples considered.

In the context of this task setting, comparing intuitive to more exhaustive strategies means to compare the relative success of small and large samples. Think of two large groups (each including 1,000 individuals): intuitive consumers who gather only about 8 observations to make a decision and exhaustive consumers who sample three times as many observations (i.e., 24). How would the intuitive group fare when compared to the exhaustive group with respect to the number of consumers who choose A, the better option? Could one imagine that the success rate of the intuitive group is similar to that attained by the exhaustive group?

A STATISTICAL MODEL FOR UNDERSTANDING THE ASSETS OF INTUITION

Indeed, statistical sampling theory tells one that under clearly specified conditions, the intuitive group may not only match the achievement of the exhaustive-search condition but may actually outperform it. That is, the number of consumers whose observed sample contingency is (correctly) positive can be higher for the intuitive group that relies on only 8 observations than for the exhaustive-strategy group with 24 observations.

How this seeming paradox is possible can be explained with reference to the model depicted in Figure 10.1 (after Kareev, 2000). The two curves represent sampling distributions of correlation coefficients for different sample sizes. Thus, when a sample of size n is drawn repeatedly from a population in which the true contingency is $\Delta = p(+/A) - p(+/B) = .8 - .4 = .4$, the distribution is like the solid line for small samples of size $n = 8$ (intuitive group). By comparison, the dashed line shows the distribution for large samples of size $n = 24$ (exhaustive group). Apparently,

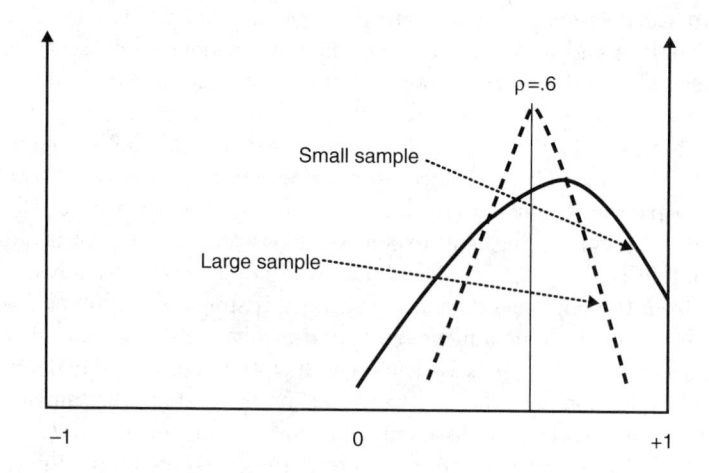

FIGURE 10.1 Skew of sampling distribution increases with decreasing sample size according to a model proposed by Kareev (1995).

the distribution of all the sample contingencies drawn that way is left-skewed, so the majority of contingencies observed in samples drawn from a population with $\Delta = .4$ is higher than $\Delta = .4$. Moreover, the skew is more apparent for the solid than the dashed curve. Over a wide range of sample sizes, the skew of the sampling distribution increases with decreasing sample size. When cases in which the correlation is undefined (e.g., all outcomes positive or all negative) are also taken into account—and this is more likely to happen the smaller the sample size—the amplifying effect of small samples reaches a maximum around $n = 7$. It is widely known that this magical number corresponds to the capacity of human working memory (cf. Kareev, 2000).

Thus, small samples in the range specified by the model in Figure 10.1 have the property of increasing the likelihood that actually existing differences can be recognized correctly, reflecting an environmental, precognitive advantage of intuitive processing. That the sample size resulting in maximum effect ($n = 7$) coincides with memory capacity suggests that evolution may have exploited (or even brought about) this intuition advantage, increasing the chance that people can hold in mind samples of data that accentuate actually existing contingencies. A good deal of empirical evidence supports the prediction derived from this model that a narrow window size can facilitate accurate decisions such as Elman's (1993) demonstration that effective language acquisition is facilitated by small samples of linguistic input or else by restricted memory capacity, both "implementing" in effect an intuitive strategy. Likewise, adult memory span is negatively correlated with performance on contingency detection tasks (Kareev, Lieberman, & Lev, 1997).

However, there are good reasons not to overstretch this notable evidence for increasing performance with decreasing sample size. On one hand, the skew in the sampling distributions of contingencies or correlations is only apparent when the actual contingency in the population is markedly different from zero. If the actual contingency is too small, no advantage of small samples will be obtained. On the other hand, the small-sample advantage depicted so far only pertains to hit rates, that is, the rate of correctly detecting a (pronounced) contingency that really exists. With respect to error rates, no doubt, small samples are also more likely to produce false alarms (i.e., indicate erroneous contingencies), although false positives seem to be less serious than false negatives (Kareev, 2005).

Fortunately, the small-sample advantage is more pervasive than the model in Figure 10.1 suggests. A more recent sampling model (Fiedler & Kareev, 2006; cf. our Fig. 10.2) demonstrates that (a) small samples may inform better decisions than large samples when population contingencies are weak, (b) the advantage of small samples is maintained when both hits and false alarms are taken into account, and (c) the equal or even superior performance of intuitive strategies generalizes across a large area of the parameter space.

The assumptions of this more recent model are simple and plausible. When repeated samples are drawn from a population in which the true contingency is, say, $\Delta = .2$, the observed sample contingency will not always exactly match the population parameter but will be scattered around the true value. As a matter of rule, the dispersion of the sample statistics will be larger for small than for large samples as shown by the solid and dashed graphs in Figure 10.2. This holds for contingencies

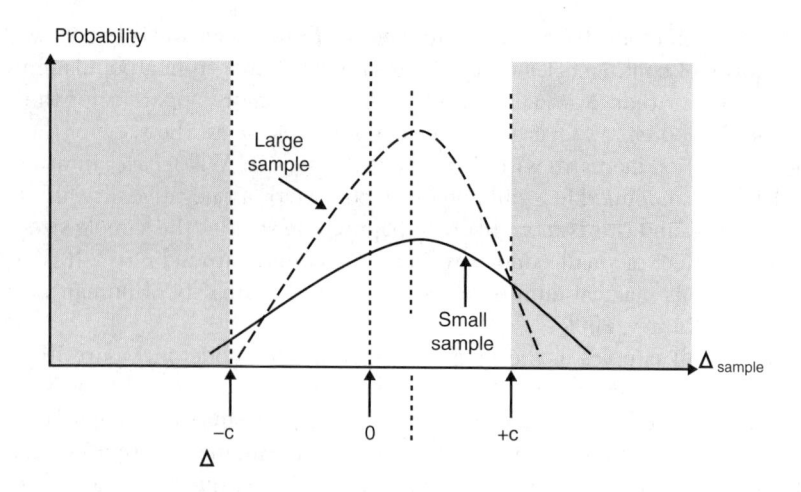

FIGURE 10.2 Dispersion of sampling distribution increases with decreasing sample size according to a model proposed by Fiedler and Kareev (2006).

of any strength; estimates of contingencies are closer to the actual value when samples are large rather than small. For very large sample size n, estimates will approximate $\Delta = .2$. For very small n, the contingencies observed in different samples vary considerably. An intermediate n will yield medium dispersion.

With respect to this universal model, the "home domain" of intuition can be easily identified with two assumptions. First, we have to introduce the distinction between estimation and choice. When the task is to make an accurate quantitative estimation of the contingency in the population, then large samples are clearly superior to small samples. This simply follows from the smaller dispersion of the dashed curve in Figure 10.2. However, when the task is only to make a qualitative choice of the better option—that is, a binary decision of whether the contingency is positive or negative, regardless of its precise size—then under a second assumption, small samples can be superior. Namely, assume that individuals do not always choose A when A dominates B (in the following denoted A $\gg$ B). Assume, rather, that for A to be chosen, the observed dominance of A over B has to be strong enough, that is, the contingency Δ_{sample} in the sample has to exceed a threshold Δ, which is often higher than the population contingency Δ. For example, whereas real differences in the environment may often be modest (such as $\Delta = .2$ in this case), a choice will only be made when the observed difference Δ_{sample} exceeds some significant criterion (say, $\Delta = .4$). When this is the case, that is, when organisms only make choices using a threshold that is higher than the real underlying difference or contingency, then small samples will most of the time produce more correct choices than large samples.

To illustrate why this happens, consider the vertical threshold lines at $\Delta = \pm.4$ in Figure 10.2. A sample difference of +.4 or larger, leading to a correct choice, will be observed more often for small than for large samples as evident from the areas under the solid and dashed line that exceed the threshold. Thus, the higher dispersion of small samples, which leads to inaccurate estimates, at the same time enables many correct threshold-based choices. To be sure, small samples will also lead to more incorrect decisions, as evident from the left distribution tails that exceed −.4. However, the intuition costs of incorrect choices on the left are clearly lower than the intuition gains of correct choices or "hits" on the right.

Evidence for the Statistical Model of Intuition

In fact, extended computer simulations confirm that intuitive decisions based on small samples outperform large samples over a wide range of sample sizes, contingency levels, thresholds, and cognitive load assumptions. Furthermore, decision makers actually do often use implicit thresholds that are higher than the contingencies to be detected, leading to a real intuition advantage. For instance, Fiedler and Kareev (2006) asked their participants to make binary choices between pairs of products or pairs of job applicants. They could sample as many observations about a pair of options (A, B) as they considered useful. At the end of this free information search, they could either choose A or B or discard a sample when they felt the sample did not allow for a choice. Across different levels of actual contingencies (i.e., true differences between A and B), ranging from $\Delta = .1$ to $\Delta = .4$, choice accuracy correlated negatively with sample size: The smaller the samples drawn, the higher the proportion of correct choices. In accordance with the line of reasoning we advanced previously, this small-sample advantage came along with judges applying rather high decision thresholds. That is, the observed differences, Δ_{sample}, that were considered sufficient to stop information choice and to make a choice tended to be higher than the real Δ that held between A and B. Consistent with this high-threshold account, the small-sample advantage was particularly pronounced when correctness (coded +1 vs. −1) was weighted with confidence of choice, reflecting the fact that confidence tends to be high at high decision thresholds. This is related, in turn, to people's well-documented tendency to overweigh strength of evidence (the strength of the observed correlation, in our case) and underweigh its weight (the number of cases on which it is based; Griffin & Tversky, 1992).

The advantage of small samples—that is, of intuitive strategies—was already evident at the environmental sampling stage: prior to the cognitive process proper. An analysis of the samples drawn at random from a universe in which A was slightly better than B [i.e., $p(+/A) \gg p(+/B)$] revealed that small samples were more likely to show an above-threshold, A advantage than larger samples. Indeed, this precognitive sampling effect exhibited the advantage of small samples more strongly than the subsequent cognitive decisions, reflecting the environmental (rather than mnemonic) origin of the phenomenon.

In similar experiments (Fiedler, Renn, & Kareev, 2006), decision makers underwent a positive or negative mood treatment (based on funny or sad films) before entering the choice task. Positive mood is a well-established determinant of intuitive processing strategies (Bless & Fiedler, 2006; Fiedler, 2001), and indeed, good-mood participants tended to base their choices on smaller samples than participants in a bad mood. Consequently, good-mood participants exhibited superior performance under specific task conditions.

Convergent findings were obtained by Kareev et al. (1997), which showed that contingency detection improved when the size of the sample made available to participants was restricted. In the "out of sight" condition of Experiment 2, participants were presented with items that varied along two continuous attributes. Items were presented one at a time and removed before the next one appeared. Sample size was smaller than, equal to, or larger than the estimated short-term memory capacity. Once the entire sample had thus been presented, judges were given one attribute value of a new item and asked to predict the value of the other attribute. Predictions were compared to the actual value, and accuracy was rewarded. Predictions were more extreme, more in the right direction, and more accurate when sample size was small.

Estimation Versus Choice

However, it is important to keep in mind that this counterintuitive advantage of intuition is but one side of the coin. It only holds for choices, not for estimation tasks. It is uncontested that quantitative estimates become more accurate with increasing sample size. For example, when participants had to figure out the proportions of correct answers given by different students in a simulated classroom environment, they arrived at more accurate performance estimates of those students whom they had asked many questions (Fiedler, Walther, Freytag, & Plessner, 2002). For example, assume two pairs of students—A, B and a,b—whose ability parameters (i.e., proportions of correct answers) differ by the same amount (e.g., A and a being 80% correct, but B and b being only 50% correct), but a larger sample of observations is available about A,B than about a,b. Then the accuracy of estimates is higher for A,B than a,b, and the estimates of A,B are less regressive (i.e., approach the actual ability differences more) than a,b estimates. This large-sample advantage holds for estimation accuracy, not for clarity and confidence of choice, which is often higher for small samples (for a similar, enlightening simulation model, see also Hertwig & Pleskac, 2006).

A synthesis of both phenomena—a choice advantage for intuition but an estimation advantage for extended information samples—was found by Fiedler, Kemmelmeier, and Freytag (1999) in the context of intergroup judgments. Information samples are normally smaller for outgroups than for ingroups, producing more intuitive judgments about outgroups than ingroups. Both computer simulations and experimental data showed that ingroup judgments were more accurate than outgroup judgments when the task called for the estimation of the precise position of groups with regard to antonymous traits. Thus, the actual position of groups on two antonymous trait dimensions—extraversion and introversion or honesty and dishonesty—was more accurately assessed for the group on which the larger sample was available (i.e., the ingroup). However, when the task called for a (forced) choice of which attribute—either extraversion or introversion—dominates, then ingroup judgments were in conflict. There was too much evidence for both antonyms to allow for the simplifying choice required. As a consequence, choices were more readily made for outgroups, apparently based on small samples and intuitive strategies that were less constrained by decision conflicts. Technically speaking, the difference in the observed evidence for two competing antonyms is more likely to exceed a threshold when outgroups rather than ingroups are being judged.

Note that estimation means to compare A and B separately to an absolute accuracy criterion, whereas choice involves a relative comparison of A versus B, regardless of their absolute level or accuracy. Small samples facilitate choices, even though exhaustive strategies involving larger samples support accurate estimation. Once this formal explication is understood, seemingly unrelated phenomena can be explained as reflecting the same influence of intuition. Thus, just as choices between two competing antonyms are easier for outgroups or small groups than for ingroups or large groups, the work of Chajut and Algom (2003) pointed to a conceptual analog in a completely different task domain. In a selective-attention task that involves a forced choice to attend to A rather than B, distracters or cognitive load that reduce the overall sample size in working memory serve to improve performance. Thus, intuitive strategies enforced through cognitive load facilitate the concentration on the task-relevant aspect, A, rather than the task-irrelevant aspect B. More exhaustive strategies in the no-load condition are more likely to induce attention conflicts.

Detecting and Affecting Change

The models and findings we have reviewed so far all assume a static environment in which the parameter values to be assessed remain stable. However, a large part of daily life calls for the assessment of changes in the environment. It is interesting to note in passing that small samples are particularly functional for the detection of change. In dynamic environments, reliance on large samples of past experience may constitute a liability rather than an asset. In contrast, monitoring but a narrow window of recent events provides the most relevant data for the detection of change. The exact size of the optimal window depends of the rate of change (the faster, the smaller the window) and the quality of the data (the noisier, the larger the window). Still, it is clear that the detection of change is best served by considering a small sample of recent events—by engaging in intuitive decision making.

Lest the force of this argument rest only on its logical appeal, we point out a list of cases in which taking into consideration even only the last, most recent item (i.e., $n = 1!$) results in effective, efficient behavior.

Situations in which the speedy detection of and reaction to change are required abound. Most prominent are interactions in dilemma situations in which two or more agents attempt to maximize their own outcomes as they compete with each other for some environmental resource. In such environments, recognizing changes in strategies and outcomes is of paramount importance. Can intuitive, small-sample-based monitoring be of any use in such situations, or is it bound to result in suboptimal, even exploitable behaviors?

To illustrate, consider a game in which each of two agents has to decide on the allocation of some units of reward. Each agent has to decide whether to award 1 unit of reward to herself or himself or to have 3 units of reward awarded to the other agent. The decision is made secretly and simultaneously by both agents and then

TABLE 10.1 Illustration of a Two-Person Dilemma Game

		Agent B	
		1 for myself	3 for the other
Agent A	1 for myself	1,1	4,0
	3 for the other	0,4	3,3

Note: The first payoff in each pair refers to Agent A, the second payoff to B.

revealed and enacted. The four possible decision combinations and the ensuing payoffs are depicted in Table 10.1.

Although the cover story may be unfamiliar, the resulting payoff matrix is that of the well-known prisoner's dilemma (PD) game. If played once, "take the one for myself" dominates "give 3 to the other," as it yields a better outcome irrespective of the other player's decision. Note, however, that mutual defection results in a lower outcome—1 for each—than would mutual cooperation. For the latter to become a stable (equilibrium) strategy requires trust and the potential for credible threats, which is available if the interaction repeats. Prominent in numerous articles dealing with the PD game are suggestions on how to play it in a way that would lead to high payoffs. As it turns out, a very simple strategy, tit for tat (TFT), which calls for monitoring the other player's last move and responding in kind on the next trial, performs amazingly well against a host of other strategies (Axelrod, 1984; Axelrod & Hamilton, 1981).

Note that the essence of TFT is an immediate, minimal-sample-based reaction. As it turns out, this intuitive strategy outperforms strategies based on more exhaustive histories employing sophisticated weighting functions. Interestingly, after years of reigning supreme as the champion of PD tournaments, TFT was beaten by another strategy, Pavlov, which is based on a win-stay, lose-shift strategy (Nowak & Sigmund, 1993)—another minimal-sample-based principle.

Consider a situation in which some resource (e.g., food) is provided to a group of consuming agents by two sources that differ in quality—one being more abundant than the other. If the overall supply is scarce, for all consumers to aggregate by the more abundant source would result in an inefficient solution. The efficient solution, known as the ideal free distribution—with the number of feeding agents at each resource proportional to its abundance—may be achieved if each organism adopts a win-stay, lose-shift strategy (Thuijsman, Peleg, Amitai, & Shmida, 1995). Thus, one sees again how an intuitive decision, based on a minimal sample, results in an efficient solution.

ENVIRONMENTAL-LEARNING CONTEXT OF INTUITION

Having introduced our sampling approach to intuition, we can now start to elaborate on several intriguing implications of this theoretical approach. In the remainder of this article, we unfold the three planes of a three-dimensional theoretical framework involving sample size × valence × psychological distance. We first discuss the relationship between (large vs. small) sample size and (positive vs. negative) valence, which turns out to be positive, reflecting search for positive and avoidance of negative information. We then turn to sample size and psychological distance, which are negatively related, as the amount of available information normally decreases with increasing distance. With regard to distance and valence, of course, positive and negative valence creates approach and avoidance, respectively.

However, although this three-fold relationship is balanced and ought to produce a stable tendency (i.e., reduced distance when samples are large due to positive valence that reduces distance further and so forth), further reflection reveals that such a perpetuating spiral must be maladaptive. If organisms sample more information only about positive objects in their close proximity, they must be ill prepared for dealing with negative information in the distance. Moreover, if many individuals strive for the same positive nearby objects, conflicts abound, and resources are soon depleted. Truly adaptive behavior has to include a device that helps the organism engage in regulation proper and thereby to avoid the perpetuating spiral. Accordingly, in a final section, we introduce a fourth dimension—we call it dynamic change—that explains how decision targets change their nature as distance decreases and sample size increases, resulting in a shift from intuition to exhaustive processing. As we show, this dynamic shift prevents the adaptive system from perpetuation.

Sample Size and Valence

One basic law of the social ecology in which adaptive learning takes place relates sample size to valence. Other things being equal, social rationality implies that positive task settings create larger samples than negative settings. Quite in line with Thorndyke's (1916) seminal law of effect, which says that reinforcement increases the probability of repeating the reinforced behavior, Denrell's (2005) recent experience-sampling approach makes a strong case for the contention that positive impressions increase the likelihood of continued interaction. In forming impressions of other people, individuals will likely break up the interaction if it is unpleasant or aversive; they will likely continue to interact if the impression is pleasant or positive. A plethora of social-psychological phenomena can be explained by this basic law: Negative initial impressions, or priming effects, are more likely to be frozen and conserved than positive initial impressions, which are likely to be revised through continued interaction. Therefore, negative impressions tend to be more stable than positive impressions, unless the environment enforces continued interaction. Negative initial impressions are more likely to be revised if they refer to proximate others who warrant continued interaction, affording a natural explanation of the self-serving bias and the ingroup-serving bias (cf. Fiedler, 1996; Fiedler & Walther, 2003).

Translating small samples to intuition, this means that intuitive strategies evolve in negatively toned environments, whereas positive toned learning environments breed more exhaustive strategies. The underlying causal influence may be bidirectional, though. Positive environments breed large samples; but at the same time, small samples may signal negative situations, whereas large samples may signal

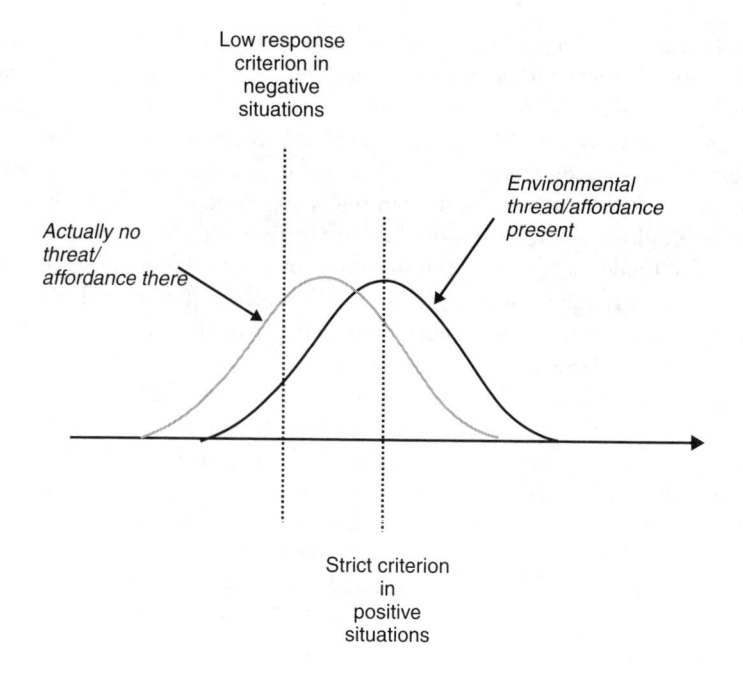

FIGURE 10.3 Lower response criterion, warranting more hits (larger proportion of area under the black curve exceeding the criterion) but also allowing for more false alarms (larger proportion of area under the grey curve exceeding the criterion) in negative as compared to positive settings.

pleasant situations. For instance, data from experiments in a simulated classroom (Fiedler et al., 2002) suggest that teachers tended to direct more questions at students they considered good rather than bad students. On one hand, this means that enlarging samples will enlarge positive information on good students more than negative information about bad students. At the same time, teachers' attentional preference is a diagnostic indicator of their implicit student evaluation.

In the context of statistical decision theories, such as signal-detection theory (Swets, Dawes, & Monahan, 2000), the intuitive strategies resulting from negative settings should induce lower decision criteria than the exhaustive strategies that characterize positive settings as illustrated in Figure 10.3. Such a response strategy is highly adaptive, to be sure, because in negative situations increasing the hit rate and avoiding misses (i.e., detecting aversive and threatening stimuli) is more important than decreasing the false-alarm rate and increasing correct rejections (i.e., wasting no energy with harmless situations). In contrast, in positive settings, a higher response criterion is functional because too high a reaction rate might interfere with the consumption and enjoyment of the pleasant situation, and overlooking another pleasant stimulus does not cause much harm. It is impossible anyway to consume many pleasant stimuli at the same time.

The assumption that negative stimulus settings trigger quick decisions based on low thresholds is consistent with several lines of evidence (cf. Dijksterhuis & Aarts, 2003) and theoretical conceptions. An analysis of cultural sign systems reveals a much higher diversity of signs signaling danger, threat, and aversive experience than signs pointing to positive referents (Fiedler, 1988), enabling organisms to react faster to negative than to positive stimuli. There are many more different negative traffic signs, action verbs, state verbs, basic emotion words, and facial expressions than positive items in the same sign systems. The very existence of highly elaborated systems of negative signs does not contradict the assumption that positive stimuli create larger samples. Indeed, elaborated sign systems in the negative domain serve to quickly identify aversive stimuli to avoid and terminate negative stimulation as nicely delineated in Taylor's (1991) mobilization-minimization model.

There is empirical and anecdotal evidence to support the somewhat counterintuitive notion that intuitive (small-sample) processes are more common in negative than in positive situations. For instance, the so-called face-in-the-crowd effect highlights the readiness to react more quickly (i.e., based on smaller sensual samples) to negative faces hidden in a crowd than to positive faces (Hansen & Hansen, 1988). Analogous findings hold for semantic stimuli (Peeters & Czapinski, 1990; Pratto & John, 1991; Wentura, Rothermund, & Bak, 2000).

Kruglanski and Webster's (1996) research on need for closure leads to the same conclusion. The tendency to come to a quick decision is facilitated by aversive states such as time pressure, processing difficulty, laborious and aversive task settings, fatigue, or noise. In contrast, the need to postpone closure and to remain open for additional information increases when the task is intrinsically enjoyable and interesting. The heightened need for closure in negative situations is also evident in an enhanced tendency to reject deviates and not to tolerate dissent (Kruglanski & Webster, 1991). A conceptual analog is the increasing tendency of eyewitnesses to identify a suspect in a lineup when the crime in question is severe and the social pressure is high (Deffenbacher, Bornstein, Penrod, & McGorty, 2004). Thus, aversive situations motivate decision makers to adopt lenient decision criteria.

More generally, there is rich evidence for the contention that people spontaneously spend more time with and search longer for positive than negative information but that they make quicker reactions and decisions about negative than positive stimulus objects or persons (Taylor, 1991). This is but a paraphrase of the well-known fact that in the realm of morality and social interaction, positive information is more common, whereas negative information is more diagnostic or informative, exactly because it is uncommon and normatively unexpected (Gidron, Koehler, & Tversky, 1993; Reeder & Brewer, 1979; Wojciszke, 1994). To be classified as honest or conscientious, a large number of observations has to confirm that someone behaves honestly or conscientiously most of the time, calling for a conservative decision criterion (say, a minimum of 90% honest behavior to constitute honesty). In contrast, to be classified in negative categories, dishonest or unreliable, a small number of one or two negative acts is sufficient.

Sample Size and Distance

An obvious ecological law says that the sample size of available information about a target object or person decreases with the psychological distance of that target. This pertains to spatial, temporal, and cultural distance just as for any other distance dimension. People know more about themselves than about others, about their own ingroup than about outgroups. People know more about their own culture than about foreign cultures. People are more informed about the present than about the distant past or the far-away future; people are exposed to larger samples of information about their own profession, hobbies, and interests than about distant topics of interest and expertise. From the rationale of our theoretical approach, therefore, it follows that decisions planned and drawn from a large distance should be typically intuitive, informed by small samples and relying on lenient response criteria.

What evidence is there to support this prediction? With regard to temporal distance, to start with, there is indeed a good deal of evidence confirming that decision options in the far away future are mentally represented in more simplified, less multidimensional ways than present decision options. For example, in an investigation by Liberman, Sagristano, and Trope (2002), the number of factors required to account for the participants' preferences among 25 daily activities was consistently lower when the activities were supposed to take place in 2 to 6 months rather than the day after.

In a similar vein, simplifying judgment tendencies such as the so-called fundamental attribution bias (Gilbert & Malone, 1995; Miyamoto & Kitayama, 2002; Ross, 1977)—explaining behavior only in terms of internal person traits while ignoring situational constraints—increases with temporal distance. Another attribution bias, the so-called actor-observer bias (Fiedler, Semin, Finkenauer, & Berkel, 1995; Jones & Nisbett, 1972; Watson, 1982) consists in the tendency to provide more simplifying, intuitive internal attributions for others' behavior than for one's own behavior. In other words, the fundamental attribution error increases not only with temporal distance (from the immediate present to the distant future) but also with social distance (from self to other attributions).

Several language analyses using the linguistic category model (Semin & Fiedler, 1988) have shown that the predicates used to describe temporally and socially distant people and behaviors tend to be more abstract and to provide less contextual detail than descriptions of closer people and behaviors (Fiedler, Semin, & Finkenauer, 1993; Semin, 2006).

Although this evidence for simplifying representations is strongly but only indirectly suggestive of smaller underlying information samples, more direct evidence comes from free information search paradigms. The tendency to concentrate information search on focal rather than distant entities has been called a positive-test strategy (Klayman & Ha, 1987). Just as scientists used to sample more data about their own theory than about alternative theory, decision makers gather more observations about the decision option under focus (i.e., the low-distance option) than about other, more remote alternative options.

Perhaps the most extensive evidence for the assumption that sample size decreases with psychological distance comes from intergroup research (Fiedler et al., 1999; Linville, Fischer, & Salovey, 1989). Simplifying tendencies in judgments of outgroups as compared with more differentiated judgments of ingroups are manifested in the outgroup homogeneity effect (Judd & Park, 1988; Park & Hastie, 1987; Park & Rothbart, 1982), the outgroup polarization effect (Linville &

Jones, 1980), as well as the outgroup covariation effect (Linville, Fischer, & Yoon, 1996). The simple assumption that smaller samples are available for outgroups than ingroups provides a sufficient account of these diverse phenomena. Consistent with this account, reversals of the outgroup-homogeneity effect are typically obtained when ingroups are minority groups, characterized by small rather than large sample size (B. Simon, 1992).

As an inevitable consequence of the negative relationship that holds between sample size and distance, more lenient criteria have to be accepted for decisions about distal objects (such as outgroups) than for proximal objects (such as ingroups). Again, the causal direction of this assumption is not quite clear. Regardless of whether sample sizes are smaller because distal decisions call for more lenient criteria or criteria have to be more lenient because the available samples for distal decisions are smaller, the result is a negative correlation, pointing to distance as a prominent environmental factor that breeds intuitive strategies.

Distance and Valence

We finally consider the relationship between distance and valence. For the triad to be balanced, or transitive, positive valence has to be associated with short distance or closeness. If positive samples are large samples, and large samples are at a nearby distance, then nearby samples ought to be positive. Indeed, a hardly contested behavioral law states that positive valence induces approach or reduced distance, whereas negative valence induces avoidance, or escape, or increased distance (Brendl, Markman, & Messner, 2005). Organisms approach pleasant things and avoid aversive things, exposing themselves to the stimuli they prefer. This notion seems so natural that we refrain here from further elaborations.

Thus, all three dyadic relations—between sample size, distance, and valence—create the consistent picture summarized in Figure 10.4. Positivity increases proximity, which increases sample size. Conversely, negativity increases distance, which decreases sample size. All three pairwise relations are mutually consistent and supported by a good deal of empirical evidence. Nevertheless, something must be wrong with the cycle depicted in Figure 10.4. A moment of reflection is sufficient to understand that such a perpetuating loop must end up in maladaptive behavior. After a longer period of increasing the relative size of positive samples in close proximity and decreasing the exposure to negative and distant information, the perspective of an organism would be severely impaired. That is, over time, the ability to foresee distant events and to prepare for aversive threats would be lost. In the remainder of this chapter, therefore, we reconcile the incontestable rules summarized in Figure 10.4 with the needs of successful adaptation and behavior regulation.

Regulation Through Dynamic Change of Decision Problems

Indeed, such an additional dimension exists, and it is not hard to find in the current literature. We call it behavior regulation. Regulation means to prevent systems from perpetuation. Within this cognitive-ecological framework, it means

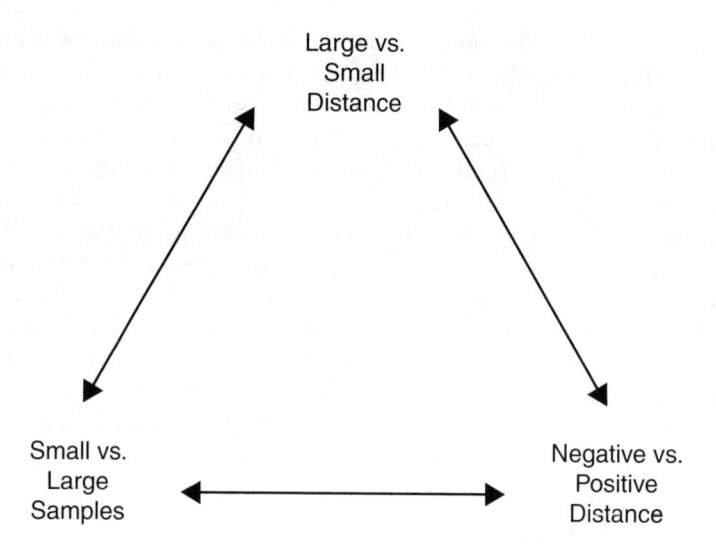

```
                    Large vs.
                     Small
                    Distance
                    ↗      ↖
                   /        \
                  /          \
                 ↙            ↘
      Small vs.                  Negative vs.
       Large        ←——————→      Positive
      Samples                     Distance
```

FIGURE 10.4 Triadic relation between sample size, valence, and distance.

avoiding an infinite loop that always increases the positivity, density, and proximity of some objects and the negativity, scarcity, and distance of others. Without such a regulatory mechanism, organisms would have no chance to recognize that proximal, familiar, and seemingly pleasant stimuli have turned into dangerous enemies or that disregarded distal alternatives have become interesting. Without such a regulatory counterforce, there could be no learning, no invention, no minority influence, and no adaptive reaction to a changing environment. Granting the need for such regulation, the crucial theoretical question then becomes how this mechanism can be described.

Indeed, an answer to this question can be found in several psychological models that speak to the interaction of cognitive and environmental factors. No doubt, there is the selective search for pleasant information and the selective truncation of unpleasant settings, which serves to increase the exposure to positive stimuli and to avoid exposure to negative stimuli. However, even though, or exactly because, avoidance and truncation behavior renders negative stimulation so scarce, negative information becomes high in diagnosticity (Skowronski & Carlston, 1989), highly salient and easy to detect (Hansen & Hansen, 1988), and is therefore given higher weight in judgment and decision making (Baumeister, Bratslavsky, Finkenauer, & Vohs, 2001; Hodges, 1974). Thus, the lower density and higher distance resulting from avoidance of negative stimuli is compensated by enhanced sensitivity, diagnosticity, and decision weight. This compensatory rule is at the heart of Taylor's (1991) mobilization-minimization model, and it was anticipated in Miller's (1944) famous notion of steeper avoidance than approach gradients. Changes in negative valence loom larger than changes in positive valence.

Miller's (1944) seminal approach to psychological distance regulation was revived and revisited in the modern research program of Trope and Liberman's (2000, 2003) construal-level theory. There is a growing body of evidence showing that the cognitive representation or construal of decision problems changes in a characteristic fashion as the distance from the decision decreases and the amount of information increases. As a matter of rule, decision problems are construed at a lower level of abstractness or at a higher level of detail when the decision comes closer. Therefore, cognitive representations of immediately faced, short-term decision problems tend to be more complex and multidimensional than representations of long-term decisions in the distant future (or in far-away places or groups). From a large distance, one clearly sees the desirability, or intrinsic value, of the central goals or intended outcomes of decision objects. In contrast, from a short distance, one also has to be concerned with the feasibility of decision plans above and beyond their ideal value or desirability.

For example, when anticipating a fancy holiday trip to Southeast Asia next summer, one's thoughts only revolve around overwhelming historical monuments, beautiful landscapes, friendly people, tasty food, and rich ancient culture. Only when departure time approaches do we begin to deal with the feasibility context, that is, bureaucratic visa affairs, inoculations, potential health threats, communication and transportation constraints, and financial requirements. Thus, with shrinking distance, the problem is getting more multidimensional, including feasibility concerns, in addition to the primary desirability dimensions (Liberman et al., 2002). Similarly, the so-called planning fallacy (Buehler, Griffin, & Ross, 1994), which refers to the underestimation of the multitude of aspects and the costs of a planned project, can be reduced by "zooming in" on the planning project (Kruger & Evans, 2004), which means to reduce its distance.

However, crucially, the representations resulting from short versus large distance not only differ in dimensionality (i.e., amount of information), but the feasibility concerns associated with short distance also create a new kind of negative valence. The positive valence of large-sample objectives in one's proximity undergoes a shift toward unpleasant, negative aspects. Whereas focusing on desirability from a large distance typically means to focus on positive aspects of desirability, struggling with the feasibility of a nearby decision problem requires one to cope with negative, unpleasant aspects of realism. Although desirability and feasibility are logically independent, it is typically low desirability and high feasibility that correlates with short distance. Recent research by Eyal, Liberman, Trope, and Walther (2004) illustrates this principle. Pro reasons to support an action were more salient when planning a decision in the distant future, whereas contra arguments were relatively more salient from a short temporal distance.

An intriguing speculation to be derived from this framework is that this shift from focusing the desirability of distant decision options to considering feasibility of nearby options comes along with a shift from choice tasks to estimation tasks. Thus, from a large distance, when information is scarce and the focus is on the intrinsic value of the options proper, one is merely concerned with choices, what is desirable. From a short distance, however, as the trade-off between the intrinsic desirability of the options and their pragmatic feasibility becomes more and more apparent, decision problems would be more likely construed as precise quantitative estimation tasks rather than simplifying qualitative choice tasks. It is important to note that such a shift from choice to estimation task construals is again adaptive because the assets of small samples can be exploited on distant choice tasks, whereas large samples can unfold their information advantages on proximal estimation tasks.

CONCLUSIONS

We believe that our three-dimensional cognitive-ecological framework—involving sample size, distance, and valence—has interesting and far-reaching implications for adaptive behavior regulation. The pairwise correlations that can be observed in the 3 two-dimensional planes of this framework can be considered functional and almost logically necessary. When making judgments and decisions from a large distance, one has to resort to intuitive strategies because larger samples are simply not available. Likewise, the natural tendency to avoid unpleasant stimuli implies, logically, that intuitive strategies are often applied to negative or aversive situations. The same axiomatic assumption—namely, that organisms approach positive and evade negative stimuli—creates a negative correlation between distance and valence.

However, apart from these logical and ecological a priori constraints, the manner in which intuition—defined as small-sample processing—correlates with valence and distance is functional and likely to increase accuracy and subjective well-being. Cost–benefit considerations within a signal-detection framework suggest that it is ecologically rational to draw quick and intuitive decisions in aversive settings based on small evidence samples and low thresholds just to minimize false positives, that is, to not overlook dangerous or painful stimuli. Similarly, it is rational to approach an object and to gather large samples of data before making quantitative estimations and being able to make quick and timely choices from a distance when only small samples are available.

However, importantly, we have shown it is also rational that the correlations that hold between valence, distance, and intuition or sample size be subject to dialectic regulation. Although positive valence induces approach behavior, reducing distance and increasing stimulus samples, it would be maladaptive if all individuals were increasingly striving for the same positive stimuli (e.g., all men trying to mate the same women; all animals searching for food in the same attractive place). So as people approach and increase the experience samples with attractive objects, there are feasibility constraints that let them discover unforeseen negative aspects in the stimuli, which turn out to be more multidimensional and less ideal than expected. In other words, what appeared to be purely positive turns out to be mixed or even negative in valence. Conversely, seemingly negative stimuli that people have been deprived of or that they have avoided long enough, may in the long run raise their curiosity and turn out to be more interesting and attractive than expected. In other words, just as the impact of hunger on eating is regulated by saturation, or just as the increase in attractiveness as a function of repeated exposure finally produces habituation (rendering frequent stimuli less attractive), the impact of valence on distance and sample size is also subject to adaptive regulation.

We believe that the statistical model we have introduced to illustrate the assets of intuitive decisions helps to go beyond the mere astonishment and the existence of proof that intuitive strategies can be quite adaptive. Rather, our model is intended to show why and under what boundary conditions this is the case. Importantly, we have shown that the assets of intuitive processes operating on small samples are confined to choice problems as distinguished from estimation problems. With regard to the causes and origins, the most intriguing implication is that the assets of intuition arise, to a considerable degree, in the environment rather than in the individual. The very statistical rules by which stimulus samples of decision objects are distributed around their true values can explain why intuitive strategies, based on small samples, may inform more accurate choices and decisions than exhaustive strategies based on large information samples.

ACKNOWLEDGMENTS

This work was supported by several grants from the Deutsche Forschungsgemeinschaft (DFG). The ideas underlying this article were created during Yaakov Kareev's guest professorship at the University of Heidelberg in 2005.

REFERENCES

Ambady, N., & Rosenthal, R. (1992). Thin slices of expressive behavior as predictors of interpersonal consequences: A meta-analysis. *Psychological Bulletin, 111,* 256–274.

Axelrod, R. (1984). *The evolution of cooperation.* New York: Basic Books.

Axelrod, R., & Hamilton, W. D. (1981). The evolution of cooperation. *Science, 242,* 1385–1390.

Baumeister, R. F., Bratslavsky, E., Finkenauer, C., & Vohs, K. D. (2001). Bad is stronger than good. *Review of General Psychology, 5,* 323–370.

Betsch, C. (2004). Präferenz für Intuition und Deliberation (PID)—Inventar zur Erfassung von affekt- und kognitionsbasiertem Entscheiden [Preference for intuition and deliberation (PID)—An inventory for assessing affect- and cognition-based decision making]. *Zeitschrift für Differentielle und Diagnostische Psychologie, 25,* 179–197.

Betsch, C. (2006). *Präferenz für Intuition und Deliberation (PID)—Messung und Konsequenzen von individuellen Unterschieden in affekt- und kognitionsbasiertem Entscheiden* [Preference for intuition and deliberation (PID)—Measurement and consequences of individual differences in affect- and cognition-based decision making]. Unpublished doctoral dissertation, University of Heidelberg, Heidelberg, Germany.

Bless, H., & Fiedler, K. (2006). Mood and the regulation of information processing and behavior. In J. P. Forgas (Ed.), *Affect in social thinking and behavior* (pp. 65–84). New York: Psychology Press.

Brendl, M., Markman, A. B., & Messner, C. (2005). Indirectly measuring evaluations of several attitude objects in relation to a neutral reference point. *Journal of Experimental and Social Psychology, 41,* 346–368.

Buehler, R., Griffin, D., & Ross, M. (1994). Exploring the "planning fallacy": Why people underestimate their task completion times. *Journal of Personality and Social Psychology, 67,* 366–381.

Chaiken, S., & Trope, Y. (Eds.). (1999). *Dual-process theories in social psychology.* New York: Guilford.

Chajut, E., & Algom, D. (2003). Selective attention improves under stress: Implications for theories of social cognition. *Journal of Personality & Social Psychology, 85,* 231–248.

Deffenbacher, K. A., Bornstein, B. H., Penrod, S. D., & McGorty, E. K. (2004). A meta-analytic review of the effects of high stress on eyewitness memory. *Law and Human Behavior, 28,* 687–706.

Denrell, J. (2005). Why most people disapprove of me: Experience sampling in impression formation. *Psychological Review, 112,* 951–978.

Dijksterhuis, A., & Aarts, H. (2003). On wildebeests and humans: The preferential detection of negative stimuli. *Psychological Science, 14,* 14–18.

Elman, J.L. (1993). Learning and development in neural networks: The importance of starting small. *Cognition, 48,* 71–99.

Epstein, S., Pacini, R., Denes-Raj, V., & Heier, H. (1996). Individual differences in intuitive-experiential and analytical rational thinking styles. *Journal of Personality and Social Psychology, 71,* 390–405.

Eyal, T., Liberman, N., Trope, Y., & Walther, E. (2004). The pros and cons of temporally near and distant action. *Journal of Personality and Social Psychology, 86,* 781–795.

Fiedler, K. (1988). Emotional mood, cognitive style, and behavior regulation. In K. Fiedler & J. P. Forgas (Eds.), *Affect, cognition, and social behavior* (pp. 100–119). Toronto, Ontario, Canada: Hogrefe.

Fiedler, K. (1996). Explaining and simulating judgment biases as an aggregation phenomenon in probabilistic, multiple-cue environments. *Psychological Review, 103,* 193–214.

Fiedler, K. (2001). Affective states trigger processes of assimilation and accommodation. In L. L. Martin & G. L. Clore (Eds.), *Theories of mood and cognition: A user's guidebook* (pp. 85–98). Mahwah, NJ: Lawrence Erlbaum Associates, Inc.

Fiedler, K., & Kareev, Y. (2006). Does decision quality (always) increase with the size of information samples? Some vicissitudes in applying the law of large numbers. *Journal of Experimental Psychology: Learning, Memory & Cognition, 32,* 883–903.

Fiedler, K., Kemmelmeier, M., & Freytag, P. (1999). Explaining asymmetric intergroup judgments through differential aggregation: Computer simulations and some new evidence. *European Review of Social Psychology, 10,* 1–40.

Fiedler, K., Renn, S. I., & Kareev, Y. (Unpublished). *Mood and the accuracy of decisions based on small versus large information samples.* University of Heidelberg, Heidelberg, Germany.

Fiedler, K., Semin, G. R., & Finkenauer, C. (1993). The battle of words between gender groups: A language based approach to intergroup processes. *Human Communication Research, 19,* 409–441.

Fiedler, K., Semin, G. R., Finkenauer, C., & Berkel, I. (1995). Actor-observer bias in close relationships: The role of self-knowledge and self-related language. *Personality and Social Psychology Bulletin, 21,* 525–538.

Fiedler, K., & Walther, E. (2003). *Stereotyping as inductive hypothesis testing.* New York: Psychology Press.

Fiedler, K., Walther, E., Freytag, P., & Plessner, H. (2002). Judgment biases in a simulated classroom—A cognitive-environmental approach. *Organizational Behavior and Human Decision Processes, 88,* 527–561.

Gidron, D., Koehler, D. J., & Tversky, A. (1993). Implicit quantification of personality traits. *Personality and Social Psychology Bulletin, 19,* 594–604.

Gilbert, D. T., & Malone, P. S. (1995). The correspondence bias. *Psychological Bulletin, 117,* 21–38.

Gilovich, T., Griffin, D., & Kahneman, D. (Eds.). (2001). *Intuitive judgment: Heuristics and biases.* New York: Cambridge University Press.

Griffin, D., & Tversky, A. (1992). The weighing of evidence and the determinants of confidence. *Cognitive Psychology, 24,* 411–435.

Hansen, C. H., & Hansen, R. D. (1988). Finding the face in the crowd: An anger-superiority effect. *Journal of Personality and Social Psychology, 54,* 917–924.

Hertwig, R., & Pleskac, T. J. (2006). *The game of life: Frugal sampling makes it simpler.* Manuscript submitted for publication.

Hodges, B. H. (1974). Effect of valence on relative weighting in impression formation. *Journal of Personality and Social Psychology, 30,* 378–381.

Hogarth, R. (2001). *Educating intuition.* Chicago: Chicago University Press.

Jones, E. E., & Nisbett, R. E. (1972). The actor and the observer: Divergent perceptions of the causes of behavior. In E. E. Jones, Kanouse, D.E., Kelley, H.H., Nisbett, R.E., Valind, S., & Weiner, B. (Eds.), *Attribution: Perceiving the causes of behavior* (pp. 79–94). Morristown, NJ: General Learning Press.

Judd, C. M., & Park, B. (1988). Outgroup-homogeneity: Judgments of variability at the individual and the group levels. *Journal of Personality and Social Psychology, 54,* 778–788.

Kareev, Y. (1995). Through a narrow window: Working memory capacity and the detection of covariation. *Cognition, 56,* 263–269.

Kareev, Y. (2000). Seven (indeed, plus or minus two) and the detection of correlations. *Psychological Review, 107,* 397–402.

Kareev, Y. (2005). And yet the small-sample effect does hold: Reply to Juslin and Olsson (2005) and Anderson, Doherty, Berg, and Friedrich (2005). *Psychological Review, 112,* 280–285.

Kareev, Y., Lieberman, I., & Lev, M. (1997). Through a narrow window: Sample size and the perception of correlation. *Journal of Experimental Psychology: General, 126,* 278–287.

Klayman, J., & Ha, Y. (1987). Confirmation, disconfirmation, and information in hypothesis testing. *Psychological Review, 94,* 211–228.

Kruger, J., & Evans, M. (2004). If you don't want to be late, enumerate: Unpacking reduces the planning fallacy. *Journal of Experimental Social Psychology, 40,* 586–598.

Kruglanski, A. W., & Webster, D. M. (1991). Group members' reactions to opinion deviates and conformists at varying degrees of proximity to decision deadline and of experimental noise. *Journal of Personality and Social Psychology, 61,* 212–225.

Kruglanski, A. W., & Webster, D. M. (1996). Motivated closing of the mind: "Seizing" and "freezing." *Psychological Review, 103,* 263–283.

Liberman, N., Sagristano, M., & Trope, Y. (2002). The effect of temporal distance on level of construal. *Journal of Experimental Social Psychology, 38,* 523–535.

Linville, P. W., Fischer, G. W., & Salovey, P. (1989). Perceived distributions of the characteristics of ingroup and outgroup members: Empirical evidence and a computer simulation. *Journal of Personality and Social Psychology, 57,* 165–188.

Linville, P. W., Fischer, G. W., & Yoon, C. (1996). Perceived covariation among the features of ingroup and outgroup members: The outgroup covariation effect. *Journal of Personality and Social Psychology, 70,* 421–436.

Linville, P. W., & Jones, E. E. (1980). Polarized appraisals of outgroup members. *Journal of Personality and Social Psychology, 38,* 689–703.

Miller, N. E. (1944). Experimental studies of conflict. In McV. Hunt (Ed.), *Personality and the behavior disorders* (pp. 431–465). New York: Ronald Press.

Miyamoto, Y., & Kitayama, S. (2002). Cultural variation in correspondence bias: The critical role of attitude diagnosticity of socially constrained behavior. *Journal of Personality and Social Psychology, 83,* 1239–1248.

Nowak, M., & Sigmund, K. (1993). A strategy of win-stay, lose-shift that outperforms tit-for-tat in the Prisoner's Dilemma game. *Nature, 364,* 56–58.

Park, B., & Hastie, R. (1987). Perception of variability in category development: Instance- versus abstraction-based stereotypes. *Journal of Personality and Social Psychology, 53*, 621–635.

Park, B., & Rothbart, M. (1982). Perception of outgroup homogeneity and levels of social categorization: Memory for the subordinate attributes of ingroup and outgroup members. *Journal of Personality and Social Psychology, 42*, 1051–1068.

Peeters, G., & Czapinski, J. (1990). Positive-negative asymmetry in evaluations: The distinction between affective and informational negativity effects. In W. Stroebe & M. Hewstone (Eds.), *European review of social psychology* (Vol. 1, pp. 33–60). Chichester, England: Wiley.

Pratto, F., & John, O. P. (1991). Automatic vigilance: The attention-grabbing power of negative social information. *Journal of Personality and Social Psychology, 61*, 380–391.

Reeder, G. D., & Brewer, M. (1979). A schematic model of dispositional attribution in interpersonal perception. *Psychological Review, 86*, 61–79.

Ross, L. (1977). The intuitive psychologist and his shortcomings: Distortions in the attribution process. In L. Berkowitz (Ed.), *Advances in experimental social psychology* (Vol. 10, pp. 173–220). New York: Academic.

Scott, S. G., & Bruce, R. A. (1985). Decision making style: The development and assessment of a new measure. *Educational and Psychological Measurement, 55*, 818–831.

Semin, G. R. (2007). Linguistic markers of social distance and proximity. In K. Fiedler (Ed.), *Frontiers of social psychology: Social communication* (pp. 389–408). New York: Psychology Press.

Semin, G. R., & Fiedler, K. (1988). The cognitive functions of linguistic categories in describing persons: Social cognition and language. *Journal of Personality and Social Psychology, 54*, 558–568.

Simon, B. (1992). The perception of ingroup and outgroup homogeneity: Reintroducing the intergroup context. *European Review of Social Psychology, 3*, 1–30.

Simon, H. A. (1956). Rational choice and the structure of environments. *Psychological Review, 63*, 129–138.

Skowronski, J. J., & Carlston, D. E. (1989). Social judgment and social memory: The role of cue diagnosticity in negativity, positivity, and extremity biases. *Psychological Bulletin, 105*, 131–142.

Swets, J., Dawes, R. M., & Monahan, J. (2000). Psychological science can improve diagnostic decisions. *Psychological Science in the Public Interest, 1*(X), 1, 1, 1–26.

Taylor, S. E. (1991). Asymmetrical effects of positive and negative events: The mobilization-minimization hypothesis. *Psychological Bulletin, 110*, 67–85.

Thorndyke, E. L. (1916). Notes on practice, improvability, and the curve of work. *American Journal of Psychology, 27*, 550–565.

Thuijsman, F., Peleg, B., Amitai, M., & Shmida, A. (1995). Automata, matching and foraging behavior of bees. *Journal of Theoretical Biology, 175*, 305–316.

Trope, Y., & Liberman, N. (2000). Temporal construal and time-dependent changes in preference. *Journal of Personality and Social Psychology, 79*, 876–889.

Trope, Y., & Liberman, N. (2003). Temporal construal. *Psychological Review, 110*, 403–421.

Watson, D. (1982). The actor and the observer: How are their perceptions of causality divergent? *Psychological Bulletin, 92*, 682–700.

Wentura, D., Rothermund, K., & Bak, P. (2000). Automatic vigilance: The attention-grabbing power of approach and avoidance-related social information. *Journal of Personality and Social Psychology, 78*, 1024–1037.

Wojciszke, B. (1994). Multiple meanings of behavior: Construing actions in terms of competence or morality. *Journal of Personality and Social Psychology, 67*, 222–232.

III

Emotion and Intuition

11

Emotion, Motivation, and Decision Making
A Feeling-Is-for-Doing Approach

MARCEL ZEELENBERG, ROB NELISSEN,
and RIK PIETERS

Tilburg University

INTRODUCTION

Anyone who has ever made an important life decision—about a partner, house, career, investment, and so forth—knows that intuition plays an important role therein. Even though people may be aware of the fact that they should make important decisions in a rational, consequential manner, and even if they try hard to do so, the reality is that when making these choices and decisions, people are often overwhelmed by preferences toward some of the options that they cannot easily verbalize. For example, when buying a house, the first impression of the house seems to be crucial. These first intuitive impressions are often based on people's initial emotional response, which does not require extensive cognitive deliberation. If it doesn't feel right, the chances are slim that a person acts on it. When the click is there, however, that person is easily prepared to overspend on it. This chapter reviews some of the emotional processes that play a role during decision processes and delineates how emotions may operate in an intuitive manner. For more general reviews of the role of affect and emotion in decision making, we refer the reader to Finucane, Peters, and Slovic (2003); Isen (2000); Ketelaar (2004, 2006); Loewenstein and Lerner (2003); and Pieters and Van Raaij (1988).

A core premise in this chapter is that emotional processes form at least part of the intuitional component of decision making (cf. T. Betsch, chap. 1, this volume).

We conceptualize emotions as motivational processes that prioritize certain goals and thereby mobilize and give direction to behavior (cf., Bagozzi, Baumgartner, Pieters, & Zeelenberg, 2000; Frijda, 1988, 2006; Nelissen, Dijker, & De Vries, 2007-a & b). This emotional influence may take place via conscious experience but may also occur more or less automatically. Put differently, we argue that emotions can implicitly activate associated goals that manifest themselves behaviorally. This motivational part of emotional experience has been relatively understudied.

In the remainder of this chapter, we first illuminate the nature of affect and of emotion. Next, we argue that to understand the effect of affect on decision making, one has to go beyond valence and study the effects of specific emotions. We then review different approaches to studying the effects of specific emotions and show how these relate to different elements of the emotional experience. We end with proposing a research agenda including issues that should be considered in research on emotion in decision making.

THE NATURE OF AFFECT

Affect is a generic term that refers to many experiential concepts including moods, emotions, attitudes, evaluations, and preferences. The defining feature is the valence dimension. *Valence* is a term borrowed from physics and chemistry (Solomon & Stone, 2002), and it refers to the positivity or negativity of an experience. Thus, any experiential concept that is valanced can be considered affective. The valence dimension is a fundamental one with respect to many psychological experiences (Osgood, Suci, & Tannenbaum, 1957; Russell, 1980). It is obvious that decision scientists have a strong interest in affect because the valence aspect of affect is so easily related to utility. Positive affect creates utility (or satisfaction) and negative affect creates disutility (or dissatisfaction; e.g., Mellers, Schwartz, & Ritov, 1999). Freud (1920/1952) even argued that "our entire psychical activity is bent upon procuring pleasure and avoiding pain" (p. 365). Thus, affect refers to positivity and negativity, to goodness and badness, to pleasantness and unpleasantness, favorability and unfavorability, and pleasure and pain. Affect is sometimes used as a synonym for emotion, but this is not only incorrect (emotions are affective, but not all affect is emotion) but also hinders progress into one's insight into the role of emotion in decision making as becomes apparent in the next sections.

THE NATURE OF EMOTION

The exact definition of *emotion* has been a matter of dispute among psychologists, philosophers, and other researchers (Kleinginna & Kleinginna, 1981) mainly because of the wide array of possible emotions that one can experience (guilt, shame, regret, disappointment, envy, gloating, anger, fear, joy, pride, to name only a few) and because there is no defining characteristic that applies to all emotions. However, there is agreement on several aspects. Emotions are acute; they are relatively momentary experiences. This differentiates emotions from moods, which typically last longer, and from other more general affects. Emotions are about something or someone: You are angry with someone; you regret a choice, and so forth. Emotions typically arise when one evaluates an event or outcome as relevant for one's concerns or preferences. One does not become emotional over something trivial. Moreover, emotions are "cognitively impenetrable": One cannot choose to have or not have emotions given certain events or outcomes that are relevant for one's concerns (Frijda, 1986, p. 468).

Emotions have multiple components, and they can be differentiated from each other on the basis of these. One of these components is the appraisal pattern that gives rise to the emotion. *Appraisal* refers to the process of judging the significance of an event for personal well-being. Appraisal theory (for a review, see Scherer, Schorr, & Johnstone, 2001), the dominant approach in emotion research, maintains that specific emotions are associated with specific patterns of cognitive appraisals of the emotion-eliciting situation. People may differ in the specific appraisals that are elicited by a particular event, but the same patterns of appraisals always give rise to the same emotions. An understanding of appraisals is important because it may help researchers to understand why specific emotions arise and hence provide a solid theoretical basis for emotion manipulation. Research on appraisal processes, however, remains relatively mute when it comes to predicting behavior (Frijda & Zeelenberg, 2001).

The other components of emotion that we address here are more closely linked to behavior. Together, these components comprise the experiential content of the emotion. Basic emotion research on experiential content (Davitz, 1969; Roseman, Wiest, & Swartz, 1994; Wallbott & Scherer, 1988) has investigated a wide range of characteristics to differentiate emotions. Roseman et al. (1994) proposed that emotions could be differentiated in terms of the following five experiential categories: feelings, thoughts, action tendencies, actions, and emotivational goals. Feelings are perceived physical or mental sensations. Thoughts are ideas, plans, conceptions, or opinions produced by mental activity. Action tendencies are impulses or inclinations to respond with a particular action. Actions include behavior that may or may not be purposive. Emotivational goals describe the goals that accompany discrete emotions (wanting to avoid danger in case of fear or wanting to recover from loss in case of sadness). These emotivational goals are similar to what Frijda (1986) has referred to as "changes in patterns of action readiness" (p. 351; Frijda, 1986, 2006). Action readiness refers to motivational states that may involve attentional focusing, arousal, muscular preparation, or actual action, goal priority, or felt readiness. Action readiness is defined by having control precedence, which means that it may overrule other goals. Many emotions can be differentiated in terms of action readiness.

The experiential content of an emotion thus reflects how emotions are felt and what emotions mean to the person experiencing them; it is the real emotional experience. Specific appraisals elicit specific emotions with specific experiential contents. In the recently developed feeling-is-for-doing approach, Zeelenberg and Pieters (2006) reserved a special role for the experiential content of emotions and for the motivational aspect that is part of it. We have proposed that this experiential content is the proximal cause of all that follows, including specific adaptive behavior. Knowing the experiential content of an emotion therefore implies knowledge of the motivations that arise during this experience. For example, when one realizes that the experience of anger in consumers goes with feelings like exploding, thoughts of unfairness and violence, and tendencies to let go and behave aggressively, it simply follows that these consumers are motivated to retaliate (Bougie, Pieters, & Zeelenberg, 2003). This knowledge allows researchers to make specific behavioral predictions. We return to this later, but first, we turn to how emotion is related to decision making.

EMOTION AND DECISION MAKING: THE NEED TO GO BEYOND VALENCE

It goes without saying that emotion plays a large role in decision making. Early theorists have recognized this, and have discussed it in quite some detail (Bentham, 1789/1948; Jevons, 1871/1965; A. Smith, 1759/1976). Despite this early interest, however, emotion never really made it into decision research. This was partly due to the fact that emotion was seen as intrinsically unstable and unpredictable and partly because it could not be measured objectively. Jevons (1871/1965), for example, stated "I hesitate to say that men will ever have the means of measuring directly the feelings of the human heart" (p. 11). Thus, although there never was any denial of the influence of emotions, it needs to be stressed that the early observations of A. Smith (1759/1976) and his contemporaries were not followed up empirically. The two early limitations, unpredictability and immeasurability, have been removed since then. The impact of emotion on behavior is actually simpler and more systematic than previously thought. First, emotions can be measured reliably in various verbal (e.g., via rating scales) and nonverbal ways (e.g., via Facial Action Coding System or facial electromyography, Larsen & Fredrickson, 1999; Parrott & Hertel, 1999). Moreover, the number of distinct emotions is fairly limited (compared to a virtual endless amount of cognitions), and they behave lawfully (Frijda, 1988, 2006). Hence, clear, stable, and predictable consequences and correlates of emotion exist.

Consequently, there is a renewed interest in the role of emotion in decision behavior from both economists and psychologists. In this current decision research (as in many fields outside core emotion theory), however, emotions are often conceptualized as valenced feeling states. That is, emotions are often equated with affect and reduced to a value on a positive–negative dimension. Positive emotions are thought to add utility, and negative emotions subtract utility. Decision making then comes down to "hedonic calculus" in which pain and pleasure are summed, and the net best alternative is picked (see also, Jevons, 1871/1965). Cabanac (1992) argued that emotions can be compared in terms of pleasure, and he referred to this as a "common currency." Also, in Mellers et al.'s (1999) "subjective expected pleasure theory," counterfactual emotions (regret, disappointment, elation, rejoicing, and surprise) are expressed via a single "pain–pleasure" dimension.

Such a one-dimensional, valence-based approach falls short for several reasons (see, for a more elaborate discussion, Zeelenberg & Pieters, 2006). First, not all negative emotions have the same effect as we review later. Second, some emotions are difficult to place on the positive–negative dimension (are pride, schadenfreude, relief, and hope unequivocally positive or negative emotions?). We thus argue that especially when one is interested in motivational and intuitive processes in decision making, a focus on the mere valence of emotions is insufficient. We came to this conviction based on a number of reasons, aptly summarized by Solomon and Stone (2002). These emotion philosophers (Solomon & Stone, 2002) recently reviewed the emotion literature and concluded that

> The analysis of emotions in terms of "valence," while it recognizes something essential about emotions . . . is an idea that we should abandon and leave behind. It serves no purpose but confusion and perpetrates the worst old stereotypes about emotion, that these are simple phenomena unworthy of serious research and analysis. (p. 431)

Thus, when interested in how emotions influence behavioral decision making, a focus on specific emotions is clearly required. Luckily, this has been realized by a number of decision researchers. We review their efforts following.

DIFFERENT APPROACHES TO EMOTION SPECIFICITY

Studies that have revealed the differential impact of specific emotions are accumulating, and several perspectives that account for these influences begin to emerge. We consider them in detail, but first, we want to make clear that for our current purposes, we are only concerned with the direct impact of specific experienced emotions. Thus, we do not discuss the influence of expected or anticipated emotions, although they prove a valuable extension to traditional expected-utility models of decision making (e.g., Mellers et al., 1999; Van der Pligt, Zeelenberg, Van Dijk, De Vries, & Richard, 1998). Neither do we discuss indirect effects of emotion on decision making, although it has been shown that emotions may bias people's judgments via the selective recall of similarly valenced memories (e.g., Bower, 1981) and by influencing the depth (i.e., heuristic or systematic) of cognitive processing (e.g., Tiedens & Linton, 2001). Our focus is on those instances in which specific emotions exert a direct impact on behavioral decisions that is not mediated by changes in the nature and content of basic cognitive processes. Hence, we highlight the more intuitive side of emotional influences on decisions.

Emotions and emotional influences can be either endogenous or exogenous (cf. Zeelenberg & Pieters, 2006). This distinction is consistent with the general role that factors can play in causal processes. We refer to emotions as endogenous when the experience is relevant to the decision at hand and an integral part of the goal-setting and goal-striving process. For example, the anxiety experienced when deliberating a risky choice or the regret experienced over an earlier investment when determining whether to invest further are endogenous. Likewise, the anger about goal frustration is endogenous. Exogenous emotions or emotional influences, on the other hand, are those that are not related to a current decision and are external to the actual goal-setting and goal-striving process, although they may—exogenously—influence this. They constitute the carryover effects of emotions or mood states resulting from a prior experience, such as watching a happy or a sad movie, on subsequent unrelated decisions. Thus, an endogenous emotion is part of current goal pursuit, whereas an exogenous emotion comes from outside, and its effects may "steam through" current goal pursuit. The distinction between endogenous and exogenous emotions is important, as it may determine the extent to which findings on emotional influences are relevant to theoretical accounts of such effects as we outlined following.

Perspectives on the direct influence of specific experienced emotions on decision making fall into either of two categories, although both are not necessarily mutually exclusive. They differ in whether they emphasize the informational or the motivational properties of emotions (Zeelenberg & Pieters, 2006). We argue for the superior suitability of motivational perspectives in accounting for effects of emotions on decision making and propose a research agenda to further theorizing on the emotional influences in decision-making processes.

Information-Based Accounts

These accounts highlight the nature of inferences that people in a particular emotional state are likely to draw. They emphasize the backward looking function of emotions highlighting the cues that emotions give about past goal performance and/or the conduciveness of the state of the world or current and future goal pursuit. Information-based accounts zoom in on the feedback function of emotions. Generally, they predict emotional influences in case of commonality between the central appraisal dimensions associated with the emotion and the principal dimension of judgment involved in a particular choice situation. Two major information-based perspectives have been outlined, the appraisal tendency approach (Lerner & Keltner, 2000, 2001), and the emotion as information model (DeSteno, Petty, Wegener, & Rucker, 2000).

The latter account in particular is heavily grounded in the seminal bodies of research that have indicated affect-congruent influences on judgment, initiated by Johnson and Tversky (1983) and Schwarz and Clore (1983). Affect congruency means that people use their feelings as a cue to infer the general state of the world, considering the world as a place where good things are likely to happen when in a positive mood or conversely, anticipating negative events when feeling bad. This mechanism became known as the "How-do-I-feel-about-it"—heuristic (Schwarz, 1990) The more recently proposed affect heuristic that refers to the fact that decision makers may simply use their intuitive affective reaction toward an object or behavior as input for their choices is another example of affect congruency (Slovic, Finucane, Peters, & MacGregor, 2002).

DeSteno et al. (2000) showed that such mood-induced biases in likelihood estimations extend to specific emotions as well, thus indicating increased likelihood estimates for events with similar "emotional overtones." For instance, inducing sadness (but not anger) increased the estimated frequency of saddening events (e.g., the number of people that will find out their best friend is moving away), whereas inducing anger (but not sadness) had similar effects for angering events (e.g., the number of criminals that will be set free because of legal technicalities).

The appraisal tendency approach (Lerner & Keltner, 2000) also emphasizes the informational function of emotions. The appraisal tendency approach conceives that each emotion activates a tendency to evaluate future events in line with the central dimensions of the appraisal that triggered the emotion. These appraisal tendencies thus are perceptual inclinations by which emotions color the cognitive interpretation of stimuli.

Support for the appraisal tendency approach initially derived from findings that indicated that anger increases tendencies to perceive other individuals as responsible for subsequent events, whereas sadness increases the tendency to ascribe responsibility to the environment (Keltner, Ellsworth, & Edwards, 1993). These patterns are consistent with the underlying appraisal patterns of sadness (situation responsible for negative outcomes) and anger (others responsible). Further support comes from a series of studies in which dispositional and situationally induced differences in people's experiences of fear and anger have been found to be associated with differences in risk perception (Lerner & Keltner, 2000, 2001). Fear and anger differ in their appraisals of control and certainty, which are low in fear and high in anger. Perceptions of risk depend mainly on people's estimates of their abilities to exert personal control in a particular situation and a sense of predictability (i.e., certainty) over the outcome of that situation. When afraid, people make more pessimistic judgments of risk (i.e., estimating the number of casualties due to various events) than people who are angry. Moreover, fear was also associated with preferences for risk-averse options, whereas anger was associated with risk-seeking preferences (Lerner & Keltner, 2001).

Taken together, both the emotion-as-information model and the appraisal tendency approach provide accounts for emotional influences on people's judgments, with the latter framework providing more encompassing and detailed predictions, as it relates emotions to a wider array of cognitive dimensions involved in judgmental processes. It is important to note that the information-based accounts take a backward looking stance with respect to goal progress. That is, emotions provide information about how one is currently doing. This affective feedback informs about the extent of goal progress, but does not provide the decision maker with clear guidelines for how to attain these goals in the future. Before evaluating the suitability of information-based frameworks in accounting for the impact of emotions on behavioral decision making in greater detail, we first introduce studies that have adopted a goal-based account to explain emotional influences.

Goal-Based Accounts

These accounts stress the implicit goals for action that are associated with an emotion to explain its influences on decisions. They emphasize the forward-looking function of emotions. That is, goal-based accounts focus on the goal setting and striving implications of emotions, which are by definition future oriented. Generally, they predict emotions to guide decisions in the direction of the outcome that is (most) conducive to the attainment of the emotional goal. In earlier research, the emotional impact on behavior has hardly ever been considered to be a goal-directed process but rather has been viewed as an accidental consequence of the operation of the emotion system (Johnson & Tversky, 1983; Schwarz & Clore, 1983). The mood maintenance hypothesis (Isen & Patrick, 1983) presents a notable exception. This hypothesis holds that when in a positive mood, people are motivated to maintain their feeling state, whereas a negative mood instigates efforts of mood repair, for instance, by motivating prosocial acts, which often result in positive affect (Schaller & Cialdini, 1990). Current goal-based perspectives on emotional influences on decision making have moved beyond a valence-based account to further understand the impact of specific emotions.

Several researchers have explicitly adopted this approach in documenting and explaining the influence of specific emotions on people's decisions. Note that the following studies (unless explicitly mentioned otherwise) all have reported effects of exogenous emotional influences, a point that we address further in the subsequent section.

Fessler, Pillsworth, and Flamson (2004) investigated the impact of anger and disgust on preferences for gambles. Fessler et al. found that disgust decreased but anger increased risk taking. Fessler et al. referred to the different implicit goals associated with anger and disgust to account for this. Specifically, Fessler et al. argued that disgust decreases risk-taking behavior because it motivates avoidance of contact. Anger, on the other hand, increased risk taking because retaliation requires to a certain extent the neglect of risk.

Raghunathan and Pham (1999) investigated the impact of fear and sadness on risk preference in choices between gambles and job options. Raghunathan and Pham predicted (and found) that fear, which they argued is associated with a goal to reduce uncertainty, decreased preference for risky options. Sadness, however, caused the opposite effect. The latter is explained by suggesting that sadness involves an implicit goal of reward replacement, inducing a tendency to favor options with highly rewarding outcomes.

Lerner, Small, and Loewenstein (2004) studied the differential impact of sadness and disgust on the endowment effect (the finding that selling prices exceed buying prices for the same object). It was found that compared to a neutral control condition in which the traditional endowment effect was replicated, buying and selling prices did not differ anymore after disgust was induced. Inducing sadness even caused a complete reversal of the endowment effect (i.e., buying prices exceeding selling prices). Rather than relying on differences in appraisal tendencies, Lerner et al. proposed a goal-based mechanism to underlie these results. Specifically, triggering the implicit goal to expel or avoid taking in (cf. Rozin, Haidt, & McCauley, 1993), disgust was hypothesized to reduce both selling and buying prices, respectively.

Zeelenberg and Pieters (1999, 2004) have compared behavioral consequences of experienced regret and disappointment in relation to failed services. Hence, these studies concerned the impact of endogeneous emotional influences. Zeelenberg and Pieters (1999) argued that such negative experiences can cause both disappointment (when service delivery falls short of prior expectancies) and regret (after a bad choice of service providers). Zeelenberg and Pieters (2004) asked consumers to recollect negative experiences with service providers and to subsequently report their feelings and behaviors in response to this encounter. Across the studies,

Zeelenberg and Pieters found different reactions following the experience of regret and disappointment. Regret was most clearly associated with switching service providers; and disappointment was also associated with negative word-of-mouth communication switching and complaining to the provider.

Finally, specific emotional influences on decisions in social dilemmas have been investigated. Social dilemmas typically model interactions between two or more people involving a motivational conflict between a decision to do what is best for the group (i.e., to cooperate) or to do what is best for oneself (i.e., to defect). Several studies have documented guilt inductions to increase the amount of cooperative decisions in ultimatum games (Ketelaar & Au, 2003) and prisoner dilemma games (Ketelaar & Au, 2003; Nelissen, Dijker, & De Vries, 2007-b). These effects have been explained by referring to the implicit goal of making-up for transgression (Nelissen et al., 2007-b), which is associated with guilt (cf. Roseman et al., 1994), or by addressing guilt's theorized status as a moral emotion (cf. Frank, 2004) that inhibits tendencies to pursue immediate self-interest (Ketelaar & Au, 2003). Finally, fear, associated with a goal to avoid risk, was found to reduce cooperation in a prisoner dilemma game, hence instigating players to make a less risky decision (Nelissen et al., 2007-b). Note that the latter study also reported interactive effects of emotion induction and social value orientations, which we turn to later.

EVALUATING INFORMATION- AND GOAL-BASED ACCOUNTS

A strict information-based perspective falls short of providing a strong account of emotional influences on decision making. First of all, the information-based perspective cannot adequately accommodate certain empirical findings. For instance, the effects of disgust and sadness on the endowment effect (Lerner et al., 2004) do not readily follow from considering the appraisal dimensions associated with both emotions. Disgust is characterized by appraisals of high certainty, human control, other responsibility, and a strong unwillingness to attend to the situation (C. A. Smith & Ellsworth, 1985). Nevertheless, it is not apparent how a tendency to appraise the situation along these dimensions causes a reduction of the endowment effect, that is, a reduction of selling prices, in particular. Similarly, it seems unclear how appraising a situation in terms of high situational control and moderate levels of certainty (as associated with sadness) would reverse the endowment effect.

Second, other empirical findings appear to contradict predictions of an information-based approach. Based on the appraisal tendency approach, similar effects would have been expected for emotions with similar appraisals. Both anger and disgust are associated with equal levels of certainty and perceived control (C. A. Smith & Ellsworth, 1985). Nevertheless, anger and disgust have differential effects on risk preferences (Fessler et al., 2004). Furthermore, sadness was found to increase rather than decrease preferences for high-risk alternatives (Raghunathan & Pham, 1999). This is odd given that sadness is primarily related to appraisals of high situational control and moderate levels of certainty, which should, in an information-based perspective, have led to reduced preference for high-risk enterprises.

Clearly, one may argue that rather than a feedback effect, emotions here had a feed-forward effect, setting goals for future pursuit rather than following the appraisals contained in experienced emotions that resulted from past events.

Third and finally, closer inspection at a theoretical level reveals that information-based accounts are more apt at accounting for judgment effects than at decision-making effects and related goal pursuits. That is, emotions clearly color or bias judgments. Such almost automatic appraisal tendency effects of emotions have been well documented. Yet, interestingly, in these studies, the emotion is the end of a goal pursuit sequence or exogenously induced, and this was followed by a moment in which judgments were called for, and the latter were obviously colored by the former. Thus, when goal pursuit ends (or did not yet initiate), and an emotion is still activated, it influences judgment in an appraisal-consistent fashion. Yet, when the emotion is part of a sequence of ongoing goal pursuit, such "appraisal consistency" effects are much less obvious. Then, one needs to know the overarching goal of people and the activated emotion to predict future behavior, as we showed earlier. Motivational perspectives, by emphasizing the implicit goals associated with current feeling states instead of foregrounding inferential processes, provide this link.

Sometimes integration is advocated for the informational and motivational functions of emotions into a single model, arguing "affective states [to] convey not only situational appraisal information, but also motivational information" (Pham, 2004, p. 363). Similarly, in its original formulation, the appraisal tendency approach was claimed to encompass not only cognitive-appraisal theories but also functional views of emotions, delineating the regulating role of emotions in shaping behavioral responses (Lerner & Keltner, 2000). Yet both assertions overlook that inference (backward looking for meaning of past states) and motivation (forward looking for desirable end states) are fundamentally distinct processes that require independent demonstration and that neither of both automatically implies the other. In other words, as we have tried to demonstrate, activation of appraisal tendencies cannot simply be equated with the activation of goals for action. Hence, suggesting that emotions cause different situational inferences and as a result will induce different goals (Pham, 2004), constitutes too big a leap in the face of current data.

It is not our intention to contest the idea that emotions have at the same time an informational and a motivational component—they do. Nor do we contradict the assertion that both can be meaningfully related as has already been noted by Frijda (1988, 2006) when discussing the "laws of emotion." As such, we find ourselves supportive to (future) attempts at integrating motivational and informational effects of emotions into a single framework. In our opinion, however, such attempts are still too premature, especially as both informational and motivational perspectives still await further validation themselves.

In sum, not only do certain research findings contradict predictions from informational accounts; such perspectives also seem to lack sufficiency and capability to explain reported effects of emotional states on decision making. These accounts seem to be better suited to explain the effect of emotion on cognitive procession. Goal-based accounts seem to be more appropriate for investigating the ways in which emotions impact the behavioral decisions people make. This is not to say that present research adopting a motivational perspective is flawless. We therefore, in the next section, present a research agenda addressing several issues that must be considered in future research investigating behavioral consequences of emotions.

TESTING GOAL-BASED ACCOUNTS: A FEELING-IS-FOR-DOING APPROACH

As we argued earlier, goal-based perspectives to account for the effects of emotions are recent, and researchers are just beginning to understand how emotions work. Zeelenberg and Pieters (2006) only recently presented a first version of their feeling-is-for-doing account of emotions. This premature version should be handled with care. This is what was proposed: When considering the potential impact of emotion on behavioral decisions, one should take seriously the fact that people may experience a whole range of different emotions, each with its idiosyncratic experiential content and associated goals. We think that this variety of feeling states exists for the sake of behavioral guidance. The specific emotion felt in a situation indicates a particular problem and prioritizes behavior that deals with this problem. Because different problems require different solutions, different emotions produce different behaviors. If one ignores emotion specificity, one would, for example, predict similar effects for regret and disappointment because both emotions have a negative valence. The feeling-is-for-doing approach predicts, therefore, differential effects for regret and disappointment and for guilt and shame and fear and anger and many other emotions that share the same valence. In addition, we expect that the same specific emotion in different situations may activate different behaviors depending on the overarching goal that people strive to. Thus, specific emotions, because of the specific meaning they convey to the decision maker, may help one to better understand the goals and motivations of the decision makers and hence predict better the specific behaviors the decision makers engage in or refrain from.

In this final section, we continue where Zeelenberg and Pieters (2006) ended, and we point out four criteria for an adequate motivational account of emotions. First, a more systematic approach to assigning goals to emotions is needed. Consider, for example, the subtle differences between implicit goals that are allegedly associated with the same emotion in several of the previously cited studies. Whereas Raghunathan and Pham (1999) declared fear to be associated with a goal to reduce uncertainty, Nelissen et al. (2007-b) stated that fear is associated with the goal of avoiding personal risks (to which uncertainty reduction would be a concomitant). Similarly, guilt is argued to relate to a tendency to disregard one's immediate self-interest (Ketelaar & Au, 2003), which would be an implicit consequence of repairing for transgression (e.g., Nelissen et al., 2007-b). Much would be lost if goal accounts are invoked post hoc to account for patterns of findings, consistent with some but not other aims of people, rather than a priori to design the appropriate experimental and control conditions to test them.

If researchers relate goals to emotions in an arbitrary manner across different studies, their results will lack comparability. This obstructs the potential for integrating findings as would be required to develop a substantial body of support for goal-based hypotheses of emotional effects. Even more problematic, the interpretation of results then acquires a post hoc flavor, for goals apparently can be inferred to match any observed effect of emotions on decision making, giving the impression that all data may support a goal-based perspective. We therefore suggest that hypotheses should be based on empirically grounded catalogues of emotion-related goals as for instance, provided by Roseman et al. (1994). Naturally, by adopting similar procedures, goals can be unambiguously ascribed to previously unstudied emotions (Bougie et al., 2003; Zeelenberg, Van Dijk, Manstead, & Van der Pligt, 1998). This procedure entails asking people to provide a detailed report about a particular emotional experience and subsequently, to answer a number of questions concerning specific feelings, thoughts, action tendencies, actions, and goals associated with this experience (cf. Roseman et al., 1994).

Second, it bears reiteration that not all feelings are clearly associated with well-defined goals for action (Frijda, 1986, 1988). Consequently, not all emotions are equally suitable for testing goal-based hypotheses of emotional influences on decision making. To collect meaningful results, behavioral consequences of emotions that are unambiguously related to a particular goal need to be singled out. More generally, it may be useful to examine in more detail which emotions are typically goal directed and which are less so, following the lead of Bagozzi, Baumgartner, and Pieters (1998). Although seemingly obvious, several of the previously cited studies have ignored this point by investigating, for instance, the impact of sadness (e.g., Lerner et al., 2004; Raghunathan & Pham, 1999). Sadness is not unambiguously characterized by a specific goal for action. If anything, it is accompanied by a loss of motivation, most likely to result in passivity. This does not mean that sadness has no function, but this function may not be directly related to the regulation of action. Apart from orchestrating behavioral responses, emotions may also serve communicative and psychological (e.g., learning) purposes. Alternatively, the influence of sadness may be more contingent on the specific overarching goal that people are pursuing than on the goal ingrained in the emotion itself.

The challenges with reports of behavioral consequences of emotions that have no clearly associated goal for action is that they are also vulnerable to impressions of post hoc reasoning to make the data match the expectations by implementing different goals on different occasions. Whereas in the endowment-effect study (Lerner et al., 2004), sadness was argued to induce a goal of changing circumstances, the impact of sadness on (increased) preferences for risky options (Raghunathan & Pham, 1999) was explained by attributing a reward-replacement goal to sadness.

Furthermore, reported behavioral effects of emotions that have no clearly associated action goal are ultimately meaningless when it comes to supporting a goal-based mechanism. Disappointment in response to failed service encounters (Zeelenberg & Pieters, 2004), for example, resulted in switching of service providers, complaining, and negative word of mouth communication. Naturally, these results outline the importance of considering specific emotions beyond global dissatisfaction when documenting consumers' reactions and clearly show a difference between two negative feelings (i.e., disappointment and regret). Nevertheless, disappointment itself is not associated with a particular goal for action.

Hence, behavioral effects may be found but it remains unclear to what underlying goal such responses are aimed at. These findings, therefore, cannot provide support for a goal-based mechanism.

Third, it is useful to focus on emotion-decision linkages that are common in decision-making practices. Highly uncommon or even weird illustrations of linkages between emotions and decision making may be exciting but less useful to a relevant theory of decision making. Consider, for example, the finding that disgust appears to reduce risk preferences (Fessler et al., 2004). Offering a speculative explanation for this effect, Fessler et al. overlooked that feelings of disgust are uncommon to say the least under natural circumstances in which individuals make risky decisions. Hence, an effect may be found, such as making less risky gambles, but how this bears on the theory of disgust, decision making, or emotions is less transparent.

Indeed, more research is needed on the functional, positive, optimal influence of emotions in regular decision making. Although it is by now commonplace to laud the functionality of emotions for decision making, as a discipline, it seems to be more attracted to the dark and grim side of emotions, which we personally believe to be uncommon, rather than to the bright sides that most people experience much more commonly. As a consequence, researchers know much more about emotional obstruction than about emotional assistance to optimality. Thus, most research as yet has emphasized carryover effects of (exogenous) emotions on judgment and decision making. Often, researchers' results derive a counterintuitive appeal from demonstrating erratic consequences and the fallibility of humans. Such findings, however, obscure awareness of the functional role emotions play in the decision-making process. Emotions that are relevant for the choice at hand (e.g., regret over foregone opportunities, fear about potential outcomes, guilt over earlier misbehavior) clearly show what emotions are and what they are for. They aid the decision maker by providing quick intuitive cues on how to solve motivational conflicts and ambiguities. Moreover, effects of exogenous emotions that seem erratic at first can often be understood if one is aware of the effects of endogenous influences. One of the strengths of a goal-based perspective is its potential to determine a priori the kind of decisions to which a particular emotion is relevant, that is, by considering how the alternative outcomes help to attain or conversely obstruct the emotional goal. At the same time, this implies that if an emotion is by no means relevant to the decision at hand, findings provide little if no support for the proposed goal-based mechanisms.

In sum, the relevance of research findings for goal-based hypotheses of emotional effects is compromised by (a) tenuous inferences of goals (i.e., a misrepresentation of the cause of an observed emotional effect), (b) the lack of goals (i.e., the inability to specify a cause), and (c) adopting irrelevant outcome measures (i.e., documenting consequences that cannot be properly related to the cause). This latter notion is especially relevant to consider when investigating exogenous effects (i.e., of experimentally induced, hence irrelevant, emotions) and warrants an increased focus on (potential) endogenous emotional influences.

Our fourth and final point concerns the need to move beyond the mere documentation of behavioral results of emotions to direct tests of the proposed goal-based mechanism underlying these effects. Although the results from previously cited studies have demonstrated congruence between observed decisional effects and emotional goals, this does not conclusively attest for the idea that goal activation as a result of emotional states causes these effects.

So far, only a single empirical study that we are aware of has indicated a goal-activation mechanism to be involved in the observed consequences of induced emotional states (Nelissen et al., 2007-b). In this study, Nielsen et al. (2007-b) reported fear to reduce and guilt to increase cooperation in a prisoner-dilemma interaction. These effects were qualified, however, by a significant interaction between the emotional state and an individual's social value orientation. Specifically, fear only decreased cooperation for prosocials, whereas only guilty proselves showed increased levels of cooperation. Social value orientations can be understood in terms of individual variation in the chronic accessibility of situation-relevant goals for action. Specifically, when confronted with a social dilemma, proselves only have their self-interest in mind and attempt to make as much as possible profit, whereas prosocials also take the other player's interest into account. Temporal goal activation due to an induced emotional state only changes the behavior of individuals to whom this goal was not already chronically accessible. Hence, fear, inducing a goal to avoid personal risk, does not affect prosocials, as they are already chronically motivated to avoid the risk of losing to the other party. Guilt, on the other hand, associated with an implicit goal to make up for transgressions, inducing a tendency to cooperate, does not affect prosocials, as they already have the other player's interest in mind. These interactions suggest that both emotions and individual dispositions operate through the same underlying mechanism of goal accessibility yet obviously present only an indirect indication thereof. Proceeding along this line, future studies should directly test whether emotional states are indeed related to increased goal activity.

SUMMARY AND CONCLUSIONS

In this chapter, we have reviewed several ways in which theorists have accounted for the effects of emotion on decision making. We differentiated between information-based accounts and motivation-based accounts. We argued in favor of motivational or goal-based accounts because we think that only this account provides a basis for emotion-specific predictions of behavioral decisions. We refer to this approach as the feeling-is-for-doing approach. This approach recognizes that the differential impact of specific emotions occurs via the strong association between emotion and motivation. Emotions arise when events or outcomes are relevant for one's concerns or preferences, and they prioritize behavior that acts in service of these concerns. As such, emotions can be understood as programs for intuitive decision making, imposing on the decision maker inclinations for action that, in a given situation, most adequately serve current strivings. Investigating these dynamics should further the understanding of both decision processes and the dynamics of emotional experiences. Put differently, when researchers realize that feeling is here for the sake of our doing, we also realize that progress in studying the intuitive decision maker cannot be made without scrutinizing emotion.

REFERENCES

Bagozzi, R. P., Baumgartner, H., & Pieters, R. (1998). Goal-directed emotions. *Cognition and Emotion, 12*, 1–26.

Bagozzi, R. P., Baumgartner, H., Pieters, R., & Zeelenberg, M. (2000). The role of emotions in goal-directed behavior. In S. Ratneshwar, D. G. Mick, & C. Huffman (Eds.), *The why of consumption: Contemporary perspectives on consumer motives, goals, and desires* (pp. 36–58). New York: Routledge.

Bentham, J. (1769/1948). *An introduction to the principles of morals and legislation.* New York: Hafner.

Bougie, R., Pieters, R., & Zeelenberg, M. (2003). Angry customers don't come back, they get back: The experience and behavioral implications of anger and dissatisfaction in services. *Journal of the Academy of Marketing Sciences, 31*, 377–391.

Bower, G. H. (1981). Mood and memory. *American Psychologist, 36*, 129–148.

Cabanac, M. (1992). Pleasure, the common currency. *Journal of Theoretical Biology, 155*, 173–200.

Davitz, J. R. (1969). *The language of emotion.* New York: Academic.

DeSteno, D., Petty, R. E., Wegener, D. T., & Rucker, D. D. (2000). Beyond valence in the perception of likelihood: The role of emotion specificity. *Journal of Personality and Social Psychology, 78*, 397–416.

Fessler, D. M. T., Pillsworth, E. G., & Flamson, T. J. (2004). Angry men and disgusted women: An evolutionary approach to the influence of emotions on risk taking. *Organizational Behavior and Human Decision Processes, 95*, 107–123.

Finucane, M. L., Peters, E., & Slovic, P. (2003). Judgment and decision making: The dance of affect and reason. In S. L. Schneider & J. Shanteau (Eds.), *Emerging perspectives on judgment and decision research* (pp. 327–364). New York: Cambridge University Press.

Forgas, J. P. (1995). Mood and judgment: The affect infusion model (AIM). *Psychological Bulletin, 117*, 39–66.

Frank, R. H. (2004). Introducing moral emotions into models of rational choice. In A. S. R. Manstead, N. Frijda, & A. Fischer (Eds.), *Feelings and emotions: The Amsterdam symposium* (pp. 422–440). New York: Cambridge University Press.

Freud, S. (1920/1952). *A general introduction to psychoanalysis.* New York: Washington Square Press.

Frijda, N. H. (1986). *The emotions.* New York: Cambridge University Press.

Frijda, N. H. (1988) The laws of emotion. *American Psychologist, 43*, 349–358.

Frijda, N. H. (2006). *The laws of emotion.* Mahwah, NJ: Lawrence Erlbaum Associates, Inc.

Frijda, N. H., & Zeelenberg, M. (2001). Appraisal: What is the dependent? In K. R. Scherer, A. Schorr, & T. Johnstone (Eds.), *Appraisal processes in emotion: Theory, methods, research* (pp. 141–155). New York: Oxford University Press.

Isen, A. (2000). Some perspectives on positive affect and self-regulation. *Psychological Inquiry, 11*, 184–187.

Isen, A., & Patrick, R. (1983). The effect of positive feelings on risk taking: When the chips are down. *Organizational Behavior and Human Performance, 31*, 194–202.

Jevons, W. S. (1871/1965). *The theory of political economy* (5th ed.). New York: Augustus M. Kelley Publishers.

Johnson, E. J., & Tversky, A. (1983). Affect, generalization, and the perception of risk. *Journal of Personality and Social Psychology, 45*, 20–31.

Keltner, D., Ellsworth, P. C., & Edwards, K. (1993). Beyond simple pessimism: Effects of sadness and anger on social perception. *Journal of Personality and Social Psychology, 64*, 740–752.

Ketelaar, T. (2004). Ancestral emotions, current decisions: Using evolutionary game theory to explore the role of emotions in decision making. In C. Crawford & C. Salmon (Eds.), *Evolutionary psychology, public policy and personal decisions* (pp. 145–168). Mahwah, NJ: Lawrence Erlbaum Associates, Inc.

Ketelaar, T. (2006). The role of moral sentiments in economic decision making. In D. De Cremer, M. Zeelenberg, & K. Murnighan (Eds.), *Social psychology and economics* (pp. 197–116). Mahwah, NJ: Lawrence Erlbaum Associates, Inc.

Ketelaar, T., & Au, W. T. (2003). The effects of feelings of guilt on the behavior of uncooperative individuals in repeated social bargaining games: An affect-as-information interpretation of the role of emotion in social interaction. *Cognition and Emotion, 17,* 429–453.

Kleinginna, P. R., & Kleinginna, A. M. (1981). A categorized list of emotion definitions, with suggestions for a consensual definition. *Motivation and Emotion, 5,* 345–379.

Larsen, R. J., & Fredrickson, B. L. (1999). Measurement issues in emotion research. In D. Kahneman, E. Diener, & N. Schwarz (Eds.), *Well-being: The foundations of hedonic psychology* (pp. 40–60). New York: Russell Sage Foundation.

Lerner, J. S., & Keltner, D. (2000). Beyond valence: Toward a model of emotion-specific influences on judgment and choice. *Cognition and Emotion, 14,* 473–493.

Lerner, J. S., & Keltner, D. (2001). Fear, anger, and risk. *Journal of Personality and Social Psychology, 81,* 146–159.

Lerner, J. S., Small, D. A., & Loewenstein, G. (2004). Heart strings and purse strings: Carryover effects of emotions on economic decisions. *Psychological Science, 15,* 337–341.

Loewenstein, G. F., & Lerner, J. (2003). The role of affect in decision making. In R. J. Davidson, K. R. Scherer, & H. H. Goldsmith (Eds.), *Handbook of affective sciences* (pp. 619–642). Oxford, England: Oxford University Press.

Mellers, B. A., Schwartz, A., & Ritov, I. (1999). Emotion-based choice. *Journal of Experimental Psychology: General, 128,* 346–361.

Nelissen, R. M. A., Dijker, A. J., & De Vries, N. K. (2007-a). Emotions and goals: Assessing relations between values and emotions. *Cognition and Emotion, 21,* 902–911.

Nelissen, R. M. A., Dijker, A. J., & De Vries, N. H. (2007-b). How to turn a hawk into a dove and vice versa: Interactions between emotions and goals in a give-some dilemma game. *Journal of Experimental Social Psychology, 43,* 280–286.

Osgood, C. E., Suci, G. J., & Tannebaum, P. H. (1957). *The measurement of meaning.* Urbana: Universtiy of Illinois Press.

Parrott, W. G., & Hertel, P. (1999). Research methods in cognition and emotion. In T. Dalgleish & M. J. Power (Eds.), *Handbook of cognition and emotion* (pp. 61–81). New York: Wiley.

Pham, M. T. (2004). The logic of feeling. *Journal of Consumer Psychology, 14,* 360–369.

Pieters, R., & van Raaij, W. F. (1988). The role of affect in economic behavior. In W. F. van Raaij, G. M. van Veldhoven, & K.-E. Warneryd (Eds.), *Handbook of economic psychology* (pp. 108–142). Dordrecht, The Netherlands: Kluwer.

Raghunathan, R., & Pham, M. T. (1999). All negative moods are not equal: Motivational influences of anxiety and sadness on decision making. *Organizational Behavior and Human Decision Processes, 79,* 56–77.

Roseman, I. J., Wiest, C., & Swartz, T. S. (1994). Phenomenology, behaviors, and goals differentiate discrete emotions. *Journal of Personality and Social Psychology, 67,* 206–211.

Rozin, P., Haidt, J., & McCauley, C. R. (1993). Disgust. In M. Lewis & J. M. Haviland (Eds.), *Handbook of emotions* (pp. 575–594). New York: Guilford.

Russell, J. (1980). A circumplex model of affect. *Journal of Personality and Social Psychology, 39,* 1161–1178.

Schaller, M., & Cialdini, R. B. (1990). Happiness, sadness, and helping: A motivational integration. In E. T. Higgins & R. M. Sorrentino (Eds.), *Handbook of motivation and cognition: Foundations of social behavior* (Vol. 2, pp. 265–296). New York: Guilford.

Scherer, K. R., Schorr, A., & Johnstone, T. (Eds.). (2001). *Appraisal processes in emotion: Theory, methods, research*. New York: Oxford University Press.

Schwarz, N. (1990). Feelings as information: Informational and motivational functions of affective states. In E. T. Higgins & R. M. Sorrentino (Eds.), *Handbook of motivation and cognition: Foundations of social behavior* (pp. 527–561). New York: Guilford.

Schwarz, N., & Clore, G. L. (1983). Mood, misattributions, and judgments of well-being: Informative and directive functions of affective states. *Journal of Personality and Social Psychology, 45*, 513–523.

Slovic, P., Finucane, M., Peters, E., & MacGregor, D.G. (2002). The affect heuristic. In T. Gilovich, D. Griffin, & D. Kahneman (Eds.), *Heuristics and biases: The psychology of intuitive judgment* (pp. 397–420). New York: Cambridge University Press.

Smith, A. (1976). *The theory of moral sentiments*. Oxford, England: Clarendon. (Original work published 1759)

Smith, C. A., & Ellsworth, P. C. (1985). Patterns of cognitive appraisal in emotion. *Journal of Personality and Social Psychology, 48*, 813–838.

Solomon, R. C., & Stone, L. D. (2002). On "positive" and "negative" emotions. *Journal for the Theory of Social Behavior, 32*, 417–443.

Tiedens, L. Z., & Linton, S. (2001). Judgment under emotional certainty and uncertainty: The effects of specific emotions on information processing. *Journal of Personality and Social Psychology, 81*, 973–988.

Van der Pligt, J., Zeelenberg, M., Van Dijk, W. W., De Vries, N. K., & Richard, R. (1998). Affect, attitudes and decisions: Let's be more specific. *European Review of Social Psychology, 8*, 34–66.

Wallbott, H. G., & Scherer, K. R. (1988). How universal and specific is emotional experience?: Evidence from 27 countries on five continents. In K. R. Scherer (Ed.), *Facets of emotion: Recent research* (pp. 31–56). Hillsdale, NJ: Lawrence Erlbaum Associates, Inc.

Zeelenberg, M., & Pieters, R. (1999). On service delivery that might have been: Behavioral responses to disappointment and regret. *Journal of Service Research, 2*, 86–97.

Zeelenberg, M., & Pieters, R. (2004). Beyond valence in customer dissatisfaction: A review and new findings on behavioral responses to regret and disappointment in failed services. *Journal of Business Research, 57*, 445–455.

Zeelenberg, M., & Pieters, R. (2006). Feeling is for doing: A pragmatic approach to the study of emotions in economic behavior. In D. De Cremer, M. Zeelenberg, & K. Murnighan (Eds.), *Social psychology and economics* (pp. 117–137). Mahwah, NJ: Lawrence Erlbaum Associates, Inc.

Zeelenberg, M., Van Dijk, W. W., Manstead, A. S. R., & Van der Pligt, J. (1998). The experience of regret and disappointment. *Cognition and Emotion, 12*, 221–230.

12

From Intuition to Analysis
Making Decisions With Your Head, Your Heart, or by the Book

ELKE U. WEBER and PATRICIA G. LINDEMANN

Columbia University

INTRODUCTION

The seemingly effortless, intuitive judgments and decisions made by experts—be they museum curators, stock traders, or chess grand masters—continue to fascinate both academia (e.g., Hogarth, 2001) and the popular imagination (Gladwell, 2005). In this chapter, we propose that expert intuition refers to processes to which the decision maker does not have conscious access either because previously conscious, analytic processes have become automated to a point in which conscious attention is no longer necessary (Goldberg, 2005) or as the result of cumulative, associative learning that has never been conscious (e.g., Plessner, Betsch, Schallies, & Schwieren, chap. 7, this volume). We also argue that nonexpert intuitive decision making is carried out in related ways.

Decision modes are the qualitatively different ways in which people make decisions. Hammond (1996) argued for a continuum of decision modes from analytic to intuitive decision strategies (see also Hamm, chap. 4, this volume). Others have provided a more detailed list of documented decision modes (Goldstein & Weber, 1995) and have proposed three classes of decision modes (Ames, Flynn, & Weber, 2004; Weber, Ames, & Blais, 2005). In this chapter, we argue that a subset of modes in the second and third categories qualify as intuitive decisions.

Although the use of different decision modes does not necessarily lead to different choices, it often does. To predict the outcome of a decision, it typically helps to know how the decision was made. People are aware of the importance of decision processes. When explaining a decision, people often focus not only on the decision outcome but also on the way they came to their decision. People's opinion of those who helped them is not just determined by the nature and magnitude of the favor but also by how they believe the person who helped them decided to help them (Ames et al., 2004). Despite the apparent importance of decision modes, decision models put forth by economists and operations researchers have tended to address only the outcomes of decisions. Decision research in psychology has shown greater concern for decision processes, using dependent measures such as decision time and confidence judgments as well as process-tracing methodologies such as information acquisition sequences and verbal protocols.

In Payne, Bettman, and Johnson's (1993) adaptive decision maker program, process-tracing techniques document that people tactically employ a wide range of decision strategies in the context of multiattribute choice in which available options can be described on a number of attributes. Each decision strategy has a characteristic way to acquire attribute values and to evaluate, combine, and compare information. The adaptive decision maker framework allows for an assessment of each strategy in terms of effort (number of processing steps required) and accuracy (likelihood of selecting the best option) and shows that decision makers tend to unconsciously select certain strategies in situations where fast and efficient processing is required and others in situations that require greater accuracy.

The adaptive decision maker framework suggests an approach that can be used to think about decision-making strategies in a broader sense, with a wider set of qualitatively different decision modes and a broader set of criteria to evaluate the appropriateness of these modes.

A FUNCTIONAL TAXONOMY OF DECISION MODES

Our functional taxonomy of decision modes is designed to explain why people (explicitly or implicitly) select one or more decision modes. We focus on three modes of decision making: calculation-, affect-, and recognition-based decisions, captured in the chapter title in colloquial terms as decisions made by the head, by the heart, and by the book. Calculation-based decisions involve analytical thought. Affect-based decisions are governed by conscious or unconscious drives or feelings. Recognition-based decisions involve recognition of the situation as one of a type for which the decision maker knows the appropriate action.

As shown in Table 12.1, decision modes differ in their inputs and their cognitive and affective processes. Calculation-based modes include normative models of multiattribute or risky choice as well as their cognitively less demanding variants (e.g., prospect theory or noncompensatory multiattribute models). Their inputs are attribute values and importance weights for multiattribute choice and probabilities and utilities for risky decisions. Psychological processes include the evaluation of outcomes and probabilities and the calculation of overall utilities for each option. These calculation-based processes for making decisions with the head are typically thought of as analytical and driven by reasoning.

TABLE 12.1 Taxonomy of Decision Modes.

Mode	Sub type	Inputs	Processes	Motivational Focus
Calculation	Traditional cost-benefit models (e.g., multi-attribute choice, risky decisions, etc.)	Attributes probabilities	Stage 1: Evaluation of utility, importance weights, decision weights Stage 2: Calculation/comparison of options	Maximization of material outcomes
	Anticipated emotions	Anticipated emotions	Stage 1: Evaluation of anticipated emotions Stage 2: Calculation/comparison of options	Maximization of emotional outcomes
Recognition	Case-based	Holistic situation	Stage 1: Implicit categorization/pattern matching Stage 2: Execution of if-then productions	Efficiency accuracy (for experts)
	Rule-based	Salient situational elements	Stage 1: Explicit categorization Stage 2: Execution of if-then productions	"Doing the right thing," justifiability-fairness/justice/self-control
	Role-based	Situational elements relevant to social role	Stage 1: Recognition of role-related obligations and rights Stage 2: Execution of role-related obligations and rights	Connectedness, Affiliation/social identity, self-confidence/self-esteem
Affect	Needs (drives)	Presence of physiological need	Physiological response: instinctive and learned Learned approach or avoidance response (operant conditioning)	Fulfillment of physiological needs
	Wants	Presence of want	Positive or negative associations (classical conditioning) Learned approach or avoidance response (operant conditioning)	Fulfillment of wants autonomy, self-affirmation
	Immediate emotions	Aroused physiological (emotional) state	Aroused physiological (emotional) state, (operant conditioning)	Autonomy, self-affirmation

When people talk about making decisions with their heart, they describe two uses of emotion in decision making. Using the heart can mean placing value on emotional outcomes and incorporating those values in the decision-making process. Looking for an apartment, you might consider cost, location, amenities, and the way you anticipate feeling in the new apartment. Including emotional consequences can be seen as putting a human face on decision making. A politician who argues for paving a playground to create a much-needed parking lot might be thought of as arguing with his head rather than his heart in the sense of failing to value the happiness of children and their families. Including anticipated emotions into decisions is, however, not qualitatively different from calculation-based decision making; the anticipated emotion is simply an additional input to the calculation.

A qualitatively different type of emotion-based decision making directs behavior when the decision maker focuses on immediate affect (i.e., affective responses experienced at the time the decision is made) rather than anticipated emotions (Loewenstein, Weber, Hsee, & Welch, 2001). Positive emotions when considering a choice alternative (desire or happiness) lead to approach; negative emotions (revulsion or fear) lead to avoidance. The affect-based decision modes we describe are not based on calculation. They include goal-oriented choices associated with drives and basic needs like food, water, shelter, sleep, or safety in which operant conditioning processes provide for the learning of behavior that results in obtaining needed reward. Affect-based decisions also include behaviors associated with the wanting of things that the decision maker has associated with positive feelings as a result of classical conditioning. Affect-based decisions also include behavior that is derived from the immediate emotional content of a situation (Zeelenberg, Nelissen, & Pieters, chap. 11, this volume). A situation that evokes anger may result in aggressive behavior, whereas a situation causing sadness may result in hesitation or withdrawal (Lerner, Small, & Loewenstein, 2004). Affective modes have an intuitive feel. People often experience the attraction–avoidance reaction as "going with their gut" because the processing leading up to this reaction is conducted at an unconscious level.

The final decision-mode category is recognition-based choice. This is decision making by the book in the sense that the decision maker carries out a behavior prescribed by an implicit or explicit rule. The decision maker using this mode is not seeking a novel approach to a problem but is relying on tried-and-true answers. Recognition-based decisions come in different variants. In case-based decisions, the decision maker is typically an expert with a memory store of specific situations in the decision domain and their appropriate associated actions. These mental representations are if–then productions, where the "if" element is a set of conditions that must be met to trigger the action in the "then" part of the production. The expert decision maker is able to unconsciously apply these production rules that have been developed through repeated experience as demonstrated by Klein (1999) with experts such as fire fighters and jet pilots operating in time-pressured, high-stakes decision domains.

Another type of recognition-based decision is rule-based decisions in which the decision maker consciously or unconsciously invokes an explicit rule of behavior.

These rules may be laws (if you are driving and come to a red light, then you must stop) or other types of regulations (parental rules, societal norms, or company rules). A final type of recognition-based decision making is role-based decisions in which the decision context elicits a rule of conduct derived from the decision maker's social role (March, 1994). Roles include positions of responsibility within society (parent or friend), group memberships (Christian or Democrat), and self-defining characteristics (honest or responsible). Each of these roles has associated obligations that can be expressed in terms of if–then productions: As a parent, if your child is very ill, then you must stay home and care for the child.

CONSTRAINED OPTIMIZATION WITH BROADER GOALS AND CONSTRAINTS

The constrained optimization view of decision making depicts decision makers as seeking the alternative that optimizes their objective function under a given set of constraints. Traditional applications define people's goals in terms of the optimization of material consequences. Our framework expands the objective function to include other types of goals. We also broaden the list of constraints that influence decision strategy selection to include factors beyond the cognitive constraints typically considered.

Although the rational-economic view of human nature assumes that people attend only to the material consequences of their choices, personality and motivation research confirms the existence of additional social motives. These include the needs for affiliation and autonomy (Hilgard, 1987; Murray, 1938), for confidence and self-esteem (Larrick, 1993), and for process-related elements such as fairness and justice (Mellers & Baron, 1993), and the justifiability of decisions (Tetlock, 1992). Philosophers also provide multifaceted views of human motivation. Habermas's (1972) taxonomy suggests three complementary types of motives: technical concern with instrumental action, practical concern with social consensus and understanding, and emancipatory concern with self-critical reflection and autonomy. We argue that when making decisions, people not only consider material outcomes but also choose a mode of making their decision that best enables them to meet additional nonmaterial goals.

The specific goals activated in a particular situation will likely vary as a function of the decision maker (personality, culture) and the content (domain) of the decision. Given the evidence for a wide range of human motives and goals as well as evidence that people use a wide range of decision modes, we propose that different decision modes coexist because they are more or less effective ways to achieve different goals. In Table 12.1, we indicate one or more motivational foci for each mode. We believe that each mode is better suited than others to address the listed motive(s). In the following, we first describe the functional significance of each decision mode and then present empirical data in support of our hypotheses.

MOTIVATIONAL FOCI OF DECISION MODES

Although calculation-based modes are best suited to addressing the traditional motive of maximizing material consequences, other modes are better suited to other goals. People wanting to justify their decisions to a supervisor would be well-served by making their decision in a rule-based fashion (e.g., following standard operating procedure) if the appropriateness of the rule is widely acknowledged. Role-based decisions, on the other hand, serve to satisfy the motive of connectedness because they activate representations of the decision maker's place in society and thus generate feelings of affiliation. Depending on the individual's personality and culture, enhancement of role identity may also increase the individual's self-confidence and self-esteem (Markus & Kitayama, 1991). The need for autonomy, counterpart to the need for affiliation and connectedness, is best met by using an affect-based decision mode. Affect-based decision making affirms that one's personal desire for an action suffices without any need to justify the decision to oneself or others.

Rule- and role-based decision making may also function as mechanisms for assuring fairness. Whereas calculation-based processing may lead the individual to act with self-interest, roles place the individual in a social context that dictates responsibilities to which individuals must adhere. For many social roles—such as friend, coworker, or community leader—the responsibilities may include placing fairness and equity over self-interest. Rules, like the categorical imperative, can promote fairness because they dictate appropriate behavior in an impartial manner.

BROADENING OF CONSTRAINTS

Simon (1956) and collaborators pioneered the addition of psychological constraints to substantive constraints, in particular, constraints provided by cognitive information-processing limitation (i.e., bounded rationality). Calculation-based decision rules that require less comprehensive and effortful processing are adaptations to information-processing constraints. More recent work has shown that emotional resource limitations further constrain optimization, preventing the operation of otherwise rational hedonic editing (Linville & Fischer, 1991). Work on mental accounting (Thaler, 1985) and precommitment strategies (Ainslie, 1975) shows that people are, at least implicitly, aware of their cognitive as well as affective shortcomings (e.g., self-control problems). Emotional constraints may restrict the selection of decision modes to those that can be reasonably implemented when self-control is an issue as, for example, the use of rules that facilitate self-control when you want to stick to your diet.

In the following, we report four studies designed to test our functional hypotheses of decision-mode usage. In two studies, we examined self-reported decision modes for scenarios that differed in situational constraints (e.g., importance and familiarity) and motives. In two additional studies, we examined dependent measures (using an explicit and implicit memory task) that can provide more circumstantial but also more objective evidence of decision-mode usage.

STUDY 1

A total of 33 Columbia University students in a decision-making class read 12 brief decision scenarios related to three content areas (relationship, school, and ethical). For example, one scenario read, "Jane has a 9 a.m. class. She woke up late and is trying to decide whether to rush over and get to class or skip it." This scenario was followed by the statement, "If I were Jane, I would:" and three possible options (mode names were not shown):

1. (Affect): Base my decision on my immediate feelings. I'd go if I feel like going and not go if I don't feel like going.
2. (Calculation): Consider how important this class will be, how likely the material is to be on the exam, how likely I am to fall asleep in class, and/or any other factors that are relevant to the decision. Then I would assess which option is better.
3. (Recognition): Recognize that it is my responsibility as a student to go to class, and so I would go.

Respondents rated their likelihood of using each strategy by distributing 6 points across the three options. Any distribution of the 6 points was allowed so long as all 6 points were used.

Finally, participants used a Likert-scale to rate each scenario on three situational characteristics (familiarity, importance, and degree of conflict experienced by the decision maker) and on two motivational characteristics—need to justify the decision to yourself and the need to justify the decision to others.

Previous studies have found that decision content influences strategy selection for reasons that include domain-related variations in information presentation (Goldstein & Weber, 1995), mental representation (Rettinger & Hastie, 2003), and social norms (Ames et al., 2004).

Based on prior research, we expected school decisions to induce calculation-based decision making because these decisions involve material consequences in terms of grades (in the short term) and career (in the long term). Relationship decisions contain an emotional element that was expected to disproportionately elicit affect-based decision making. For the ethical decisions, prior work provided less guidance. Using our taxonomy of decision-mode selection, we reasoned that ethical questions often have deontological solutions related to social roles (religious or other social identities). Consequently, we hypothesized that ethical decisions would activate strong usage of role-based decision making.

As shown in Figure 12.1, the pattern of mode-use across the three content domains confirmed our expectations. Calculation-based processing was most frequent for the school domain, whereas affect-based processing was most frequent for the relationship domain and role-based decisions most frequent for the ethics domain.

In regression analyses, we examined which situational and motivational factors (assessed independently for each decision scenario) determined use of each of the three decision modes and whether decision domain predicted decision mode usage above and beyond these situational and motivational factors. We coded domain

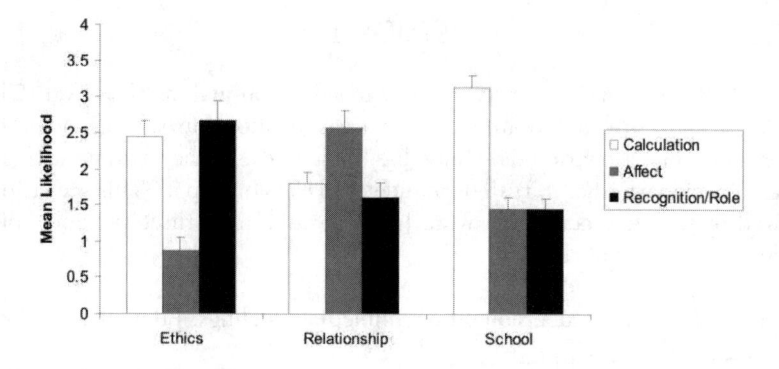

FIGURE 12.1 Likelihood of making calculation-, affect-, and recognition/role-based decisions in ethical, relationship, and school-related decisions in Study 1.

by two contrasts (relationship and ethics), with school decisions as the reference category.

Table 12.2 shows that use of the calculation-based mode is strongly influenced by situational variables: Importance and decision difficulty (i.e., degree of conflict experienced by the decision maker) increases its likelihood, whereas familiarity with the decision situation decreases it. Important decisions may focus the decision maker on their material outcomes and consequences, thereby creating a motivational state well served by calculation-based decision making. Difficult decisions may be difficult, in part, because the more intuitive (and easier) recognition and affective modes of decision making do not arrive at a satisfactory conclusion, thus necessitating more

TABLE 12.2 Regression Analysis: Likelihood of Mode Use in Study

	Calculation		Affect		Recognition/Role	
Predictor	Beta	Sig.	Beta	Sig.	Beta	Sig.
Situational Factors						
Importance	0.13	0.04 °	−0.08	0.21	−0.06	0.36
Degree of Conflict	0.13	0.03 °	−0.01	0.90	−0.13	0.03 °
Familiarity	−0.15	0.01 °	0.00	0.97	0.16	0.01 °
Motivational Factors						
Self-Justify	−0.09	0.21	−0.04	0.55	0.13	0.06
Other-Justify	−0.08	0.23	−0.09	0.13	0.16	0.01 °
Domain						
Relationship	−0.34	0.00 °	0.28	0.00 °	0.07	0.25
Ethical	−0.23	0.00 °	−0.08	0.17	0.30	0.00 °

Notes: Three separate regressions were conducted (for calculation-, affect-, and recognition/role-based modes) on situational factors, motivational factors and domain. Shown are regression coefficients (beta) and their significance level. Asterisks mark coefficients that are significantly different from zero at the .05 level.

effortful calculation-based processing. Familiar decisions, on the other hand, can be handled by the less effortful and seemingly intuitive recognition-based mode.

For the recognition-based mode, both situational and motivational factors come into play. As predicted, familiarity was a significant positive predictor, as it invokes if–then rules that typically develop over time with experience in a decision situation. As predicted in Table 12.1, recognition-based decision making was positively related to self-justification and especially, other-decision justification.

None of the situational and motivational factors influenced use of the affect mode, which was however more frequently found for relationship decisions as already illustrated in Figure 12.1. Above and beyond the influence of situational and motivational factors that differed across domains, the calculation-based mode was still more frequent for school decisions and recognition/role-based mode more frequent for ethical decisions.

Although Study 1 was exploratory research, it was also used as a teaching exercise, and the decision-mode structure was simplified for this reason by restricting the recognition mode to role-based decision making, the calculation mode to standard cost–benefit analysis, and eliminating the anticipated-affect mode. In Study 2, we used a broader range of decision modes and also allowed respondents to rate their likelihood of using each mode independently, making it possible to express strong preferences for multiple modes.

STUDY 2

A total of 57 Columbia undergraduate students were recruited by campus fliers and paid for their participation. First, respondents read descriptions of five decision modes: cost–benefit and anticipated affect (calculation-based modes), rule and role (recognition-based modes), and the affect-based mode. Then, participants used a Likert scale to rate their likelihood of using each decision mode in 12 different decision scenarios, answering questions such as "How likely would you be to make this decision based on your *immediate feelings* or *gut reaction* to the situation?" We told participants that they could endorse multiple modes (or no mode) for each scenario. As a separate dependent measure, they also indicated which single mode they would use if they had to choose only one mode. Finally, respondents rated each decision scenario on three situational factors (importance, familiarity, and emotionality) and two motivational factors (need to self-justify and need to justify to others).

A new group of scenarios was used for this study, which represented five content domains: consumer, work/school, relationship, ethical, and routine/everyday decisions. Many of the scenarios drew from two or more content domains. These mixed content scenarios were meant to emulate real-life decisions in which modes may be in conflict as when a student must choose between hanging out with friends (relationship domain, likely to result in affect-based processing) and studying for exams (work/school domain, likely to result in calculation-based processing).

Respondents also completed a questionnaire developed by Kruglanski et al. (2000) that evaluates self-regulatory motivation on two orthogonal dimensions: locomotion and assessment. People high in locomotion are motivated to approach

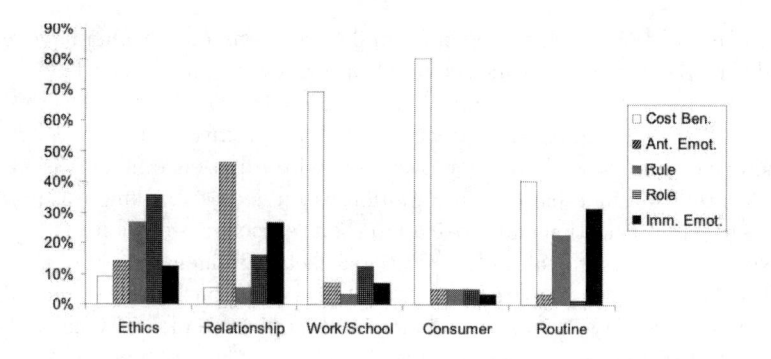

FIGURE 12.2 Percentage of participants selecting indicated decision mode for single content domain scenarios in Study 2. Ben. = benefit; Ant. Emot. = anticipated emotion; Imm. Emot. = immediate emotion.

problems quickly and efficiently to move on. People high in assessment are interested in careful evaluation to select the optimal alternative. Field data suggested that personality differences on these measures may be related to differences in preferred decision modes, making people more or less comfortable with quick intuitive versus effortful analytic decision modes (Hansen, Marx, & Weber, 2004).

Results for the first dependent measure, the mode respondents would select if they could choose only one mode, are shown in Figure 12.2 for the scenarios that relate to only one content domain. None of the ethics questions fell purely within the ethics domain, and so data from the question that most strongly emphasized the ethics domain is presented. As in Study 1, recognition-based (role- and rule-based) processing is dominant in the ethics domain. In the relationship domain, affective processing continues to be critical, although it is now divided between anticipated affect and immediate affect. For the work/school domain, standard cost–benefit approaches are dominant. Consumer decisions show the strongest pattern of preference for the cost–benefit decision mode, whereas routine decisions are made by relying on three different strategies—cost-benefit calculation, rule, and immediate affect. Immediate affect may be evoked by these routine decisions (e.g., which toothpaste to buy, which route to take to class) because they are of low importance and may provide the opportunity to "give in" to whims in a way that is not acceptable for less routine matters.

For scenarios involving multiple domains, we hypothesized that different aspects of the scenario would invoke different modes, leading to the use of more decision modes than single-domain scenarios. We coded mode ratings of 4 or higher (above midpoint) as indicating mode use, and we counted the number of modes used for a given scenario. A paired t test comparing the number of modes used for single-domain versus multiple-domain scenarios confirmed our hypothesis. For single-domain decisions, respondents indicated using on average 2.56 modes; but for multiple-domain decisions, they used on average 3.12 modes, $t(56) = 6.01, p \ll .01$.

Regression analyses of the second dependent measure—namely, the likelihood-of-use ratings for each mode—are presented in Table 12.3. Situational factors, the

TABLE 12.3 Regression Analysis: Likelihood of Mode (or Sub-Mode) Use in Study 2

| | Calculation |||| | Recognition |||| | Affect ||
| | Cost Benefit || Anticipated Emotion || Rule || Rule || Immediate Emotions ||
Predictor	Beta	Sig.	Beta	Sig.	Beta	Sig.	Beta	Sig.	Beta	Sig.
Situational Factors										
Importance	0.30	0.00 °	−0.05	0.30	0.07	0.24	0.11	0.05 °	−0.43	0.00 °
Emotionality	−0.05	0.27	0.07	0.07	−0.01	0.76	0.04	0.29	0.15	0.00 °
Familiarity	−0.28	0.00 °	0.44	0.00 °	−0.01	0.87	0.16	0.01 °	0.48	0.00 °
Motivational Factors										
Self-Justify	0.15	0.01 °	0.01	0.91	−0.08	0.19	0.00	0.95	0.08	0.16
Other-Justify	0.05	0.30	−0.04	0.47	0.28	0.00 °	0.21	0.00 °	−0.09	0.07
Assessment	0.09	0.03 °	0.06	0.11	−0.10	0.02 °	0.05	0.23	0.00	0.96
Locomotion	-0.01	0.83	−0.01	0.76	0.13	0.00 °	−0.08	0.03 °	−0.05	0.20
Domain										
Relationship	−0.14	0.01 °	−0.01	0.87	−0.08	0.20	0.00	0.95	0.01	0.85
Work/School	0.05	0.41	−0.05	0.40	0.06	0.33	0.23	0.00 °	−0.07	0.25
Ethics	−0.26	0.00 °	−0.04	0.54	0.04	0.59	0.16	0.02 °	0.02	0.75
Routine	0.07	0.16	−0.25	0.00 °	0.13	0.02 °	0.02	0.66	−0.12	0.01 °
Consumer	0.10	0.04 °	−0.07	0.14	−0.02	0.71	0.02	0.63	−0.09	0.08

Notes: Separate regressions were conducted for each mode or sub-type—calculation (cost-benefit and anticipated emotions), recognition (rule and role), and affect (immediate emotions). Likelihood of using each mode was regressed on situational factors, motivational factors, and decision domain. Shown are regression coefficients (beta) and their significance level. Asterisks mark coefficients that are significantly different from zero at the .05 level.

first set of predictors, included the newly added variable emotionality as well as decision importance and familiarity. Almost as a manipulation check, degree of emotionality predicts use of the two affective modes and reduces use of the cost–benefit mode, which confirmed the notion that matters of the heart are typically not ruled by reason. More emotionality was also associated with an increase in role-based decision making, which suggested that the need for affiliation hypothesized to trigger role-based decision making had an affective component. Decision importance again increased use of the calculation-based mode but also of the role-based mode, which suggested that nonmaterial needs can rank high in importance. Decision importance decreased use of the immediate-affect mode. Contrary to prediction and Study 1, familiarity did not lead to a significant increase in recognition-based processing but instead increased use of both the immediate- and anticipated-affect modes, which suggested that a broad set of decision scenarios from different domains ought to be used to obtain stable results.

Motivational factors were the second set of predictors. The need for other justification increased use of the rule- and role-based modes. Although our taxonomy emphasizes rule-based decision making as useful for justifying decisions to others, role-based decision making seems to serve the same purpose. Interestingly, self-justification needs predicted increased use of cost–benefit processing. The newly added personality traits of assessment focus and locomotion focus affected decision-mode use as predicted. Individuals higher in assessment were more likely to use cost–benefit analysis and less likely to use recognition-based decision making. Locomotion-oriented individuals were more likely to use recognition-based decision making.

The final set of predictors were dummy-coded variables indicating content domain of the decision: relationship, work/school, ethics, routine, or consumer decisions. Included in the regression, these variables showed whether decision domain predicts mode use above and beyond the effects of situational and motivational factors that vary between domains. Consistent with Study 1, we found such effects. The cost–benefit mode was more likely for consumer decisions and less likely for relationship and ethics decisions. Rule-based decision making was more likely for routine decisions with ample opportunity to develop a rule. The role-based mode was more frequent for work/school decisions (in which respondents could be expected to identify closely with the student role) and ethics decisions (for reasons we outlined earlier).

Studies 1 and 2 clearly indicate that decision-mode usage is related to situational and motivational factors; however, even when we take these factors into consideration, content domain still exerts a strong effect. Social norms for handling different types of decisions are in part responsible for this (Ames et al., 2004). Thus, people believe that large consumer purchases should be made with the head and that social decisions should be made with the heart or by social roles. It appears to be inappropriate to calculate material costs and benefits in social situations, although calculating emotional costs and benefits to oneself and to others is perfectly acceptable.

In the next two studies, we attempted to provide nonsubjective evidence of decision-mode use given that self-reports of cognitive processes are often unreliable (Ericsson & Simon, 1980). Reliance on introspection alone as a source of evidence is questionable. Thus, we sought an alternative and more objective method of diagnosing mode usage in the form of explicit or implicit memory tests. Using the cloud-chamber metaphor of particle physics in which elementary particles cannot be directly observed, but their presence can be inferred from the trail they leave behind in cloud chambers, we designed Study 3 to test whether use of a particular decision mode would detectably change the representation and subsequent memory of a decision. To do this, we asked participants to use specific decision modes to make substantive decisions—modes that were sometimes incompatible with the content domain of the decision. We then used memory measures to assess memory representations. Our unanticipated results indicate that participants resisted using assigned decision modes that were incompatible with decision content, which highlighted the importance of social norms for decision-mode use.

STUDY 3

We randomly assigned 39 Columbia students (paid for their participation) to one of three decision modes (calculation-, role-, or affect-based decision making) and told them to role-play a person who makes their decisions in the assigned mode (which was described to participants). Participants read three richly detailed decision problems that included multiple details relevant for each of the three decision modes: information about outcomes, social obligations, and experienced emotions. We hypothesized that participants assigned to use of a specific mode would focus on mode-relevant information, leaving it more accessible than other information, with manifestations in a subsequent recall task. Because the memory task was a surprise, each respondent only made one of the three decisions.

The scenarios came from different domains: a career decision in which a graduating student was deciding whether to pursue music or medicine, an ethical decision in which a woman was deciding whether it was right to place her mother in a nursing home, and a consumer decision in which a middle-aged father was deciding between a practical minivan and an exciting sports car. In hindsight, it should have been clear to us that social norms suggest different modes as most appropriate for the three decisions: calculation-based decision making for the career and consumer scenario and role-based decision making for the ethical scenario.

After making their decision in their assigned mode, respondents were asked to write a letter telling a friend about the decision (the memory task). These letters were coded for predominantly calculation-, role-, or affect-based informational details by two independent coders who were blind to the experimental conditions and hypotheses and had high interrater agreement (92%). Contrary to our initial hypothesis, there was no association between assigned mode and the mode judged to predominate in the subsequent tell-a-friend account, $\chi^2(4, N=39) = 4.89, p \gg .10$. However, as shown in Table 12.4, tell-a-friend accounts differed significantly by scenario in the direction expected by social norms about domain-specific mode usage, $\chi^2(4, N = 39) = 11.26, p \ll .05$; the calculation-based mode was modal for the career and consumer scenarios, and the role-based mode was modal for the ethical scenario.

Implicit decision-mode selection based on overlearned social norms seems to have overridden explicit task instructions about mode usage in those cases in which

TABLE 12.4 Predominant Mode Used in Tell-a-Friend Responses in Study 3

Predominant Mode in Tell-a-Friend	Career Scenario	Ethical Scenario	Consumer Scenario	Total
Calculation	10	4	8	22
Role	4	7	0	11
Affect	1	1	4	6
Total	15	12	12	39

Notes: Number of responses falling within each mode category (calculation-, role-, and affect-based) for each scenario is indicated.

we tried to induce participants to adopt domain-incompatible modes. In Study 4, we provided an additional test of the hypothesis that use of a specific decision mode leaves behind a memory trail.

STUDY 4

We selected respondents from among the participants in Study 1. We used their responses to that study to determine their chronic disposition to operate in an affect-based or a calculation-based mode (i.e., we tallied the number of points each respondent allocated to each of the two modes across the 12 scenarios). We placed the top analytic responders ($n = 4$) in the calculation-based group, and we placed the top affective responders ($n = 5$) in the affect-based group. We told participants of their classification and instructed them to make the ensuing decision in their naturally preferred and assigned mode (either calculation or affect).

We presented a decision scenario as an audio recording of a dialogue interspersed with narration. Participants listened to the audio recording while viewing slides of the decision maker, the decision maker's conversational partners, and other relevant elements of the story. We used this audiovisual presentation to bring the situation to life. The decision situation was an expanded version of the career decision from Study 3 in which the relationship and emotional elements of the story were heightened so that both the affect-based mode and the calculation-based mode might be considered legitimate. The male student in the story was torn between the more practical career choice of attending medical school, the option his parents wished him to pursue, and the less practical path of taking a small part in a traveling theatre production to pursue his dream of becoming an actor. The dialogue reflected a strong heart versus head conflict, with the student's feelings pulling him toward acting and analysis suggesting that medicine was the right path.

Respondents viewed this information with the instructions to make the decision in their naturally preferred and assigned mode (either calculation or affect) and had to subsequently justify it in writing. They then completed an implicit memory task in an unrelated-task paradigm, which we designed to assess differential activation of respondents' semantic memory as the result of differences in their assigned/preferred decision mode. Respondents saw a list of 40 word prompts (equated for word frequency in the English language), each followed by a blank, and we asked them to write down the first word that came to mind after reading each prompt. Some prompts were known to trigger more calculation-based associations ("cost," "buying," "demand"), others more affect-based associations ("pleasure," "loss," "wish"), whereas others were expected to do neither ("become," "carpet"). The cloud-chamber metaphor suggests that the process of making a decision in a calculation-based mode should leave concepts and constructs associated with this mode more accessible, thus increasing the likelihood of making calculation or cost–benefit related associations, especially to those prompts designed to trigger calculation-based associations. In contrast, we expected to see a larger number of affective associates in those respondents who had been asked to make the decision using an affect-based mode.

Two raters naïve to the experimental hypotheses and conditions coded the content of the free associations produced by the 9 respondents as related to cost–benefit calculation, affect, or neither. The two raters agreed 97% of the time and resolved their small number of disagreements by discussion. The results suggest that the prescribed decision mode did indeed activate mode-consistent constructs in memory, $\chi^2(1, N = 111) = 12.31, p \ll .001$. Of the 49 affect-related associates (e.g., "love," "happy," "feel," "grief," "hurt"), 71% were generated by respondents who had been asked to make the decision in the affect-based mode. Of the 62 cost–benefit-related associates ("supply," "money," "cost," "probability"), 65% were generated by respondents who had been asked to make the decision in the calculation-based mode.

This result suggests that evidence of mode-specific processing can be obtained that is more objective than self-reports (e.g., implicit memory tests such as the one just described or possibly functional MRI measures of differential brain activation in regions known to be associated with different modes of processing). Unlike self-reports, such measures do not depend on introspection and will allow us to further validate our hypotheses about the functions of different decision modes summarized in Table 12.1.

CONCLUSIONS

The first two studies we described in this chapter suggest that people are well aware of possessing a repertoire of decision modes ranging from quick intuitive responses based on either affective reactions or overlearned associations at one end of the continuum to the more or less automatic application of rules of conduct or social obligations and to the effortful calculation of relative costs and benefits at the other end of the continuum. Reported decision-mode use followed clear and consistent patterns that were guided by both abstract decision characteristics (importance and familiarity) and the domain of the decision. Reported differences in mode use and social norms about domain-appropriate mode use reported elsewhere (Ames et al., 2004) were consistent with the hypothesized differences in motivational foci of the decision modes. Different human motives are activated to different degrees in different content domains. Maximization of material outcomes is a much greater priority in consumer or financial decisions than in social decisions. To the extent that calculation-based decision making is best suited to satisfy this objective, we should expect to find more calculation-based decisions in these domains.

Personality differences or cultural differences on variables known to increase the chronic salience of different motivations have also been shown to be associated with differences in the use of decision modes that are better equipped to satisfy those motivations. Thus, respondents with a greater chronic need for locomotion (making a decision quickly) were more likely to use quicker intuitive decision modes, whereas respondents with a greater need for assessment (making careful and optimal decisions) were more likely to use effortful analytic decision modes. Weber et al. (2005) showed that decision makers in a collectivist culture (China) with its emphasis on affiliation were more likely to make role-based decisions, whereas decision makers in an individualist culture (United States) with its emphasis on autonomy were more likely to make affect based decisions.

Situational characteristics and the needs and motives of the decision maker thus combine to determine the implicit choice of one or more modes by which a decision gets made (see also C. Betsch, chap. 14, this volume). Future research will determine the relationship between the use of multiple decisions modes with common or conflicting conclusions and people's confidence in their decision. The last two studies we reported in this chapter point the way to more objective diagnostics of decision-mode use that can be enlisted to provide additional support for the proposed functional framework of decision-mode selection.

Our results show that intuitive decisions that are reached without any conscious deliberation (based on immediate affect or an automatically triggered if–then rule) can be expected to occur in certain types of situations (in social decisions more likely than career decisions) and for certain types of decision makers (for people who have a lot of familiarity with the decision in question, i.e., domain experts, and for decision makers oriented toward locomotion and with low needs for assessment). In other situations, one can expect to see greater evidence of more effortful analytic modes of decision making.

ACKNOWLEDGMENT

The research reported in this chapter was supported by National Science Foundation Grant SES–0079664.

REFERENCES

Ainslie, G. (1975). Specious reward: A behavioral theory of impulsiveness and impulse control. *Psychological Bulletin, 82,* 463–496.

Ames, D. R., Flynn, F. J., & Weber, E. U. (2004). It's the thought that counts: On perceiving how helpers decide to lend a hand. *Personality and Social Psychology Bulletin, 30,* 461–474.

Ericsson, K. A., & Simon, S. (1980). Verbal reports as data. *Psychological Review, 87,* 215–251.

Gladwell, M. (2005). *Blink: The power of thinking without thinking.* New York: Little, Brown.

Goldberg, E. (2005). *The wisdom paradox: How your mind can grow stronger as your brain grows older.* New York: Gotham Books.

Goldstein, W. M., & Weber, E. U. (1995). Content and its discontents: The use of knowledge in decision making. In J. R. Busemeyer, R. Hastie, & D. L. Medin (Eds.), *Decision making from a cognitive perspective: The psychology of learning and motivation* (Vol. 32, pp. 83–136). New York: Academic.

Habermas, J. (1972). *Knowledge and human interests* (J. Shapiro, Trans.). London: Heinemann.

Hammond, K. R. (1996). *Human judgment and social policy.* New York: Oxford University Press.

Hansen, J., Marx, S., & Weber, E. U. (2004). *The role of climate perceptions, expectations, and forecasts in farmer decision making: The Argentine Pampas and South Florida* (Tech. Rep. No. 04–01). Palisades, NY: International Research Institute for Climate Prediction.

Hilgard, E. R. (1987). *Psychology in America: A historical survey.* New York: Harcourt Brace Jovanovich.
Hogarth, R. M. (2001). *Educating intuition.* Chicago: University of Chicago Press.
Klein, G. (1999). *Sources of power: How people make decisions.* Cambridge, MA: MIT Press.
Kruglanski, A. W., Thompson, E. P., Higgins, E. T., Stash, M. N., Pierro, A., Shah, J., et al. (2000). To "do the right thing" or to "just do it": Locomotion and assessment as distinct self-regulatory imperatives. *Journal of Personality and Social Psychology, 79,* 793–815.
Larrick, R. P. (1993). Motivational factors in decision theories: The role of self-protection. *Psychological Bulletin, 113,* 440–450.
Lerner, J. S., Small, D. A., & Loewenstein, G. (2004). Heart strings and purse strings: Effects of specific emotions on economic transactions. *Psychological Science, 15,* 337–341.
Linville, P. W., & Fischer, G. W. (1991). Preferences for separating and combining events: A social application of prospect theory and the mental accounting model. *Journal of Personality and Social Psychology, 60,* 5–23.
Loewenstein, G. F., Weber, E. U., Hsee, C. K., & Welch, E. (2001). Risk as feelings. *Psychological Bulletin, 127,* 267–286.
March, J. G. (1994). *A primer of decision making: How decisions happen.* New York: The Free Press.
Markus, H. R., & Kitayama, S. (1991). Culture and self: Implications for cognition, emotion and motivation. *Psychological Review, 98,* 224–253.
Mellers, B. A., & Baron, J. (Eds.). (1993). *Psychological perspectives on justice: Theory and applications.* New York: Cambridge University Press.
Murray, H. A. (1938). *Explorations in personality.* New York: Oxford University Press.
Payne, J. W., Bettman, J. R., & Johnson, E. J. (1993). *The adaptive decision maker.* Cambridge, England: Cambridge University Press.
Rettinger, D. A., & Hastie, R. (2003). Comprehension and decision making. In S. L. Schneider & J. Shanteau (Eds.), *Emerging perspectives on judgment and decision research* (pp. 165–200). New York: Cambridge University Press.
Simon, H. A. (1956). Rational choice and the structure of the environment. *Psychological Review, 63,* 129–138.
Tetlock, P. E. (1992). The impact of accountability on judgment and choice: Toward a social contingency model. *Advances in Experimental Social Psychology, 25,* 331–376.
Thaler, R. H. (1985). Mental accounting and consumer choice. *Marketing Science, 4,* 199–214.
Weber, E. U., Ames, D., & Blais, A.-R. (2005). How do I choose thee? Let me count the ways: A textual analysis of similarities and differences in modes of decision making in China and the United States. *Management and Organization Review, 1,* 87–118.

13

In the Forest of Value
Why Moral Intuitions Are Different From Other Kinds

JONATHAN HAIDT and SELIN KESEBIR

University of Virginia

INTRODUCTION

Suppose we ask you whether shoplifting is more or less common than theft from automobiles in your country. How would you answer? You might have little more to go on than a vague intuition, based on the availability to your memory of the time something was stolen from your car, and pick the second choice. Or you might think about which crime the average teenager is more likely to commit and (again, relying on a hunch) pick shoplifting. The answer, at least in the United States, is theft from automobiles. All we have to do to get you to accept that fact is to assert it and include a footnote,[1] which you probably will not check.

However, now suppose we ask you whether it would be better to chop off a thief's finger each time he is caught stealing rather than put him in jail. How would you answer? You probably have a strong intuition that this is not a better policy. Yet suppose we asserted that it was a better policy, and we included a footnote justifying our claim. Suppose we referred to studies on the ineffectiveness of jail time at reducing recidivism; on the suffering that each thief causes to his dozens or

---

[1] *Crime in the United States 2004.* Uniform Crime Reporting. Retrieved January 22, 2006, from http://www.fbi.gov/ucr/cius_04/. Of course, both crimes are usually not reported to the police, and it may be that shoplifting is more heavily underreported. However, if we could cite a definitive study here, it would settle the matter.

hundreds of victims; on the tax money it takes to keep prisons running; and on the greater effectiveness of pain, shame, and fear of mutilation as deterrents to criminal activity.[2] Suppose we could show that an amputation policy was better from a utilitarian point of view than the current policy of repeated incarcerations for large numbers of poor men. Would you change your mind? Probably not. In this second case, you are more likely to check the footnote, challenge the research, and change the terms of the debate. You would try to bring in additional considerations such as decency, dignity, and the irreversibility of amputation.

Why are these cases so different? At first glance it seems obvious that the first case is a matter of fact—a matter of what is—whereas the second case is a matter of value—of what ought to be. This ancient philosophical distinction might serve as an organizing principle for research on intuition. Put simply, researchers have a green light to study intuitions anywhere in the domain of facts: Which of two gambles has a higher payoff? Which way will a ball roll when released from a circular tube? Which signs of heart disease do the best diagnosticians rely on when making their recommendations? In these cases, there are demonstrably right answers, and researchers can study the process of how people reach or fail to reach these answers as well as whether intuitive methods are superior to more analytical methods (as they sometimes are; Gigerenzer, Todd, & The ABC Research Group, 1999; Plessner & Czenna, chap. 15, this volume). However, intuition in matters of value promises to be much more difficult: Which of two paintings is more beautiful? Which cuisine is better, Thai or Mongolian? What should we do with thieves: put them in jail or cut off their fingers? There seems to be a red light flashing, a warning to researchers that they are about to enter a dark forest where the light of objective truth does not penetrate the dense canopy of personal tastes. Researchers are free to study how people make such judgments, but they will have trouble showing that one judgment is better or more accurate than any other.

In recent years, several intrepid researchers have ventured into the forest of value and created a few clearings. Baron (1998) and Sunstein (2005) have both examined the heuristics and intuitions that people use when thinking about moral matters. For example, Baron (1998; Baron & Spranca, 1997; Haidt & Baron, 1996) has documented that people's moral decisions are affected in a seemingly irrational way by the status quo, the omission–commission distinction, and whether a chemical or toxin was manmade or natural. Sunstein (2005) offered an overlapping catalogue of moral heuristics including the following: Do not knowingly cause human death, do not permit wrongdoing for a fee, punish betrayals of trust, and do not tamper with natural processes for biological reproduction. The tool that Baron (1998) and Sunstein (2005) have both used to create these clearings in the forest—these places where moral intuitions could be evaluated as right or wrong—was consequentialism: the doctrine that consequences (harms and benefits) matter. All else equal, people and policymakers ought to prefer the decision, law, or procedure that leads to better consequences rather than worse. Sunstein (2005) called his benchmark for evaluating moral heuristics weak consequentialism because it does not require anyone to adopt utilitarianism; it just requires acceptance of the proposition

---

[2] We have no such evidence. However, if we did, would you accept it?

that when choices have different effects on a valued class of outcomes (lives saved, suffering avoided), ceteris paribus, more is better than less.

In many of Baron's (1998) and Sunstein's (2005) specific examples, the unit of comparison is that most widely agreed on metric: lives saved. Sunstein, for example, offered the fascinating fact that many people are horrified that air bags occasionally kill the people they were designed to protect even though, on the whole, air bags save a great many lives. In one experiment, people on average preferred a car that produced a higher overall risk of death to one with a lower total risk but a higher risk of death caused by the air bag (Koehler & Gershoff, 2003). This choice, Sunstein (2005) suggested, shows the inappropriate application of a moral heuristic (about betrayal by the air bag that was supposed to protect you) to a consumer decision, which leads to a worse outcome (from a consequentialist perspective). It can reasonably be called an error. This consequentialist perspective can be applied to many situations involving quantifiable levels of death and suffering such as trolley problems (switch a train to a track where it will kill one person, to save the lives of five?), medical decisions (kill quickly and painlessly, or let a person die slowly, painfully, and naturally?), and vaccination programs (vaccinate millions knowing that a few will be killed by the vaccine?).

Consequentialism is indeed a powerful tool, but to venture more deeply into the dark forest of value, more tools will be necessary. Most real moral dilemmas force people to make trade-offs across classes of values: the rights of the mother versus the life of the fetus?, death versus dishonor?, autonomy versus obedience?, and loyalty versus fairness? Weak consequentialism cannot help people solve these problems, because they do not present people with choices in which ceteris is paribus. Furthermore, almost any truly difficult or longstanding moral dilemma is likely to tap into subcultural and generational differences within a society. In the United States, at least, political liberals and conservatives often take different sides on policy issues with moral overtones. (We would bet, e.g., that political conservatives would be more supportive than liberals of our proposal to chop off the fingers of thieves.) If people succeed in evaluating specific moral intuitions as right or wrong, better or worse, will they have to declare that some cultures and subcultures are morally superior to others? If so, then research in the forest of value will have many more social and political implications than research on the open plain of objective fact.

We believe that the time is right for empirical researchers to charge into the forest, and we believe that, with the right tools, research can be done effectively. In the rest of this chapter, we provide a preliminary map of the terrain and a possible taxonomy of the creatures that live there. We do not describe the entire domain of value (whose other residents include at very least aesthetics and humor); we focus on the part that we ourselves have explored—morality—and we explain how and why research on moral intuitions is different from research on intuitions about objective facts. First, we comment on the last 20 years of research on intuition and identify three major perspectives: intuition as a personality trait, intuition as a guide for behavior, and intuition as a way of knowing truth. Second, we examine whether moral facts really exist and if so, what kind of thing they are. We propose (following Wiggins, 1987) a distinction between *anthropocentric* facts (which emerge from and depend on the perceptual abilities of fully enculturated human beings) and plain facts (which do not). Third, we provide a classification scheme for studying moral intuitions. We propose that there are five psychological systems that act like social "taste buds" to make people respond affectively to properties of the social world around them. These five psychological systems are the universal foundations on which cultures create divergent though heavily constrained moralities. Fourth, we give several reasons why intuitions about morality (a kind of anthropocentric truth) are different from intuitions about plain facts. These differences must be noted before research methods can be imported from the plain of objectivity into the forest of value. We conclude the chapter by discussing three implications of our intuitionist approach for research on morality and for public policy debates.

A TAXONOMY OF RESEARCH ON INTUITION

In 1982, Bastick published *Intuition: How We Think and Act,* the most comprehensive work ever done on intuition. Bastick (1982) opened the book with a literature review using all of the abstracting services available in 1979, which gave him a universe of 2,692,000 articles, reports, and theses. Of this set, only 91 had the word *intuition* in the title or abstract; and of these articles, only 24 were really studies of intuition. Bastick (1982) offered the understated conclusion that "there is very little modern research into intuition" (p. 4).

To see how things have changed since 1979, we conducted a similar review. Using only the American Psychological Association's PsycINFO database (which is much more focused than Bastick's [1982] approach yet still yields 2.1 million entries) and scanning for the word *intuition* in any field now yields 2,888 records.[3] To reduce this corpus to a more manageable and codable set, we changed the terms of the search: We collected the abstracts of all articles in the PsycINFO database in which the words *intuition, intuitive,* or *intuitionist* appeared in the title. We limited our search to peer-reviewed journal articles published in the last 20 years (1985–2004). We excluded book reviews and studies that used the word *intuition* in an incidental way—that is, they were not really about intuition. We ended up with 355 abstracts, which we read and coded based on their content or approach.[4]

We found three broad classes of research articles as depicted in Figure 13.1. One class (9% of all coded articles) focused on intuition as a *personality variable* tracing back to Carl Jung's original use of the term and included many studies exploring the sensing-intuition dichotomy of the Myers-Briggs Type Indicator®. Other studies in this group had examined the intuitive/experiential and analytical/rational thinking styles proposed by Epstein (1990; chap. 2, this volume) in his cognitive-experiential self-theory.

The second class (35%) we labeled *behavioral,* for these articles had approached intuition as a form of gradually developing expertise related to action. This class included many studies of how people become skilled in particular content

---

[3] Search conduced on January 21, 2006, using EBSCO databases.
[4] Search conducted on October, 13, 2005, using EBSCO databases.

```
                    ┌─────────────┐
                    │  INTUITION  │
                    └──────┬──────┘
         ┌─────────────────┼─────────────────┐
┌────────────────────┐           ┌────────────────────────┐
│ Personality Variable│          │      Behavioral        │
│ e.g., Meyers-Briggs,│          │ e.g., expertise, decision-│
│   Epstein's CEST   │           │ making, problem-solving,│
└────────────────────┘           │    physical action     │
                                 └────────────────────────┘
              ┌──────────────┐
              │ Propositional│
              └──────┬───────┘
       ┌─────────────┴──────────────┐
┌──────────────┐           ┌─────────────────────┐
│  Plain Truth │           │ Anthropocentric Truth│
├──────────────┤           ├─────────────────────┤
│ e.g., pattern detection,│ e.g., moral, ontological,│
│ statistical, mathematical,│ religious, linguistic, legal,│
│ reasoning about the │    │ metaphysical, or political│
│ physical world      │    │ reasoning about the social│
│                     │    │      world.         │
└──────────────┘           └─────────────────────┘
```

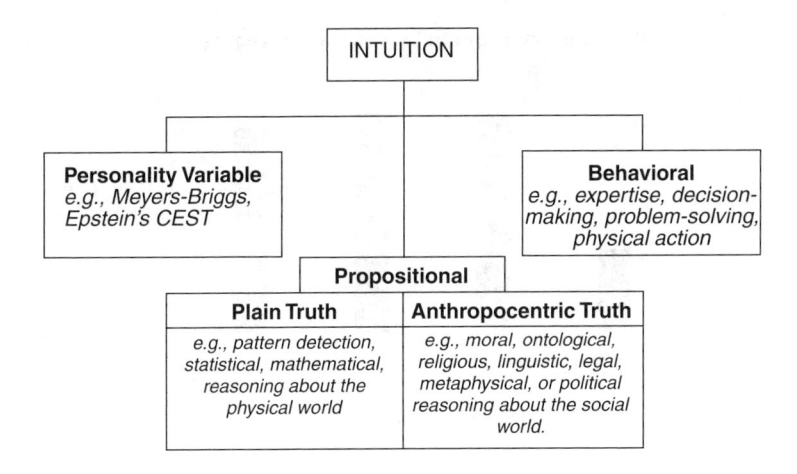

FIGURE 13.1 Major categories of research on intuition.

domains such as sports, music, teaching, nursing, parenting, engineering, management, entrepreneurship, and psychotherapy. Other work we put in this class had examined insight and creativity in problem solving, physical action, and action on the social world including the self (e.g., pretending and affect regulation).

The third and largest class (55%) we labeled *propositional,* for the concern in these articles had been on how people guess or figure out facts about the world. Of course, coming to know facts is a part of expertise, so the distinction between our behavioral and propositional classes was not always sharp; but we relied on a heuristic to separate them: Is intuition in the service of *doing* such that one can speak of more or less skilled performance? Or is intuition in the service of *knowing* so that one can speak of better or worse mental representations, beliefs, and feelings? Is the criterion effective action or accurate representation of facts about the world?

Within the third class, we made a further distinction between propositions that were about plain facts (31% of the total including intuitions about probabilities, pattern detection, and reasoning about the physical world) and propositions that were about anthropocentric facts, which we explain more fully in a moment (24% of the total including intuitions about morality, grammaticality, religion, law, and politics). As a first pass, plain facts are propositions that are demonstrably true out on the flat plain of objectivity. They can be proven by logic (as in the Linda-the-banker problem) or by experiment (as in testing children's erroneous intuition that a ball rolled through a curved tube would continue to curve). Plain facts would generally pass the "alien test": If intelligent aliens were to visit Earth from another solar system, people would expect interstellar agreement about things that are plain facts about the universe independent of human perception of them. For example, the Earth is the third planet from the sun, and gold is a better conductor of electricity than is iron. Both of those statements are true, and they were true long before any human being knew they were true. We would not, however, expect intelligent aliens to

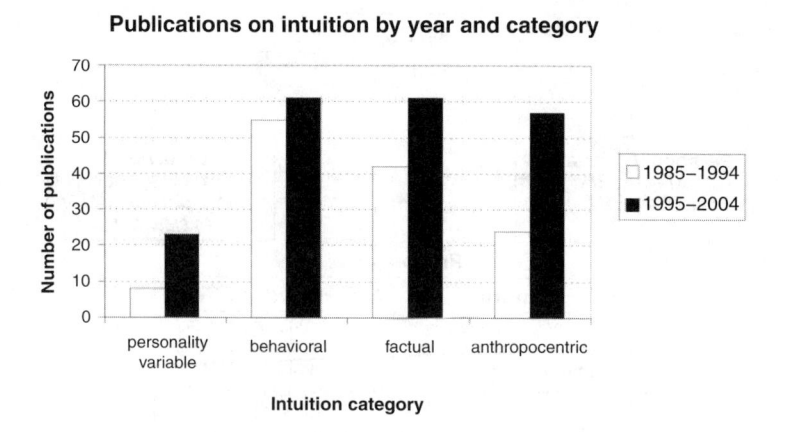

Publications on intuition by year and category

FIGURE 13.2 Number of publications within each category.

agree with human beings about other things that depend on the human sensorium (e.g., that ammonia smells bad) or on human-constructed standards (e.g., that Shakespeare is a better writer than Dickens). These latter propositions are anthropocentric facts–they have a truth value but only with respect to biological facts about human beings (for ammonia) or cultural facts about particular interpretive communities (for Shakespeare).

Using this classification scheme, we examined trends over the last 20 years. Figure 13.2 shows that in the first 10 years of the period reviewed (open bars), the behavioral category was the largest—55 articles that accounted for 43% of the articles in that period. However, in the second 10 years, the behavioral category grew only slightly—by 11%, which is well below the 49% rate of "inflation" in the number of research articles in the PsycINFO database. The plain facts category grew at the rate of inflation (45%). The two categories that grew faster than the rate of inflation were personality (188% growth due largely to the work of Epstein) and anthropocentric facts (138% growth due largely to the increasing use of the term *intuition* in social cognition work). The rapid growth of research on anthropocentric facts is confirmed by returning to Bastick's (1982) review in which he found that nearly all experimental studies of intuition examined intuitions that could be tested against an objective criterion such as asking people to guess the true mean of a set of numbers or to intuit the next number or word in a series of numbers or words. It appears, therefore, that researchers really are venturing in ever-increasing numbers into the forest of value where the tools used to study intuitions about plain facts may or may not apply.

ARE THERE MORAL FACTS?

Because of our evolutionary history, we humans are extremely good at thinking about two kinds of things: objects moving in response to physical forces in the physical world and agents acting in response to their beliefs and desires in the social world. The developmental psychologist Bloom (2004) suggested that people have what amounts to two separate computational systems in their heads: one to solve physical problems and one to solve social problems. When a question fits neatly into one of these computers (e.g., Why is the door stuck? or Why won't Bob speak to Mary?), people are quite good at getting the answer. However, when a question requires radically different kinds of thinking, as often happens in modern physics (How can matter be made of waves or strings?) and occasionally in psychology (What is consciousness?), lay people are quite bad at it, and only years of specialized training can enable a person to think about the problem effectively. The theory of evolution exemplifies this difficulty: Biologists with PhDs understand and overwhelmingly support Darwin's theory of evolution, which requires thinking about how phenotypes emerge and vary over thousands of generations. No physical force or intentional agent pushes on the phenotype, so evolutionary change cannot be imagined easily using either of the two computers. The lay public, at least in the United States, finds it difficult to understand that design can emerge without a designer, and so they find creation theories more intuitively sensible. (According to a Harris poll conducted in 2005, only 22% of adult Americans believe that human beings evolved from other species; 64% endorsed direct creation by God, and an additional 10% endorsed intelligent design.)

A similar problem bedevils morals. The lay public all around the world is composed of moral realists—people who believe that moral statements (such as "it is wrong to kill," or "women should obey their husbands")—refer to plain facts: objective, unchangeable, unquestionable truths. People have found ways to use both of their computational systems to support their moral realism. In Hinduism, the moral law ("dharma") is thought of as a kind of physical law, as pervasive and inescapable as the law of gravity. For Christian fundamentalists, the moral law is just as inescapable, but it is founded on the beliefs and desires of God the creator. Even Westerners who are not religious fundamentalists are generally moral realists, believing in universal human rights and quick to take offense at the negative treatment of women in many non-Western countries. James (1897/1912) noted this tendency and said that people are "absolutists by instinct" (p. 14).

The problem with people's default state of universalist/absolutist moral realism is diversity. The ancient Greeks were well aware—through trade, travel, and warfare—that customs varied greatly around the Mediterranean world and that moral statements might be different from plain facts. Aristotle (Nichomachean Ethics, Book V, 7) noted that fire burned both in Greece and in Persia, but men's notions of justice appeared to vary from city to city. The fact that people in other cultures held their values just as dearly as did the Greeks led some Greek philosophers (but not Aristotle) to abandon moral realism and adopt moral relativism—the idea that actions can be right or wrong only relative to some standard or framework, yet that standard or framework itself cannot be justified as the uniquely correct one (Levy, 2002). For most relativists, morals are understood using the social computer, but rather than being grounded in the unchanging beliefs and desires of God, morals are evaluated relative to the beliefs and desires of particular individuals or groups at particular times.

Relativism, however, is profoundly threatening to lay people and specialists alike because when morals are said to be nothing more than individual or communal tastes, it becomes difficult to criticize behavior people find abhorrent, and the rules and prohibitions of society seem to rest on no foundation at all. Chaos and self-indulgence are widely seen as the handmaidens of subjectivism and relativism. To ward off this threat, moral philosophers have struggled for 2,500 years to find a foundation for morals—to create a defensible moral realism. Most have tried to build this foundation out of plain facts such as deductive logic or utilitarian calculation. Descartes tried to ground a morality based on the goodness of God in a chain of deductions beginning with his famous *"cogito, ergo sum."* Kant tried to ground morals in the logic of noncontradiction with his "categorical imperative." The utilitarians tried to ground morality in simple math: Act only in such a way that you bring about the greatest overall good. It is as though moral philosophers have been trying (until recently) to justify a morality that would pass the alien test—a morality that would be true for and accepted by any rational creature anywhere in the universe.

The project failed (see MacIntyre, 1981). No philosopher has yet discovered a foundation for ethics that satisfies. (If philosophers cannot even convince each other, what luck would they have with aliens?) Of course, moral realism and moral relativism both have many versions and in the past 30 years, many philosophers have fruitfully explored the middle ground—versions of realism in which moral facts exist yet depend in some way on facts about human beings (e.g., Blackburn, 1993; McDowell, 1985; Smith, 1994; Wiggins, 1987) or versions of relativism that still allow people to evaluate and criticize the practices of other cultures (e.g., Harman, 1977).

There are a variety of emergent properties and entities that exist, even though they are hard for people to think about correctly because they do not fit neatly into either of their two computers. For example, philosophers have long been comfortable with the realization that color and smell are not exactly in the objects; rather, these properties emerge from the interaction of the human eye and nose with objective (plain fact) properties of objects. These emergent facts (blood is red, ammonia smells bad) are easy to accept because eyes and noses are pretty much the same wherever you go. Blood is just as red and ammonia smells just as bad in Persia as it does in Greece, so people are not threatened by the specter of diversity. The redness of blood and the unpleasantness of ammonia are anthropocentric facts, but they are true for all anthropic beings, so people can treat them as if they were plain facts, and can say that a person is wrong (color blind or anosmic) if her perceptions differ.

But why stop there? Why insist that anthropocentric facts must be agreed on by all nondefective human beings? Here is a fact about human nature that is exactly as true and universal as the rods and cones of human vision: Humans are obligatory culturalists. Any group of people that lives together for a few years will create standards of value with regard to behavior, food, music, and many other things that they evaluate affectively as good or bad. As the anthropologist Geertz (1973) wrote, "man is an animal suspended in webs of significance he himself has spun, [and] I take culture to be those webs" (p. 5). Honeybees are obligatory hive creatures, and one can only make sense of their behavior with respect to the physical and social entity—the hive—that emerges from their interaction. Human beings, like honeybees, ants, termites, many wasps, and naked mole rats, are ultrasocial creatures (Campbell, 1983), and one can only make sense of human behavior with respect to the physical and social entities—the cultures—that emerge from people's interactions. (Of course, the mechanism behind peoples' ultrasociality is radically different from that of the other ultrasocial animals: It probably involves multilevel cultural and genetic selection; see Richerson & Boyd, 1998; D. S. Wilson, 2002.) Cultures create narrative traditions, frames of reference, and patterns of reward and punishment that make most objects and actions easily classifiable as good or bad in their contexts. So are these classifications just arbitrary subjectivism? Are they nothing more than the whim of each individual person? No, they are not. Only a person who has become "culture blind" could fail to see that social facts (as Durkheim, (1951/1897) called them) have a reality of their own that is more than just the sum of the beliefs of individuals.

Moral facts are social facts. They are anthropocentric facts that are not necessarily shared across all cultures but are facts within a culture. There are many other kinds of facts that are similar: Some writers really are better than others. Some foods really taste better than others. Some jokes really are funnier than others. Some people really are more beautiful than others. Some students' papers deserve higher grades than others. One should not expect any of these statements (when filled in with particular cases) to pass the alien test—judgments of taste, humor, beauty, academic ability, and virtue all require a working human sensorium and an enculturated human mind. Nor should one expect these statements to hold true in other cultures, for their truth value depends on the emergent social facts of a particular culture at a particular time (although in practice, cultures usually agree on these judgments at levels way above chance). Also, one should not even expect these statements to be endorsed by 95% of all people within a given nation, tribe, or organization. Any social group contains diversity—often more diversity within than across groups—and people participate in many nonconcentric groups and have many nonnested identities. So anthropocentric facts are often messier and harder to measure than plain facts. However, they are facts of a certain kind; they are not just the whims of individuals. The dark forest of value contains many truly subjective entities (such as a person's preference for flavors of yogurt), but it is also full of anthropocentric facts, which include the emergent moral norms of a group.

Anthropocentric moral facts are not the kind that most lay people want; they want murder, slavery, and the veiling of women to be wrong with no footnotes about emergent social facts. So our position would be labeled as a kind of relativism by some philosophers and by many commentators on the cultural right (for whom relativism is the new communism—the new all-purpose enemy). However, we think our position can be made more realistic and less threatening to chaos-fearing realists by drawing on recent research and theory on moral intuition.

WHAT ARE THE SPECIES OF MORAL INTUITION?

To use a zoological analogy, we hope we have established that many moral statements are members of the ontological order *anthropocentrica* and not, as some have thought, the orders *subjectivica* or *objectivica*. Other families within this order include beauty, humor, cuisine, and good writing. Within the family of morality, can one be more specific? Are there recognizable genera and species as well? Several theorists have already proposed classifications. Fiske (1991; 2004) has offered a comprehensive theory in which all social interactions are guided by four "relational models." The four are communal sharing (in which people are interchangeable members of a single cooperative entity), authority ranking (in which relationships are structured hierarchically; superiors must protect subordinates who in turn owe respect and deference), equality matching (in which people trade turns, favors, or goods in an exact one-to-one match), and market pricing (in which people trade goods, labor, or money based on proportions and ratios). In Fiske's (1991) approach, cultures vary in which of the models they use to structure particular interactions and in how they set various implementation rules for each model. Moral intuitions are then just the expectations people have for the right way to do things, using their universal models in culture-specific ways, and the emotionally laden reactions people have to violations of these expectations.

Shweder (1990) offered a different but related classification based on his analysis of the content of moral discourse in several cultures. Shweder (1990) and Shweder, Much, Mahapatra, and Park (1997) have found that people generally frame their moral arguments using one or more of three ethics or clusters of interrelated moral goods: the ethics of autonomy (focusing on individuals and relying on notions of harm, rights, and justice), the ethics of community (focusing on the integrity of groups and relying on notions such as duty, obedience, and loyalty), and the ethics of divinity (focusing on souls and the human relationship with God and relying on notions such as purity, sacredness, piety, and sin).

Haidt and Joseph (2004) analyzed the theories of Fiske (1991) and Shweder et al. (1997) along with two other lists of moral goods, values, or practices said to be common around the world (Brown, 1991; Schwartz & Bilsky, 1990). Haidt and Joseph also included de Waal's (1996) description of the precursors of human morality in other animals, which included sympathy, hierarchy, and reciprocity. These five lists showed a great deal of overlap with each other, yet no one system could neatly incorporate all the others. So Haidt and Joseph searched for lower level components—the patterns of social behavior that were said to trigger some sort of evaluative response in people or chimpanzees—and concluded that there were three indisputable candidates: harm/care, fairness/reciprocity, and authority/respect. All five of the works surveyed said that humans (and chimpanzees) notice and care about events in their social world in which individuals are harmed, reciprocity is violated, or hierarchical role expectations are not fulfilled. After trying to ground the virtues of diverse cultures in these three sets of intuitions, Haidt and Joseph concluded that two other sets of intuitions were necessary, intuitions that were mentioned by most (but not all) of the five authors: ingroup/loyalty and purity/sancity. Haidt and Joseph noted that all five of their proposed "foundational intuitions" had been discussed in evolutionary terms—that is, there was already a plausible story being told in the evolutionary literature as to why highly social primates would have evolved to be sensitive to harm/care, fairness/reciprocity, authority/respect, ingroup/loyalty, and purity/sanctity. Haidt and Joseph also noted that this list of five foundations was not meant to be exhaustive but that it was meant to explain the great majority of moral judgments made in any human culture.

Haidt and Joseph (2004) were wary of evolutionary reductionism, and they wanted to capture both the evident similarities and the florid differences in morality across cultures. Haidt and Joseph proposed that the key analytical move was to examine the relationship between foundational intuitions, which are shaped by evolution and are innate in some sense, and virtues, which are emergent social facts of the sort that we discussed previously. Virtues are rooted in foundational intuitions, yet they grow to become part of the dense and complex "webs of significance" (Geertz, 1973, p. 5) that each culture spins.

The example of cuisine—another genus of *anthropocentrica*—may help illustrate this claim. Our tongue comes equipped with five kinds of taste buds, each one responsive to plain facts about the world that were crucial for the survival of our omnivorous ancestors. Sweet and sour receptors are obvious adaptations for gauging the sugar level of fruits. Bitter receptors alert us to classes of chemicals that are often poisonous to us. Taste buds that respond to salt and glutamate help us evaluate molecules common in meat. These five kinds of taste buds convert plain facts about the chemicals present in potential foods into affective reactions of like and dislike. However, we cannot really judge one meal to be better or worse than another by comparing their scores on the five foundational tastes (except in the extreme case of a very high score on bitterness). Rather, we must examine the cuisine that developed within each culture: Greek cuisine favors the use of olive oil, tomatoes, and lamb; Southern Indian cuisines favor the use of fish, rice, and hot chili peppers. Cuisines are emergent cultural products shaped jointly by the physical properties of the food-giving world (what options are available?), the affect-giving properties of our tongue (and nose), and the meaning-giving properties of cultural history (e.g., Indian cuisines are shaped by religious ideas about purity, violence, and heat). Within a cuisine zone, some cooks, meals, or restaurants can be judged better than others, but one would expect foreigners to show less agreement (although not a complete lack of agreement) with such judgments. We would expect judgments of food quality to completely fail the alien test.

The five kinds of taste buds constrain what cuisines are possible, but within those constraints, there is enormous room for cultural creativity. We believe the same situation holds for morality. The five foundational intuitions are, like taste buds, innate perceptual systems that make people emotionally responsive to patterns in their social world that were important during the evolution of their ultrasocial species. We do not specify how foundational intuitions are innate in this chapter; we leave that for another one (Haidt & Joseph, in press). For our present purposes, it does not matter whether these intuitions are products of a massively modularized mind (Tooby & Cosmides, 1992; Sperber, 1994) or a mind that has no modules at all for higher cognitive processes (Prinz, 2006). All we need here is the notion of evolutionary preparedness (Seligman, 1971): It is easy to teach monkeys (and children) to fear snakes but hard to teach them to fear flowers (LoBue & DeLoache, 2005; Mineka & Cook, 1988). Similarly, we believe it is easy to teach children to pick out and react appropriately to cases involving harm, unfairness, group membership, hierarchical rank, and social disgust. These abilities are not present at birth, but they emerge on a predictable developmental timetable (Fiske, 1991), and socializing agents would face a steep uphill struggle to teach children virtues that contradicted their sociomoral preparedness, for example, to love their enemies, or to love all people equally, or to prefer getting less than their age-mates in a distribution of resources. Some moral goods are more easily learnable than others.

Yet, even though all children are born with the same preparedness to build on the foundational intuitions, cultures vary widely in the degree to which they actually do build on each. For example, in the United States, the current "culture war" pits liberals, who build virtues almost exclusively on the harm and fairness foundations, against conservatives who build virtues on all five foundations (Haidt & Graham, in press). Most controversial issues in this war involve conservatives asserting virtues related to in-groups (patriotism, unquestioning loyalty to the group), authority (respect for teachers, parents, and the president), and purity (notions of sacredness and sin), which liberals do not recognize as virtues. Dissent during wartime is called courageous by liberals, but it is treason to conservatives. Spanking is child abuse for many liberals, but it is the proper discipline for disobedience for many conservatives; and allowing gay people to marry is a matter of compassion and justice for many liberals, but it is perversity and sacrilege for many conservatives. A similar struggle is now playing out in Western Europe between tolerant secular societies (based on highly developed notions of compassion and fairness embodied in welfare states) and Islam (based on all five foundations, with heavy emphasis on group loyalty, respect for and submission to God, and religious notions of purity and pollution).

The five intuitive foundations leave a great deal of room for cultures to develop different sets of virtues, but they do constrain the universe of possible moralities. Just as no human culture could create a cuisine based entirely on bitterness, or even on sweetness, no human culture could create a morality based entirely on selfishness or even on love. Various utopian communal schemes have been tried in which all members shared all property and were discouraged from forming special relationships with their own children or with particular sexual partners, but such schemes have always failed (McCord, 1990). They were simply too incongruent with human nature.

WHY MORAL INTUITIONS ARE DIFFERENT

We have argued that moral intuitions are a kind of social-perceptual system that allows one to see and feel a class of anthropocentric facts. If moral intuitions pick up real (although emergent and not plain) properties of the world, then we can begin to talk about the accuracy of moral intuitions; and if we can talk about accuracy, then perhaps we can build on the initial expeditions of Sunstein (2005) and Baron (1998) to create a science of moral judgment and decision making that uses the same experimental paradigms as does other research on judgment and decision making. However, before we can do so, we must state clearly the differences between moral intuitions and intuitions about plain facts. We believe there are three main differences that make a difference.

Assessments of Accuracy for Moral Intuitions Require Social Consensus; Assessments of Accuracy for Intuitions About Plain Facts Do Not

Accuracy is easy to assess in studies of intuitions about plain facts: Dortmund is a larger city than is Bonn, even if most Americans believe the opposite (Goldstein, & Gigerenzer, 2002) and even if most Germans were to believe the opposite. A ball will roll in a straight line when released from a curved tube, even if every person on Earth thought it would continue to curve. So researchers in these cases can specify their own benchmark—the objective truth—and proceed with their studies. However, research on moral intuition is harder, and we know of only two general strategies for assessing the accuracy or quality of moral intuitions. First, researchers can constrain the study to focus on a single moral good that they know is highly valued within the culture to which researchers, researchers' participants, and researchers' eventual readers belong. In most research on morality, this value is the avoidance of harm. (See Haidt & Graham, in press, on why Western researchers have inappropriately narrowed the domain of morality to issues of harm.) Once the moral space is narrowed to issues of harm, then one can apply consequentialism to examine when and how moral intuitions fail or succeed in minimizing harm. For example, Ritov and Baron (1990) showed that the intuitive preference for harm by omission over harm by commission leads many people to reject vaccination programs that would save large numbers of lives because a few children would die from the vaccine itself. In principle, this approach ("narrow the field, then quantify") could work for values other than harm. One can imagine a group of religious scholars narrowing the field of consideration to a single holy book and then evaluating a person's actions solely on the basis of how many commandments the action violated. The crucial step is to restrict the domain of consideration so tightly that social consensus can be assumed on what is left within the domain. A simple procedure such as counting lives saved or laws broken can then be used to make judgments of better and worse.

The more difficult strategy is to assemble panels of experts who serve as benchmarks. In the Olympic sport of figure skating, there really are better and worse performances, but these judgments cannot be made solely by counting the number of falls or the height of the jumps. Panels of experts do apply checklists and formal criteria, but some part of the judgment is intuitive. Judges sharpen their intuitions after many years of involvement with the sport, and they rely (perhaps) on some innate mental mechanisms that give them an affective response to graceful versus clumsy movements. Figure skating stands in contrast to the 100-m dash in which the domain of consideration has been narrowed to a single metric: time to go from point A to point B, which can be measured by counting. The evaluation strategy used in figure skating allows for the integration of multiple sources of value such as innovation, grace, physical strength, and charisma. Moral judgment researchers might try a similar strategy of assembling a panel of people who are known and respected for their moral wisdom and have them pass judgment on people's morally questionable actions or on a research participant's moral intuitions about a complex situation. This strategy is obviously quite difficult to carry out in the laboratory; and as far as we know, nobody has tried it. The European system of having criminal trials conducted by a panel of judges, however, is a version of this strategy used to arrive as close as possible to moral truth.

Moral Facts Have Existential Implications; Plain Facts Usually Do Not

The tasks used to demonstrate biases and errors in decision making are fun. When students say that Linda is more likely to be a bank teller active in the feminist movement than she is to be a bank teller, they can usually be disabused of this notion with a simple Venn diagram. Some students resist at first and search for a justification of their initial judgment; but for nearly all students, there soon comes a moment when they "get it"—they see their error and the reason for their error. Students can quickly be gotten to change their minds on the Wason (1969) card task, the bat-and-ball task,[5] or any number of other problems in which intuitions trick one into misperceiving a plain fact about cost or probability. Not only do students change their minds; they enjoy the process and sometimes ask for more such puzzles. These puzzles all pass what Sunstein (2005, p. 531) called the embarrassment test: People come to realize their mistakes and feel embarrassed at their former intuitions. It is easy to admit your mistake and change your mind because nothing is at stake; nothing is threatened if Linda turns out to be a bank teller who is not active in the feminist movement.

Intuitions about moral facts play out quite differently. Haidt, Koller, and Dias (1993) and Haidt and Hersh (2001) have constructed dozens of vignettes that are moral analogues of the standard judgment and decision-making problems: taboo violations that feel intuitively wrong yet in which nobody is harmed. Examples include a family that ate its dog after the dog was killed by a car, a woman who used her old American flag to clean her toilet, an adult brother and sister who had consensual sex using two forms of birth control, and a variety of people who engaged in unusual or disgusting (but harmless) sexual acts (Haidt & Hersh, 2001; Haidt et al., 1993). Highly educated political liberals usually say that these acts are morally acceptable because they maintain a relatively narrow moral domain in which people should be free to do what they want as long as they do not hurt anyone. However, the majority of people condemn these actions, in large part because of the flash of negative affect that the stories produce (Haidt et al., 1993; Wheatley & Haidt, 2005). Participants who condemn these actions then struggle to find reasons to justify their condemnation. When the interviewer points out that nobody is harmed in the stories, people rarely change their minds. Often they change facts or make assumptions in a desperate attempt to find a victim (e.g., "she'll feel guilty for the rest of her life"). Sometimes they confess to being "morally dumbfounded": They feel that they know, deeply and intuitively, that the action is wrong, but they just do not know how to explain why (Haidt, 2001). Never is there a moment when participants

---

[5] A bat and a ball cost $1.10 in total. The bat costs $1.00 more than the ball. How much does the ball cost? Many people erroneously guess 10 cents (Kahneman & Frederick, 2002).

get it—realize that there is no harm, and that therefore, their former opposition was groundless. Moral problems do not pass Sunstein's (2005) embarrassment test. Even when people can be pressured into changing their judgments (as in studies that use a cross-examiner who challenges the participant's flimsy post hoc justifications), these new judgments are usually offered reluctantly and often with qualifiers (e.g., "well, I guess it's OK for the brother and sister to have sex, but I still don't think it's a good idea"). These new judgments are expressions of dual attitudes (T. D. Wilson, Lindsey, & Schooler, 2000) in which System 2 (explicit attitudes) has been pushed by logic and conversational pressure to say "yes," whereas System 1 (implicit attitudes) is still saying "no, no, no!"

People are so much more reluctant to change their minds about incest than about Linda because so much more is at stake. As we stated previously, human beings are, in a way, hive creatures like honeybees, and the hive is constructed out of anthropocentric facts, many of which are shared moral values. A person who questions whether human life is always more important than animal life, or who suggests that rich people should get two votes, or who thinks it is fine for brothers and sisters to have sex is ripping out a piece of the hive and holding it up for debate. All the work that was done to make an emergent truth feel like an absolute/universal truth comes undone, and the structural integrity of the rest of the hive is weakened. Moral beliefs hold groups together, so people are not free to change their moral beliefs as they please. Changing one's moral beliefs sometimes threatens one of the most basic human needs: the need to belong (Baumeister & Leary, 1995). Imagine what would happen in a tight-knit psychology department in which nearly all members shared an intense dislike of a particular politician, and they routinely made jokes or sarcastic comments about the politician to each other. However, then suppose that one member announced that he or she was going to vote to reelect that politician because he or she agreed with his policies on terrorism. How would the others react? Exactly this situation happened in our department at the University of Virginia in 2004, and the professor who expressed dissenting views reported reactions ranging from disbelief to anger to ostracism.[6]

Moral beliefs also give people a sense of purpose and meaning in life (Baumeister, 1991), so threats to moral beliefs are sometimes threats to a person's deepest goals and commitments. Moral beliefs are therefore fraught with existential entailments, whereas the Linda problem is not. It is as though the domain of morality is covered with a complex network of invisible fences—the kind used to keep suburban dogs from wandering by giving them a shock when they get too near the property lines. Just try looking at things from Hitler's perspective—it hurts. In people's minds, they can roam freely around the Linda problem, and they can inspect counterfactual objective worlds (suppose the sun suddenly vanished, what would happen to the Earth?). However, it is much harder and more painful for people to think about alternative moral worlds and perspectives ("Suppose Bin Laden is right about Western civilization?" or "What if human life were not really valuable?"). For all these reasons, moral intuitions are different from other kinds—they

---

[6] Because of the passion about this particular politician within the academic community, we feel compelled to declare that the professor was not an author of this chapter.

are "stickier" than most intuitions about plain facts because they have so many personal, social, and existential entailments.

In the Moral Domain, System 2 Is Usually a Servant of the System 1; on the Plain of Objective Fact, System 2 Has More Independence

Dual-process models generally present the mind as being composed of two systems that can operate (to some extent) independently: System 1 uses ancient, rapid, automatic, intuitive processes to reach its conclusions; whereas System 2 uses more evolutionarily recent, controlled, slow, conscious reasoning processes to reach its conclusions (Chaiken & Trope, 1999; Deutsch & Strack, chap. 3, this volume; Epstein, chap. 2, this volume; Sloman, 1996). Yet what is the relationship between these two processes? In many dual-process models, people are said to be cognitive misers who try to solve problems using System 1 whenever they can, and they call on the more expensive (effortful) System 2 only when System 1 is not up to the task (e.g., Chaiken, 1980). System 2 is therefore like a wise consultant who is hired only when needed or like a monitor who checks the work of System 1 and occasionally overrides its conclusions. On this view, System 2 is the more rational, reasoned, and reliable system, and the errors that Sunstein (2005) and Baron (1998) have found in moral judgment are due largely to the failure of System 2 to check and revise the moral intuitions of System 1. Sunstein (2005) proposed that people should be wary of such unmonitored moral intuitions and should strive to rely more on System 2.

In the moral domain, however, System 2 may be less useful than it is out on the plain of objective fact. Whenever strong emotions and desires are at work, people are likely to engage in motivated reasoning (Kunda, 1990). When existential threats and invisible fences are at work, the pressures on System 2 to reach the right conclusion—the one that backs up System 1—may be overwhelming. So is the solution to strive to free System 2 from all affective influences and let it do its job coolly and rationally? No, it is not. Hume (1739/1969) long ago challenged the belief common among philosophers that reasoning could lead to substantive moral conclusions without substantial reliance on the passions (feelings, sentiments, affect). Modern research on the role of emotion and affectively laden intuition in moral judgment has indicated that Hume was correct (Damasio, 2003; Haidt, 2001); gut feelings and emotions are essential for proper moral functioning.

Out on the plain of fact, System 1 and System 2 can each operate independently, and much of the research on dual-process models of cognition has concerned the many interesting cases in which the two systems reach different conclusions. In these cases, the dispute must be resolved by System 2. That does not mean that System 2 was always right in the first place, as Gigerenzer et al. (1999) showed; but because verification usually requires calculation, formal logic, or consulting published facts, System 2 is the final arbiter of truth. In the forest of value, however, System 2 (reasoning) simply cannot operate on its own. The interesting creatures are mostly *anthropocentrica*, and culturally tuned intuitions are the only way that these creatures can be perceived and evaluated. So reason must have a partner—intuition—and it is an open and currently debated question which one of these partners makes the better leader, which one is better suited to be an assistant, and how much work each partner in fact does (see various positions in Greene, in press; Haidt, 2001; Pizarro & Bloom, 2003).

IMPLICATIONS: INTUITIONISM IN A MORALLY DIVERSE SOCIETY

We have advocated an intuitionist approach to the study of anthropocentric truths in general and morality in particular. We have suggested that the human mind comes prepared to learn moral virtues related to the five foundations of harm/care, fairness/reciprocity, ingroup/loyalty, authority/respect, and purity/sanctity. We have claimed that moral intuitions are a kind of social-perceptual system that enables people to perceive the emergent social facts that constitute the cultures within which they live. We believe that this perspective has many interesting and, we hope, provocative implications for researchers and for public policy debates as well. The following are three of these:

1. Charge into the forest. It is often said *de gustibus non est disputandum* (there is no dispute about taste), but morality is not just a matter of taste. Within a culture, some actions are better than others, and some judgments are better than others. Researchers can evaluate the quality and accuracy of moral judgments as long as they do not mistake anthropocentric truths for plain facts.
2. Look beyond harm. Research on moral judgment has so far focused almost exclusively on harm, examining when and why people make nonutilitarian choices. However, harm is just one of (at least) five genera within the family of moral concerns. If researchers do not expand the scope of their investigation, they are bound to misunderstand most of the world's moralities, which build on all five foundations. Liberals, in particular, have a hard time understanding conservative moral concerns, which they often dismiss as racism, sexism, and narrow-minded fears about change disguised in moral terminology. This dismissal is an error—it is a failure of social perception that can be fixed by reading ethnographies and case studies of conservative cultures and subcultures (e.g., Abu-Lughod, 1986; Ault, 2005).
3. Study the destabilizing effects of moral diversity. Nearly all academic articles on diversity have praised it, and many have discussed the benefits of participating in a diverse workplace or educational environment. Yet there are reasons to be careful about promoting or "celebrating" diversity. Tajfel's (2005) "minimal group" studies showed just how easy it is to divide people on the basis of trivial differences. When the differences are tribal markers such as language, race, or national origin, emphasizing differences produces much stronger divisions (see review in Berreby, 2005). However, a democracy can be diverse in the origins of its people while still creating a rich, thick, consensual moral world in which its citizens can thrive. The American motto of e pluribus unum (from many,

one) captures this ideal of unity forged out of diversity. The real threat to the moral order is not ethnic diversity, it is moral diversity—a lack of consensus on basic values. When there is no such consensus, many social facts vanish, and society enters the state Durkheim (1951/1897) called "anomie." People are left to search for meaning on their own or in small and often unstable groups (as described in Bellah, Madsen, Sullivan, Swidler, & Tipton, 1985). Haidt, Rosenberg, and Hom (2003) presented evidence that people respond to ethnic and moral diversity very differently. Perhaps diversity is like cholesterol: There are two kinds, and one should strive to maximize one while reducing the other.

In conclusion, social scientists are studying intuition in increasing numbers, and the area of greatest growth is intuitions about anthropocentric truths (see Figure 13.2). Baron (1998) and Sunstein (2005) have documented some of the intuitions that people use when thinking about moral issues and have shown how these intuitions can be evaluated as better or worse. In this chapter, we have attempted to extend Baron and Sunstein's work, which is anchored in the easily quantified variables of physical harm and mortality. We agree that public policy should be based primarily on utilitarian calculations (at least, in Western democracies, and arguably in other nations too), and we agree that harm has pride of place in utilitarian calculations. The only caveat we add is this: In their utilitarian considerations, policymakers should take an expanded view of utility in which they recognize that the people they serve care about more than just lives and money saved. People want to live in a well ordered moral world in which crime is punished (even in cases where it does not make directly utilitarian sense to do so) and the government does not hurt innocent people (even when a government sponsored vaccination program would, overall, save lives). Policymakers need not always defer to citizens' moral intuitions—sometimes (as with the deep intuitive opposition to racial integration in the American South) it should mount a campaign to educate and change those intuitions. However, a truly utilitarian approach to public policy would take into account many moral goods that may not be obvious to all policymakers; it would have to recruit moral intuition as a guide and ally of reasoning to help it understand the forest of value it is trying to improve.

ACKNOWLEDGMENTS

We thank Jonathan Baron, Joshua Greene, Neil Levy, Henning Plessner, and Nina Strohminger for helpful comments on the first draft.

REFERENCES

Abu-Lughod, L. (1986). *Veiled sentiments*. Berkeley: University of California Press.

Ault, J. M. J. (2005). *Spirit and flesh: Life in a fundamentalist Baptist church*. New York: Knopf.

Baron, J. (1998). *Judgment misguided: Intuition and error in public decision making.* New York: Oxford University Press.
Baron, J., & Spranca, M. (1997). Protected values. *Organizational Behavior and Human Decision Processes, 70,* 1–16.
Bastick, T. (1982). *Intuition: How we think and act.* Chichester, England: Wiley.
Baumeister, R. (1991). *Meanings of life.* New York, Guilford.
Baumeister, R. F., & Leary, M. R. (1995). The need to belong: Desire for interpersonal attachments as a fundamental human motivation. *Psychological Bulletin, 117,* 497–529.
Bellah, R. N., Madsen, R., Sullivan, W. M., Swidler, A., & Tipton, S. M.. (1985). *Habits of the heart: Individualism and commitment in American life.* New York: Harper & Row.
Berreby, D. (2005). *Us and them: Understanding your tribal mind.* New York: Little, Brown.
Blackburn, S. (1993). *Essays in quasi-realism.* New York: Oxford University Press.
Bloom, P. (2004). *Descartes' baby: How the science of child development explains what makes us human.* New York: Basic Books.
Brown, D. E. (1991). *Human universals.* New York: McGraw-Hill.
Campbell, D. T. (1983). The two distinct routes beyond kin selection to ultra-sociality: Implications for the humanities and social sciences. In D. L. Bridgeman (Ed.), *The nature of prosocial development: Interdisciplinary theories and strategies* (pp. 11–41). New York: Academic.
Chaiken, S. (1980). Heuristic versus systematic information processing and the use of source versus message cues in persuasion. *Journal of Personality and Social Psychology, 45,* 752–766.
Chaiken, S., & Trope, Y. (1999). *Dual-process theories in social psychology.* New York: Guilford.
Damasio, A. (2003). *Looking for Spinoza.* Orlando, FL: Harcourt.
de Waal, F. (1996). *Good natured: The origins of right and wrong in humans and other animals.* Cambridge, MA: Harvard University Press.
Durkheim, E. (1951/1897). *Suicide* (J.A. Spalding & G. Simpson, Trans.). New York: The Free Press.
Epstein, S. (1990). Cognitive-experiential self-theory. In L. Pervin (Ed.), *Handbook of personality theory and research* (pp. 165–192). New York: Guilford.
Fiske, A. P. (1991). *Structures of social life: The four elementary forms of human relations.* New York: Free Press.
Fiske, A. P. (2004). Relational models theory 2.0. In N. Haslam (Ed.), *Relational models theory: A contemporary overview* (pp. 3–25). Mahwah, NJ: Lawrence Erlbaum Associates, Inc.
Geertz, C. J. (1973). *The interpretation of cultures.* New York: Basic Books.
Gigerenzer, G., Todd, P. M., & The ABC Research Group. (1999). *Simple heuristics that make us smart.* New York: Oxford University Press.
Goldstein, D. G., & Gigerenzer, G. (2002). Models of ecological rationality: The recognition heuristic. *Psychological Review, 109,* 75–90.
Greene, J. (in press). The secret joke of Kant's soul. In W. Sinnott-Armstrong (Ed.), *Moral psychology.* Vol. 2: The Cognitive Science of Morality. Cambridge, MA: MIT Press.
Haidt, J. (2001). The emotional dog and its rational tail: A social intuitionist approach to moral judgment. *Psychological Review, 108,* 814–834.
Haidt, J., & Baron, J. (1996). Social roles and the moral judgement of acts and omissions. *European Journal of Social Psychology, 26,* 201–218.
Haidt, J., & Bjorklund, F. (in press). Social intuitionists answer six questions about morality. In W. Sinnott-Armstrong (Ed.), *Moral psychology: Vol. 2. The cognitive science of morality.* Cambridge, MA: MIT Press.

Haidt, J., & Graham, J. (in press). When morality opposes justice: Conservatives have moral intuitions that liberals may not recognize. *Social Justice Research*.
Haidt, J., & Hersh, M. A. (2001). Sexual morality: The cultures and reasons of liberals and conservatives. *Journal of Applied Social Psychology, 31*, 191–221.
Haidt, J., & Joseph, C. (2004, Fall). Intuitive ethics: How innately prepared intuitions generate culturally variable virtues. *Daedalus*, 55–66.
Haidt, J., & Joseph, C. (in press). The moral mind: How 5 sets of innate intuitions guide the development of many culture-specific virtues, and perhaps even modules. In P. Carruthers, S. Laurence & S. Stich (Eds.), *The Innate Mind, Vol. 3*.
Haidt, J., Koller, S., & Dias, M. (1993). Affect, culture, and morality, or is it wrong to eat your dog? *Journal of Personality and Social Psychology, 65*, 613–628.
Haidt, J., Rosenberg, E., & Hom, H. (2003). Differentiating diversities: Moral diversity is not like other kinds. *Journal of Applied Social Psychology, 33*, 1–36.
Harman, G. (1977). *The nature of morality*. New York: Oxford University Press.
Hume, D. (1969). *A treatise of human nature*. London: Penguin. (Original work published 1739)
James, W. (1912). *The will to believe and other essays in popular philosophy*. Norwood, MA: The Plimpton Press. (Original work published 1897)
Kahneman, D., & Frederick, S. (2002). Representativeness revisited: Attribute substitution in intuitive judgment. In T. Gilovich, D. Griffin, & D. Kahneman (Eds.), *Heuristics and biases: The psychology of intuitive judgment* (pp. 49–81). New York: Cambridge University Press.
Koehler, J. J., & Gershoff, A. D. (2003). Betrayal aversion: When agents of protection become agents of harm. *Organizational Behavioral and Human Decision Processes, 90*, 244–261.
Kunda, Z. (1990). The case for motivated reasoning. *Psychological Bulletin, 108*, 480–498.
Levy, N. (2002). *Moral relativism: A short introduction*. Oxford, England: Oneworld.
LoBue, V., & DeLoache, J. (2005). *Human infants associate snake and fear*. Unpublished manuscript, University of Virginia, Charlottesuille, VA.
McCord, W. M. (1990). *Voyages to utopia: From monastery to commune: The search for the perfect society in modern times*. New York: Norton.
McDowell, J. (1985). Values and secondary qualities. In Honderich, T., editor, Morality and Objectivity: A Tribute to J.L. Mackie, pp. 110–129. Routledge and Kegan Paul, London.
Mineka, S., & Cook, M. (1988). Social learning and the acquisition of snake fear in monkeys. In T. Zentall & B. G. Galef (Eds.), *Social learning: Psychological and biological perspectives* (pp. 51–73). Hillsdale, NJ: Lawrence Erlbaum Associates, Inc.
Pizarro, D., & Bloom, P. (2003). The intelligence of the moral emotions: A comment on Haidt (2001). *Psychological Review, 110*, 293–296.
Prinz, J. (2006). Is the mind really modular? In R. Stainton (Ed.), *Contemporary debates in cognitive science*. New York: Blackwell, 22–36.
Richerson, P. J., & Boyd, R. (1998). The evolution of human ultra-sociality. In I. Eibl-Eibesfeldt & F. K. Salter (Eds.), *Indoctrinability, ideology, and warfare: Evolutionary perspectives* (pp. 71–95). New York: Berghahn.
Ritov, I., & Baron, J. (1990). Reluctance to vaccinate: Omission bias and ambiguity. *Journal of Behavioral Decision Making, 3*, 263–277.
Schwartz, S. H., & Bilsky, W. (1990). Toward a theory of the universal content and structure of values: Extensions and cross-cultural replications. *Journal of Personality and Social Psychology, 58*, 878–891.
Seligman, M. E. P. (1971) Phobias and preparedness. *Behavior Therapy, 2*, 307–320.
Shweder, R. (1990). In defense of moral realism: Reply to Gabennesch. *Child Development, 61*, 2060–2067.

Shweder, R. A., Much, N. C., Mahapatra, M., & Park, L. (1997). The "big three" of morality (autonomy, community, divinity), and the "big three" explanations of suffering. In P. Rozin & A. Brandt (Eds.), *Morality and health* (pp. 119–169). New York: Routledge.

Sloman, S. A. (1996). The empirical case for two systems of reasoning. *Psychological Review, 119*, 3–22.

Smith, M. (1994). *The moral problem*. Oxford, England: Blackwell.

Sperber, D. (1994). The modularity of thought and the epidemiology of representations. In L. A. Hirschfeld & S. A. Gelman (Eds.), *Mapping the mind: Domain specificity in cognition and culture* (pp. 39–67). New York: Cambridge University Press.

Sunstein, C. R. (2005). Moral heuristics. *Behavioral and Brain Sciences, 28*, 531–573.

Tajfel, H. (1982). *Social identity and intergroup behavior*. Cambridge, England: Cambridge University Press.

Tooby, J., & Cosmides, L. (1992). The psychological foundations of culture. In J. Barkow, L. Cosmides, & J. Tooby (Eds.), *The adapted mind: Evolutionary psychology and the generation of culture* (pp. 19–136). New York: Oxford University Press.

Wason, P.C. (1969). Regression in reasoning? *British Journal of Psychology, 60*, 471–480.

Wheatley, T., & Haidt, J. (2005). Hypnotically induced disgust makes moral judgments more severe. *Psychological Science, 16*, 780–784.

Wiggins, D. (1987). *Needs, values, truth*. Oxford. England: Blackwell.

Wilson, D. S. (2002). *Darwin's cathedral: Evolution, religion, and the nature of society*. Chicago: University of Chicago Press.

Wilson, T. D., Lindsey, S., & Schooler, T. (2000). A model of dual attitudes. *Psychological Review, 107*, 101–126.

14

Chronic Preferences for Intuition and Deliberation in Decision Making
Lessons Learned About Intuition from an Individual Differences Approach

CORNELIA BETSCH
University of Heidelberg

INTRODUCTION

Feeling and thinking are two modes of information processing that influence our decision making every day. Sometimes choosing one particular alternative feels better than choosing something else, and sometimes an elaborated analysis reveals the advantages of one alternative over the other. Although each individual can engage in either strategy of making a decision—deciding based on feelings or on thoughts—there is evidence that not everybody is equally fond of both strategies. Instead, people have preferences regarding decision-making strategies: whereas some people generally prefer to make their decisions intuitively in an affect-based manner, others prefer deliberate, thoughtful decision making (C. Betsch, 2004). These chronic preferences influence information processing during and after the decision-making process. In the next paragraph, I clarify what intuition and deliberation actually mean in this context. Thereafter, I outline the method for measuring individual differences in the preference for intuition and deliberation. In the main part of the chapter, I provide a broad overview of recent findings on how the individual preference for intuition and deliberation impacts information processing, decisions, and postdecisional affect. In the final section,

I summarize what such an individual differences approach can teach researchers about intuition.

THE HEAD OR THE HEART? INTUITION AND DELIBERATION AS STRATEGIES IN DECISION MAKING

The decision maker can choose among a variety of strategies to make a choice. Intuition and deliberation are two of these strategies. Over the last decades, it has been repeatedly shown that affect plays an important role in fast and intuitive decision making (e.g., see Damasio, 1994; Schwarz & Clore, 1983; Slovic, Finucane, Peters, & MacGregor, 2001). The essence of the findings can be cast in a new definition of an emotion-bound type of intuition:

> Intuition is a process of thinking. The input to this process is mostly provided by knowledge stored in long-term memory that has been primarily acquired via associative learning. The input is processed automatically and without conscious awareness. The output of the process is a feeling that can serve as a basis for judgments and decisions. (T. Betsch, chap. 1, this volume, p. 4)

On a theoretical level, intuition is usually settled as one of two processing modes in a variety of dual-process theories (e.g., Deutsch & Strack, chap. 3, this volume; Epstein, chap. 2, this volume; Hammond, Hamm, Grassia, & Pearson, 1987; Hogarth, 2001; Sloman, 1996). The models postulate a deliberate mode of thinking as a counterpart to the intuitive mode. Accordingly, deliberation is an analytic mode that reflectively processes mainly cognitive contents such as beliefs, arguments, and reasons.

The two major points explicated in the previous definition of intuition are that (a) intuition is based on implicit knowledge and (b) that intuition uses the feeling or affect toward options as a criterion for decisions. Even though different definitions of intuition propose different roots of intuition, the consensus seems to have developed that intuition is based on implicit knowledge (Hogarth, 2001; Lieberman, 2000; Plessner, 2006; Reber, 1989). The learning of this knowledge "usually cannot be accessed by introspection and therefore cannot be verbalized. [As such,] intuitive processing resembles Greenwald and Banaji's (1995) concept of implicit cognition" (T. Betsch, chap. 1, this volume, p. 4). Given that people differ in their reliance on intuition, one can deduce that people will therefore also differ in their reliance on implicit knowledge. In a later section of this chapter, I go into more detail on this issue and present data testing this assumption.

The second part of the definition relates to the feelings aspect of intuition: the feeling or affect connected to an option or the feeling of risk evoked by uncertain alternatives. These feelings can influence decisions directly without cognitive mediation (e.g., Loewenstein, Weber, Hsee, & Welch, 2001; Slovic et al., 2001), and thus they can be the crucial information at the time of the decision. The affective primacy hypothesis (Zajonc, 1980) poses that the affective reaction toward objects is a basic, primary, and automatic reaction when an object is encountered. Reliance on this affect allows for fast decisions. All subsequent cognitive operations will need time for elaboration and deliberation. Individual differences in the reliance on affect will therefore result in different decision times: Intuitive people should be able to make faster decisions. Moreover, parameters sensitive to the influence of affective or cognitive information will also show different values for intuitive and deliberate people. As I show in the following, one such parameter is the utility function (i.e., the function that allocates a continuous utility value to an increasing amount of money). Various findings have shown that the use of affect as a judgment and decision mode influences the shape of the utility function (Hsee & Rottenstreich, 2004; Schunk & C. Betsch, 2006). I reveal details in the respective section following.

The possibility to use multiple strategies poses the old question of when each strategy is used (e.g., Payne, Bettman, & Johnson, 1993). Regarding the intuitive versus deliberate strategies, it has been a consensual assumption that factors within the environment trigger the selection of a strategy. Physiological needs, for example, are said to trigger affect, whereas the presence of probabilities triggers the use of deliberate strategies (Epstein, chap. 2, this volume; Hammond et al., 1987; Weber & Lindemann, chap. 12, this volume). Probably the most prominent approach to strategy selection describes the selection of a strategy as a result of an internal metacalculus process (Payne et al., 1993; for an overview, see T. Betsch, Haberstroh, & Höhle, 2002). The individual selects the strategy yielding the highest effectiveness and efficiency, referring back to learning experiences with the strategy. The learning experiences are stored in metacognitive production rules. However, the decision maker does not always have to undergo such demanding metachoice processes, as Bröder (2003) pointed out: Strategies can turn into routines when they have repeatedly worked out in the past. In a similar manner, individuals can also develop preferences for a strategy, for example, due to different learning experiences in the past (C. Betsch, 2004). Thus, besides situational factors or metacalculus processes, chronic and stable factors within the person can also determine strategy selection and make the use of intuition and deliberation more or less likely.

ASSESSING INDIVIDUAL DIFFERENCES IN INTUITION AND DELIBERATION

Various attempts to assess these individual differences in the use of intuition, of affect, of thinking, or of different judgment and decision strategies have led to the existence of a series of inventories with varying goals and operationalizations of intuition. Affect and cognition are sometimes assessed by one scale and are thus intermixed, or affect is not even considered. Epstein, Pacini, Denes-Raj, and Heier (1996) and Pacini and Epstein (1999) have found that people differ in their inclinations to rely on the experiential and on the rational system (rational experiential inventory; Epstein et al., 1996). People with a high need for cognition enjoy thinking and are willing to spend large amounts of cognitive effort to solve problems. People with high faith in intuition mainly process in a heuristic manner using cognitive shortcuts; following emotions represents only a subpart of faith in intuition. The Myers–Briggs Type Indicator® (MBTI; Myers & McCaulley, 1986), an inventory widely used in the United States, captures mainly the disposition to behave in an intuitive manner. Affect plays no major role in the MBTI Intuition scale (Langan-Fox & Shirley, 2003). The individual need for affect is assessed by the need for affect scale (Maio & Esses, 2001) and captures the individual's motivation to approach or avoid emotion-inducing situations. The relation to emotional decision making is not yet assessed, and it is therefore unclear if people who approach emotional situations also utilize affect for making decisions. The constructs locomotion and assessment (Kruglanski et al., 2000) constitute two goal pursuit orientations that express a tendency to "just do it" (locomotion) and to "do the right thing" (assessment). Whereas just doing it might represent one aspect of intuition, the locomotion scale lacks the important facet of affect-driven behavior and instead assesses the action orientation and the degree of being energized during actions. The assessment scale mainly pertains to aspects of self-evaluation and other evaluation, not to the decision-relevant evaluation of options or actions.

To summarize, various scales capture similar but different aspects of individual differences in intuition, in emotional behavior, or in the tendency to think and to evaluate. As I outlined previously, the difference between using affect and using cognition as a decision criterion has increasingly gained interest in the decision literature. As none of the existing scales was created to assess affect- versus cognition-based decision making, a new scale was constructed with the goal of capturing individual preferences for either strategy (C. Betsch, 2004). In the next paragraphs, I outline how individual strategy preferences (i.e., individual differences in intuition and deliberation) can be assessed in a reliable, fast, and economical way.

The focus of the Preference for Intuition and Deliberation Scale (PID; C. Betsch, 2004) is the assessment of preferences for intuition and deliberation. *Intuition* is defined as a basic decision mode that uses direct affective reactions toward the decision option as the decision criterion (affect-based decision making). Deliberation follows cognitions (beliefs, evaluations, reasons; cognition-based decision making). PID consists of two independent scales with nine items each, preference for intuition (PID–Intuition; e.g., "I listen carefully to my deepest feelings"), and preference for deliberation (PID–Deliberation; e.g., "I prefer making detailed plans rather than leaving things to chance"). On a 5-point scale ranging from 1 (I very much disagree) to 5 (I very much agree), individuals can express their agreement or disagreement with the statements. The two scales are usually slightly negatively correlated ($< -.20$). The appendix reveals the German original of the scale and its English and Dutch translations including reliability data, instructions for participants, and scoring instructions.

The individual preference for a decision strategy is a strong predictor for strategy choice. In a study, C. Betsch (2004) asked people directly which strategy they would rely on in different situations (those requiring intuition or deliberation to different degrees). People adapted to the requirements of the situation by choosing an appropriate strategy. For example, when intuition was the appropriate strategy, the majority chose intuition. However, beyond the situational requirement, the preferred strategy still significantly explained variance in strategy selection (C. Betsch,

2004, Study 3), leading intuitive people to choose intuition more frequently than deliberation across all scenarios.

The correlates (reported in C. Betsch, 2004) of preference for intuition indicate that people with a high preference for intuition are inclined to quick and emotional behavior and personality traits. PID–Intuition correlates positively with quick decision making, extraversion, and agreeableness. Preference for deliberation, on the other hand, correlates with conscientiousness, perfectionism, and the need for structure. Both scales are independent of the ability to think logically and of intelligence. This fosters the idea that people indeed have a preference for one strategy and do not just use or avoid the strategy they happen to be good or bad at (e.g., thinking). Other findings point in the same direction. An indirect measure of the attitude toward intuition and deliberation corresponded to the preferences as assessed by PID: Individuals with a high preference for intuition had a more positive attitude toward intuition as compared to deliberation; the reverse was true for people with a higher preference for deliberation (pretest in C. Betsch & Kunz, 2006).

Intuition is not the opposite of deliberation (cf. also Epstein, 1990). Thus, intuition and deliberation are not two poles of one dimension, but they are rather two independent dimensions (for a discussion and results of a confirmatory factor analysis, see C. Betsch, 2004, Study 2). This implies that people can be high on one scale, such as preference for intuition (PID–Intuition), and low on the other, preference for deliberation (PID–Deliberation). This offers the possibility to constitute types of decision makers (in this case, the person is an intuitive person; henceforth, the types are called the intuitives vs. deliberates: empirically, each type constitutes about one third of a random sample). People can also be high or low on both scales, indicating that they use intuition and deliberation without clear preferences for either strategy (about one third of a random sample). In fact, most of our everyday decisions involve a mixture of the two modes (Hsee & Rottenstreich, 2004). After a deliberate search for information, for example, a person can still make an intuitive decision or vice versa; the emotions involved in a decision process can be cognitively processed and be subject to deliberation. Therefore, a high scale value on the intuition scale and a low value on the deliberation scale, for example, do not mean that one exclusively relies on feelings; however, it suggests a strong shift in the weight of emotional information.

In the next three sections, I spotlight findings from different studies that have used the PID Scale. By and large, the results demonstrate that the individual preference for intuition and deliberation can account for diverse and apparently unrelated effects in different areas.

INDIVIDUAL STRATEGY PREFERENCES AND THE RELIANCE ON IMPLICIT KNOWLEDGE

The idea that intuition is based on implicit knowledge raises the question of whether individual differences in intuition are caused by different implicit learning processes or by a differing usage of the existing knowledge. Reber, Walkenfeld, and Hernstadt (1991) argued that there are no individual differences in the acquisition of implicit knowledge. As a consequence, there should not be any individual differences in intuition. However, even though all individuals acquire implicit knowledge in a similar manner, people might differ in their reliance on this knowledge. Whereas intuitive people might rely on their implicit knowledge when they make judgments (e.g., on their implicit attitude) deliberate people might not do so and instead use their explicit attitude.

The attitude toward objects and actions serves as a means to make predictions about behavior, for example, to predict the choice between two consumer products say, an apple or a candy bar (e.g., Karpinski & Hilton, 2001). When someone has a favorable attitude toward a particular product, he or she is more likely to buy this product. Recent theories in social psychology assume that people may have two different attitudes toward an object at the same time, one that is explicit and one that is implicit (Fazio, 1990; Greenwald & Banaji, 1995; Wilson, Lindsey, & Schooler, 2000). In general, it has been suggested that implicit attitudes guide spontaneous behavior, whereas more deliberative behavior is influenced more by explicit attitudes (Fazio, 1990; Fazio & Towles-Schwen, 1999; Wilson et al., 2000).

Recent research has shown that when people have to be spontaneous (e.g., when they cannot think deliberately because of imposed time pressure), the implicit attitude predicts their behavior. Without time pressure, however, the explicit attitude turned out to be a better predictor of behavior (Friese, Wänke, & Plessner, 2006). Thus, particularly for uncontrolled behavior such as spontaneous choices, implicit attitudes represented better predictors than explicit attitudes. Besides factors within the situation (such as time pressure), other factors within the person can also determine the degree of deliberation such as the individual preference for intuition and deliberation. As I pointed out previously, people with a preference for deliberation are inclined to think a lot before making a decision, whereas people with a preference for intuition like to go with their gut feelings and decide based on affect.

Given the idea that the implicit attitude predicts spontaneous behavior, and the explicit attitude predicts deliberate behavior, one can assume that for people with a preference for deliberation, the explicit attitude is a predictor of behavior, whereas the behavior of intuitive people should be predictable by their implicit attitude. The definition of intuition I gave previously proposes that intuition refers to automatic, nonattentionally acquired implicit knowledge. The goal of a study (C. Betsch, 2006) that tested and confirmed this assumption was to predict participants' choice between an apple and a candy bar as a take-away gift at the end of the study. C. Betsch (2006) therefore assessed the implicit attitude (via the Implicit Association Test; Greenwald, McGhee, & Schwartz, 1998) and explicit attitude, the behavior shown by the participants and the individual preference for intuition and deliberation. When the participants made their choice, there was no time pressure or any instruction to deliberate. This enabled the participants to choose in an unconstrained situation, which should foster the use of the preferred decision strategy.

Across all participants, there were no differences between the implicit and explicit attitude in the power to predict behavior: Both the implicit and explicit attitude were significant predictors of behavior (C. Betsch, 2006). To assess whether the behavior of intuitive people can be better predicted by the implicit attitude and that of deliberate people by the explicit attitude, Betsch conducted separate regression analyses for dominantly intuitive and dominantly deliberate individuals. As expected, for intuitive participants, only the implicit attitude was a significant predictor, and the explicit attitude was not significant. The pattern reversed for deliberate participants: Their behavior could be predicted by the explicit attitude, whereas the implicit attitude was no significant predictor of behavior. This reversal indicates that intuitive and deliberate people base their choices on different sources of knowledge. Whereas intuitive people use their implicit attitude to make a choice, deliberate people use their explicit attitude.

It can be concluded that intuition, the behavioral representation of spontaneous and uncontrolled action, refers to implicit knowledge and that deliberation (i.e., controlled and thoughtful behavior) capitalizes on explicit knowledge. The PID seems to be a moderator for the prediction of implicit and explicit measures (Richetin, Perugini, Adjali, & Hurling, 2006). The sketched data are certainly only a beginning in determining the knowledge bases of intuition and deliberation. Additional studies should experimentally manipulate the acquisition and the kind of knowledge used for decision making.

The second point I raised in the previous definition of intuition is that decisions made intuitively are strongly influenced by affect toward the decision alternative. In the following section, I summarize a study in the field of risky decision making showing that intuitive people are more strongly influenced by feelings than deliberate individuals are.

INDIVIDUAL STRATEGY PREFERENCES AND THE RELIANCE ON FEELINGS

Decisions made under risk are a very suitable area in which to assess the influence of affect on decisions. Risk provokes feelings (e.g., fear, excitement), and risk elicits thoughts (what might be the pros and cons of taking the risk?). A decision made under risk can be based on either kind of information (e.g., Loewenstein et al., 2001; Slovic et al., 2001). Affective information can influence the decision with or without cognitive mediation ("risk as feelings" hypothesis; Loewenstein et al., 2001). If intuitive people use affect elicited by risk in a different fashion than do deliberate people, this difference should be observable in their decision behavior. How can it be detected whether participants use their feelings or cognitive information to make a decision? First, one can assess decision latencies. The longer one takes to make a decision, the more likely one engages in cognitive reflections and the weighing of pros and cons. The faster one decides, the more likely one relies on instantly accessible information, which is very likely affective information (cf. affective primacy hypothesis; Zajonc, 1980). As a second indicator of affect or cognition as a basis for a decision under risk, one can assess the risk attitudes of the participants. The risk attitude is assessed by estimating the person's utility function. The utility function allocates a continuous utility value to an increasing amount of money. A risk-neutral attitude is expressed by a linear utility function. If one uses affect in her or his decision, the risk attitude will not be neutral, but it will express risk aversion or a risk-seeking attitude (therefore, by definition, the utility function should be curved). Hsee and Rottenstreich (2004) demonstrated this in a study in which they experimentally manipulated the mode in which participants judged the utility of various goods. Hsee and Rottenstreich found that when their participants were primed to use evaluation by affect, the utility functions were curved, which expressed nonneutral risk attitudes. When they were primed to use evaluation by calculation, the utility function was nearly linear, which expressed a risk-neutral attitude. Therefore, in addition to the time taken to make a decision, one can see a curved risk attitude as a further indicator for affect-driven behavior, whereas a more linear function indicates deliberate and thoughtful evaluation.

In a study (Schunk & C. Betsch, 2006), the assessment of the curvature of the utility function served to test whether participants with a preference for intuition relied more on affect than did deliberate participants. The hypothesis was that intuitive participants would rely more on their feelings when they made decisions, which should result in nonneutral risk attitudes (= curved utility functions). Deliberate participants, on the other hand, should instead have risk-neutral attitudes expressed by linear utility functions. The participants had to make repeated choices between lotteries. Their choices allowed them to estimate their utility function and for calculation of a curvature index. The results revealed that intuitive participants relied more on affect than did deliberate ones: Intuitive participants were (a) faster in their decisions and (b) had a more curved utility function than deliberate participants as indicated by correlations of PID–Intuition and PID–Deliberation with the curvature index. This means that intuitive people showed risk attitudes that were not neutral; that is, the feeling provoked by the risk was not ignored but integrated in the decision. Deliberate people, on the other hand, took more time to decide and showed rational, neutral-risk attitudes (as indicated by more linear utility functions). This difference shows that intuitive people relied more on feelings than deliberates did.

THE CONSEQUENCES OF A FIT BETWEEN THE PREFERRED AND APPLIED STRATEGY (DECISIONAL FIT)

The studies I have sketched so far deal with the main effects of the individual preference for intuition and deliberation. As I have implied in the preceding discussion, the habitual, spontaneous use of intuition and deliberation is infrequently measured, but it is usually manipulated. When a person in the laboratory is forced to use either strategy, he or she still has a preference for intuition or deliberation. In this section, I deal with the interaction of the preference for intuitive and deliberate decision strategies and the actual exertion of such strategies. Imagine someone with a stable preference for intuition. In most situations, this person will try to use intuition as her or his default strategy for decision making. As a matter of fact, people strive to surround themselves with an environment in which they can use their preferred strategy (Pfeifer, 2005). However, some situations might impede intuitive decision making, for example, when others request explicit justifications for the choice or when the decision has to comply with social or external norms and standards. In these situations, the person will have to break with routines and preferences and think about the decision. Recent research in social psychology showed that whether a person can or cannot use a preferred or chronic strategic means is an important factor, as was also shown in the domain of regulatory fit (Higgins, 2000). Regulatory fit is the fit between a chronic approach versus avoidance motivation and the actual approach/avoidance behavior. Regulatory fit positively influences the perception of value (upvaluation of a chosen good; Higgins, Idson, Freitas, Spiegel, & Molden, 2003; for an overview, see Higgins, 2005), achievement (Bianco, Higgins, & Klem, 2003; Förster, Higgins, & Idson, 1998; Keller & Bless, 2006; Shah, Higgins, & Friedman, 1998), and motivation (Förster et al., 1998; Shah et al., 1998).

Similar findings occurred in the field of the individually preferred intuitive or deliberate decision strategy (C. Betsch & Kunz, 2006). A fit between preferred and applied decision strategy, a so-called decisional fit, led to an increase in liking of the chosen object (upvaluation effect) and a decrease in negative emotions after a decision with a negative outcome (buffer effect). In the following, I briefly summarize the two positive effects of decisional fit.

In one study (C. Betsch & Kunz, 2006, Study 2), participants evaluated different attitude objects (such as spiders, blood donation, chocolate) and reported how they felt and how they thought about the objects. C. Betsch & Kunz (2006) found that when participants used the evaluation mode that fit their preferred decision strategy (e.g., evaluation by feelings and a preference for intuition), the objects were evaluated more positively than when the two modes did not fit together (e.g., evaluation by thinking and a preference for intuition). This implies that decisional fit apparently created positive value that did not stem from the objects themselves but from using the preferred strategy.

A series of follow-up studies (C. Betsch & Kunz, 2006) showed further that decisional fit can lead to an upvaluation of the chosen object. The participants had the choice between two thermos coffee pots and made their decision either in a mode that fit or did not fit their preferred strategy (C. Betsch & Kunz, 2006, Study 1). The estimated monetary value of the pot increased as a function of decisional fit: Those who were allowed to choose according to their preferred mode assigned a higher value to the pot. This effect also occurred when participants failed to gain an expected prize as a result of their decision (i.e., when the outcome of the decision was negative; C. Betsch & Kunz, 2006, Study 3). After decisions with decisional fit, the missed object was evaluated more positively as indicated by a higher willingness to pay to get the object. The studies have indicated that decisional fit (i.e., the application of one's preferred strategy) increases the value of the focal object.

Following decisions with negative outcomes, people often experience regret (e.g., Zeelenberg, Nelissen, & Pieters, chap. 11, this volume). Two studies (C. Betsch & Kunz, 2006) tested whether regret is reduced following decisions made with decisional fit. In one study, participants reported two past decisions with negative outcomes. They reported one intuitive and one deliberate decision and subsequently evaluated how much they regretted their decisions. In another study (C. Betsch & Kunz, Study 5), participants made two decisions that had negative outcomes—again one decision was made intuitively, the other deliberately. As dependent variables, they rated how much they regretted their choices. In both studies, C. Betsch and Kunz (2006) found a buffer effect of decisional fit: When the applied strategy fit the preferred strategy, participants regretted their choices less than when they used a mode they did not prefer. Decisional fit thus worked as a buffer against the experience of regret.

It seems that using the preferred strategy activates the positive attitude held toward the strategy (Fazio, Sanbonmatsu, Powell, & Kardes, 1986). C. Betsch and Kunz (2006) proposed that the positive attitude or valence spreads to related nodes (objects such as the chosen object) in the semantic network (Bower, 1981; cf. evaluative conditioning and the spreading attitude effect; Walther, 2002). The evaluated object profits from this valence, as the decision maker misattributes the feeling of valence and attributes it to the outcome in which it produces the upvaluation effect. Similarly, this activation of positive valence should make negative outcomes become less negative, which might lead to the reduction of regret. Furthermore, the experience of "doing it the right way" can also reduce regret (Connolly & Reb, 2003), and this should be the case when people use their preferred strategy.

Individuals' psychological immune system provides all sorts of mechanisms that allow the individuals to influence their feelings in a positive way following a decision (Gilbert, Pinel, Wilson, Blumberg, & Wheatley, 1998). Keeping in mind the decisional fit results together with the large literature on the positive effects of regulatory fit, it seems worthwhile to list another protective shield in line with rationalization, dissonance reduction, motivated reasoning, and so forth (for a more extensive list, see Gilbert et al., 1998, p. 619): the fit between a chronic orientation (such as strategy preferences or regulatory focus; cf. Higgins, 2000) and the actual applied strategy.

LESSONS LEARNED ABOUT INTUITION

The findings I have reported previously show that the behavior of intuitive people can be better predicted by their implicit attitude rather than explicit attitude (it is the other way around for deliberate people; C. Betsch, 2006); they show that the utility function of intuitive people is more curved than that of deliberate people (which is more linear; Schunk & C. Betsch, 2006); and they show that intuitive people like their decisions better and regret their decisions less when the decisions are made intuitively instead of deliberately (vice versa for deliberate people; C. Betsch & Kunz, 2006). One can draw conclusions about intuition and deliberation from the different behavior and information processing displayed by intuitive and deliberate people.

First, people actually differ in the extent to which they rely on intuition and deliberation. Researchers know from studies in which decision modes have been manipulated (e.g., C. Betsch, Betsch, & Haberstroh, 2004; Wilson et al., 1993;

Wilson & Schooler, 1991) that people are basically able to engage in both intuitive and deliberate decision strategies when the experimenter makes them do so or when the situation obviously requires either strategy (C. Betsch, 2004, Study 3). Most decision makers' attitudes, however, are not neutral toward the strategy used. As I discussed previously, individuals have chronic preferences for one mode or the other: They either like or dislike intuition or deliberation (C. Betsch & Kunz, 2006), and they show a higher tendency to use this preferred strategy even though situational requirements might be opposing (C. Betsch, 2004, Study 3). This preference variable seems to moderate the prevalence of the occurrence of intuition (and deliberation) in unconstrained situations.

As a second conclusion, the findings provide evidence for the notion that intuition capitalizes on implicit knowledge. Although there is evidence that there are no individual differences in implicit learning (Reber et al., 1991), there seem to be individual differences in the reliance on this kind of knowledge. The implicit attitude differentially predicted the choice behavior of intuitive but not of deliberate people (C. Betsch, 2006). Thus, the decision of the intuitive people in the study was more strongly influenced by implicit knowledge than by explicit knowledge.

The idea that implicit knowledge constitutes the basis for intuition also has implications for the ease with which intuitive knowledge can be changed. Changes in implicit knowledge occur only following numerous learning experiences. This is also suggested by the literature on implicit attitude formation (T. Betsch, Plessner, & Schallies, 2004). Imagine that the implicit knowledge about the desirability of an alternative was acquired by frequent encounters with the alternative. Only further frequent encounters will teach the information-processing system a reliable change in its desirability. As the new information is not integrated consciously but implicitly, only slow changes in the knowledge about the alternative's value occur (see also Haberstroh, chap. 16, this volume). Even though intuitive people make decisions more quickly, their decisions should reflect the product of slow learning processes, and as a consequence, they should be more prone to errors resulting from slow change processes in the environment. Deliberate people may be better able to compass changes in the environment because of their tendency to deliberately and explicitly integrate information (even though this may take some time). This fictitious pattern of results could be a crucial test to consolidate the notion that intuition rests on implicit knowledge, whereas deliberation uses explicit knowledge.

The third lesson learned about intuition is that the variable that guides the decision is often a feeling. Intuitive people listen to their feelings as indicated by the positive correlations of emotional personality variables (extraversion, agreeableness, openness to experience, faith in intuition) with a preference for intuition. Although these correlations may suggest that intuition uses feelings as a decision criterion, they are by no means proof of this idea. However, the results of Schunk and C. Betsch (2006) point in the same direction: Results from a priming study in which participants were primed to use an affective decision mode (Hsee & Rottenstreich, 2004) were replicated by letting intuitive people make decisions (Schunk & C. Betsch, 2006). This further supports the idea that intuition and affect are strongly linked.

Decision objects provoke feelings, which can or cannot be used to make the decision. When people are primed to use these feelings, their decisions mirror this feeling. Their willingness to pay for 5 versus 10 CDs of Madonna's music, for example, no longer depends on the number of CDs but on how much the individual likes Madonna (Hsee & Rottenstreich, 2004). Likewise, the feelings provoked by the risk in a lottery choice were used by intuitive people but not by deliberate ones. The prospect of risk made intuitive participants fear or seek risk (i.e., they showed an attitude toward the risk; Schunk & C. Betsch, 2006). Deliberate people, however, tried to abstract from this feeling in time-consuming operations and showed behavior, which was nearly risk neutral. This finding is complemented by the differences in decision time, as intuitives were faster than deliberates.

Feelings are often a result of the integration of a huge amount of information. Intuition is assumed to exploit the capability of a person's mind to process information in parallel (T. Betsch, chap. 1, this volume; Glöckner, chap. 19, this volume). In contrast to sequential processing, parallel processing again implies shorter decision times. The shorter decision times found by Schunk and C. Betsch (2006) may be a result of more parallel processing by intuitive people and more sequential processing by deliberate people. Whereas the encounter with a risky situation elicits a feeling that is instantly used by an intuitive person, this feeling has to be consciously dealt with by deliberate individuals. Should it be taken into account? Should it be discarded? What else should further be taken into account? How should the information be weighted? These questions illustrate that deliberation can only be a sequential process. Future studies should test whether intuitive people are more inclined to or even better than deliberate people in parallel processing.

The fourth lesson learned pertains to the question: Is one particular strategy "better"? The reported findings on decisional fit suggest that this question per se is inadequate. At least in respect to subjective variables of decision quality (regret, perceived value of the chosen object), the findings did not reveal advantages of either strategy. Rather, they showed that both strategies can be advantageous given that the user prefers it. The positive attitude toward the strategy used becomes activated on using the strategy and transfers to the object (C. Betsch & Kunz, 2006). The decisional fit data show that a factor within the person, namely, the preferred decision strategy, plays a crucial role in determining when which strategy is better. Most research on predictors of good intuitive and good deliberate decisions has concentrated on factors within the situation or the environment such as the sampling process or the kind of knowledge considered (Hogarth, 2005; chap. 6, this volume; Plessner & Czenna, chap. 15, this volume; Unkelbach & Plessner, chap. 17, this volume). The goodness of the decision often equals the accuracy of judgments in relation to some absolute standard (e.g., the judged vs. actual performance of shares on the stock market; T. Betsch, Kaufmann, Lindow, Plessner, & Hoffmann, 2006). The current research on individual preferences has only considered personal standards such as the experienced value of a chosen good. Future research should also address the question of whether the individual preference for a decision strategy makes people better in respect to objective criteria.

SUMMARY AND CONCLUSION

Taken together, the essence of the implications I discussed previously reads as follows:

1. People differ in the way they rely on their heads or their hearts. Even though virtually everybody is able to feel and to think, people follow their strategy preferences if they have the chance to.
2. The knowledge base of intuition seems to be implicit knowledge, whereas deliberation is based on explicit knowledge.
3. Intuition often uses a feeling as a criterion for a decision, whereas deliberation uses cognitions.
4. It does matter which decision strategy a person uses: When the individually preferred strategy can be applied (i.e., the person experiences decisional fit), the subjective evaluation of the decision outcome is more positive (less negative).

The fact that effects of strategy preferences were found in such different content areas stresses the importance of the differentiation between affective and cognitive judgment and decision strategies and especially its consideration as an individual difference variable. If affect-based intuition is the subject of a researcher's experimental interest, it seems useful to include the short and economical PID (see appendix) scale in the design. As the presented research has shown, it is advantageous to control for variance due to individual differences and especially, to control for potential interactions between the preferred and the applied strategy.

REFERENCES

Betsch, C. (2004). Präferenz für Intuition und Deliberation. Inventar zur Erfassung von affekt- und kognitionsbasiertem Entscheiden [Preference for Intuition and Deliberation (PID): An inventory for assessing affect- and cognition-based decision-making]. *Zeitschrift für Differentielle und Diagnostische Psychologie, 25*, 179–197.

Betsch, C. (2006). *Using the head or the heart: Improving the prediction of choice by the assessment of individual preferences for intuitive and deliberate decision making.* Manuscript submitted for publication.

Betsch, C., Betsch, T., & Haberstroh, S. (2004). Intuition: Wann Sie Ihren Bauch entscheiden lassen können. *Wirtschaftspsychologie, 6*, 81–83.

Betsch, C. & Kunz, J. J. (2006). *The fit between preferred and applied decision strategy as protective shield: Effects of decisional fit.* Manuscript submitted for publication.

Betsch, T., Haberstroh, S., & Höhle, C. (2002). Explaining and predicting routinized decision making: A review of theories. *Theory & Psychology, 12*, 453–488.

Betsch, T., Kaufmann, M., Lindow, F., Plessner, H., & Hoffmann, K. (2006). Different principles of information integration in implicit and explicit attitude formation. *European Journal of Social Psychology, 36*, 887–905.

Betsch, T., Plessner, H., & Schallies, E. (2004). The value-account model of attitude formation. In G. R. Maio & G. Haddock (Eds.), *Contemporary Perspectives on the Psychology of Attitudes* (pp. 252–273). London: Psychology Press.

Bianco, A. T., Higgins, E. T., & Klem, A. (2003). How "fun/importance" fit impacts performance: Relating implicit theories to instructions. *Personality and Social Psychology Bulletin, 29*, 1091–1103.

Bower, G. H. (1981). Mood and memory. *American Psychologist, 36*, 129–148.
Bröder, A. (2003). Decision making with the "adaptive toolbox": Influence of environmental structure, intelligence, and working memory load. *Journal of Experimental Psychology: Learning, Memory, & Cognition, 29*, 611–625.
Connolly, T., & Reb, J. (2003). Omission bias in vaccination decision: Where's the "omission"? Where's the "bias"? *Organizational Behavior and Human Decision Processes, 91*, 186–202.
Damasio, A. (1994). *Descartes' error: Emotions, reason, and the human brain*. New York: Grosset/Putnam.
Epstein, S. (1990). Cognitive-experiential self-theory. In L. A. Pervin (Ed.), *Handbook of personality: Theory and research* (pp. 165–192). New York: Guilford.
Epstein, S., Pacini, R., Denes-Raj, V., & Heier, H. (1996). Individual differences in intuitive-experiential and analytical-rational thinking styles. *Journal of Personality and Social Psychology, 71*, 390–405.
Fazio, R. H. (1990). Multiple processes by which attitudes guide behavior: The MODE model as an integrative framework. In M. P. Zanna (Ed.), *Advances in experimental social psychology* (Vol. 23, pp. 75–109). San Diego, CA: Academic.
Fazio, R. H., Sanbonmatsu, D. M., Powell, M. C., & Kardes, F. R. (1986). On the automatic activation of attitudes. *Journal of Personality and Social Psychology, 50*, 229–238.
Fazio, R. H., & Towles-Schwen, T. (1999). The MODE model of attitude-behavior processes. In S. Chaiken & Y. Trope (Eds.), *Dual-process theories in social psychology* (pp. 97–116). New York: Guilford.
Förster, J., Higgins, E. T., & Idson, L. C. (1998). Approach and avoidance strength during goal attainment: Regulatory focus and the "goal looms larger" effect. *Journal of Personality and Social Psychology, 75*, 1115–1131.
Friese, M., Wänke, M., & Plessner, H. (2006). Implicit consumer preferences and their influence on product choice. *Psychology and Marketing, 23*, 727–740.
Gilbert, D. T., Pinel, E. C., Wilson, T. D., Blumberg, S. J., & Wheatley, T. P. (1998). Immune neglect: A source of durability bias in affective forecasting. *Journal of Personality and Social Psychology, 75*, 617–638.
Greenwald, A. G., & Banaji, M. R. (1995). Implicit social cognition: Attitudes, self esteem, and stereotypes. *Psychological Review, 102*, 4–27.
Greenwald, A. G., McGhee, D. E., & Schwartz, J. L. K. (1998). Measuring individual differences in implicit cognition: The implicit association test. *Journal of Personality and Social Psychology, 74*, 1464–1480.
Hammond, K. R., Hamm, R. M., Grassia, J., & Pearson, T. (1987). Direct comparison of the efficacy of intuitive and expert cognition in expert judgment. *IEEE Transaction on Systems, Man, and Cybernetics, 5*, 753–770.
Higgins, E. T. (2000). Making a good decision: Value from fit. *American Psychologist, 55*, 1217–1230.
Higgins, E. T. (2005). Value from regulatory fit. *Current directions in psychological science, 14*, 209–213.
Higgins, E. T., Idson, L. C., Freitas, A. L., Spiegel, S., & Molden, D. C. (2003). Transfer of value from fit. *Journal of Personality and Social Psychology, 84*, 1140–1153.
Hogarth, R. M. (2001). *Educating intuition*. Chicago: University of Chicago Press.
Hogarth, R. (2005). Deciding analytically or trusting your intuition? The advantages and disadvantages of analytic and intuitive thought. In T. Betsch & S. Haberstroh (Eds.), *The routines of decision making* (pp. 67–82). Mahwah, NJ: Lawrence Erlbaum Associates, Inc.

Hsee, C. K., & Rottenstreich, Y. (2004). Music, pandas, and muggers: on the affective psychology of value. *Journal of Experimental Psychology: General, 133,* 23–30.

Karpinski, A., & Hilton, J. L. (2001). Attitudes and the Implicit Association Test. *Journal of Personality & Social Psychology, 81,* 774–788.

Keller, J., & Bless, H. (2006). Regulatory fit and cognitive performance: the interactive effect of chronic and situationally induced self-regulatory mechanisms on test performance. *European Journal of Social Psychology, 36,* 393–405.

Kruglanski, A.W., Thompson, E. P., Higgins, E. T., Atash, M. N., Pierro, A., Shah, J. Y., et al. (2000). To "do the right thing" or to "just do it": Locomotion and assessment as distinct self-regulatory imperatives. *Journal of Personality and Social Psychology, 79,* 793–815.

Langan-Fox, J., & Shirley, D. A. (2003) The nature and measurement of intuition: Cognitive and behavioral interests, personality and experiences. *Creativity Research Journal, 15,* 207–222.

Lieberman, M. D. (2000). Intuition: A social cognitive neuroscience approach. *Psychological Bulletin, 126,* 109–137.

Loewenstein, G., Weber, E., Hsee, C. K., & Welch, E. (2001). Risk as feelings. *Psychological Bulletin, 127,* 267–286.

Maio, G. R., & Esses, V. M. (2001). The need for affect: Individual differences in the motivation to approach or avoid emotions. *Journal of Personality, 69,* 583–615.

Myers, I. B., & McCaulley, M. H. (1986). *Manual: A guide to the development and use of the MBTI.* Palo Alto, CA: Consulting Psychologists Press.

Pacini, R., & Epstein, S. (1999). The relation of rational and experiential information processing styles to personality basic beliefs, and the ratio-bias phenomenon. *Journal of Personality and Social Psychology, 76,* 972–987.

Payne, J. W., Bettman, J. R., & Johnson, E. J. (1993). *The adaptive decision maker.* Cambridge, England: Cambridge University Press.

Pfeifer, B. (2005). The relation of decisional fit and self-regulation in the domain of career choice. Unpublished master's thesis, University of Heidelberg, Heidelberg, Germany.

Plessner, H. (2006). The smartness of intuition and its boundaries. In A. Scherzberg (Ed.), *Kluges Entscheiden* (pp. 109–120). Tübingen, Germany: Mohr Siebeck.

Reber, A. S. (1989). Implicit learning and tacit knowledge. *Journal of Experimental Psychology: General, 118,* 219–235.

Reber, A. S., Walkenfeld, F. F., & Hernstadt, R. (1991). Implicit and explicit learning: Individual differences and IQ. *Journal of Experimental Psychology: Learning, Memory, and Cognition, 17,* 888–896.

Richetin, J., Perugini, M., Adjali, I., & Hurling, R. (2006). *Intuitive versus Deliberative preferences in decision making process: A moderator for the prediction of implicit and explicit measures.* Manuscript submitted for publication.

Schunk, D., & Betsch, C. (2006). Explaining heterogeneity in utility functions by individual preferences for intuition and deliberation. *Journal of Economic Psychology, 27,* 386–401.

Schwarz, N., & Clore, G. L. (1983). Mood, misattribution, and judgments of well-being: Informative and directive functions of affective states. *Journal of Personality and Social Psychology, 45,* 513–523.

Shah, J. Y., Higgins, E. T., & Friedman, R. (1998). Performance incentives and means: How regulatory focus influences goal attainment. *Journal of Personality and Social Psychology, 74,* 285–293.

Sloman, S. A. (1996). The empirical case for two systems of reasoning. *Psychological Bulletin, 119,* 3–22.

Slovic, P., Finucane, M., Peters, E., & MacGregor, D. G. (2002). The affect heuristic. In T. Gilovich, D. Griffin, & D. Kahneman (Eds.), *Heuristics and biases: The psychology of intuitive judgement* (pp. 397–420). New York: Cambridge University Press.

Walther, E. (2002). Guilty by mere association: Evaluative conditioning and the spreading attitude effect. *Journal of Personality and Social Psychology, 82*, 919–934.

Wilson, T. D., Lindsey, S., & Schooler, T. (2000). A model of dual attitudes. *Psychological Review, 107*, 101–126.

Wilson, T. D., Lisle, D. J., Schooler, J., Hodges, S. D., Klaaren, K. J., & LaFleur, S. J. (1993). Introspecting about reasons can reduce post-choice satisfaction. *Personality and Social Psychology Bulletin, 19*, 331–339.

Wilson, T. D., & Schooler, J. (1991). Thinking too much: introspection can reduce the quality of preferences and decisions. *Journal of Personality and Social Psychology, 60*, 181–192.

Zajonc, R. B. (1980). Feeling and thinking: Preferences need no inferences. *American Psychologist, 35*, 151–175.

APPENDIX

GERMAN, ENGLISH, AND DUTCH VERSION OF THE PREFERENCE FOR INTUITION AND DELIBERATION SCALE (PID)

Item	Preference for Intuition, PID–Intuition
2.	Ich beobachte sorgfältig meine innersten Gefühle. I listen carefully to my deepest feelings. Ik let heel goed op mijn diepste gevoelens.
4.	Bei den meisten Entscheidungen ist es sinnvoll, sich ganz auf sein Gefühl zu verlassen. With most decisions it makes sense to completely rely on your feelings. Bij de meeste beslissingen is het zinnig om op je gevoelens te vertrouwen.
5. (–)	Ich mag Situationen nicht, in denen ich mich auf meine Intuition verlassen muss. I don't like situations that require me to rely on my intuition. Ik houd niet van situaties waarin ik op mijn intuïtie moet vertrouwen.
8.	Ich ziehe Schlussfolgerungen lieber aufgrund meiner Gefühle, Menschenkenntnis und Lebenserfahrung. I prefer drawing conclusions based on my feelings, my knowledge of human nature, and my experience of life. Ik geef de voorkeur aan conclusies trekken op basis van mijn gevoelens, mijn kennis van de menselijke natuur en mijn levenservaring.
9.	Bei meinen Entscheidungen spielen Gefühle eine große Rolle. My feelings play an important role in my decisions. Mijn gevoelens spelen een belangrijke rol in het nemen van beslissingen.
12.	Wenn es darum geht, ob ich anderen vertrauen soll, entscheide ich aus dem Bauch heraus. When it comes to trusting people, I can usually rely on my gut feelings. Als het op mensen vertrouwen aankomt, dan kan ik gewoonlijk vertrouwen op mijn goede gevoelens.
15.	Ich mag lieber gefühlsbetonte Personen. I prefer emotional people. Ik geef de voorkeur aan emotionele mensen.

Item	Preference for Intuition, PID–Intuition
17.	Ich bin ein sehr intuitiver Mensch.
	I am a very intuitive person.
	Ik ben een heel intuïtief persoon.
18.	Ich mag emotionale Situationen, Diskussionen und Filme.
	I like emotional situations, discussions, and movies.
	Ik houd van emotionele situaties, discussies en films.

Item	Preference for Deliberation, PID–Deliberation
1.	Bevor ich Entscheidungen treffe, denke ich meistens erst mal gründlich nach.
	Before making decisions I first think them through.
	Ik denk goed na voordat ik beslissingen neem.
3.	Bevor ich Entscheidungen treffe, denke ich meistens erst mal über meine Ziele nach, die ich erreichen will.
	Before making decisions I usually think about the goals I want to achieve.
	Voordat ik beslissingen neem, denk ik gewoonlijk na over de doelen die ik will bereiken.
6.	Ich denke über mich nach.
	I consider myself.
	Ik denk over mezelf na.
7.	Ich schmiede lieber ausgefeilte Pläne, als etwas dem Zufall zu überlassen.
	I prefer making detailed plans rather than leaving things to chance.
	Ik maak liever gedetailleerde plannen dan dat ik iets aan het toeval overlaat.
10.	Ich bin perfektionistisch.
	I am a perfectionist.
	Ik ben een perfectionist.
11.	Wenn ich eine Entscheidung rechtfertigen muss, denke ich vorher besonders gründlich nach.
	I think about a decision particularly carefully if I have to justify it.
	Wanneer ik een beslissing moet nemen, denk ik daar bijzonder zorgvuldig over na.
13.	Ich nehme bei einem Problem erst mal die harten Fakten und Details auseinander, bevor ich mich entscheide.
	When I have a problem I first analyze the facts and details before I decide.
	Wanneer ik een probleem heb, analyseer ik eerst de feiten en details voordat ik een beslissing neem.
14.	Ich denke erst nach, bevor ich handle.
	I think before I act.
	Ik denk na voordat ik iets doe.
16.	Ich denke über meine Pläne und Ziele stärker nach als andere Menschen.
	I think more about my plans and goals than other people do.
	Ik denk meer over mijn plannen en doelen na dan andere mensen.

Note. (–) = recode.

RELIABILITY

German version: Cronbach's α for PID–Intuition between .76 and .81 and PID–Deliberation between .76 and .79; English translation, Cronbach's α for PID–Intuition = .77 and PID–Deliberation = .79; Dutch translation: Cronbach's α for PID–Intuition = .78 and PID–Deliberation = .84.

TEMPORAL STABILITY

PID–Intuition = .76 and PID–Deliberation = .74 after 6 months; similar results after 1 week (M. Perugini, personal communication, 2006).

INSTRUCTION FOR PARTICIPANTS

Please answer all the following questions about your life in general. Your answers should correspond to the way you generally make decisions. Circle the number that best represents your opinion: 1 means that you very much disagree, 5 means that you very much agree.

SCORING INSTRUCTIONS

Calculate the sum or mean of all items of each scale (PID–Intuition; PID–Deliberation). PID–Intuition and PID–Deliberation can be correlated with other variables of interest or used as predictors in a regression. To compare intuitive and deliberate types, perform two median splits, one on each variable, and classify the people above the median of PID–Intuition and below the median of PID–Deliberation as intuitive, and the people above the median of PID–Deliberation and below the median of PID–Intuition as deliberate. Experience showed that a randomly acquired sample contains about one-third intuitive and one-third deliberate people and one third of people who score either high or low on both scales.

IV

The Assets and Deficits of Intuition

15

The Benefits of Intuition

HENNING PLESSNER and SABINE CZENNA

University of Heidelberg

INTRODUCTION

*I*n many everyday decisions, people do not go consciously through steps of searching, weighing evidence, and inferring a conclusion before they act. Instead, people rely on instant responses including affective valences or "gut feelings," which are reached with little apparent effort. These spontaneous judgment processes are what can be defined as *intuition* (e.g., T. Betsch, chap. 1, this volume; Epstein, chap. 2, this volume; Haidt, 2001; Hogarth, 2001). Now assume that you have to make an important decision, and for some reason, the analytic thinking process that you have applied points in a different direction than your immediate gut feeling. Should you, nevertheless, rely on your intuition? Does intuition bear some benefit beyond its apparent effortlessness? How do you know when you can trust your intuition, and under what circumstances would it be better to obey your reflective thoughts? Given the vast amount of literature, with a focus on biases, errors, and shortcomings in intuitive (or heuristic) judgments and decisions (e.g., Barron, 1998; Kahneman, Slovic, & Tversky, 1982), the answer seems to be clear. A statement such as "being more analytic and less intuitive should help you to develop more effective and rewarding solutions to the difficult managerial judgment and decision-making challenges that lie ahead" (Kardes, 2002, p. 402) appears to be self-evident. Accordingly, the assumption of a general superiority of reflective processes in comparison to more intuitive ones has been prevalent in classical models of rational choice (for an overview, see, e.g., Hastie & Dawes, 2001). However, one reason for the increasing (or renewed) interest in the concept of intuition in the domain of judgment and decision making stems from the observation that at least sometimes spontaneous responses can outperform more deliberate ways of thinking. This finds its expression, for example, in the reference to hidden sources of knowledge and the "power of thinking without thinking" (Gladwell, 2005).

Indeed, there are an impressive number of empirical demonstrations that question the assumption of a general superiority of analytic processes (e.g., Wilson, 2002). For example, several studies that were conducted on the theoretical background of the adaptive toolbox program (Gigerenzer, Todd, & the ABC Research Group, 1999) have shown that simple heuristics can perform as well as or better than normative models of cognition (e.g., linear regression) that use complex, compensatory methods of weighing all the different options (see also Catty & Halberstadt, chap. 18, this volume). This line of research adds to the long list of studies that have compared intuitions directly with some sort of external accuracy criteria (cf. Bastick, 1982; Hammond, Hamm, Grassia, & Pearson, 1987). However, two aspects fall relatively short in the research that has conceptualized intuition as the use of fast and frugal heuristics (Gigerenzer et al., 1999). One aspect is the proof that people actually rely on such heuristics under conditions that trigger intuitive processes (e.g., time pressure). For instance, Glöckner (chap. 19, this volume) found that only a few people's decision strategies in corresponding tasks could be classified as the use of fast and frugal heuristics. The other aspect that falls short is a lack of empirical comparisons of people's spontaneous responses with people's deliberate judgments on the same task in relation to a good–bad dimension (cf. Hammond et al., 1987; Hogarth, 2005). To answer the question of whether people should go with their gut feeling or with the result of their deliberation in a given judgment or decision situation, one would need exactly this as a basis: a comparative evaluation of the processes that people actually use in the same task under conditions of spontaneous versus deliberate judgments and decisions.

In the remainder of this chapter, we start with a quick review of research that has directly compared spontaneous and deliberate judgments in reference to an objective criterion. Afterward, we describe a theoretical framework that allows for the determination of situations in which spontaneous judgments are likely to outperform deliberative ones. Finally, we present the results of some recent experiments that support the assumptions that are derived from this framework.

SPONTANEOUS VERSUS DELIBERATIVE JUDGMENTS AND DECISIONS

A problem that automatically arises when one starts to investigate whether people are better off with spontaneous or with deliberate judgments and decisions is the determination of what *better* means. For example, when the judgment is about the taste of strawberry jam, one could ask whether the correspondence to an evaluation of expert taste testers of a consumer magazine (as it has been used in a study by Wilson & Schooler, 1991) is a fair and valid comparison criterion. Such preference judgments can be considered as falling in the broad category of "matters of value" that are dealt with in this volume, for example, by Haidt and Kesebir (chap. 13). To circumvent the difficult discussions that accompany the good–bad or better–worse distinction in judgments about matters of value, we restricted our review of research that has directly compared spontaneous with deliberative judgments and decisions to those tasks that are about "matters of fact." A good example of such research is Halberstadt and Levine's (1999) study about the prediction of basketball results. In Halberstadt and Levine's study, participants who were classified as basketball experts made predictions of the outcomes of basketball games in an American college basketball tournament. Half of the participants were asked to analyze reasons for their predictions before making them, whereas the other half were asked to rely on their spontaneous feelings. Afterward, the predictions of both groups were compared with the factual outcomes of the games. Among other results, it was found that those participants that reasoned ahead of time chose the winning teams less often and predicted scores that deviated more extremely from the actual scores than the participants that made spontaneous predictions. Thus, this study showed that intuitive predictions could be objectively better than reasoned ones.

With the study by Halberstadt and Levine (1999) as a kind of prototype in mind, we conducted a literature search using the PsycINFO database to find empirical studies in which spontaneous and deliberative processes on the same task were compared with an incontrovertibly objective criterion for quality. To get a manageable set of studies, we reduced the corpus of about 3,000 records that appears when one scans the word *intuition* (cf. Haidt & Kesebir, chap. 13, this volume) by searching for peer-reviewed journal articles that have included combinations of *intuition* with *time pressure, decision mode, reasoning, cognitive load, verbalization,* and the like. We also searched directly for some of these words (e.g., *time pressure*) because several authors in the domain of judgment and decision making avoid the use of the term *intuition*. From the resulting set of about 500 articles, we read the abstracts and chose those articles that matched our "prototype study" (Halberstadt & Levine, 1999) regarding the comparison of spontaneous with deliberative judgments in relation to an objective criterion. Our search ended with a relatively small sample of 21 studies, which surely does not claim to cover all research that could be of interest here (for an older but more complete review, see Bastick, 1982).

As can be seen in Table 15.1, among this final set are almost as many studies that found deliberate judgments to outperform spontaneous ones as studies that found the opposite pattern or no superiority of either of these modes. However, the focus of our literature search on judgments about matters of fact may have led to an actual underestimation of the potential of intuitive processes. For example, Hammond et al. (1987) suggested that tasks with analytic-inducing characteristics (e.g., judgments about uncertain facts) are generally better handled in an analytic mode, whereas tasks with intuition-inducing characteristics are better handled in an intuitive mode (see also McMackin & Slovic, 2000). Nevertheless, even with our limited PsyINFO search, we found a significant number of studies that have found people to benefit from their intuition beyond their deliberation when compared with an objective criterion. In other words, the assumption of a general superiority of analytic processes proves to be wrong even in the domain of judgments about matters of fact.

TABLE 15.1 A Sample of Studies That Directly Compares Spontaneous and Deliberate Judgments in Reference to an Objective Criterion

Authors	Manipulation	Task	The Winner
Bartlett, Till, & Levy (1980)	Instruction: Verbalization	Picture Recognition Picture "Resemblance"	No Effect Deliberation
Clare & Lewandowsky (2004)	Instruction: Verbalization	Face Recognition in Different Line-Ups Not Present-option Forced-choice	2 Studies: Intuition 2 Studies: No Effect
Dougherty & Hunter (2003)	Time Pressure	Probability Judgments: Subadditivity	Deliberation
Fallshore & Schooler (1995)	Instruction: Verbalization	Face Recognition for Different Races Own-Race & Upright Own-Race & Inverted Other-Race & Upright Other-Race & Inverted	2 Studies: Intuition 1 Study: No Effect 2 Studies: No Effect 1 Study: No Effect
Fiore & Schooler (2002)	Instruction: Verbalization	Route Recognition Featural Knowledge Configural Knowledge	No Effect Intuition
Gilbert & Rappoport (1975)	Instruction: Analytic vs. Aesthetic (feeling)	Quantity Estimation Detection of an Embedded Figure	Deliberation Intuition
Goodie & Crooks (2004)	Time Pressure	Probability Judgments: Base Rates	1 Study: Intuition 2 Studies: No Effect 1 Study: Deliberation
Halberstadt (2005)	Instruction: Verbalization	Emotion Recognition & Upright Emotion Recognition & Inverted Emotion Recognition & Masked Face Recognition Feature Recognition	2 Studies: Intuition No Effect 2 Studies: No Effect No Effect Intuition
Halberstadt & Levine (1999)	Instruction: Verbalization	Basketball Predictions	Intuition
Itoh (2005)	Instruction: Verbalization	Face Recognition Weak Memory Strong Memory No Memory Manipulation	Deliberation No Effect Deliberation
Klimesch (1980)	Instruction: Verbalization	Picture Recognition	Deliberation

TABLE 15.1 A Sample of Studies That Directly Compares Spontaneous and Deliberate Judgments in Reference to an Objective Criterion (Continued)

Authors	Manipulation	Task	The Winner
Kruglanski & Freund (1983)	Time Pressure	Anchoring in Conjunctions and Disjunctions	Deliberation
Melcher & Schooler (1996)	Instruction: Verbalization	Wine Recognition No Expertise Perceptual Expertise Verbal Expertise	 Deliberation Intuition Deliberation
Melcher & Schooler (2004)	Instruction: Verbalization	Mushroom Recognition: Perceptual Training / Expertise Conceptual Expertise/Training	 Intuition Deliberation
Memon & Bartlett (2002)	Instruction: Verbalization	Face Recognition in Young and Older Adults Young Adults Older Adults	 No Effect No Effect
Memon & Rose (2002)	Instruction: Verbalization	Face Recognition in Children	No Effect
Perfect, Hunt, & Harris (2002)	Instruction: Verbalization	Voice Recognition	Intuition
Schooler & Engstler-Schooler (1990)	Instruction: Verbalization	Face Recognition Face Recognition & Speed Test Face Recognition & Self Paced Test Color Recognition	4 Studies: Intuition 1 Study: No Effect 1 Study: Intuition 1 Study: Intuition
Schroyens, Schaeken, & Handley (2003)	Time Pressure	Evaluation of Conditional Inferences	Deliberation
Silverberg & Buchanan (2005)	Instruction: Verbalization	Picture Recognition	Deliberation
Windschitl & Chambers (2004)	Time Pressure	Probability Judgments: Dud-Alternative Effect	Deliberation
Windschitl & Krizan (2005)	Time Pressure	Probability Judgments Winning Raffles	2 Studies: Deliberation

Itoh, Y. (2005). The facilitating effect of verbalization on the recognition memory of incidentally learned faces. *Applied Cognitive Psychology, 19,* 421–433.

WHEN DOES INTUITION BEAT REFLECTION?

On a theoretical level, the observation of differences in the outcome of spontaneous and deliberative thinking processes has led to the development of several dual-system theories in the domain of judgment and decision making that have been summarized, for example, by Hogarth (2001). Among others, Hogarth (2001) concluded that although there are important differences in details, most theories share the basic assumption that the two systems differ by the presence or absence of cognitive effort. One system, which Hogarth (2001) called *tacit*, is triggered to operate automatically, works typically without conscious awareness, and provides quick responses, for example, in the form of feelings. The other system, the *deliberate*, involves explicit reasoning and deliberation and also requires effort and attention.

Quite compatible with Hogarth's (2001) approach, as well as with many other dual-process theories (e.g., Deutsch & Strack, chap. 3, this volume; Epstein, chap. 2, this volume; Lieberman, 2000; Stanovich & West, 2000), is the following description of two systems of judgment and decision making in which a distinction is made between an intuitive and a reflective system (see Fig. 15.1). The intuitive system works mainly on the basis of implicit knowledge and expresses itself above all other systems in spontaneous judgments and decisions. In contrast, the reflective system deals with explicit knowledge and is most likely to become effective under conditions of deliberate judgment and decision making. The distinction between implicit and explicit knowledge in this framework follows, for example, social psychology's distinction between implicit and explicit attitudes (e.g., Greenwald & Banaji, 1995; Wilson, Lindsey, & Schooler, 2000). According to social psychologists, people may have two contradictory attitudes toward one object at the same time (e.g., a

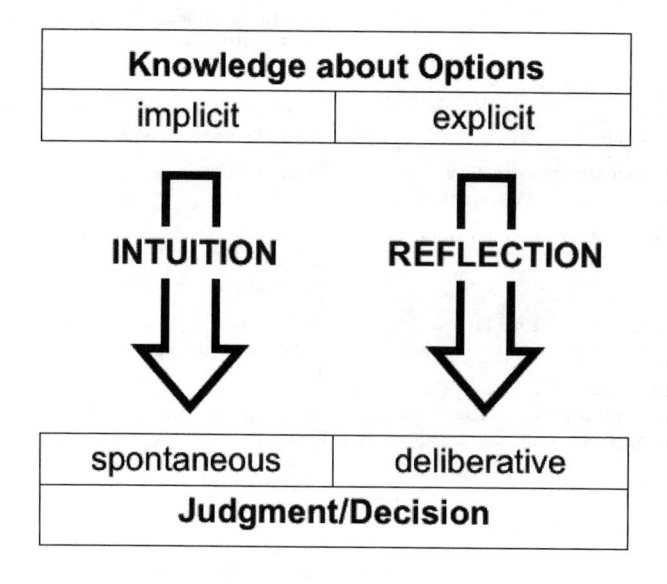

FIGURE 15.1 Two systems of judgment and decision making as proposed by Plessner (2006).

negative implicit and a positive explicit attitude). In addition, it has been suggested that implicit attitudes guide spontaneous behavior, whereas deliberative behavior is influenced more by explicit attitudes (e.g., Fazio, 1990; Fazio & Towles-Schwen, 1999). Implicit attitudes are generally defined as evaluative responses toward attitude objects that are activated automatically and, in contrast to explicit attitudes, are not necessarily subject to introspection. Moreover, implicit attitudes are assumed to result from basic processes of associative learning (e.g., Betsch, Plessner, Schwieren, & Gütig, 2001; Walther, Nagengast, & Trasselli, 2005). In contrast, it is assumed that explicit attitudes are constructed on the spot (e.g., on the basis of immediately available information; Schwarz, 2000). According to the value account model of attitude formation (Betsch, Plessner, & Schallies, 2004), these assumptions can be summarized by stating that implicit attitude formation is guided by a summation principle, whereas explicit attitude formation is guided by an averaging principle (see also Betsch, Kaufmann, Lindow, Plessner, & Hoffmann, 2006). Thus, implicit attitudes are likely to reflect the entire information about an attitude object that one has encountered before, whereas explicit attitudes are more likely to reflect a subsample of this information. For example, in an experiment by Betsch et al. (2001, Experiment 3), participants were presented with a huge amount of information about the returns of several shares at the same time that they were concentrating on a cognitive task. Additionally, particular return events were made salient during encoding to enhance memory for exemplar information. Afterward, attitudinal judgments that had to be made within 6 sec reflected the differences of the sum of returns between the shares. However, judgments that had to be expressed without a time limit were biased toward the values of those returns that had been made salient during encoding. In other words, participants in the intuitive condition (time pressure) were able to accurately respond to factual differences between the shares, whereas participants in the reflective condition (no time pressure) relied on explicitly memorable, although unrepresentative, information about single returns. Similar findings could be obtained, for example, in the domain of frequency judgments by Haberstroh (chap. 16, this volume).

Three requirements from the two systems framework (Fig. 15.1) must be fulfilled to expect an advantage of people's spontaneous judgments and decisions over their deliberative judgments and decisions. At first, people must posses knowledge that is based on prior experiences with the relevant options (e.g., concerning their value and frequency). Although, this requirement is fulfilled in many everyday situations, this is not the case in the majority of paradigms that are used in research on judgment and decision making (cf. T. Betsch, chap. 1, this volume). Second, implicit and explicit knowledge about the relevant options must be dissociated; that is, the different learning processes underlying implicit and explicit knowledge acquirement must produce different results. If implicit and explicit knowledge are equal, one would expect both systems to produce almost identical outcomes, and thus, the judgment mode would not matter. Third, implicit knowledge qualities must match the demands of a given judgment or decision task; that is, it must be useful to solve a task. As we said previously, implicit knowledge is assumed to reflect one's entire prior experiences with a judgmental object or a decision option. As such, it can contain the integration of much more information than one would be able to handle explicitly and thus provides a valuable resource for judgment and decision making (e.g., Plessner, Betsch, Schallies, & Schwieren, chap. 7, this volume). However, implicit knowledge does not contain information about how representative the prior experiences are because it is blind to the constraints that are inherent in the sampling processes that underlie its formation (Fiedler, 2000; Unkelbach & Plessner, chap. 17, this volume). Therefore, the usefulness of implicit knowledge for a given judgment or decision task depends on several features of the environment in which it has been acquired (e.g., if it stems from a "wicked" or a "kind" learning environment; Hogarth, 2001; chap. 6, this volume). In addition, judgment and decision tasks can differ to the extent in which they favor representative, selective, biased, or corrected samples of information (Kruglanski, 1989).

Taken together, on the basis of our two systems framework, we expect people to benefit from their intuition when they possess implicit knowledge that goes beyond their explicit knowledge in a given judgment or decision task. In the following, we present corresponding results from experiments in two different domains: predicting football results and the classical anchoring paradigm.

PREDICTING SOCCER RESULTS

Although great interest is taken in experts' predictions of sporting events (e.g., in the betting market), so far, little is known about the circumstances that allow experts to make accurate predictions. Some studies have even found no differences between the forecasting performances of soccer experts and nonexperts (e.g., Andersson, Edman, & Ekman, 2005). In addition, Halberstadt and Levine (1999) found that experts in basketball were better at predicting the outcomes of games when they relied on their spontaneous feelings instead of on their deliberate thoughts, when they were asked to recollect reasons before they made their predictions. Thus, the combination of expertise and deliberative reasoning does not seem to guarantee the most accurate predictions of sporting events. On the basis of the two systems framework that we introduced previously (Fig. 15.1), we argue that these findings are due to the specific qualities of the knowledge on which intuitive and reflective predictions are based. For example, a soccer expert attending to information about game results over several years is likely to acquire implicit knowledge about the strength of national soccer teams that reflects their actual performance differences as they are expressed, for example, in the world ranking of the Fédération Internationale de Football Association (FIFA). Relying on this knowledge would lead to fairly accurate predictions (e.g., Andersson et al., 2005). On the other hand, an expert's explicit knowledge can be distorted toward salient but unrepresentative events (e.g., the "shooting streak" of a single player or a bad performance in a test match; Cantinotti, Ladouceur, & Jacques, 2004). Therefore, it is expected that an expert's intuition is even more likely to outperform his reflection in the prediction of soccer results when information with little or no diagnostic value is available before the start of a game.

To test this hypothesis, Plessner, Freiberger, Kurle, and Ochs (2006) recruited 80 participants who were categorized as experts on the basis of a soccer-expertise test and asked them to make predictions for the first round of games of the FIFA Confederation Cup 2005. In the first round, 12 games were played between some of the best national teams in the world including Brazil, Argentina, and Germany. As in the study conducted by Halberstadt and Levine (1999), half of the participants were asked to analyze reasons before making predictions, whereas the other half were asked to rely on their spontaneous feelings. In addition, time of prediction was varied by asking half of the participants to make their predictions 4 weeks before the Confederation Cup and the other half to make their predictions directly in the week before the start of the Cup. The reasoning behind this manipulation was as follows. At 4 weeks before the Confederation Cup, there were relatively few specific media reports concerning the event. At the same time, the national championships and European cup tournaments were still taking place. However, one week before the Confederation Cup, the sport pages of German newspapers had almost nothing else to report than the latest stories about the Confederation Cup and the participating teams. Thus, if people were likely to use immediately available information in their deliberative predictions, even when their predictions were of little diagnostic value, prediction accuracy would be worse in the week before the event than 4 weeks earlier.

After all first round games were played, comparing participants' predictions with the real outcomes assessed the accuracy of their predictions. The results are depicted in Figure 15.2. As expected, predictions were generally better when participants relied on their intuition instead of on reflection. In addition, it was found that this effect was more pronounced in the predictions that were made in the week before the Confederation Cup than in the earlier predictions 4 weeks before. Thus, these results confirm the assumption that people are most likely to benefit from their intuitions when they posses implicit knowledge that is of use in a given judgment or decision task and dissociated from explicit knowledge.

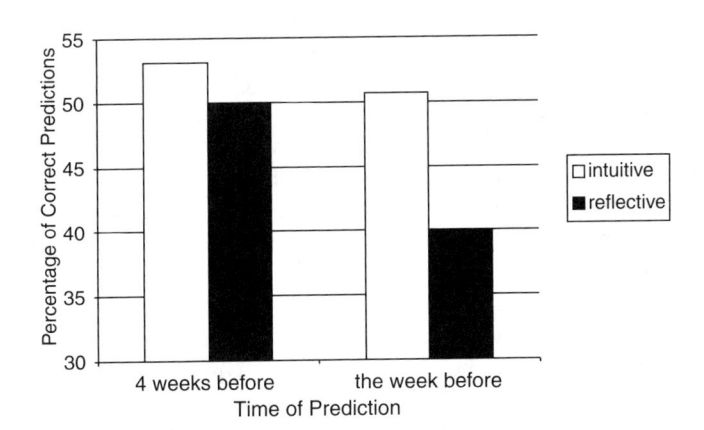

FIGURE 15.2 Accuracy of expert predictions of first-round matches at the Fédération Internationale de Football Association Confederations Cup 2005 by judgment mode and time of prediction (Plessner, Freiberger, Kurle, & Ochs, 2006).

In a recent follow-up study concerning predictions for the FIFA World Cup 2006, we were able to replicate the advantage of intuitive predictions but only as expected for soccer experts. Participants who failed to reach a certain level in a soccer-expertise test were, on average, worse than the experts, and it did not matter if they had made their predictions in an intuitive or a deliberative manner. Together, these studies clearly have shown that soccer experts who possess valid implicit knowledge about the strength of certain teams are, on average, better off to rely on their intuitive responses than on their reflective processes when making predictions about the results of soccer games.

ANCHORING

The anchoring effect is one of the most robust phenomena in the social judgment literature (e.g., Epley, 2004; Mussweiler & Strack, 1999). People seem to be inevitably biased in their judgments (e.g., frequency estimation) by a prior consideration of an anchor stimulus (e.g., a number). In most cases, this leads to an assimilation of the final judgment toward the anchor. For a long time, this effect has been explained by people's use of an anchoring and adjustment heuristic, which has been considered an intuitive judgment strategy (Tversky & Kahneman, 1974). Others have explained these effects by a numeric priming of the anchor value, which has been considered as an almost automatic process (e.g., Wilson, Houston, Etling, & Brekke, 1996). According to the selective accessibility model by Mussweiler and Strack (1999), anchoring effects are explained by a comparably more reflective judgment process, although one could debate the reflective versus intuitive nature of this process (cf. Epley, 2004). However, the model assumes that people compare a judgmental target with the anchor stimulus by testing the possibility that the target's value is similar to the anchor. In most cases, this leads to a selective increase in the accessibility of anchor-consistent knowledge about the target. Subsequent judgments are assumed to be based primarily on this knowledge. Because the active generation of knowledge plays a central role in this model, it is assumed that anchoring effects that are mediated by selective accessibility are more likely to occur when people are in a reflective judgment mode than when they rely on their intuition. As we have outlined before, intuition can be conceptualized as a process that relies primarily on implicit knowledge (Fig. 15.1) that stems from all prior experiences with the judgmental targets. Therefore, one could assume that an anchor only influences intuitive judgments when no corresponding implicit knowledge about the target has been previously acquired. However, in the majority of anchoring studies, judgmental objects are used when people have little or no prior experiences that would be of help to answer a question correctly.

Plessner, Czenna, and Betsch (2005) conducted an experimental study to test the assumption that people with valid implicit knowledge are able to resist the influence of anchors. Following the classical anchoring paradigm, participants made two consecutive judgments (comparative and absolute) about the same target object. First, participants indicated if the average temperature in a certain town

BENEFITS OF INTUITION   261

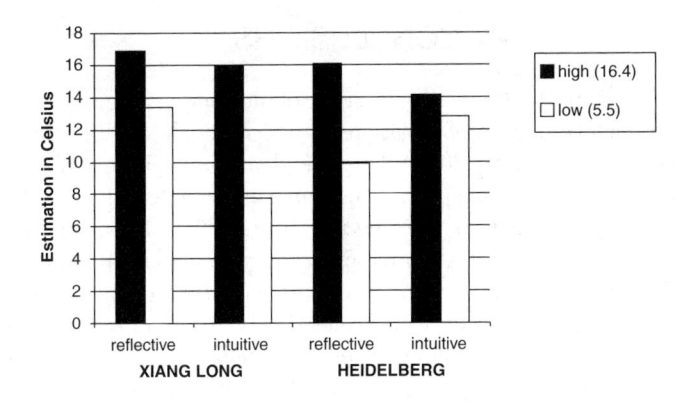

FIGURE 15.3 Estimation of the average annual temperature in judges' home town (Heidelberg) versus an unknown place (Xiang Long) by anchor and judgment mode (Plessner, Czenna, & Betsch, 2005).

was higher or lower than a given temperature (the anchor). Subsequently, they estimated the actual average temperature. To control the influence of prior knowledge on participants' judgments, half made estimations about the average temperature in their hometown (Heidelberg), and the other half estimated the average temperature in an unknown town (Xiang Long). Anchors were used that were either clearly above or below the actual average temperature in Heidelberg. In addition, the mode of judgment (intuitive vs. reflective) varied by instruction (use of spontaneous feelings vs. deliberate thinking). The results of Plessner et al.'s (2005) study can be seen in Figure 15.3. The anchors influenced participants' estimations of their hometown's average temperature only if they judged in a reflective mode. Participants who estimated the average temperature in the unknown town, Xiang Long, obtained the reversed pattern in which the anchors only affected their intuitive judgments. Thus, the mediating process of selective accessibility led to an anchoring effect only when participants had time to think and were able to generate anchor-consistent knowledge. Obviously, participants could not generate such knowledge when they estimated the average temperature of the unknown town, Xiang Long. The intuitive judgments, on the other hand, reflected participants' entire experiences with the towns' temperatures in both conditions. In the case of Xiang Long, judgments were restricted to the provided anchors. Accordingly, the strongest anchoring effect was found in this condition. In the case of the hometown, participants' implicit knowledge comprised all the daily experiences with the temperature. Therefore, the provided anchors were of minor significance in this condition. Together, this research points to the fact that under certain conditions, people may overcome anchoring effects when they rely on their intuition. This finding partly contradicts the common view of anchoring as the product of an intuitive judgment strategy. However, in our opinion, it is compatible with the selective accessibility model of judgmental anchoring.

CONCLUSIONS

One of the most important issues in the study of intuition in judgment and decision making is the determination of situations in which people can benefit from their intuitive responses (Hogarth, 2005). This would allow one, for example, to answer the following question: "If in a given situation, can I scientifically decide between either using analytic thought or trusting my intuition?" An important attempt has been made to answer this question by analyzing people's learning environments. For example, Hogarth's (2001; chap. 6, this volume) distinction between wicked learning environments (with little or no feedback) and kind environments (with accurate feedback) suggests benefits of intuition only for the latter. Based on his approach, Hogarth (2001) suggested several measures that can be developed with the aim of educating people's intuitive skills. Other researchers (e.g., Hammond et al., 1987) have emphasized the interaction of type of cognition and type of task to assess the validity of intuitive responses. According to this alternate approach, intuition should have an advantage in intuitive tasks, whereas reflection or analysis should be more valid in analytic tasks (McMackin & Slovic, 2000).

In our two-systems framework (Fig. 15.1), we combine both of the preceding approaches with social psychology's assumptions about possible dissociations between implicit and explicit attitudes. With our framework, we propose that the specific fit between the qualities of a judge's implicit versus explicit knowledge and the demands of a given judgment task allows for the determination of situations in which either intuitive or reflective processes lead to better performance. Corresponding evidence for this assumption could be found, for example, in studies on the prediction of football results and the classical anchoring paradigm (see also Haberstroh, chap. 16, this volume).

An important limitation of our framework is that it is only applicable to judgment and decision situations that involve options in which the judge or decider has prior experiences concerning, for example, value and frequency. However, in our opinion, this requirement is fulfilled in most everyday judgment and decision situations.

ACKNOWLEDGMENTS

The research underlying this chapter was supported by a grant from the Deutsche Forschungsgemeinschaft via the Sonderforschungsbereich 504 (TP A10) to H. Plessner. Many thanks to Michael Miller for his helpful comments on a draft version of this chapter.

REFERENCES

Andersson, P., Edman, J., & Ekman, M. (2005). Predicting the World Cup 2002 in soccer: Performance and confidence of experts and non-experts. *International Journal of Forecasting, 21,* 565–576.

Baron, J. (1998). *Judgment misguided: Intuition and error in public decision making.* New York: Oxford University Press.

Bartlett, J. C., Till, R. E., & Levy, J. C. (1980). Retrieval characteristics of complex pictures: Effects of verbal encoding. *Journal of Verbal Learning and Verbal Behavior, 19,* 430–449.

Bastick, T. (1982). *Intuition: How we think and act.* New York: Wiley.

Betsch, T., Kaufmann, M., Lindow, F., Plessner, H., & Hoffmann, K. (2006). Different mechanisms of information integration in implicit and explicit attitude formation. *European Journal of Social Psychology, 36,* 887–905.

Betsch, T., Plessner, H., & Schallies, E. (2004). The value-account model of attitude formation. In G. R. Maio & G. Haddock (Eds.), *Contemporary perspectives on the psychology of attitudes* (pp. 252–273). Hove, England: Psychology Press.

Betsch, T., Plessner, H., Schwieren, C., & Gütig, R. (2001). I like it but I don't know why: A value-account approach to implicit attitude formation. *Personality and Social Psychology Bulletin, 27,* 242–253.

Cantinotti, M., Ladouceur, R., & Jacques, C. (2004). Sports betting: Can gamblers beat randomness? *Psychology of Addictive Behaviors, 18,* 143–147.

Clare, J., & Lewandowsky, S. (2004). Verbalizing facial memory: Criterion effects in verbal overshadowing. *Journal of Experimental Psychology: Learning, Memory, and Cognition, 30,* 739–755.

Dougherty, M. R. P., & Hunter, J. (2003). Probability judgment and subadditivity: The role of working memory capacity and constraining retrieval. *Memory and Cognition, 31,* 968–982.

Epley, N. (2004). A tale of tuned decks? Anchoring as accessibility and anchoring as adjustment. In D. J. Koehler & N. Harvey (Eds.), *The Blackwell handbook of judgment and decision making* (pp. 240–256). Oxford, England: Blackwell Publishers.

Fallshore, M., & Schooler, J. W. (1995). Verbal vulnerability of perceptual expertise. *Journal of Experimental Psychology: Learning, Memory, and Cognition, 21,* 1608–1623.

Fazio, R. H. (1990). Multiple processes by which attitudes guide behavior: The MODE model as an integrative framework. In M. P. Zanna (Ed.), *Advances in experimental social psychology* (Vol. 23, pp. 75–109). San Diego, CA: Academic.

Fazio, R. H., & Towles-Schwen, T. (1999). The MODE model of attitude-behavior processes. In S. Chaiken & Y. Trope (Eds.), *Dual process theories in social psychology* (pp. 97–116). New York: Guilford.

Fiedler, K. (2000). Beware of samples! A cognitive-ecological sampling approach to judgment biases. *Psychological Review, 107,* 659–676.

Fiore, S. M., & Schooler, J. W. (2002). How did you get here from there? Verbal overshadowing of spatial mental models. *Applied Cognitive Psychology, 16,* 897–909.

Gigerenzer, G., Todd, P. M., & the ABC Research Group. (Eds.). (1999). *Simple heuristics that make us smart.* New York: Oxford University Press.

Gilbert, G. S., & Rappoport, L. (1975). Categories of thought and variations in meaning: A demonstration experiment. *Journal of Phenomenological Psychology, 5,* 419–424.

Gladwell, M. (2005). *Blink: The power of thinking without thinking.* New York: Little, Brown.

Goodie, A. S., & Crooks, C. L. (2004). Time pressure effects on performance in a base-rate task. *Journal of General Psychology, 131,* 18–28.

Greenwald, A. G., & Banaji, M. R. (1995). Implicit social cognition: Attitudes, self-esteem, and stereotypes. *Psychological Review, 102,* 4–27.

Haidt, J. (2001). The emotional dog and its rational tail: A social intuitionist approach to moral judgment. *Psychological Review, 108,* 814–834.

Halberstadt, J. B. (2005). Featural shift in explanation-biased memory for emotional faces. *Journal of Personality and Social Psychology, 88,* 38–49.

Halberstadt, J. B., & Levine, G. M. (1999). Effects of reasons analysis on the accuracy of predicting basketball games. *Journal of Applied Social Psychology, 29,* 517–530.

Hammmond, K. R., Hamm, R. M., Grassia, J., & Pearson, T. (1987). Direct comparison of the efficacy of intuitive and analytical cognition in expert judgment. *IEE Transactions on Systems, Man, and Cybernetics, 17,* 753–770.
Hastie, R., & Dawes, R. M. (2001). *Rational choice in an uncertain world—The psychology of judgment and decision making.* Thousand Oaks, CA: Sage.
Hogarth, R. (2001). *Educating intuition.* Chicago: The University of Chicago Press.
Hogarth, R. (2005). Deciding analytically or trusting your intuition? The advantages and disadvantages of analytic and intuitive thought. In T. Betsch & S. Haberstroh (Eds.), *The routines of decision making* (pp. 67–82). Mahwah, NJ: Lawrence Erlbaum Associates, Inc.
Kahneman, D., Slovic, P., & Tversky, A. (Eds.). (1982). *Judgment under uncertainty: Heuristics and biases.* Cambridge: Cambridge University Press.
Kardes, F. R. (2002). *Consumer behavior and managerial decision making* (2nd ed.). Upper Saddle River, NJ: Prentice Hall.
Klimesch, W. (1980). The effect of verbalization on memory performance for complex pictures. *Zeitschrift für Experimentelle und Angewandte Psychologie, 27,* 245–256.
Kruglanski, A. W. (1989). The psychology of being "right": The problem of accuracy in social perception and cognition. *Psychological Bulletin, 106,* 395–409.
Kruglanski, A. W., & Freund, T. (1983). The freezing and unfreezing of lay-inferences: Effects on impressional primacy, ethnic stereotyping, and numerical anchoring. *Journal of Experimental Social Psychology, 19,* 448–468.
Lieberman, M. D. (2000). Intuition: A social cognitive neuroscience approach. *Psychological Bulletin, 126,* 109–137.
McMackin, J., & Slovic, P. (2000). When does explicit justification impair decision making? *Journal of Applied Cognitive Psychology, 14,* 527–541.
Melcher, J. M., & Schooler, J. W. (1996). The misremembrance of wines past: Verbal and perceptual expertise differentially mediate verbal overshadowing of taste memory. *Journal of Memory and Language, 35,* 231–245.
Melcher, J. M., & Schooler, J. W. (2004). Perceptual and conceptual training mediate the verbal overshadowing effect in an unfamiliar domain. *Memory and Cognition, 32,* 618–631.
Memon, A., & Bartlett, J. (2002). The effects of verbalization on face recognition in young and older adults. *Applied Cognitive Psychology, 16,* 635–650.
Memon, A., & Rose, R. (2002). Identification abilities of children: Does a verbal description hurt face recognition? *Psychology, Crime and Law, 8,* 229–242.
Mussweiler, T., & Strack, F. (1999). Comparing is believing: A selective accessibility model of judgmental anchoring. In W. Stroebe & M. Hewstone (Eds.), *European review of social psychology* (Vol. 10, pp. 135–168). Chichester, England: Wiley.
Perfect, T. J., Hunt, L. J., & Harris, C. M. (2002). Verbal overshadowing in voice recognition. *Applied Cognitive Psychology, 16,* 973–980.
Plessner, H., Scherzberg, A., Betsch, T., Blanke, H.-J., Walgenbach, P., Waschkuhn, A., & Wegner, G. (2006). Die Klugheit der Intuition und ihre Grenzen [The smartness of intuition and its boundaries]. In A. Scherzberg et al. (Eds.), *Kluges Entscheiden* (pp. 109–120). Tübingen, Germany: Mohr Siebeck.
Plessner, H., Czenna, S., & Betsch, C. (2005, September). *Intuition beyond heuristic reasoning: Less anchoring by less thinking.* Paper presented at the 6th European Social Cognition Network Meeting in Vitznau, Switzerland.
Plessner, H., Freiberger, V., Kurle, A., & Ochs, K. (2006, May). *Besser früh und spontan als spät und analytisch: Die Genauigkeit von Expertenvorhersagen für den FIFA Confederations Cup 2005* [Better early and spontaneous than late and analytic: The accuracy of expert predictions concerning the FIFA Confederations Cup 2005]. Paper presented at the 36th Meeting of the Arbeitsgemeinschaft Sportpsychologie in Münster, Germany.

Schooler, J. W., & Engstler-Schooler, T. Y. (1990). Verbal overshadowing of visual memories: Some things are better left unsaid. *Cognitive Psychology, 22,* 36–71.

Schroyens, W., Schaeken, W., & Handley, S. (2003). In search of counter-examples: Deductive rationality in human reasoning. *Quarterly Journal of Experimental Psychology: A. Human Experimental Psychology, 56,* 1129–1145.

Schwarz, N. (2000). Social judgment and attitudes: Warmer, more social, and less conscious. *European Journal of Social Psychology, 30,* 149–176.

Silverberg, N., & Buchanan, L. (2005). Verbal mediation and memory for novel figural designs: A dual interference study. *Brain and Cognition, 57,* 198–209.

Stanovich, K. E., & West, R. F. (2000). Individual differences in reasoning: Implications for the rationality debate. *Behavioral and Brain Sciences, 23,* 645–665.

Tversky, A., & Kahneman, D. (1974). Judgment under uncertainty: Heuristics and biases. *Science, 185,* 1124–1131.

Walther, E., Nagengast, B., & Trasselli, C. (2005). Evaluative conditioning in social psychology: Facts and speculations. *Cognition and Emotion, 19,* 175–196.

Wilson, T. D. (2002). *Strangers to ourselves: Discovering the adaptive unconscious.* Cambridge, MA: Harvard University Press.

Wilson, T. D., Houston, C., Etling, K. M., & Brekke, N. (1996). A new look at anchoring effects: Basic anchoring and its antecedents. *Journal of Experimental Psychology: General, 4,* 387–402.

Wilson, T. D., Lindsey, S., & Schooler, T. Y. (2000). A model of dual attitudes. *Psychological Review, 107,* 101–126.

Wilson, T. D., & Schooler, J. W. (1991). Thinking too much: Introspection can reduce the quality of preferences and decisions. *Journal of Personality & Social Psychology, 60,* 181–192.

Windschitl, P. D., & Chambers, J. R. (2004). The dud-alternative effect in likelihood judgment. *Journal of Experimental Psychology: Learning, Memory, and Cognition, 30,* 198–215.

Windschitl, P. D., & Krizan, Z. (2005). Contingent approaches to making likelihood judgments about polychotomous cases: The influence of task factors. *Journal of Behavioral Decision Making, 18,* 281–303.

16

Intuitive and Deliberate Strategies in Frequency Estimation

SUSANNE HABERSTROH
University of Osnabrück

INTRODUCTION

People use a variety of strategies to accomplish most cognitive tasks. This strategic variability has been shown in various domains such as frequency judgments (Betsch, Siebler, Marz, Hormuth, & Dickenberger, 1999; Brown, 1995, 1997, 2002), numerosity judgments (Luwel & Verschaffel, 2003; Luwel, Verschaffel, Onghena, & de Corte, 2003), decision making (Payne, Bettman, & Johnson, 1988, 1993), answering questions from memory (Reder, 1987), or subtraction tasks (Siegler, 1987). To predict judgments and decisions, the crucial question is under which condition each strategy is used. Consequently, a lot of research has dealt with the question of strategy selection when solving cognitive tasks. Referring to decision-making research, Payne et al. (1993) identified three factors that moderate strategy selection. The first factor refers to features of the strategies such as the effort required to employ the strategy or its accuracy. Second, individual differences can influence strategy selection (e.g., C. Betsch, chap. 14, this volume). In this chapter, I concentrate on the third factor Payne et al. (1993) discussed: contextual variations while the judgment or decision is made. These contextual factors might refer to task characteristics, such as the wording of questions (e.g., Blair & Burton, 1987; Reder, 1987), or situational demands such as time pressure. Severe time pressure can cause a shift from more effortful decision strategies, such as the weighted additive rule, to less effortful rules such as elimination by aspects (Tversky, 1972). According to *The Adaptive Decision Maker* (Payne et al., 1993) approach, a trade-off between effort and accuracy determines strategy choice. For a given situational constraint, the decision maker adopts the best strategy that is available in the strategy repertoire (see also

Betsch, Brinkmann, Fiedler, & Breining, 1999; Payne et al., 1988, 1993; Svenson & Maule, 1993; Weber & Lindemann, chap. 12, this volume).

In this chapter, I extend these ideas to the effect of situational constraints on strategy selection when people estimate event frequencies. I argue that estimation strategies differ on the intuition-deliberation dimension. The use of these estimation strategies yields some counterintuitive predictions: I show that under specific circumstances, an intuitive estimation strategy leads to more accurate frequency judgments than does the use of a deliberate strategy.

INTUITIVE AND DELIBERATE FREQUENCY ESTIMATION STRATEGIES

In research on frequency judgments, there has been a rather heterogeneous collection of theories and findings regarding the strategies people use when estimating frequencies (e.g., Brown, 1995, 1997, 2002; Dougherty & Franco-Watkins, 2002; Gallistel & Gelman, 1992; Hasher & Zacks, 1979, 1984; Sedlmeier & Betsch, 2002; Tversky & Kahneman, 1973). Accordingly, the notion of multiple strategies for frequency estimation has been introduced into the frequency research (Betsch, Siebler, et al., 1999; Brown, 1995, 1997, 2002) that has stated that people can use various estimation strategies, which they apply selectively. However, the critical question remains: Under which conditions are estimation strategies used, and to what extent does strategy selection influence the accuracy of judgments?

Until now, many strategies for frequency estimation have been described and some attempts have been made to identify conditions under which these strategies are used. Most of this research has focused on the distinction between enumeration strategies and nonenumeration strategies introduced by Brown (1995, 1997, 2002). In Brown's (1995, 1997, 2002) framework, the selection of a strategy is influenced by two factors: first, by properties of the event itself, such as the distinctiveness of single events (Brown, 1995) or the absolute number of events (Blair & Burton, 1987; Burton & Blair, 1991). Second, properties of the event memory impact strategy selection (Brown, 1997). These two factors Brown (1995, 1997, 2002) described refer to properties of the event itself and the representation of the events in memory. Strategy selection so far has only rarely been linked to the retrieval of information, that is, to properties of the judgment process; only one study (Blair & Burton, 1987) addressed this issue: Research on estimating behavioral frequencies in survey interviews has shown that the wording of the question can influence the selection of a judgment strategy: "How often" questions lead to the more frequent use of repetition rates as the basis for frequency judgments than do "How many times" questions.

In this chapter, I elaborate on another broad categorization of estimation strategies suggested earlier (Haberstroh & Betsch, 2002). This broad categorization of estimation strategies into online strategies and memory-based strategies integrates many estimation strategies that have been described in the frequency literature. *Online strategies* are based on a frequency record, which is stored during the encoding of information, whereas *memory-based strategies* utilize a memory sample drawn at the time of judgment to arrive at a frequency estimate.

I incorporate this distinction of strategies in a model that predicts the use of online and memory-based strategies in particular situations. The model assumes that in the research on strategy selection, one important factor has been neglected so far: the degree of deliberation while the frequency judgment is made. I show that online strategies are more likely to be used in intuitive judgments, whereas memory-based strategies are more likely in deliberate judgments. This should lead to differences regarding the accuracy of judgments.

This understanding of intuitive judgments is rooted in the so-called learning perspective on intuition (e.g., T. Betsch, chap. 1, this volume; Hogarth, 2001). This line of research suggests that people have extraordinary capacities in establishing mental representations of number, time, space, and value during encoding (e.g., Hasher & Zacks, 1979, 1984; Betsch, Plessner, Schwieren, & Gütig, 2001). Intuitive judgments utilize these records of prior experiences and consequently are not the result of inference processes at the time of judgment. If the encoded sample of information is representative for the criterion to be judged, intuitive judgments can be remarkably accurate. This has been shown in a variety of domains such as value judgments (Betsch et al., 2001; Plessner, Betsch, Schallies, & Schwieren, chap. 7, this volume) or frequency judgments (Haberstroh & Betsch, 2002; Hasher & Zacks, 1979, 1984; Zacks & Hasher, 2002).

THE STRATEGY-APPLICATION MODEL

Previous research has provided profound empirical evidence for the use of many different strategies for frequency estimation. The strategy-application model does not add more strategies to this selection. Rather, it aims at integrating some of them, and it proposes estimating intuitively versus deliberately as one moderating variable for the use of the respective categories.

One aim of the model is to show that characteristics of the encoded stimuli as well as characteristics of the retrieval process of these stimuli can influence deliberate frequency judgments. As an example of stimuli characteristics, the model incorporates the influence of the valence of stimuli on judgments about their frequency. The valence of stimuli is one of the basic characteristics of human experience (e.g., Zajonc, 1980) and has so far received surprisingly little attention in the frequency research.

Moreover, as an example of characteristics of the retrieval process, the model deals with one very frequently studied topic in the frequency literature: the influence of the availability of exemplars on frequency judgments (Tversky & Kahneman, 1973). Researchers in this field have been and are confronted with rather contradictory findings: Some studies have shown the influence of availability on frequency judgments, whereas others have not. By differentiating between intuitive and deliberate judgments, the model I propose here is able to shed some light on this controversy.

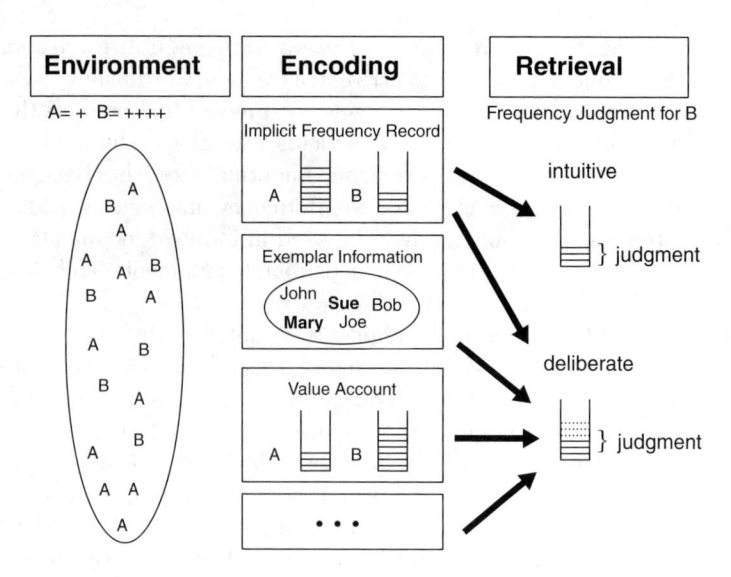

FIGURE 16.1 The strategy-application model.

Selecting valence and availability as parameters in this model does not exclude other factors from exerting a similar impact on frequency judgments.

Encoding of Information

Figure 16.1 shows an overview of the model. The left oval represents the environment, which for simplicity contains only two events, A and B—for example the male (A) and female (B) persons you met at a party. In this example, the two events differ with respect to their frequency of occurrence (you met more men than women at the party) and with respect to their valence (you liked the women much better than the men).

With respect to the encoding of information, the model assumes that during encoding, the frequency information is automatically and nonintentionally integrated in a unitary memory structure. This idea was first proposed within the so-called automatic encoding models (e.g., Hasher & Zacks, 1979, 1984). Researchers promoting this idea have proposed that the frequency of occurrence is a fundamental aspect of an experience, which is continuously and automatically encoded and incremented into a unitary memory structure (e.g., Alba, Chromiak, Hasher, & Attig, 1980; Hasher & Zacks, 1979, 1984; Watkins & LeCompte, 1991; Whalen, Gallistel, & Gelman, 1999; Zacks & Hasher, 2002). In a subsequent judgment, the individual can simply read out the magnitude of this structure without retrieving concrete instances from memory (Church, 1984; Gibbon, 1992). Here, this memory structure is called implicit frequency record (IFR).

Within the class of automatic encoding models, there are different views of how such frequency representations are formed. Some theories have used the metaphor of a "cognitive counter" (Alba et al., 1980; Underwood, 1969) to illustrate the accumulative properties of the underlying memory process. Accordingly, counters are assumed to be attached to superordinate categories in memory and to tag instances of occurrence of category exemplars. At any time, the individual may read the current state of the counter to form a frequency judgment. The cognitive counter notion is challenged by the fact that absolute frequency judgments are systematically distorted even though the relative accuracy in frequency estimation is high. The literature on animals, however, provides one with a variant of the automatic encoding approach, which is capable of explaining the distortions in absolute frequency judgments. According to this approach, the formation of mental magnitudes is not described as a binary process in which each occurrence of an event contributes equally to the mental representation. Rather, each event is thought to deliver an impulse of activation to the encoding system, which varies in intensity dependent on context factors such as the time elapsed between consecutive events (Church, 1984; Gallistel & Gelman, 1992). This variant of the automatic encoding approach can also account for the influence of noise and has been recently supported in studies with human participants (e.g., Whalen et al., 1999). With increasing frequencies, the weight of each entry decreases, thus yielding a logarithmic function of input frequencies. Early entries have stronger weights. This resulting logarithmic function is similar to basic laws of psychophysics such as Weber's (1834) Law or Fechner's (1860) Law or to the utility function (Bernoulli, 1738/1954). The logarithmic function resulting from different weights for each entry can also account for the frequently replicated empirical finding that frequency judgments are "regressed," meaning that low frequencies are overestimated and high frequencies are underestimated (e.g., Fiedler, 1991; Hintzman, 1969; Sedlmeier, Hertwig, & Gigerenzer, 1998). Rather than absolute accuracy, this approach predicts relative accuracy in frequency judgments. The state of IFRs are not expected to mirror the actual frequencies in an absolute sense; instead, as each event delivers an impulse into the system, the relation between frequencies should be mirrored in the states of the IFRs. Thus, frequency judgments, which are based on IFRs, should be high in relative accuracy in that they should maintain the rank order of frequencies.

Furthermore, Gallistel and Gelman (1992) argued that the processes that underlie the representation of numerosities are analogous to histogram arithmetic. This implies that people can perform operations on these numerosities as if they were represented as columns of different height. For example, people can detect which of two columns (e.g., numerosities and frequencies) is higher, or they can perform simple mathematical operations on these numerosities such as adding two columns.

In this model, I take over these assumptions of Whalen et al. (1999) and Gallistel and Gelman (1992) regarding the formation of the IFRs. These properties of the IFR have some important consequences for accumulating frequencies. First, whenever the IFR is based on a representative sample of the relevant information, the state of the IFR should be high in relative accuracy. This means that as the histogram algebra implies, the IFR should mirror which of two events has been encountered more frequently. However, as I outlined previously, the IFR is not necessarily accurate in absolute terms. Second, the IFR should not systematically reflect other aspects of the encoded information (availability, valence of information, etc.) apart from the frequency information. In Figure 16.1, event A occurs more often in the environment than event B. Therefore, the IFR for A shows a higher state than the IFR for B.

Besides the IFR, other pieces of information are stored in memory during encoding as well. For example, if you meet male (event A in Figure 16.1) and female (event B) persons at a party, you will be able to recall some of the male and female names represented in the second box in Figure 16.1. Thus, part of the information about the events is kept in memory and can later be retrieved as exemplar information. The exemplars may differ with respect to the ease with which they can be retrieved (i.e., their availability in memory). This difference may be due to several factors such as the recency of encoding. In Figure 16.1, events of category A are more available, as indicated by the bold type.

In addition to the IFR and event memory, the strategy-application model also assumes that the valence of stimuli is aggregated and stored during encoding. Regarding the evaluation of encoded events, an approach by Betsch, Plessner, and Schallies (2004) and Betsch et al. (2001) is adopted that predicts the formation and use of implicit attitudes. This approach assumes that the mere encoding of value-charged stimuli is a sufficient condition to initiate implicit online formation of summary evaluations. The intensities of positive and negative valences are thought to accumulate in a unitary memory structure called *value account*. This process is summative. A value account is more easily accessible in memory than concrete traces of past experiences. In Figure 16.1, the valence of event B is four times higher than the valence of event A. Due to the summation of valences, the value account for B shows a higher positive state than the one for event A, even though event A has been encountered more often than event B. The slightly higher frequency of A cannot compensate for the much higher valence of B.

Finally, the blank box represents other cognitive processes, which might be instigated by the encoding of events such as the update of general knowledge structures like schemata or stereotypes.

Retrieval

As I have shown, various pieces of information are stored in memory during the encoding of events. The model predicts under which conditions this information is used in frequency judgments.

The model proposes that the most important knowledge basis in estimating frequencies is the IFR. Just like the value account (Betsch et al., 2001), the IFR is highly associated with the respective category whose frequency is accumulated. Whenever the category is activated, the activation spreads to the IFR and to its current state. Consequently, when people have to judge the frequency of an event or a category, the IFR is automatically activated, and therefore, its state comes to mind automatically as a "first guess." However, due to the implicit nature of the aggregation and activation processes, people do not have an insight into the source of this first guess (Greenwald & Banaji, 1995: "[T]races of past experience affect some performance, even though the influential earlier experience is not remembered in the usual sense—that is, it is unavailable to self-report or introspection" [pp. 4–5]). However, as long as they do not have the chance to consider more pieces of information due to situational constraints, they have to rely on this first guess. When people make intuitive judgments induced, for example, by time pressure or by the instruction to "guess spontaneously," they do not have the resources to consider more pieces of information. Therefore, intuitive judgments should be based on the momentary state of the IFR. This strategy is what Haberstroh and Betsch (2002) subsumed under the label online strategies because the judgment is based on a memory structure, which was built during encoding.

As I outlined previously, only the frequency information is aggregated in this memory structure. Therefore, relying on the IFR should be the most successful strategy to arrive at valid frequency judgments. Intuitive judgments should be high in relative accuracy and not influenced by other factors such as the availability or the valence of events. To summarize, this model predicts that intuitive judgments, which are arrived at without extensive deliberation, should be most accurate. Consequently, the intuitive judgment for event B in the upper row in Figure 16.1 is equal to the state of the IFR for event B.

What happens if people make a deliberate judgment and thus do not have to rely on the first guess that comes to their mind? Because of its high level of association to the respective event, the IFR is also activated in deliberate judgments. However, because people do not have an insight into this implicit aggregation process, they doubt the validity of their first guess. When Hasher and Zacks (1984) presented their idea of automatic encoding, they also raised this idea. However, they did not elaborate or pursue it:

> Are there circumstances under which stored frequency information will not be used? The answer is probably yes. People seem largely unaware of the quality of their stored frequency knowledge and of the range of information for which this knowledge exists. To the extent that a situation depends on conscious reasoning, frequency knowledge may not be used. (p. 1385)

Thus, the first guess does not seem to be experienced as a valid basis for a frequency judgment because people do not know about its source, and therefore, they do not use this information in their judgment. Rather, they try to activate information that subjectively seems more valid than the vague first guess elicited by the IFR. In this case, various aspects of the events can impact frequency estimates. First, the model proposes that judgments can be influenced by properties of the recall content such as the actual number of exemplars retrieved (enumeration strategy; Brown, 1997, 2002), the representativeness of retrieved exemplars for the category (Tversky & Kahneman, 1974), or the valence of the retrieved stimuli (Betsch et al., 2001). Second, judgments can be influenced by properties of the retrieval process itself such as echo intensity (Dougherty & Franco-Watkins, 2002; Dougherty, Gettys, & Ogden, 1999), feelings of familiarity (Hintzman & Curran, 1994), or the availability of exemplars (Tversky & Kahneman, 1973). In many natural settings, these properties of the recall content and the retrieval process are highly correlated with the actual frequency of occurrence. However, this does not necessarily have to be the case, as, for example, Tversky and Kahneman (1973) demonstrated repeatedly. When they are uncorrelated, the model predicts that deliberate judgments should be less accurate than intuitive frequency judgments.

In Figure 16.1, the deliberate judgment for event B is not only based on the state of the IFR, but additional information is activated and integrated. Thus, the deliberate judgment should be biased by the availability of information or by the valence of stimuli.

EMPIRICAL EVIDENCE

So far, two factors that can influence deliberate frequency judgments have been identified and tested experimentally: the availability of exemplars and the valence of stimuli.

Availability of Exemplars

The strategy-application model can account for the fact that the availability of exemplars sometimes influences frequency judgments but not always. As Tversky and Kahneman (1973) pointed out, "one may estimate probability by assessing availability" (p. 208). In the model's terms, the availability of an exemplar can influence frequency judgments in addition to the IFR: When people think about their judgments, they activate exemplar information that can influence their estimates. Therefore, as Tversky and Kahneman (1973) and others have shown in experiments on the availability heuristic (for an overview, see Schwarz, 1989), categories with highly available exemplars should be judged as being more frequent than categories with less available exemplars. However, the strategy-application model makes more precise predictions than the availability heuristic because it postulates moderating conditions under which the availability should have an influence on frequency judgments. More specifically, this effect should only occur when people think about their judgments (deliberate judgments) and not in intuitive judgments. In the latter judgment type, they only base their estimates on the state of the IFR. However, when they think about their estimates, they activate additional exemplar information. In this case, the availability of exemplars will be used to estimate frequencies. I note that this prediction contradicts current research about the use of heuristics in judgment and decision making in which heuristics are assumed to be "rules of thumb" that can be applied effortlessly in contrast to more costly judgmental strategies (Kahneman, Slovic, & Tversky, 1982).

Because the model proposes that intuitive frequency judgments are based on IFR, it is predicted that judgments will reflect frequencies of actual occurrence. Because IFRs provide a holistic record of prior frequency of experiences, the resulting judgments should reveal a high degree of relative accuracy. As I outlined previously, that does not imply a high degree of absolute accuracy but rather that the rank order of actual frequencies should be maintained in intuitive judgments. Judgments should not be biased by the availability of exemplars or by the valence of stimuli.

Moreover, in deliberate judgments, people activate additional information at the time of evaluation. Frequency judgments can then be influenced by properties of the recall process itself (e.g., availability of exemplars) or by properties of the recall content (e.g., valence of stimuli). In cases when this additional information is not correlated with the actual frequencies, deliberation should decrease relative accuracy in frequency judgments.

This idea has been tested in a series of experiments (Haberstroh & Betsch, 2002; Haberstroh, Betsch, & Aarts, 2005). In these experiments, Haberstroh and Betsch (2002) and Haberstroh et al. (2005) have manipulated the availability of exemplars within participants by varying the repetition rates of exemplars of two categories. Each participant's task was to judge the frequency of occurrence for the two categories; for this estimate, they were either instructed to think carefully or to guess spontaneously. In the paradigm that has been employed for these experiments, participants had to perform a computerized task: they had to repeatedly "feed" animals of two fictitious genera (*Amanepes* and *Oropholus*) with either meat or plants using mouse clicks. They were instructed to always feed the animals of only one genus either meat or plants. On each trial, first the name of a fictitious animal (e.g., "Stong") appeared on the computer screen. Then the category (i.e., the genus of the respective animal, either "Amanepes" or "Oropholus") was presented. Each participant's task was to click on one of two buttons (meat or plants) to feed the animal. At the end of this feeding task, in a final questionnaire, they were asked how often they had fed animals of the two genera. In these experiments, the frequency of the two behaviors ranged from 20 to 45. In all experiments, the availability of exemplars was manipulated by the repetition rate of the exemplars within a category. One category consisted of only a few names, which were repeated often during the feeding trial. The other category consisted of many different animals, which were only presented once or twice during the feeding phase. Due to the unfamiliarity of names, this manipulation led to a low recall rate. Thus, as in many other experiments, the availability of exemplars has been manipulated by the number of exemplars participants were expected to be able to recall (e.g., Curt & Zechmeister, 1984; Lewandowsky & Smith, 1983; Tversky & Kahneman, 1973). When participants gave their frequency estimates, Haberstroh and Betsch (2002) and Haberstroh et al. (2005) have manipulated the judgment mode, that is, the degree of deliberation: Participants were either instructed to guess spontaneously or to think carefully about how often they had fed animals of each genus. Because the judgment mode was manipulated after the information had been presented, the encoding phase was identical for both conditions and independent of the degree of deliberation during the judgment.

This series of experiments has tested the hypothesis that intuitive judgments reflect the relation (i.e., the rank order of frequencies) of the two behaviors and do not reflect the availability of exemplars, whereas deliberate judgments should be biased by the availability of exemplars.

In fact, when both behaviors were performed the same number of times, intuitive frequency judgments were not influenced by the availability of exemplars. Participants gave similar estimates for both categories. However, deliberate judgments were strongly biased by the availability: Participants indicated that the behavior with the more available exemplars was performed more often than the behavior with the less available exemplars. Thus, participants perceived a difference in the two frequencies, which in fact did not exist (Haberstroh et al., 2005).

This effect was even more pronounced when the two behaviors were not performed the same number of times. In another experiment (Haberstroh et al., 2005), frequency of occurrence and availability of exemplars were manipulated in the opposite direction: The behavior with the more available exemplars was performed less often, and the behavior with the less available exemplars was performed more often. In this experiment, only participants with the instruction to guess spontaneously were able to detect the actual difference between the two frequencies. When people thought about their judgment, they did not perceive the existing difference at all.

Taken together, these experiments have provided evidence for the idea that intuition versus deliberation moderates the use of estimation strategies. Intuitive judgments, which were arrived at using a spontaneous guess, were more accurate in relative terms. The rank order of actual frequencies was maintained in the frequency judgments. However, when participants invested more cognitive resources in their judgments and thought about them carefully, judgments were biased by the availability of exemplars.

Valence of Stimuli

So far, I have shown that a property of the retrieval process, availability of exemplars, can influence frequency estimates at the time of judgment when people carefully consider them. If this additional information is not correlated with the objective frequencies, deliberation leads to less accurate judgments. Still, people activate this information if they do not trust their first guess in the search for more valid information.

The same reasoning should apply to the content of the retrieved information such as the valence of events. Based on this assumption, I predict that the valence of information, automatically aggregated in the value account, can influence frequency judgments in a similar way. When people search for information about the event, the value account is activated (Betsch et al., 2001). People then use this information to infer the presentation frequency. The value account gives them a "positive feeling" toward an event (Betsch et al., 2001), and they use this feeling to judge the frequency of the event. The model assumes that events with a more positive valence are considered to have been presented more frequently than events with a less positive valence.

Taken together, the model predicts that only if people are asked to deliberately form frequency judgments will their judgments reflect the valence of stimuli. When they judge intuitively, judgments should mirror the state of the IFR, which is not correlated with valence. So far, the interdependence of value and frequency has only been studied in the opposite direction (i.e., frequency of occurrence influences value judgment). This phenomenon is widely known as the "mere exposure effect" and has received vast empirical support (e.g., Brooks & Watkins, 1989; Lee, 2001; Zajonc, 1968). The strategy-application model suggests that interdependence also exists in the other direction: Value of events influences frequency judgments.

This idea has been tested experimentally in a series of studies (Haberstroh et al., 2005). In these studies, Haberstroh et al. adopted a paradigm developed by Betsch et al. (2001) to study the aggregation of valence information in the value account. In this paradigm, participants saw commercial advertisements on the computer monitor. They were told that their primary task was to answer some questions about these advertisements afterward. As a secondary task, ostensibly to distract their attention away from the advertisements, a running caption was presented on the bottom of the screen that showed stock quotes on different trading days (e.g., "Wednesday, September 4, Frankfurt: Supan + 14, Elskar + 6, Pittler + 22"). These numbers do not describe absolute prices of these stocks but rather value increases compared to the previous trading day. To ensure encoding, participants were asked to read this information aloud. The amount of information that was presented was sufficiently high to keep participants from intentionally monitoring the sum or frequency of occurrence of the stocks. At the end of the presentation, participants were asked how often each single stock had been presented. Again, they were either asked to guess spontaneously or to think carefully about their judgment. In the material that was presented, there were always two focal stocks, which differed with respect to their valence (i.e., with respect to the sum of their outcomes).

When the two stocks were presented the same number of times, Haberstroh et al. (2005) found the same effect that could be observed for the availability of exemplars: When participants estimated the frequencies intuitively, judgments reflected the fact that both stocks were presented equally often. However, when participants thought about their judgment, they were biased by the valence of stimuli: The stock with the higher sum of outcomes was judged to have been presented more frequently than the stock with the lower sum of outcomes.

Again, this effect was even more pronounced when frequency and valence were manipulated in opposite directions, that is, the more frequent stock had the lower sum of outcomes than the less frequent stock. In this experiment (Haberstroh et al., 2005), only intuitive judgments maintained the rank order of the frequencies (i.e., that only those participants judged the stock with the lower sum as more frequent). Again, when participants thought about their judgment, they were influenced by the valence of information. The results even showed a significant reversal in the judgments: Deliberate judgments were in fact higher for the less frequent stock, which had the higher sum of outcomes.

Taken together, these experiments have provided evidence for the idea that properties of the recall content can also be used in frequency judgments when people think about those judgments. In this case, they do not rely solely on their first guess but activate more pieces of information, which might then influence frequency estimates. Earlier research has repeatedly demonstrated the mere exposure effect (e.g., Zajonc, 1968), which describes the effect when the valence of a stimulus is judged more positively if it has been presented repeatedly. The Haberstroh et al. (2005) experiment provided first evidence for the reverse effect: Frequencies were estimated to be higher when the valence of the stimulus was more positive, in this case, a higher sum of outcomes. This reverse effect only occurred for deliberate frequency judgments and was so pronounced that even a significant reversal of actual frequencies in the deliberate judgments occurred. Deliberate frequency judgments here reflected the rank order of valence, not the rank order of frequencies like the intuitive judgments.

GENERAL DISCUSSION

In this chapter, I proposed a model that introduces intuition versus deliberation as an important factor for strategy selection in frequency judgments. Previous research had shown that participants use a large number of estimation strategies to arrive at frequency judgments and some attempts have been made to identify moderating conditions (e.g., Betsch, Siebler, et al., 1999; Brown, 1995, 1997, 2002). However, the characteristics of the judgment situation, such as the amount of deliberation participants spend in making their judgment, has mostly been neglected so far. In the experiments I have reported here, intuitive judgments have been induced by an instruction to guess spontaneously (Haberstroh et al., 2005). However, other methods lead to the same effect such as employing explicit time pressure (for frequency judgments, see Haberstroh & Betsch, 2003; for valence judgments, see Betsch et al., 2001). Aside from instructing participants to think carefully about their judgment, other methods can be used to evoke deliberate judgments: In another series of experiments, Haberstroh and Betsch (2003) paid participants according to their performance on the frequency judgment task and found similar results.

The results show that intuitive judgments were more accurate in relative terms than were deliberate judgments. This is a rather counterintuitive result because there are lines of research, such as the heuristics-and-biases research (Kahneman et al., 1982), that predict the opposite pattern: Deliberation should lead to a higher accuracy of judgments. I argue that the accuracy of deliberate judgment strategies depends on the applicability of conscious judgmental strategies. In our paradigms, we (Haberstroh & Betsch, 2002; Haberstroh, et al., 2005) employed an information overload by presenting many unfamiliar animal names or stocks so that participants could not retrieve a representative memory sample of the stimuli they had to judge. There was no analytical strategy available that might have enabled participants to increase accuracy. This differentiates these paradigms from those used in the heuristics-and-biases research, such as the combination task ("How many groups of 8 or groups of 2 can be formed from a population of 10 people?") or variations of arithmetical problems ("What is the product of 8x7x6x . . . x1 vs. 1x2x3x . . . x8?"; Tversky & Kahneman, 1973) and explains why our results (Haberstroh et al., 2005) deviate from this research.

Intuition outperforms deliberation in frequency estimates when the following conditions are met. The relevant information has to be encoded completely or a representative sample of the information has to be encoded. In this case, the IFR mirrors the distribution of events in the environment so that a judgment based on the IFR will lead to a highly accurate estimation. In addition, another condition has to be satisfied to arrive at a valid IFR: The relevant category has to be activated during encoding so that the IFR can be formed for the respective category. For example, if "rose" has been encoded as a flower (and not as a girl's name), an IFR for "flowers" will be built, and the occurrence of "rose" will be aggregated in this IFR. Consequently, if later on an estimate for "girls' names" is asked for, participants will not be able to retrieve a valid IFR because the category has not been activated during encoding. The information "rose" cannot retrospectively be recoded as an input for this new, nonexistent IFR. Thus, the estimate for "girls' names" will not mirror the actual frequencies (Betsch, Siebler, et al., 1999). These two conditions are necessary to form a valid IFR. Relying on the first guess maximizes the probability that this information is used in the judgment so that under these conditions, intuitive judgments outperform deliberation.

REFERENCES

Alba, J. W., Chromiak, W., Hasher, L., & Attig, M. S. (1980). Automatic encoding of category size information. *Journal of Experimental Psychology: Human Learning and Memory, 6*, 370–378.

Bernoulli, D. (1954). Expositions of a new theory on the measurement of risk. *Econometrica, 22*, 23–26. (Original work published 1738)

Betsch, T., Brinkmann, J., Fiedler, K., & Breining, K. (1999). When prior knowledge overrules new evidence: Adaptive use of decision strategies and the role of behavioral routines. *Swiss Journal of Psychology, 58*, 151–160.

Betsch, T., Plessner, H., & Schallies, E. (2004). The value-account model for attitude formation. In G. R. Maio & G. Haddock (Eds.), *Contemporary perspectives on the psychology of attitudes* (pp. 252–273). Hove, England: Psychology Press.

Betsch, T., Plessner, H., Schwieren, C., & Gütig, R. (2001). I like it, but I don't know why: A value-account model to implicit attitude formation. *Personality and Social Psychology Bulletin, 27*, 242–253.

Betsch, T., Siebler, F., Marz, P., Hormuth, S., & Dickenberger, D. (1999). The moderating role of category salience and category focus in judgments of set size and frequency of occurrence. *Personality and Social Psychology Bulletin, 25*, 463–481.

Blair, E., & Burton, S. (1987). Cognitive processes used by survey respondents to answer behavioral frequency questions. *Journal of Consumer Research, 14*, 280–288.

Brooks, J. O., & Watkins, M. J. (1989). Recognition memory and the mere exposure effect. *Journal of Experimental Psychology: Learning, Memory, & Cognition, 15*, 968–976.

Brown, N. R. (1995). Estimation strategies and the judgment of event frequency. *Journal of Experimental Psychology: Learning, Memory and Cognition, 21*, 1539–1553.

Brown, N. R. (1997). Context memory and the selection of frequency estimation strategies. *Journal of Experimental Psychology: Learning, Memory and Cognition, 23*, 898–914.

Brown, N. R. (2002). Encoding, representing, and estimating event frequencies: A multiple strategy perspective. In P. Sedlmeier & T. Betsch (Eds.), *Etc. frequency processing and cognition* (pp. 37–53). Oxford, England: Oxford University Press.

Burton, S., & Blair, E. (1991). Task conditions, response formulation processes, and response accuracy for behavioral frequency questions in surveys. *Public Opinion Quarterly, 55*, 50–79.

Church, R. M. (1984). Properties of the internal clock. *Annals of the New York Academy of Sciences, 423*, 566–582.

Curt, C. L., & Zechmeister, E. B. (1984). Primacy, recency, and the availability heuristic. *Bulletin of the Psychonomic Society, 22*, 177–179.

Dougherty, M. R. P., & Franco-Watkins, A. (2002). A memory models approach to frequency and probability judgment: Applications of Minerva 2 and Minerva DM. In P. Sedlmeier & T. Betsch (Eds.), *Etc. frequency processing and cognition* (pp. 121–136). Oxford, England: Oxford University Press.

Dougherty, M. R. P., Gettys, C. F., & Ogden, E. (1999). Minerva DM: A memory process model for judgments of likelihood. *Psychological Review, 106*, 180–209.

Fechner, G. T. (1860). *Elemente der Psychophysik* [Elements of psychophysics]. Leipzig, Germany: Breitkopf & Hartel.

Fiedler, K. (1991). The tricky nature of skewed frequency distributions: An information loss account of distinctiveness-based illusory correlations. *Journal of Personality and Social Psychology, 60*, 24–36.

Gallistel, C. R., & Gelman, R. (1992). Preverbal and verbal counting and computation. *Cognition, 44*, 43–74.

Gibbon, J. (1992). Ubiquity of scalar timing with a Poisson clock. *Journal of Mathematical Psychology, 36*, 283–293.

Greenwald, A. G., & Banaji, M. R. (1995). Implicit social cognition: Attitudes, self-esteem, and stereotypes. *Psychological Review, 102*, 4–27.

Haberstroh, S., & Betsch, T. (2002). Online strategies versus memory-based strategies in frequency estimation. In P. Sedlmeier & T. Betsch (Eds.), *Etc. frequency processing and cognition* (pp. 205–220). Oxford, England: Oxford University Press.

Haberstroh, S., & Betsch, T. (2003). [Manipulating degree of deliberation by time pressure and payment]. Unpublished raw data.

Haberstroh, S., Betsch, T., & Aarts, H. (2005). *The role of deliberation in frequency judgments*. Manuscript submitted for publication.

Hasher, L., & Zacks, R. T. (1979). Automatic and effortful processes in memory. *Journal of Experimental Psychology: General, 108*, 356–388.

Hasher, L., & Zacks, R. T. (1984). Automatic processing of fundamental information: The case of frequency of occurrence. *American Psychologist, 12*, 1372–1388.

Hintzman, D. L. (1969). Apparent frequency as a function of frequency and the spacing of repetitions. *Journal of Experimental Psychology, 80*, 139–145.

Hintzman, D. L., & Curran, T. (1994). Retrieval dynamics of recognition and frequency judgments: Evidence for separate processes of familiarity and recall. *Journal of Memory & Language, 33*, 1–18.

Hogarth, R. (2001). *Educating intuition*. Chicago: The University of Chicago Press.

Kahneman, D., Slovic, P., & Tversky, A. (1982). *Judgments under uncertainty: Heuristics and Biases*. New York: Cambridge University Press.

Lee, A. Y. (2001). The mere exposure effect: An uncertainty reduction explanation revisited. *Personality and Social Psychology Bulletin, 27*, 1255–1266.

Lewandowsky, S., & Smith, P. W. (1983). The effect of increasing the memorability of category instances on estimates of category size. *Memory & Cognition, 11*, 347–350.

Luwel, K., & Verschaffel, L. (2003). Adapting strategy choices to situational factors: The effect of time pressure on children's numerosity judgement strategies. *Psychologica Belgica, 43*, 269–295.

Luwel, K., Verschaffel, L., Onghena, P., & de Corte, E. (2003). Strategic aspects of numerosity judgment: The effect of task characteristics. *Experimental Psychology, 50*, 63–75.

Payne, J. W., Bettman, J. R., & Johnson, E. J. (1988). Adaptive strategy selection in decision making. *Journal of Experimental Psychology: Learning, Memory and Cognition, 14*, 534–552.

Payne, J. W., Bettman, J. R., & Johnson, E. J. (1993). *The adaptive decision maker*. Cambridge, England: Cambridge University Press.

Reder, L. M. (1987). Strategy selection in question answering. *Cognitive Psychology, 19*, 90–138.

Schwarz, N. (1989). Accessible content and accessibility experiences: The interplay of declarative and experiential information in judgment. *Personality & Social Psychology Review, 2*, 87–99.

Sedlmeier, P., & Betsch, T. (Eds.). (2002). *Etc. frequency processing and cognition.* Oxford, England: Oxford University Press.

Sedlmeier, P., Hertwig, R., & Gigerenzer, G. (1998). Are judgments of the positional frequencies of letters systematically biased due to availability? *Journal of Experimental Psychology: Learning, Memory, and Cognition, 24,* 754–770.

Siegler, R. S. (1987). Strategy choices in subtraction. In J. A. Sloboda & D. Rogers (Eds.), *Cognitive processes in mathematics* (pp. 81–106). Oxford, England: Clarendon Press.

Svenson, O., & Maule, A. J. (Eds.). (1993). *Time pressure and stress in human judgment and decision making.* London: Plenum.

Tversky, A. (1972). Elimination by aspects: A theory of choice. *Psychological Review, 79,* 281–299.

Tversky, A., & Kahneman, D. (1973). Availability: A heuristic for judging frequency and probability. *Cognitive Psychology, 5,* 207–232.

Tversky, A., & Kahneman, D. (1974). Judgment under uncertainty: Heuristics and biases. *Science, 185,* 1124–1130.

Underwood, B. J. (1969). Attributes of memory. *Psychological Review, 76,* 559–573.

Watkins, M. J., & LeCompte, D. C. (1991). Inadequacy of recall as a basis for frequency knowledge. *Journal of Experimental Psychology: Learning, Memory, and Cognition, 17,* 1161–1176.

Weber, E. H. (1834, 1996). De tactu. Annotationes anatomicae et physiologicae. Leipzig: Koehler. Translated in H.E. Ross & D.J. Murray (1996) (Eds) E.H. Weber on the tactile senses. 2nd edition. Hove (UK): Erlbaum; Taylor & Francis.

Whalen, J., Gallistel, C. R., & Gelman, R. (1999). Nonverbal counting in humans: The psychophysics of number representation. *Psychological Science, 10,* 130–137.

Zacks, R. T., & Hasher, L. (2002). Frequency processing: A twenty-five year perspective. In P. Sedlmeier & T. Betsch (Eds.), *Etc. frequency processing and cognition* (pp. 21–36). Oxford, England: Oxford University Press.

Zajonc, R. B. (1968). Attitudinal effects of mere exposure. *Journal of Personality and Social Psychology, 9*(Suppl. 2, Pt. 2).

Zajonc, R. B. (1980). Feeling and thinking: Preferences need no inferences. *American Psychologist, 35,* 151–175.

17

The Sampling Trap of Intuitive Judgments

CHRISTIAN UNKELBACH and HENNING PLESSNER

University of Heidelberg

INTRODUCTION

There is good evidence that intuitive judgments can be superior to or at least as good as deliberative judgments even if one is to take objective criteria as a benchmark (Plessner & Czenna, chap. 15, this volume). In this chapter, however, we deal with the limitations of intuitive judgments. We approach this topic by considering the sampling processes that have been proposed to underlie social judgments (Fiedler, 2000). From this perspective, we address the following question: When should people trust their intuition and when not?

To do so, at first it is necessary to discuss shortly how and when intuitive judgments can be superior to deliberate judgments; that is, if one takes normatively correct decisions as a standard, how is it possible that if one has the necessary information and the appropriate integration rules that a suboptimal decision or judgment is reached? As a starting example, we consider the case of a female teacher who has to grade her students for the last year. The information is available (e.g., the grades in the written exams of the last year), and the integration rule is simple (e.g., the mean of these grades). However, there is also the oral performance during class of the students that has to be considered in the final grade. Now the situation differs in the respect that not all the information is directly available. Our teacher could now employ a deliberative strategy and try to remember as much as possible of each student's classroom performance, mentally grade the performances, and then average across these mental grades to form a judgment about the overall oral performance. Yet, such memory-based judgments have been shown to be prone to a multitude of biases (Hastie & Park, 1986).

A student's good test performance might cue the memory for good oral performances (e.g., Cooper, 1981), the very first and the more recent episodes have a memory advantage and might be unduly weighted (e.g., Schwarz & Strack, 1991), or the information search is truncated too early (e.g., Wyer & Srull, 1989). Even more, the mental effort to employ this strategy is enormous and probably beyond the average mental capacity of the working memory (Baddeley, 1994). A more parsimonious strategy would be if the teacher made an intuitive judgment about the student's oral performance, if we follow Haidt's (2001) definition of *intuition* as "the sudden appearance in consciousness of a . . . judgment, including an affective valence (good–bad, like–dislike), without any conscious awareness of having gone through steps of searching, weighting evidence, of inferring a conclusion" (p. 818). In accordance with the theoretical work of Hogarth (2001) and others (cf. T. Betsch, chap. 1, this volume), we believe that this spontaneous appearance is based on an implicit or automatic part of the human cognitive system, which, in contrast to the willful and controllable part, stores the full stream of experiences and information that is offered to the organism. Whereas the controllable part is subject to the limitations of the working memory or the attention span, this implicit part works without these limitations. Again, the literature on intuitive judgments and decisions has demonstrated that there are many occasions when the latter, the intuitive judgment, is a preferable strategy just because the underlying mechanisms have fewer limitations than the mechanisms that serve a deliberative strategy. In this example, an intuitive strategy would save the teacher a lot of effort and would possibly avoid the judgmental biases that come into play if a judgment is made deliberatively. However, to rephrase the initial question, how can the teacher know whether she should follow a deliberate or an intuitive strategy given that she wants the most accurate and fair assessment of a student's performance? Can she trust her intuition? To answer that question, we introduce the sampling theory of inductive (i.e., based on input from the environment) social judgments by Fiedler (2000).

APPLYING A SAMPLING THEORY TO INTUITIVE JUDGMENTS

Many social judgments, intuitive or deliberative, are concerned with latent attributes that are not directly available for assessment, for example, the ability of a student, the talent of an athlete, or the prospect of a company's shares on the stock market. Although everyday language sometimes foils people into believing that they can actually measure and judge these constructs, they are distal and need to be inferred from proximal information (Brunswik, 1957). The available proximal information for a student's ability might be the student's grades in written exams; for an athlete, it might be a performance in a competition; and for a company's shares, it might be the average return on investment in the last year. Note, however, that these informational instances represent by no means attributes such as "ability" or "talent" themselves. What people use to judge these attributes is a sample of information that links the hidden properties of the environment with the cognitive mechanisms that are concerned with judgment formation (Fiedler, 2000). For example, if the task is to estimate the probability of having a car accident given that the driver is drunk, one might immediately think of all the reported cases when alcohol was involved in car accidents. Yet the actual number of people who drive intoxicated and do not have an accident is not accessible just because only accidents are reported but not nonaccidents. Therefore, it is impossible to know whether the probability estimated from the available sample is accurate. Thus, people have to rely on the information they have, what we call a sample of information. Therefore, to get an accurate representation of the environment and its properties, people need representative and applicable samples of information. However, in many cases, the interplay of environment and cognition does not allow for representative samples, as in the case when all drunk people who get home safely with their car do not show up in any statistics.

Let us apply this approach to the teacher's problem of her student's final grades. In the case of written exams, the mean of the grades from the last year should be exactly the representative and applicable sample that is needed. Far more interesting is the case of oral performances when the necessary information is not readily available but needs to be sampled from memory. Intuitive judgments might be superior in this case because they are based on the full stream of information, which by design should be more representative of the environment than deliberatively constructed information samples. To reiterate, deliberation necessarily needs to be selective, mainly due to the limitations of the working memory (Baddeley, 1994; Dijksterhuis, 2004; Kareev, 2000), but also because retrieval of information is often biased or because information is just not willfully accessible at the time of judgment (e.g., Schwarz, 1998).

For example, Fiedler, Walther, Freytag, and Plessner (2002) had participants teach a virtual school class of 16 students over an extended time period. Participants could select questions for the students and got feedback whether a called-on student gave a correct or incorrect answer to a selected question. The provided information amount was enormous, and basically none of the participants could deliberately remember many singular instances of correct and incorrect answers. The awarded grades, however, reflected clearly the information they had sampled about the students during their teaching without deliberately remembering or integrating the presented information. This example represents then the case in which the sample of prior experiences is perfectly applicable for the judgment task at hand.

THE SAMPLING TRAP

When judging the performance of students, a teacher's experience in the classroom might be as good a sample as it gets; and as research has shown, people are remarkably sensitive to the information in a sample (Fiedler, Brinkmann, Betsch, & Wild, 2000; Fiedler et al., 2002). However, there is also the case when the prior experiences that are implicitly stored and on which the intuitive judgment is presumably based are not applicable for the judgment at hand. Then, the exact great sensitivity of implicit cognition and the accuracy of automatic data integration, which leads to good intuitive judgments, work against judgment accuracy just because the sample of information is not applicable. The easiest case of such non-applicability is given when prior experiences are not representative; as the statistical metaphor of sampling suggests, samples need to be representative for the population of interest to make valid inferences. To illustrate that case, imagine you had to judge the talent of a soccer player. Again, talent is a distal variable that cannot be assessed directly but needs to be inferred from proximal information. For a soccer player, this information might be direct observations obtained during games the player participated in, news reports about the players, or word of mouth from other people. Even if we stay with the probably most unbiased source of information, firsthand observations, the sample is constrained in the respect that the game might be against a weak opponent, resulting in an excellent performance, or against a very strong opponent, resulting in a poor performance. So, after watching either one of these two games, the experience is constrained by the strength of the opponent. We suspect that intuitive judgments, however, do not correct for such constraints. That is, the automatic part of the cognitive system that serves as input for intuitive judgments is metacognitively blind for any constraints that can make a sample of prior experiences not applicable for a given judgment task at hand (Fiedler & Wänke, 2004).

EXPERIMENTAL EVIDENCE 1: JUDGING JAN SIMAK

To test this assumption, we used a well-documented effect in social psychology research, the category-split effect: When people estimate the frequency of instances in a social category, the overall estimate is higher when the category is split into smaller subcategories (Fiedler & Armbruster, 1994; Rottenstreich & Tversky, 1997; Van Boven & Epley, 2003). For example, if participants are asked how many Japanese cars there are on an average German highway, they give lower estimates compared to the question of how many Honda, Mitsubishi, Toyota, and Mazda cars there are. The category Japanese cars is split into subcategories or instances of the superordinate category. In terms of the sampling approach, we could say that splitting a category results in a far richer sample of proximal cues to estimate the actual distal frequency in the population. So far, this is not problematic because there is no reference point. However, if people are asked whether there are more American cars or more Honda, Mitsubishi, and Toyota cars on an average German highway, they should realize that the informational cues that serve as input for the judgment are far more constraining for the American cars than for the Japanese cars. Note in particular that all things being equal, the estimate for American cars should be relatively higher than the estimate for Japanese cars just because the superordinate category encompasses all American cars, whereas only specific types of Japanese cars are asked. The actual instances of Japanese cars, however, provide judges with a richer experiential sample to use in their judgment. Again, intuitive judgments are most likely blind to such manipulations of data generation, and therefore, judgments should vary systematically with the number of subcategories provided.

We employed the described procedure not for judgments about mere frequency but for judgments about the quality of an athlete (Unkelbach & Plessner, 2007). The basic idea was that splitting the positive features of an athlete should result in a more favorable judgment when the negative features are not split and vice versa when the negative features are split and the positive features are not. The athlete of our choice was Jan Simak, a striker in the team of Hannover 96, at that time a German second-league soccer club. His positive feature was his excellent technical skill, and his negative feature was a lack of physical fitness. Our participants were 40 sport coaches from the vicinity of Heidelberg, Germany, who were recruited for an experiment "concerning the ability of sport coaches to judge sportsmen." As basis for the judgment, we compiled a presentation about Jan Simak, which—besides some background information about age, former clubs, and so forth—contained an equal amount of positive and negative information: The former always related to his technical skill, the latter always related to his lacking fitness. After participants saw this presentation, the crucial category-split manipulation followed. This manipulation was embedded in a simple questionnaire. Half of the participants were assigned to a positive split condition and were asked about Jan Simak's passing game, dribbling, shots, and ball security, all items that actually appeared in the presentation and fell under the general category of technical skill. However, the actual amount of information about his technical skill was larger than these four items. In comparison, they were asked about Jan Simak's physical fitness in general. The remaining participants were assigned to a negative split condition and evaluated his technical skill in general, whereas the category physical fitness was split into the instances of speed, jump, stamina, and aggressiveness; again, all these items actually appeared in the presentation but represented only a subset of all the information that was given. Nevertheless, splitting the category into subcategories should provide a richer experiential sample as a basis for the judgment. Finally, the dependent variables were assessed. First, participants were asked to evaluate Jan Simak's quality as a soccer player on a 9-point scale ranging from 1 (*very poor*) to 9 (*very good*). Second, participants were asked whether they would hypothetically hire Jan Simak for their team, again on a scale ranging from 1 (*for sure*) to 9 (*not ever*). The results are displayed in Figure 17.1. Given that the positive category was split, judges evaluated Jan Simak more positively and expressed greater interest in buying him for their own team. Note that all judges had the same information from the initial presentation, and the non-split category in both conditions actually contained more possible information. Yet, splitting the category provided a richer experiential sample to base the judgment on. As we suspected, participants were blind for this sampling manipulation and did not correct their judgment accordingly. Interestingly, this unjustified reversal of judgments might be due to the full use of all the available experiences, which usually creates an advantage for intuitive judgments. Thereby, category split represents a nice example of how a sample of information might not be representative for the underlying distribution (in this case, the original presentation) but is still uncritically used in judgments.

In the case of the sport coaches, we could clearly show that strategic manipulations of the information samples, using the category-split effect, results in biased

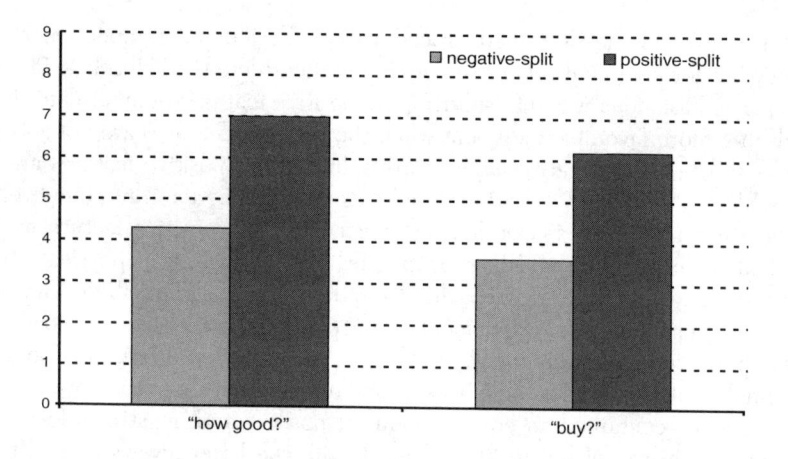

FIGURE 17.1 Mean judgments of the sport coaches on how good Jan Simak is and whether they would buy him for a soccer team. Note that for reasons of clarity, for both ratings, higher values indicate a more positive evaluation. The difference between the positive and negative split conditions is highly reliable for both ratings, multivariate $F(2, 35) = 16.07$, $p < .001$.

judgments. This bias is not introduced by faulty cognitive processes (such as availability, halo-effects, etc.; see previous discussion), to which intuitive judgments should be immune, but by the simple nonrepresentative nature of the provided sample for the underlying distribution. This leads to the paradoxical situation that the judgments were the more biased the more the information from a sample of experiences was used. Yet, Unkelbach and Plessner (2007) used an almost unfair strategy to bias the information sample, that is, to make it nonapplicable. Maybe, when the strategic manipulation is more blatant, people might be able to metacognitively control whether their experiences are appropriate for a given task and thereby escape the trap that is set by the structure of the cognitive system. Or maybe people are doomed to always use their experiences when making intuitive judgments; after all, they are based on implicit knowledge and often operationalized as spontaneous judgments (Betsch, chap. 1, this volume).

EXPERIMENTAL EVIDENCE 2: REPETITION EFFECTS

The most obvious way to manipulate the experiential sample is the mere repetition of information. For example, if you watch a news show on TV and later you see a videotaped version of the exact same show, you do not learn anything new, nor is there a gain in validity of the information. This emptiness of repeated information was already noted by Wittgenstein (1955/1977) who gave the example of a person who is "buying several copies of the morning paper to ensure that the content is true" (p. 147). If the implicit learning process that is presumably responsible for the effectiveness of intuitive judgments is sensitive regarding manipulations of the information sample, it should be visible in the case of artificial inflation through repetition. However, if the underlying mechanism is indeed blind for these constraints, and the show presents good news about, for example, the performance of a company, your spontaneous evaluation of this company should be more positive after watching the show twice then only watching the show once. For sure, the reverse should be true for negative news.

To test whether people can monitor this information repetition, the same idea used in the example was implemented in an experiment with the following general outline (Unkelbach, Fiedler, & Freytag, 2007, Experiment 3): Participants were asked to take the perspective of a person who wants to invest money in the stock market. They were told to observe the market before choosing a stock for their investment. They were presented with a fictitious setting in which information about the stock market was provided by two consecutive evening news shows, which presented identical information about the performance of 10 different shares on the market. For reasons of simplicity, the performance information was dichotomous—either a share gained value on a given day or it did not. Participants watched the news for a simulated time of 16 days and evaluated the shares afterwards. The crucial manipulation was whether participants watched only one or both shows for a given day. Thus, a very complex information environment was created that required observing 10 shares for 16 simulated days, including the repetition of information on some of these days. The reasoning underlying this design is as follows: If people can metacognitively escape the sampling trap, there should be no difference between shares that gained value on a day when both shows were watched compared to shows when only one of the shows was watched. However, if, as Unkelbach et al. (2007) suspected, implicit learning is blind to such sampling constraints as repetition, shares that gained value on days when both shows were watched should be preferred compared to shares that gained value when only one show was watched. In other words, are the preference ratings for the shares a function of the number of days a share gains value or are the preferences a function of the number of days plus the repetition of this information on some of the days?

To investigate this, Unkelbach et al. (2007) created a distribution of the days the 10 shares (Numbers 1 to 10) gained values that pitted shares with the same number of "winning days" but with different repetition days against each other. Even more, some shares were only seen as winners on days with two news shows, whereas other shares only gained value when there was only one news show, thereby creating pairs of shares in which the actual better share was seen less often as a winner in the 16-days sample. Three shares gained value on 8 days (i.e., 1 to 3), four gained value on 6 days (i.e., 4 to 7), and the remaining three gained value on only 4 days (i.e., 8 to 10). These three sets represented the only actual and valid difference between the shares. Within each set, there should be no difference in preferences. However, in each set, one share gained value only on days with repetition (i.e., when both shows were watched; 1, 4, and 8), and one share gained value only on days without repetition (i.e., when one show was watched; 3, 7, and 10). The remaining shares of each set were equally distributed across repetition and nonrepetition days (i.e., 2, 5, 6, and 9), resulting in the distribution visible in the lower part of Figure 17.2.

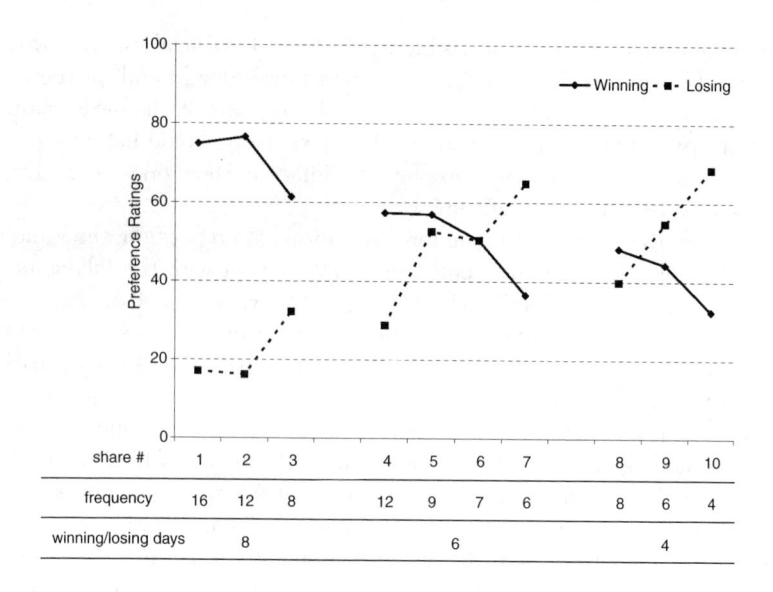

Figure 17.2 Mean liking judgments of participants for 10 shares with varying days of winning and presentation frequency of that information. Higher preference ratings indicate a more positive evaluation. All visible effects for frequency and number of winning/losing days are statistically reliable.

In this experiment (Unkelbach et al., 2007), 68 students of the University of Heidelberg participated, and after watching the news shows over the simulated 16 days, they provided preference ratings for the 10 different shares. As already mentioned, they were informed that their task would be to make judgments about shares on the stock market. To do so, they would have the chance to watch the stock report of two news shows over a simulated time of 16 days. On half of the days, either both shows were watched, thereby introducing repetition of the same information, and on the remaining 8 days, only one show was watched. It was ensured that all participants understood the fact that the second news show on the same day represents only repeated information and does not offer any valid, additional information. After this observation phase, participants rated how much they liked each share individually using a scale ranging from 0 (*not at all*) to 100 (*very much*).

These ratings provide a clear answer to the question whether people can metacognitively control the representativeness or applicability of a provided information sample. The general pattern is presented with the solid winning lines in Figure 17.2. First, although the information environment was very complex, participants clearly distinguished between the three sets of shares (i.e., shares that gained value on 8, 6, or 4 days). As can be seen, on average, the 8-day shares ($M = 70.93$) received the highest preference ratings followed by the 6-day shares ($M = 50.23$) and the 4-day shares ($M = 41.81$). This linear trend was statistically highly reliable and reflected the actual properties of the presented information environment. More interestingly, within each set, those shares that were seen more often as winners, although this increase was artificially created by mere repetition, were preferred over shares without this presentation repetition. All the linear trends for the presentation frequency within the three sets were highly reliable. Even more, for Shares 7 and 8, there was a significant reversal of the preferences such that Share 8, actually the better share, was preferred less than Share 7, which appeared only on repetition days, whereas the former share appeared only on nonrepetition days. Thus, the evaluations of the shares were influenced as predicted by the higher frequency of positive information in the experiential sample, although this increase was created by an obvious and blatant manipulation, the simple repetition of information. People seem to be unable to monitor whether the information sample on which their judgment is based is directly applicable for the task at hand or if correction is called for. In other words, participants in this experiment relied uncritically on their experiences, although they knew that these were strategically manipulated.

One might argue that this preference for shares that were presented more frequently is due to a mere exposure effect. Zajonc (1968) and Monahan, Murphy, and Zajonc (2000) have shown convincingly that people prefer stimuli (people, Chinese ideograms, etc.) to which they were previously exposed. Although such a mechanism, which is generally of adaptive value, might also contribute to intuitive judgments, it offers a different explanation than the presented sampling approach. To show that it is indeed the uncritical use of an information sample that is responsible, Unkelbach et al. (2007) replicated the experiment with only a minor change: Instead of days a share gained in value, that is, participants were now told that they would receive binary information whether a share lost value on a given day or not.

In this experiment (Unkelbach et al., 2007, Exp. 2), 20 additional students from the University of Heidelberg participated, and the results are presented by the dotted lines in Figure 17.2. As Figure 17.2 shows, the results were an almost perfect reversal of the data obtained when the presentation frequency refers to winning rather than to losing days. Now, participants liked the 4-day shares best ($M = 54.35$) followed by the 6-day shares ($M = 49.21$) and the 8-day shares ($M = 21.32$). In addition, within each of these sets, there was the same linear trend to prefer the high frequency shares as in the experiment with winning shares but in the reverse direction. From this data, we are safe to conclude that it was not a mere exposure effect, which should influence preference independently from the accompanying predicate (i.e., whether the occurrence means that the share lost or gained value). Rather, the more likely candidate is the uncritical use of the available information sample. Again, in both studies (Unkelbach et al., 2007; Unkelbach & Plessner, 2007), participants showed a remarkable sensitivity to the provided information—however, they were almost blind to the constraints imposed on the generation of this sample, even in the most blatant case of mere information repetition.

DISCUSSION

Our starting assumption was that intuitive judgments can be superior to deliberative judgments because they utilize the full stream of information from past experiences (Plessner & Czenna, chap. 15, this volume). Whereas deliberative judgments are prone to all sorts of biases in the process of information encoding, storage, retrieval, and integration, intuitive judgments circumvent many of these possible biases. However, there is a lack of control whether the information that is presumably used by an intuitive judgmental process is really applicable for the task at hand. In other words, although the information provided in an environmental sample is fully and correctly utilized, there exists a metacognitive myopia regarding the constraints of the respective sample (Fiedler, 2000; Fiedler & Freytag, 2004; Fiedler &Wänke, 2004). In this chapter, we shortly outlined two such cases in which the provided information sample was not representative of the underlying information distribution; and the results show clearly that albeit the information was strategically manipulated, there is no correction process for the constraints imposed on the experiential samples: neither when the constraints were subtle as with the category-split effect (Unkelbach & Plessner, 2007), nor when the constraints were blatant as with the repetition effect (Unkelbach, Fiedler, & Freytag, 2007). Thus, when an information sample is not applicable for a given judgment task, this leads to the paradoxical situation that the final judgments are the more biased the more fully and accurately the sample is utilized. The amazing capability of intuition to arrive at correct conclusions from vast amounts of data, usually too vast to process it deliberatively mostly because the attention span and working capacity of conscious thought is limited (Dijksterhuis, 2004), has now been demonstrated in many studies (e.g., Betsch, Plessner, Schwieren, & Gütig, 2001; Lewicki, Hill, & Czyzewska, 1992). Despite the often astonishing accuracy of automatic processing and intuitive judgments, we believe that the underlying cognitive processes are blind to important constraints of the processed information sample (but see also Sedlmeier, 2006). Blatant constraints are, for example, the repetition or the negation of information, but more subtle constraints, which are due to the interplay of the cognitive system and the structural properties of the environment on the other side (e.g., the example of driving drunk and having an accident), might even go totally unnoticed.

CONCLUSIONS: HOW TO ESCAPE THE SAMPLING TRAP?

Human cognition seems to be very sensitive to all the information that is presented as input; this input, as far as our and others' research has demonstrated, seems almost impossible to control for constraints that are imposed on it. Thus, the spontaneous valence-laden judgments that emerge spontaneously as intuition based on this input cannot be regulated metacognitively. Yet, whether one uses this impression for judgments, and even more important for behavior, is open to control. The initial question, whether to trust intuition, can now be reframed as to whether one has the appropriate sample of experience for the task at hand. The teacher from the beginning example is probably well off when she is making an intuitive judgment concerning the oral performance of her students. Her experience covers a large sample of information that is as applicable as it gets, thereby representing a case in which intuitive judgments might be superior to deliberation in assessing the true properties of the environment. The sport coaches, however, are advised to take a sketch pad and keep close track of their observations and experiences. Especially small samples have a good chance to convey biased samples of information just as small samples in statistics are less reliable than large samples (but see also Fiedler & Kareev, chap. 10, this volume). The extreme case was provided in the experiments we discussed involving the repetition effect: Although people cannot help the immediate impression that winning shares with repetition are better than without repetition, they should not use this immediate and effortless judgment.

In the end, the way to escape the sampling trap of intuitive judgments is the same as for deliberative judgments, namely, to decide whether your information sample is applicable for the task. Interestingly, this leads again to two ways in which people can make this decision. They could trust or distrust their intuition intuitively or deliberatively: the latter when they have no experience with their own intuitive judgments and the former when they have the experiences with previous intuitive decisions, given that the sample of experiences is appropriate for the task, that is.

REFERENCES

Baddeley, A. (1994). The magical number seven: Still magic after all these years? *Psychological Review, 101,* 353–356.

Betsch, T., Plessner, H., Schwieren, C., & Gütig, R. (2001). I like it but I don't know why: A value-account approach to implicit attitude formation. *Personality and Social Psychology Bulletin, 27,* 242–253.

Brunswik (1957). Scope and aspects of the cognitive problem. In H. Gruber, K. R. Hammond, & R. Jessor (Eds.), *Contemporary approaches to cognition* (pp. 5–31). Cambridge, MA: Harvard University Press.

Cooper, W. H. (1981). Ubiquitous halo. *Psychological Bulletin, 90,* 218–244.

Dijksterhuis, A. (2004). Think different: The merits of unconscious thought in preference development and decision making. *Journal of Personality and Social Psychology, 87,* 586–598.

Fiedler, K. (2000). Beware of samples! A cognitive-ecological sampling approach to judgment biases. *Psychological Review, 107,* 659–676.

Fiedler, K., & Armbruster, T. (1994). Two halfs may be more than one whole: Category-split effects on frequency illusions. *Journal of Personality and Social Psychology, 66,* 633–645.

Fiedler, K., Brinkmann, B., Betsch, T., & Wild, B. (2000). A sampling approach to biases in conditional probability judgments: Beyond base rate neglect and statistical format. *Journal of Experimental Psychology: General, 129,* 399–418.

Fiedler, K., & Freytag, P. (2004). Pseudocontingencies. *Journal of Personality and Social Psychology, 87,* 453–467.

Fiedler, K., Walther, E., Freytag, P., & Plessner, H. (2002). Judgment biases in a simulated classroom—A cognitive-environmental approach. *Organizational Behavior & Human Decision Processes, 88,* 527–561.

Fiedler, K., & Wänke, M. (2004). On the vicissitudes of cultural and evolutionary approaches to social cognition: The case of meta-cognitive myopia. *Journal of Cultural and Evolutionary Psychology, 2,* 23–42.

Haidt, J. (2001). The emotional dog and its rational tail: A social intuitionist approach to moral judgment. *Psychological Review, 108,* 814–834.

Hastie, R., & Park, B. (1986). The relationship between memory and judgment depends on whether the judgment task is memory-based or on-line. *Psychological Review, 93,* 258–268.

Hogarth, R. M. (2001). *Educating intuition.* Chicago: University of Chicago Press.

Kareev, Y. (2000). Seven (indeed, plus or minus two) and the detection of correlations. *Psychological Review, 107,* 397–403.

Lewicki, P., Hill, T., & Czyzewska, M. (1992). Nonconscious acquisition of information. *American Psychologist, 47,* 796–801.

Monahan, J. L., Murphy, S. T., & Zajonc, R. B. (2000). Subliminal mere exposure: Specific, general, and diffuse effects. *Psychological Science, 11,* 462–466.

Rottenstreich, Y., & Tversky, A. (1997). Unpacking, repacking, and anchoring: Advances in support theory. *Psychological Review, 104,* 406–415.

Schwarz, N. (1998). Accessible content and accessibility experiences: The interplay of declarative and experiential information in judgment. *Personality and Social Psychology Review, 2,* 87–99.

Schwarz, N., & Strack, F. (1991). Context effects in attitude surveys: Applying cognitive theory to social research. In W. Stroebe & M. Hewstone (Eds.), *European review of social psychology* (Vol. 2, pp. 31–50). Sussex, England: Wiley.

Sedlmeier, P. (2006). Intuitive judgments about sample size. In K. Fielder & P. Juslin (Eds.), *Information sampling and adaptive cognition* (pp. 53–71). Cambridge, England: Cambridge University Press.

Unkelbach, C., Fiedler, K., & Freytag, P. (2007). *Information repetition in evaluative judgments: Easy to monitor, hard to control. Organizational Behavior and Human Decision Process, 103,* 37–52.

Unkelbach, C., & Plessner, H. (2007). "Category-Split" bei Urteilen über Sportlerinnen, Sportler und Sportarten. [Category-split in judgments about sports and athletes]. *Zeitschrift für Sozialpsychologie, 38,* 111–121.

Van Boven, L., & Epley, N. (2003). The unpacking effect in evaluative judgments: When the whole is less than the sum of its parts. *Journal of Experimental Social Psychology, 39,* 263–269.

Wittgenstein, L. (1977). *Philosohpische Untersuchungen* [Philosphical investigations]. Frankfurt, Germany: Suhrkamp. (Original work published 1955)

Wyer, R. S., & Srull, T. K. (1989). *Memory and cognition in its social context.* Hillsdale, NJ: Lawrence Erlbaum Associates, Inc.

Zajonc, R. B. (1968). Attitudinal effects of mere exposure. *Journal of Personality & Social Psychology, 9,* 1–27.

18

The Use and Disruption of Familiarity in Intuitive Judgments

STEVE CATTY and JAMIN HALBERSTADT

University of Otago

INTRODUCTION

*I*ntuition has become the "black box" of modern psychology. By their very nature, intuitive judgments elude analysis; although many people share a cultural understanding of what it is to be intuitive, describing, quantifying, and modeling the process of intuition have proved to be much more difficult. Indeed, early models of cognition ignored intuition altogether, postulating that all judgments were based on reasoned, statistically analytic processes (e.g., Janis & Mann, 1977; von Neumann & Morgenstern, 1944). Gradually, however, intuition has become more and more central in the understanding of cognitive processes (T. Betsch, chap. 1, this volume).

Recent treatments of intuition have attempted to characterize it as a distinct "mode" of processing qualitatively different from analytic thought. For example, one such "dual-processing" model postulates one mode of cognition that provides reflexive, intuitive answers and a parallel mode that deliberatively analyzes possible outcomes (Gilbert, 2002). More recent theory and research have suggested that the intuitive mode may be based on a small set of simple processes using easily accessible information, for example, making judgments based solely on whether the stimuli are recognized (Goldstein & Gigerenzer, 1999). At the same time, recent research on "reasons analysis" in social psychology has provided convergent data in the form of disruptions to affect and cognition caused by highly analytical judgment strategies.

In this chapter, we explore the nature of intuitive processes by drawing on these bodies of research. In our view, intuition is simply the use of subjective feeling states as direct cues to judgment, what Gigerenzer and Todd (1999) called "fast and frugal" or "simple" heuristics. In what follows, we first trace the evolution of simple heuristics as an answer to classical but cognitively implausible models of rationality, ultimately situating them in the context of more general dual-processing models of cognition. We then review the literature on reasons analysis and document the disruptive effects of analytic thought on attitude and judgment quality. Next, we attempt to understand reasons analysis effects in terms of simple heuristics theory and postulate in particular that analytic impairment occurs as the result of an overcomplication of judgments that would otherwise be inferred directly from subjective feeling states; and we report the results of two studies that illustrate the overcomplication effect. Finally, we evaluate the value of subjective familiarity as a mechanism of accurate intuition more generally.

A FOUNDATION FOR MODELING INTUITIVE JUDGMENTS

Common wisdom suggests that explicit analyses of decisions can only improve them; the more people deliberate on a decision—the more exhaustive a list of pros and cons they create—the better that decision will be and the more satisfied people will be with the decision they make. This assumption is formalized in classical models of rational choice in which individuals are "rational actors" who make a decision "by assessing the probability of each possible outcome, discerning the utility to be derived from each, and combining these two assessments. The option pursued is the one that offers the optimal combination of probability and utility" (Gilovich & Griffin, 2002, p. 1). The notions of optimal search and maximization of expected outcomes are pervasive assumptions of rational human behavior in psychology as well as other disciplines such as economics, law, and medicine. Their implication is that, for any given decision, a person accurately makes calculations of probability and multiattribute utility and that any deviations from these calculations are unsystematic errors.

Objecting to this classical model of rational choice, Simon (1957) recognized that human cognitive processing has limited capacity, hence the unlimited rationality implied by rational choice models sets an unrealistic standard for human cognition (Gilovich & Griffin, 2002). Simon (1957) introduced the concept of "bounded rationality" in which human rationality is expressed in psychologically plausible terms, emphasizing both humans' limited cognitive capacity and the strong influence of the structure of the environment in which their cognitive limitations evolved. As an alternative to the complex statistical computations leading to the optimal solution, as posited by the classical rational model, Simon introduced the notion of "satisficing." Rather than looking for the best of all available options relative to all relevant criteria, a "satisficer" searches for a solution that is satisfactory with respect to a single, subjective criterion. The change in focus from finding an optimal solution to finding a satisfactory one relieves the burden of unrealistic cognitive demand and thereby provides a more psychologically plausible and cognitively simple model of human decision making.

Following Simon's (1957) notion of bounded rationality, the simple heuristics program (Gigerenzer, Todd, & the ABC Research Group, 1999) described the human mind as an "adaptive toolbox," a collection of domain-specific, psychologically plausible, fast and frugal heuristics that have evolved to exploit the relationships between subjective internal cues and external reality. Proponents of this program have shown that just a handful of heuristics, all with simple searching, stopping, and decision rules, can perform as well as or better than normative models of cognition (such as Bayesian probability or linear regression) that use complex, compensatory methods of weighing all the different options to find an optimum solution (Gigerenzer & Goldstein, 1999). The crucial benefit of these simple heuristics is that they are psychologically plausible—that is, able to be implemented with limited time and capacity—and hence are ideal candidates for modeling human cognition (see also Raab & Johnson, chap. 8, this volume).

An exemplary set of studies by Goldstein and Gigerenzer (2002) have shown the use of the "recognition heuristic," the simplest of simple heuristics on which many of the relatively more complex heuristics are based. The recognition heuristic is used when deciding which of a set of objects is valued higher on some criterion (e.g., "which of these two books has sold more copies worldwide?") and states that "if one of two objects is recognized and the other is not, then infer that the recognized object has the higher value with respect to the criterion" (Goldstein & Gigerenzer, 2002, p. 76). For example, when asked which of two cities, Munich or Dortmund, has a higher population, a person who recognized Munich but not Dortmund would (correctly) infer that Munich has a higher population.

This heuristic firmly embodies the notion of bounded rationality by emphasizing both the limited cognitive capacity required to make apparently complex judgments and the critical importance of the structure of the environment in decision-making processes. Indeed, this heuristic can only work when there is a nonarbitrary relationship between the structure of the environment and people's sense of recognition with objects in that environment. Given this relationship, a decision maker requires no knowledge of the judgment criterion (e.g., the populations of Munich and Dortmund) but only awareness of their own subjective responses to the stimuli—whether either Munich or Dortmund feels familiar. Armed with only this subjective cue, a decision maker can make accurate intuitive judgments on stimuli in a complex environment by letting the relationship between the cue and the structure of the environment do the work.

DUAL-PROCESSING MODELS

Incorporating the simple heuristics program into the broader framework of a dual-processing model, we can develop a more sophisticated understanding of intuitive processes. Dual processing models of cognition, many of which are variations on Epstein's (e.g., 1994; chap. 2, this volume) foundational cognitive-experiential self-theory, have become prolific in recent years (e.g., Deutsch & Strack, chap. 3, this volume; Sloman, 1996). Epstein's (1994) theory proposes two fundamentally different modes of cognition: experiential processes that are personalized, affective, quick, and effortless and cognitive processes that are analytic, slow, and effortful.

Combining cognitive-experiential self-theory with its descendants, Stanovich and West (2002), used the more generic labels of "System 1" (experiential) and "System 2" (cognitive) processes in which System 1 processes represent those that are not deliberative but rather based on quicker, more reflexive processes less available to consciousness (Gilovich & Griffin, 2002). System 2 processes reflect the antithesis of System 1 processes and involve slow, rule-based information processing that requires high cognitive effort and systematic reasoning (Chaiken & Trope, 1999). Discussing the two systems, Stanovich and West (2002) noted that they fundamentally differ with regard to task construal—whereas System 1 tasks are "highly contextualized, personalized, and socialized," System 2 processes "serve to decontextualize and depersonalize problems" (p. 436).

In many versions of dual-processing theory, System 1 processes provide quick intuitive answers to judgments, and System 2 processes monitor these answers, correcting or overriding them as necessary. For example, Gill and Gilbert (1999, as cited in Gilbert, 2002) had participants rate adjectives describing their personality after completing a mood manipulation (listening to happy or sad music). Participants in a "hurried" condition were told to respond "as quickly as you can," whereas participants in an "unhurried" condition were told to "take your time and think carefully about your answers." Gill and Gilbert (1999, as cited in Gilbert, 2002) hypothesized that all participants would infer their personality from their current mood ("I'm tapping my toes and feeling pretty happy, so I guess I'm generally a happy person"), but when given time, they would correct these inferences ("Of course, I've just been listening to samba music, so maybe that's why I can't stop moving"); and results conformed to these expectations (Gilbert, 2002, p. 177). In terms of dual-processing theory, Gill and Gilbert's study (as cited in Gilbert, 2002) provides an example of the disruption (in this case, correction) of a heuristic, System 1 process (using current mood as a cue to infer the criterion of personality) by a controlled, analytic, System 2 process.

REASONS ANALYSIS

The adequacy of the classical model of rationality has also been challenged by a body of psychological research that has suggested that at least one type of System 2 process—explicitly analyzing the reasons for one's decision—can sometimes impair the decision relative to a nonreasoned or intuitive strategy. In a study representative of this research, Wilson et al. (1993) asked participants to evaluate two types of art posters, with half of the participants analyzing their reasons for their evaluations before providing them. Pretests had shown that one type of poster (impressionist paintings) was much more popular than the other type (humorous, "contemporary" posters), but in the main experiment, reasoning participants chose the humorous posters more often than controls and more often chose to take these posters home with them after the experiment. Immediately after the experiment, both reasoners and controls were equally satisfied with their choice of poster, but when contacted several weeks later, reasoners were significantly less satisfied with the poster they had selected than were controls, which showed a decrease in judgment quality after reasoning, at least when quality was measured by the participant's own satisfaction.

More controversially, there is also some evidence that reasoned judgments can be objectively worse than intuitive ones. Wilson and Schooler (1991, Study 1) found that people who analyzed their reasons for liking different brands of strawberry jam expressed preferences that corresponded less well to those of experts (i.e., taste testers at the magazine *Consumer Reports*), compared to people who did not analyze reasons. In a second study, participants were given information about psychology courses in which they could enroll the following semester. Compared to nonreasoners, reasoners recalled less of the information rated important by experts (i.e., faculty at the university) and were less likely to enroll in highly rated courses. Although there is some question in these studies as to the appropriateness of equating expert judgment and quality, Halberstadt and Green (2004) replicated the results in a domain with formal and systematic quality criteria: Olympic dives. In Halberstadt and Green's study, participants rated Olympic dives by watching video footage of eight individual dives from the 1996 Atlanta Summer Olympics representing a range of skill as indicated by the actual scores they received from Olympic judges. Participants rated the dives twice over and were asked to judge the dives as if they were the official Olympic judges, with reasons analysis as a within-subjects manipulation. Ratings made after performing reasons analysis were significantly poorer than those made without analysis, relative to the official scores given by Olympic judges. The within-subjects design, unusual for this type of research, was also able to show asymmetric effects of System 1 and System 2 processing. Reasons-based impairment carried over to subsequent judgments made under nonreasoning conditions, but intuitive judgments did not protect against subsequent reasoning. Analytic thought, in other words, impaired judgment accuracy regardless of when it occurred in the experiment.

Furthermore, Halberstadt and Levine (1999) found that reasoning impaired judgments with an incontrovertibly objective criterion for quality: the factual outcomes of basketball games. In this study, basketball experts (self-described) were asked to predict the winners and scores of 16 games in a national college basketball tournament in the United States. As in Halberstadt and Green's (2004) study, participants who analyzed their reasons made predictions that deviated further from experts' ratings than did controls' predictions. Furthermore, participants in the reasoning condition also chose the winning teams less often and predicted scores that deviated more extremely from the actual scores, which showed that reasoned predictions can be objectively worse than intuitive ones.

The most common explanation for the so-called reasons analysis effect (e.g., Wilson, Dunn, Kraft, & Lisle, 1989) is that reasoning changes the information on which an attitude is based. When people are asked to analyze the reasons for their attitude, they provide reasons they believe underlie the attitude in question. However, not having direct access to all (or any) of the reasons for an attitude, they instead provide reasons that are easiest to verbalize, most cognitively accessible, or most plausible (Nisbett & Wilson, 1977). They then report (and temporarily adopt) the attitude implied by this biased set of reasons. This process can be seen in Wilson and Schooler's (1991) poster study in which reasoning theoretically overemphasized the most verbalizable components of participants' attitudes toward the posters. These components favored the contemporary posters, leading to more positive attitudes and behaviour toward them. However, the influence of momentarily salient reasons diminished over time so that participants soon readopted their original (unreasoned) attitudes; and if their original attitudes conflicted with their behavior, participants were less satisfied with their selected posters. This account has also been used as an explanation for reasons analysis effects in studies using objective external criteria. Halberstadt and Levine (1999) proposed that the reasons brought to mind for which team would win a basketball game were the most verbalizable and cognitively accessible reasons for the judgment. If analyzed predictions were based on momentarily salient reasons, and if these reasons were biased toward the losing team, accuracy would be impaired.

REASONS ANALYSIS AS A DISRUPTION OF SIMPLE HEURISTICS

The "biased subset" account of reasons analysis effects has important implications for the nature of intuition. Implicitly, intuitive judgments are portrayed as being based on information and information processing too complex for the conscious, analytic mind to replicate. However, the simple heuristics and dual-processing models of cognition provide one with an alternative: that intuitive judgments are not highly complex but rather based on simple, affect-based, System 1, heuristic processes and that reasons analysis may simply represent a more deliberative, System 2 cognitive mode that overcomplicates these otherwise accurate intuitive judgments.

For example, Halberstadt and Levine's (1999) research on basketball predictions can be seen in terms of simple heuristic processes that are disrupted by reasons analysis. The most fundamental simple heuristic, recognition, could not itself have been used by participants in this study because all teams were presumably recognized, but a related cue, subjective familiarity, was available. Although familiarity data were not recorded in the study, a post hoc examination of proxies for familiarity indicated that participants could have used familiarity as a simple and effective cue in the experimental task. For example, the most recent year a team previously appeared in the tournament plausibly relates to the team's familiarity. For eight out of nine of the games discernible on this cue, the more familiar team won (an accuracy of .89). For the remaining seven games in the study, both teams appeared most recently in the same year and so were not discernible on this cue; but even if the winner of these remaining games was chosen randomly (with an accuracy of .5), this pseudofamiliarity heuristic achieves an accuracy of .69 across all games, which is very similar to the actual accuracy rates achieved by the expert participants in the study (reasoners = .652, control = .704). That a simple cue can predict such an objective and complex criterion as accurately as self-described experts is testimony to the potential power of simple heuristic processes. If participants' predictions in the Halberstadt and Levine study were based on a simple subjective cue similar to this familiarity proxy, analyzing their reasons could have disrupted the heuristic use of this cue and resulted in poorer performance. Understanding reasons analysis effects in this way provides both a plausible model of intuitive judgments, firmly grounded in Simon's (1957) notion of bounded rationality, as well as a clear explanation of why and when a reasoned decision will be systematically less accurate than an intuitive one.

EXPERIMENTAL INVESTIGATIONS

With the simple heuristics literature that has shown that people do use such simple cues in heuristic ways to make their judgments, what remains to be tested is whether reasons analysis can disrupt the use of these cues. Investigating this question experimentally, we conducted two studies in the domain of music popularity and looked at the use of a *familiarity heuristic*—a generalization of the recognition heuristic—as a simple System 1 process used in these judgments. Reasons analysis in this case, we argued, could prompt the use of more complicated, perhaps more plausible, but ultimately less valid cues than recognition. In general, in terms of dual-process theory, reasons analysis may cause interference in intuitive System 1 processes by unnecessarily engaging analytic System 2 processes.

We tested this hypothesis in a series of studies in which we investigated participants' use of subjective familiarity as a cue for judgments about the popularity of music. We chose this stimulus domain for several reasons: First, we expected subjective familiarity to be strongly predictive of the objective popularity of the stimuli—short clips of popular songs—in which popularity was indicated by where the stimuli fell on a New Zealand 2001 "top singles" chart. We based this expectation on the assumption that the better a song's ranking, the more familiar it would be to participants via radio and television exposure. Second, this domain affords an external objective criterion (the song's position on the chart) against which to test the accuracy of intuitive and reasoned judgments. Last, musical passages are meaningful stimuli on which to perform a reasons analysis. This is an important factor to consider, as reasons analysis may not disrupt a simple use of familiarity when the only cue on which the decision may be based is the familiarity of the stimulus.

To validate the assumption that subjective familiarity and objective popularity are strongly related, we conducted a pretest in which we measured both variables for a set of songs that were popular in New Zealand in 2001. Results of the pretest confirmed our assumption and showed that subjective familiarity correlated strongly with both the objective popularity of the songs ($r = -.79$) and with participants' estimations of where the songs fell on the chart ($r = -.73$), which showed that this was a domain in which the familiarity heuristic may well be used.

A more indicative measure of how accurate the familiarity heuristic would be in any given environment is given by calculating the proportion of times a more familiar object has a higher criterion value than a less familiar object across all possible pairs of objects within that domain. This value, which ranges from 0 to 1, is known as "cue validity" (Goldstein & Gigerenzer, 1999, 2002). Goldstein and Gigerenzer (2002) found that recognition was a high valid cue for many stimulus domains including largest Indian cities (validity = .95), largest deserts (validity = .80), longest rivers (validity = .69), and largest seas (validity = .64). The familiarity validity of music popularity, as calculated from our pretest, was .67.

Although reasons analysis could theoretically disrupt the use of familiarity in any domain, this disruption should only make judgments less accurate when reasons analysis shifts the basis of the judgment away from a cue that validly predicts the criterion in question, that is, when familiarity validity is high. In domains in which cue validity is low, reasons analysis will shift the basis of the judgment away from a cue that does not accurately predict the criterion in question and hence will not impair (and may in fact improve) the judgment.

Having shown the strong relationship between familiarity and music popularity, in our first main experiment, we investigated whether participants did in fact use familiarity for their decisions in this domain and if so, whether reasons analysis would disrupt participants' use of familiarity and hence impair the accuracy of their decisions. We placed each participant in either a reasoning condition or a control condition, and we presented all participants with 10 two-option, forced-choice trials; we presented the beginning of two of the songs used in the pretest and asked participants which of the two songs had a better ranking in the top singles list. Whereas participants in the control condition were not given any specific instructions for making their decisions, reasoning participants were told to "think about and analyze *why* one song might have been more or less popular than the other," and for each decision, we asked them to list some of their reasons before guessing which song had the better ranking. After the 10 trials, all participants rated their familiarity of all 20 songs used in the study.

Use of familiarity was calculated as the proportion of trials on which a participant chose as more popular the subjectively more familiar song based on his or her own familiarity ratings. Accuracy was calculated as the proportion of trials on which a participant chose as more popular the song with the higher ranking in the top singles list.

Participants in both reasoning and control conditions chose the more familiar song significantly more often than chance (82% and 84%, respectively) and were significantly more accurate than chance (76% and 77%, respectively). However, the two conditions did not differ from each other on either measure.

To determine whether effects of reasons analysis on familiarity use were moderated by idiosyncratic familiarity validity, we calculated validity for each participant in the experiment. Average familiarity validity was very similar to that of the pretest. However individual validities ranged greatly. Splitting participants into high-valid and low-valid groups at the median, an interaction emerged such that the high-valid group showed a significant reasons-analysis effect; reasoners chose the more familiar of the two songs as more popular (i.e., chose in accordance with the familiarity heuristic) less often than intuition participants ($M = .82$ vs. $M = .94$, respectively). Among participants with low familiarity validity, reasoners used familiarity nonsignificantly more than controls ($M = .82$ and $M = .74$, respectively). Interestingly, the main effect of validity was significant such that participants with low validities chose the subjectively familiar songs significantly less often than participants with high validities ($M = .78$ vs. $M = .88$, respectively), implying selective use of familiarity. Familiarity use across all participant groups is depicted in Figure 18.1.

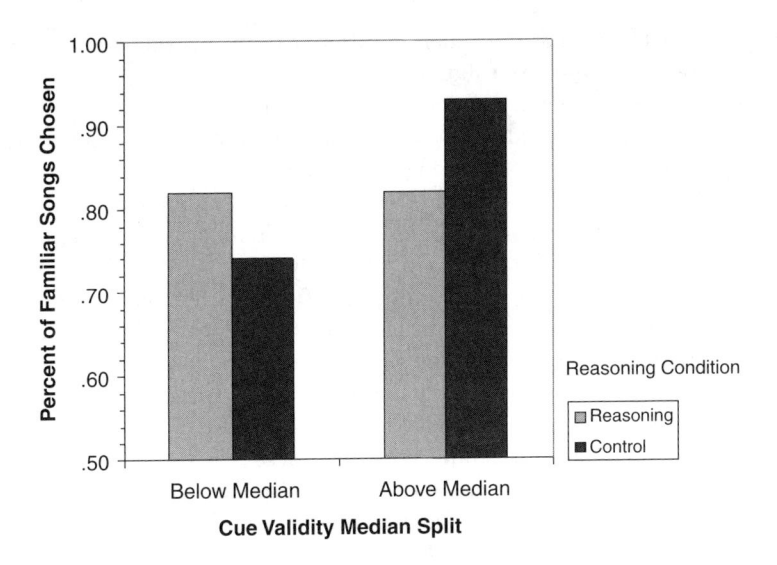

FIGURE 18.1 Average proportion of familiar songs chosen as a function of reasoning condition and cue validity.

Because familiarity was in fact a good predictor of popularity, the interaction between familiarity validity and reasoning condition was also reflected in the accuracy of participants' popularity judgments. Participants with low familiarity validities were significantly less accurate than participants with high validities ($M = .71$ vs. $M = .83$, respectively), and among participants with high validities, reasoning participants were less accurate than intuiting participants ($M = .76$ vs. $M = .87$, respectively). Among participants with low validities, reasoners were marginally more accurate than controls ($M = .76$ vs. $M = .66$, respectively).

The differential use of familiarity, based on familiarity validity, was an interesting result, for although familiarity validity is a measure of how predictive familiarity is of the criterion judged, these two factors are theoretically independent; it is possible to use familiarity in judgments in which there is low validity, and conversely, familiarity need not be used despite being highly valid. Empirically demonstrating the relationship between these two factors, then, suggests that familiarity is used strategically. Indeed, correlational analyses revealed that control participants appropriately modulated their use of familiarity in accordance with its validity ($r = .42$), whereas reasoning participants did not ($r = .04$), a difference also reflected in the correlations between accuracy and familiarity validity ($r = .59$ for control participants and $r = .15$ for reasoning participants).

Although this first experiment gives credibility to reasons-analysis effects being caused by the interference of simple heuristical processes, the results are only correlational in at least two senses: First, familiarity with the songs was measured, not manipulated. This means that although participants were clearly choosing popular songs in accordance with the familiarity heuristic a large proportion of the time, it is not clear that they were choosing popular songs because they were more familiar. Second, and relatedly, familiarity validity was not manipulated, which allowed the possibility that the apparent differences in this variable were due to another factor associated with validity.

Therefore, we conducted a second study to address the causal roles of both familiarity and familiarity validity in the use and disruption of simple heuristics. We manipulated familiarity by exposing participants to half of the stimuli—here 20 of 40 short bass guitar solos—early in the experiment. In a pretest, we confirmed that this manipulation induced a sense of subjective familiarity in the participants; the exposed bass solos were rated as significantly more familiar than novel bass solos ($M = 5.26$ and $M = 4.58$, respectively, on a 10-point scale ranging from 0 to 9). We manipulated familiarity validity by changing the judgment domain. In a posttest to our first experiment, we found that although familiarity was a high-valid cue for predicting the objective position of the songs, it was a relatively low-valid cue for predicting participants' liking of the songs. We therefore investigated participants' use of (manipulated) familiarity across these two domains. We predicted that participants would choose in accordance with the familiarity heuristic, using their experimentally induced sense of familiarity as a cue for their popularity judgments, and that reasons analysis would disrupt this use of familiarity. Second, this effect was hypothesised to occur when predicting a criterion with high familiarity validity (popularity), but not one with low familiarity validity (liking).

After manipulating participants' sense of familiarity by exposing them to the stimuli, we presented them with two bass solos—one of which was previously presented (the familiar bass solo) and one of which was novel (the unfamiliar bass solo)—and asked them to choose which solo they thought was higher on a (supposed) popularity rating list (based on the number of times each solo was downloaded from the Internet) or to rate which solo they liked more. The hypotheses were supported: Control participants chose the familiar bass solos as more popular significantly more often than chance ($M = .57$) and significantly more often than reasoning participants ($M = .48$), but there was no statistical difference between reasoners and control participants in the liking judgment conditions.

These results support the findings of the first experiment and show that familiarity was indeed the basis for judgments about music popularity rather than just a correlate of these judgments. Familiarity was also used strategically depending on the familiarity validity of the criterion, whether the sense of familiarity is measured or experimentally induced. Thus, it appears that the dual-processing framing of reasons analysis, instantiated as the use and disruption of familiarity, is a plausible account to explain the disruption of judgments by reasons analysis, at least in this stimulus domain.

FAMILIARITY AS THE BASIS FOR INTUITION

Although we have concentrated on the use and disruption of familiarity in this chapter, our analysis does not depend on familiarity per se. Any subjective feeling state could theoretically be used as the basis for intuitive System 1 processes if it accurately predicted the external criterion in question. Other subjective feeling states may well underlie simple cognitive processes as well as or instead of familiarity. One strong candidate is the "affect heuristic" postulated by Slovic, Finucane, Peters, and MacGregor (2002) in which automatic affective evaluations of an object underlie cognitive judgments (see also Glöckner, chap. 19, this volume). Slovic et al. (2002) reviewed a wide scope of literature that has demonstrated the central role of automatic, affectively based positive or negative reactions to stimuli in judgments, ranging from risk and benefit analyses of different technologies to preferences for living or holidaying in different cities or states. An example of the use of affect in cognitive judgments is given by Schwarz and Clore (1983) whose participants based judgments of their overall life satisfaction on a simple evaluation of their mood state (which itself was caused by a mood induction task or, in a second study, the weather at the time of the judgment). Gill and Gilbert (1999, as cited in Gilbert, 2002) provided a similar demonstration of affect use in judgments as we reported previously.

A diverse body of research has shown, however, that familiarity is a promising mechanism of intuition in social judgment more generally, providing a basis for such basic cognitive processes as recognition, preference, and categorization. Jacoby, Kelley, Brown, and Jasechko (1989), for example, found that participants misjudged as famous nonfamous names shown earlier in the experiment. Subjective familiarity also significantly and independently predicts attractiveness judgments in a variety of social and nonsocial stimuli (Halberstadt & Rhodes, 2000; Halberstadt, Rhodes, & Catty, 2003) and has been implicated as an evolutionary cue to the safety of a stimulus (Zajonc, 1980). Familiarity through past exposure is also a potent cue in a number of judgments. Stimuli that have been seen before are judged more positively than new ones (the "mere exposure effect"; Zajonc, 1980; see Bornstein, 1989, for a review), and this effect has been shown even (and especially) in the absence of stimulus recognition (e.g., Kunst-Wilson & Zajonc, 1980). Halberstadt and Badland (2006) found that objective exposure, via its effects on affect, influenced social categorization such as the judged likelihood of two individuals being friends. Such unconscious use of familiarity is particularly interesting from the point of view of intuition, which is in part defined by its implicit and inaccessible nature.

Whether the processes underlying intuition are based on familiarity, defining intuition in terms of the use of subjective feeling states provides a mechanism, via the logic of simple heuristics, for intuitive accuracy—quite simply, our subjective feeling states are in fact sometimes predictive of the real world. In addition, to the extent that explicit or analytic thought is incompatible with the detection and use of feeling states, our analysis provides insight into the mechanisms of reasons-based disruption of attitudes and judgments. We hope that it will also provide a starting point for mapping out the domains in which intuitive judgments could and should be used.

REFERENCES

Bornstein, R. F. (1989). Exposure and affect: Overview and meta-analysis of research 1968–1987. *Psychological Bulletin, 106,* 265–289.

Chaiken, S., & Trope, Y. (1999). *Dual-process theories in social psychology.* New York: Guilford.

Epstein, S. (1994). Integration of the cognitive and the psychodynamic unconscious. *American Psychologist, 49,* 709–724.

Gigerenzer, G., & Goldstein, D. G. (1999). Betting on one good reason: The take the best heuristic. In G. Gigerenzer, P. Todd, & The ABC Research Group (Eds.), *Simple heuristics that make us smart* (pp. 75–96). New York: Oxford University Press.

Gigerenzer, G., & Todd, P. M. (1999). Fast and frugal heuristics: The adaptive toolbox. In G. Gigerenzer, P. Todd, & The ABC Research Group (Eds.), *Simple heuristics that make us smart* (pp. 3–34). New York: Oxford University Press.

Gilbert, D. T. (2002). Inferential correction. In T. Gilovich, D. Griffin, & D. Kahneman (Eds.), *Heuristics and biases: The psychology of intuitive judgment* (pp. 167–184). New York: Cambridge University Press.

Gilovich, T., & Griffin, D. (2002). Introduction—Heuristics and biases: Then and now. In T. Gilovich, D. Griffin, & D. Kahneman (Eds.), *Heuristics and biases: The psychology of intuitive judgment* (pp. 1–18). New York: Cambridge University Press.

Goldstein, D. G., & Gigerenzer, G. (1999). The recognition heuristic: How ignorance makes us smart. In G. Gigerenzer, P. Todd, & The ABC Research Group (Eds.), *Simple heuristics that make us smart* (pp. 37–58). New York: Oxford University Press.

Goldstein, D. G., & Gigerenzer, G. (2002). Models of ecological rationality: The recognition heuristic. *Psychological Review, 109,* 75–90.

Halberstadt, J. B., & Badland, C. (2006). Mere exposure-based emotional response categorization. *Polish Psychology Bulletin, 37,* 23–30.

Halberstadt, J. B., & Green, J. (2004, April). *Explicit reasoning impairs judgments of Olympic dives.* Paper presented at the 31st Australasian Experimental Psychology Conference, Dunedin, New Zealand.

Halberstadt, J. B., & Levine, G. M. (1999). Effects of reasons analysis on the accuracy of predicting basketball games. *Journal of Applied Social Psychology, 29,* 517–530.

Halberstadt, J. B., & Rhodes, G. (2000). The attractiveness of nonface averages: Implications for an evolutionary explanation of the attractiveness of average faces. *Psychological Science, 11,* 285–289.

Halberstadt, J. B., Rhodes, G., & Catty, S. (2003). Subjective and objective familiarity as explanations for the attraction to average faces. In S. P. Shohov (Ed.), *Advances in psychology research* (Vol. 22, pp. 35–49). New York: Nova Science Publishers, Inc.

Jacoby, L. L., Kelley, C., Brown, J., & Jasechko, J. (1989). Becoming famous overnight—Limits on the ability to avoid unconscious influences of the past. *Journal of Personality and Social Psychology, 56,* 326–338.

Janis, I. L., & Mann, L. (1977). *Decision making: A psychological analysis of conflict, choice, and commitment.* New York: Free Press.

Kunst-Wilson, W. R., & Zajonc, R. B. (1980). Affective discrimination of stimuli that cannot be recognized. *Science, 207,* 557–558.

Nisbett, R. E., & Wilson, T. D. (1977). Telling more than we can know: Verbal reports on mental processes. *Psychological Review, 84,* 231–259.

von Neumann, J., & Morgenstern, O. (1944). *Theory of game and economic behavior.* Princeton, NJ: Princeton University Press.

Schwarz, N., & Clore, G. L. (1983). Mood, misattribution, and judgments of well-being: Informative and directive functions of affective states. *Journal of Personality & Social Psychology, 45,* 513–523.

Simon, H. A. (1957). *Models of man: Social and rational.* New York: Wiley.

Sloman, S. A. (1996). The empirical case for two systems of reasoning. *Psychological Bulletin, 119,* 3–22.

Slovic, P., Finucane, M., Peters, E., & MacGregor, D. G. (2002). The affect heuristic. In T. Gilovich, D. Griffin, & D. Kahneman (Eds.), *Heuristics and biases: The psychology of intuitive judgment* (pp. 397–420). New York: Cambridge University Press.

Stanovich, K. E., & West, R. F. (2002). Individual differences in reasoning: Implications for the rationality debate? In T. Gilovich, D. Griffin, & D. Kahneman (Eds.), *Heuristics and biases: The psychology of intuitive judgment* (pp. 421–439). New York: Cambridge University Press.

Wilson, T. D., Dunn, D. S., Kraft, D., & Lisle, D. J. (1989). Introspection, attitude change, and attitude-behavior consistency: The disruptive effects of explaining why we feel the way we do. *Advances in experimental social psychology, 22,* 287–343.

Wilson, T. D., Lisle, D. J., Schooler, J. W., Hodges, S. D., Klaaren, K. J., & LaFleur, S. J. (1993). Introspecting about reasons can reduce post-choice satisfaction. *Personality & Social Psychology Bulletin, 19,* 331–339.

Wilson, T. D., & Schooler, J. W. (1991). Thinking too much: Introspection can reduce the quality of preferences and decisions. *Journal of Personality and Social Psychology, 60,* 181–192.

Zajonc, R. B. (1980). Feeling and thinking: Preferences need no inferences. *American Psychologist, 35,* 151–175.

19

Does Intuition Beat Fast and Frugal Heuristics?
A Systematic Empirical Analysis

ANDREAS GLÖCKNER

Max Planck Institute for Research on Collective Goods

INTRODUCTION

*I*n numerous recent publications (Betsch, 2005; Damasio, 1994; Dougherty, Gettys, & Ogden, 1999; Haidt, 2001; Kahneman & Frederick, 2002) as well as in the previous chapters of this volume (e.g., T. Betsch, chap. 1, this volume; Deutsch & Strack, chap. 3, this volume; Epstein, chap. 2, this volume; Hogarth, chap. 6, this volume; Weber & Lindemann, chap. 12, this volume), the importance of automatic processes and intuitive strategies in decision making has been highlighted. Despite the increased interest in this topic, rigorous empirical tests that measure how many people indeed use such intuitive strategies compared with simplifying fast and frugal heuristics (Gigerenzer, Todd, & the ABC Research Group, 1999) and complex-rational serial weighted additive strategies (Payne, Bettman, & Johnson, 1988) are still rare. At least two reasons for this can be identified. First, some of the automatic models make it hard to derive testable and unique predictions (e.g., Damasio, 1994; Slovic, Finucane, Peters, & McGregor, 2002). Second, classical methods to detect decision strategies like information search analysis (Payne et al., 1988) or analysis of think-aloud protocols (Montgomery & Svenson, 1983) are not capable of detecting intuitive decision strategies and might even hamper their application (Glöckner & Betsch, 2006; Hamm, chap. 4, this volume). My aims in this chapter are to outline a method that avoids these problems and to present data from a research program that closes the empirical gap.

First, I describe the relevant classes of strategies—namely complex-rational, simplifying, and intuitive strategies—that decision makers might apply. With the consistency-maximizing strategy (CMS; Glöckner, 2006), I introduce one specific intuitive decision strategy that allows for deriving testable and distinguishable predictions. After that, I outline a methodological approach that allows for detecting the intuitive CMS. Finally, I summarize and discuss empirical data from six experiments that shed light on the question of which class of decision strategies accounts for the majority of individuals' decision behavior.

COMPLEX-RATIONAL DECISION STRATEGIES

In a complex world, decision situations are usually characterized by many pieces of available information. Classical decision theories, like expected utility theory and its successors (Edwards, 1954; Kahneman & Tversky, 1979; von Neumann & Morgenstern, 1944), have postulated that decision behavior can be understood as a complex process of information integration. It was assumed that individuals integrate utilities and (subjective) probabilities of consequences according to a weighted sum algorithm and choose the option with the highest weighted sum. More generally, such strategies can be called *weighted additive strategies* (WADD). The deliberate application of such complex-rational strategies was traditionally used as a prescriptive standard for decision behavior (Baron, 2000; for a different position, see Todd & Gigerenzer, 2000).

SIMPLIFYING DECISION STRATEGIES

People might attempt to apply such complex-rational strategies. However, as has been argued in earlier publications, most individuals are not able to use these cognitively demanding strategies in the majority of everyday decision situations because of limited computational capacity (H. A. Simon, 1955, 1982). They might use simplifying strategies instead. In this tradition, Gigerenzer et al. (1999) have postulated several so-called fast and frugal heuristics. According to Gigerenzer et al. (1999; Gigerenzer & Goldstein, 1996; Gigerenzer et al., 1999; see also Catty & Halberstadt, chap. 18, this volume; Raab & Johnson, chap. 8, this volume), decision makers reduce the complexity of decision situations by using only a small part of the available information as well as simple serial rules for information integration.

One special kind of decision task that has been explored by Gigerenzer et al. (1999) is decisions that are based on probabilistic inferences. Thereby, individuals estimate a criterion (e.g., unknown size of a city) from discriminative predictors (e.g., the city is a state capital) to select the option that is better on this criterion. Following a Brunswikian (Brunswik, 1955) approach, predictors are called *cues* and differ in *validity*, that is, in their correlation with the criterion. The "drosophila" of recent research on probabilistic inferences is the city size paradigm in which participants have to decide which of two cities has more inhabitants based

TABLE 19.1   Decision Strategies

Strategy	Information Integration	Usage of Information	Procedure
WADD	serial	all	choose the option with the highest weighted sum of cues and their validity
TTB	serial	only most valid cue	choose the option that has the better value on the most valid cue; if the values are equal use the second most valid cue etc.
REC	serial	only recognition	choose the option you know/recognize
EQW	serial	only values, no cue-validities	choose the option that has the higher sum of cue values (without weighting them by their validity); if the sums are equal choose randomly
RAND	none	none	choose one option randomly
CMS	automatic	all activated	use an automatically formed consistent representation of the decision situation to select an option

on dichotomous cues. This paradigm was also used in most of the studies reported in this chapter.

Gigerenzer et al. (1999) specified several fast and frugal heuristics that might be used adaptively in natural environments. The most important heuristics are one-reason decision strategies like the take the best heuristic (TTB) and the recognition heuristic (REC) and tallying strategies like the equal weight rule (EQW; also called Dawes's rule) (Gigerenzer et al., 1999). The computational steps of these strategies are summarized in Table 19.1. Because fast and frugal strategies are based on the idea of reducing complexity by ignoring information and using simple integration rules, these strategies should be called *simplifying strategies*. Czerlinski, Gigerenzer, and Goldstein (1999) and Goldstein and Gigerenzer (1999) could have demonstrated that the application of fast and frugal heuristics would lead to a surprisingly high accuracy of choices in real world environments. However, recent studies have repeatedly shown that fast and frugal heuristics are under many conditions not the predominantly used decision strategies (e.g., Bröder, 2000; 2003; Bröder & Schiffer, 2003b; Newell, Weston, & Shanks, 2003). The studies have shown that individual choice patterns are often in line with predictions of a WADD strategy. Glöckner and Betsch (2006) observed extremely low decision times that could not be explained by a serial computation of a WADD strategy.

INTUITIVE DECISION STRATEGIES

The best explanation for this surprising result is one that has been long ignored in behavioral decision research, namely, that individuals base their decisions on automatic processes (T. Betsch, chap. 1, this volume; Kahneman & Frederick, 2002). It has been recently argued by several authors (Beach & Mitchell, 1996; Betsch, 2005;

Busemeyer & Townsend, 1993) that individuals choose options based on the results of automatic processes in which information is quickly integrated according to complex compensatory algorithms. Hammond, Hamm, Grassia, and Pearson (1987) postulated a continuum between these so-called intuitive and analytic strategies. Hammond et al. described intuitive strategies by the following properties. Pieces of information are quickly integrated with low cognitive control and low conscious awareness. Thereby, the organizing principle is weighted averaging. Because of the large variety of automatic cognitive processes, many different classes of intuitive strategies with different properties and application areas are likely to exist. Some might be based on memory retrieval of multiple memory traces (Dougherty et al., 1999); others could rely on affective information, which represents individual learning histories (Betsch, 2005; Damasio, 1994; Slovic et al., 2002).

Along with the increased interest in intuitive decision strategies, one central idea of Gestalt psychology (Köhler, 1947; see also Cartwright, 1941; Cartwright & Festinger, 1943) has made its way back to decision research, namely, that decisions are based on automatic processes of perception (Read, Vanman, & Miller, 1997). According to this idea, individuals immediately form a consistent impression of a decision situation on perceiving it, which is in turn used to choose an option. Consequently, models of perception could be appropriate to model intuitive decision behavior. Of particular interest seem to be parallel constraint satisfaction (PCS) network models, which have been the computational core of important models of perception (McClelland & Rumelhart, 1981; Read & Miller, 1998). In this line of thought, different authors (Betsch, 2005; Glöckner, Betsch, & Schindler, 2006; Holyoak & Simon, 1999; Thagard & Millgram, 1995) have argued that individuals use PCS processes in decision making.

The basic idea behind PCS models is that automatic processes of information structuring set in when individuals perceive a decision situation. In a holistic process, pieces of information favoring one or another alternative are being weighed against each other. The processing system modifies information and seeks to find a consistent mental representation of the situation. Note that consistency maximizing in decision situations can mainly be reached by dominance structuring, that is, by changing information so that one option is clearly dominating the other. The resulting consistent mental representation might then be used to make a decision. With the CMS, I propose one specific intuitive decision strategy for probabilistic inferences that is based on a PCS network.

The CMS

The CMS postulates three steps of decision making (Glöckner, 2006). When encountering a decision situation, individuals first activate associated and salient information in memory and form a mental representation from given and memory-stored information. This mental representation can be understood as a temporarily activated network of information. Immediately after activating the network, automatic processes operate toward maximizing consistency in the network. By spreading activation, inconsistencies between pieces of information are reduced, and a consistent representation is formed. In a third step, the individual might use

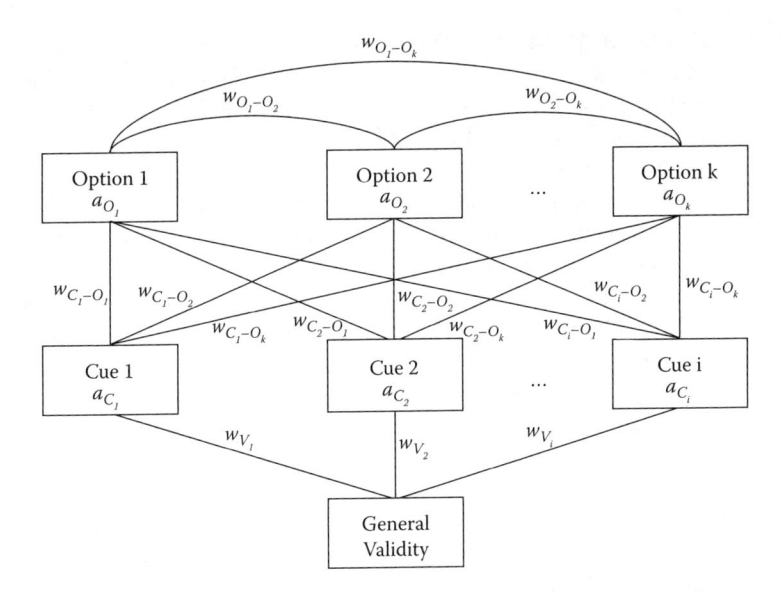

FIGURE 19.1. A general model for basic probabilistic inferences. Boxes represent nodes; lines represent links, which are all bidirectional. Connection weights can range from −1 to +1 and are labelled w. Using the iterative updating algorithm, coherence is produced in the network by changing activations (a). The special node "General Validity" has a constant activation of +1 and is used to supply the network with energy. The indexes o and c refer to option and cue nodes, the index v refers to connections with the general validity node.

the resulting representation—in which one option usually is clearly dominating—to make a decision. It is assumed that deliberate processes might be used to alter the network in the activation phase and in the consistency-maximizing phase to support consistency-maximizing processes (cf. supervisor mode; Betsch, 2005).

Structure of the PCS model. I (Glöckner, 2006) developed a general PCS network model that allows for simulating the automatic processes of the consistency-maximizing phase. The general model for basic probabilistic inferences is presented in Figure 19.1. As I described previously, probabilistic inferences are one important class of decisions in which options are chosen based on probabilistic cues. Accordingly, the network consists of options and cues, which are represented as nodes. The option nodes are interconnected by inhibitory links because only one option should be chosen. The links represent the relations between cues and options, for instance, if one cue speaks for or against an option. The general validity node stands for a generally stable concept of validity. The links between the general validity node and the cues represent the initial validity of each cue.

The variables a and w refer to the activations of nodes and to the strength of links. The indexes c and o specify cues and options. For instance, a_{o2} refers to the activation of option 2 and w_{c1-o2} refers to the strength of the link between cue 1 and option 2. The index v refers to connnections with the general validity node.

Computational algorithm. The process of maximizing consistency can be simulated by an iterative updating algorithm in which the activation of all nodes *a* changes over time. In this process, positively activated nodes activate other nodes with which they are connected by positive (excitatory) links and lower the activation of nodes with which they are connected by inhibitory links. The reverse pattern of activation occurs for negatively activated nodes. Note that all links in the model are bidirectional, which means that activation flows not only from cues to options but also from options to cues. (The specific activation function can be found in the appendix.) In a process of self-organization, over time, a stable state of the network will be reached in which activation stops changing. The state represents a minimum of contradiction and energy in the system (Read et al., 1997). This solution is the consistent representation of the situation, which is characterized by specific activations of options and cues. High activations of options stand for positive evaluations of these options; high activation of cues stand for high subjective validities. Note that there is a difference between fixed initial cue validities (represented by links between the general validity node and cue nodes) and variable resulting cue validities (represented by the activation of cue nodes). The number of iterations that are necessary to reach a stable state can be interpreted as an estimate of the time it will take to form a consistent representation and therefore for the decision time.

An example illustrates the process. If an individual has to decide which of two cities has more inhabitants, that individual would activate associated cues and cue information in memory, for instance, City A is a state capital, City B has a university, City B has a major league sports team. The available options as well as the activated cues and cue values would form a network as presented in Figure 19.1. In the second step, pieces of information would be weighed against each other and information would be thereby modified, for instance, the subjective validity of the cue state capital could be decreased and the validity of the cues university and major league sports team could be increased to form a consistent representation in which City B dominates City A. Based on this representation, City B could be chosen.

Predictions of CMS. Using systematic simulations of the network and theoretical considerations, I (Glöckner, 2006) derived the following predictions of CMS: (a) the choices of individuals who use CMS approximate the choices predicted by a weighted additive strategy, (b) decision times are generally short, (c) decision times increase with increasing inconsistency in the decision situation, and (d) subjective validities are changed within the decision process.

These predictions differ from the predictions of simplifying fast and frugal heuristics as well as from the predictions of complex-rational strategies. Simplifying strategies predict that individuals are not able to use complex decision strategies quickly, that decision times depend on the number of computational steps needed to come to a decision only (Brandstätter, Gigerenzer, & Hertwig, 2006), and that the validities of cues are stable. A serial WADD strategy predicts approximately the same choices as CMS, but the strategy further predicts that individuals need a certain amount of time to calculate the correct choice. Furthermore, decision times should be constant for all decision situations with equal numbers of options and cues because the number of computational steps is always the same (Payne et al., 1988). Finally, according to WADD, cue validities should not be modified in the decision process.

These different predictions allow for identifying the use of simplifying fast and frugal heuristics, of an intuitive CMS, and of a rational weighted additive strategy (Glöckner, 2006). To improve understanding of the later reported results, I present methodological issues and the general research paradigm first.

METHODOLOGICAL ISSUES

One of the challenges of decision research is the individual classification of decision strategies without influencing the decision behavior itself. This is particularly true if decision strategies that include automatic processes will be investigated. As argued elsewhere (Glöckner & Betsch, 2006), classical methods of behavioral decision research, such as "mouselab" (e.g., Payne et al., 1988) and think-aloud protocols (e.g., Montgomery & Svenson, 1983), are not capable of capturing automatic processes and might even hinder individuals in using them. With the Bayesian strategy classification, Bröder and Schiffer (2003a) developed a statistically sound alternative method that is based on the analysis of choice patterns only. Bröder and Schiffer could demonstrate that decision strategies such as WADD, TTB, and EQW can be efficiently identified by that method. Although a milestone in individual strategy classification, this innovative method has one obvious fundamental shortcoming. If two decision strategies predict the same choice patterns, the method will not be capable of distinguishing between these strategies. Thus, Bayesian strategy classification is not capable of separating WADD users from CMS users because the predicted choices are approximately equal. Recall that the major difference pertains to the process through which the decision is made, deliberately and in a serial fashion versus intuitively by parallel processing.

Three-Step Classification Method

I (Glöckner, 2006) proposed that for an unambiguous strategy classification, a three-step classification method can be used that is based on analysis of choices and decision times. In a first step, a test is done to see whether an individual applied a complex WADD strategy by analyzing decision times. For that, the lower time limit for the application of a WADD strategy was measured in a preliminary study (Glöckner, 2006) in which participants were explicitly instructed to use WADD. A time of 12 s was used, which was the lower limit of the 95% confidence interval of decision times after five training decisions. If observed decision times are below this limit, time is not sufficient for the application of a WADD strategy and its application can be ruled out. Furthermore, reliability of repeated choices is computed to detect users who selected options randomly. These participants are classified as random strategy (RAND) users. In a second step, choices are analyzed using the Bayesian strategy classification method. Participants are thereby classified as TTB, EQW, or CMS users according to their choices using maximum likelihood estimation (Bröder & Schiffer, 2003a). In a third step of classification, decision times for different decision tasks are compared for verifying classifications of TTB and EQW. This is necessary because under specific constellations of cue validities, more complex decision strategies like WADD and CMS can always predict the same choices as simple heuristics like TTB and EQW,[1] which could lead to an overestimation of the prevalence of these simple strategies. Specifically, a comparison is made to see if decision times for different decision tasks differ significantly in contradiction to the predictions of the respective simple strategy.[2] If significant differences are found in line with the predictions of a more complex strategy (for instance, CMS), individuals are classified as users of that more complex strategy.

Briefly summarized, individuals who showed repeated decision times of more than 12 s were classified as WADD users. Participants who showed choices in line with the predictions of TTB and EQW and no significant deviations from their predictions concerning decision times were classified as users of these strategies. Individuals who showed a low reliability were classified as RAND users. Finally, participants were classified as CMS users if (a) choices can only be explained by CMS or WADD, and decision times are lower than 12 s; or (b) choices can be explained by TTB, EQW, or CMS, but decision times can be explained by CMS only.

Research Paradigm

The previously mentioned city size paradigm was used in most of the later reported experiments. Participants decided which city has more inhabitants based on information from several probability cues. In the majority of our experiments (Glöckner, 2006; Glöckner & Hodges, 2006) these cues were: (a) the city is or is not a state capital, (b) the city has or does not have a university, and (c) the city has or does not have a major league sports team. To assure external validity of the studies, cue validities were not specified by instruction but had to be constructed by the participants based on their knowledge of the world. Existing cities were used that were unfamiliar to the participants. The cities were selected to allow for the construction of the cue patterns depicted in Table 19.2.

From the structure of the cue patterns, the following predictions were derived concerning choices. TTB users chose Option A in all six cue patterns. Participants who used EQW chose Option B in cue pattern 4. Furthermore, they randomly chose between Option A and B in cue patterns 1 to 3. WADD and CMS users with low cue dispersion chose Option B in cue Pattern 4 and Option A in all other

---

[1] If cue validities are almost equal to each other, serial WADD and CMS predict the same choices as EQW. If the validity of the most valid cue is much higher than the validity of the subsequent cues, serial WADD and CMS predict the same choices as TTB.

[2] Specifically, it is tested against the null hypothesis that decision times for cue Patterns 4 and 6 (Table 19.2) are equal. The null hypothesis should be retained if participants used TTB or EQW. The alternative hypothesis is that decision time for Pattern 4 is higher than for Pattern 6. According to CMS, a big difference would be expected because inconsistency in Pattern 4 is much higher. Paired t tests were used for comparisons.

TABLE 19.2   Cue Patterns

	Pattern 1		Pattern 2		Pattern 3		Pattern 4		Pattern 5		Pattern 6	
	A	B	A	B	A	B	A	B	A	B	A	B
Cue 1	+	−	+	−	−	−	+	−	+	−	+	−
Cue 2	−	+	−	−	+	−	−	+	−	−	+	−
Cue 3	−	−	−	+	−	+	−	+	+	−	−	+

Note: The table shows the six general cue patterns used in Experiments 1 to 4. A and B represent options. Cue 1 is the most valid cue, cue 2 is the second cue and cue 3 is the least valid cue. Plus (+) and minus (−) stand for positive or negative cue values.

cue patterns. WADD and CMS users with high cue dispersion chose Option A in all six cue patterns and could be differentiated from TTB users by decision time analysis only. Each cue pattern was repeatedly presented using different cities. To increase reliability, side-reversed versions of each comparison were added. Choices and decision times were recorded.

Using the three-step strategy classification method, it was determined whether individuals used RAND, WADD, EQW, TTB, or CMS. To prepare strategy classifications, individual cue hierarchies had to be detected. These subjective cue hierarchies were measured on an individual level using so-called detect decision in which cities were compared that only had one positive cue value each (cf. cue patterns 1 to 3 in Table 19.2). For instance, if one person always chose cities with only a university as being larger than cities with only a major league sports team, for this person, university should be a more valid cue than major league sports team. Based on the measured individual cue hierarchies, predictions for choices and decision times for the different decision strategies were derived.

DECISIONS FROM OPENLY PRESENTED INFORMATION

In Glöckner (2006), two experiments were carried out to determine decision strategies in probabilistic inferences. The city size paradigm and the three-step strategy classification method were used. In both experiments, cue information from the cities was openly presented on a screen as displayed in Table 19.2. In the first experiment ($N = 63$), participants completed 48 decision tasks, which represented eight versions of the six cue patterns depicted in Table 19.2. They were instructed to make good decisions as quickly as possible. Strategy classification revealed a clear dominance of CMS. Of the participants, 63% were classified as users of CMS, 24% used TTB, and only 2% used a serial WADD strategy (Table 19.3). Furthermore, it was found that the aggregated decision times were in line with the predictions of CMS and varied dependent on the consistency in the cue patterns, with Patterns 4 and 6 showing the highest and lowest decision times, respectively. Interestingly, decision times did not differ significantly between users of TTB and CMS and were generally very low ($M = 2.52$ s, $SD = 1.77$ s).

The second experiment ($N = 89$) explored to what degree the complexity of the decision task influences strategy selection. Complexity was manipulated within

TABLE 19.3   Decision Strategies Used by Participants

	Decision Strategies					
	WADD	TTB	EQW	CMS	RAND	Not class
	Decisions from openly presented information					
Exp. 1: 3 cues	1 (2%)	15 (24%)	0 (0%)	40 (63%)	2 (3%)	5 (8%)
Exp. 2a: 3 cues	1 (1%)	15 (17%)	2 (2%)	54 (61%)	14 (16%)	2 (3%)
Exp. 2b: 6 cues	1 (1%)	21 (24%)	0 (0%)	45 (51%)	0 (0%)	22 (25%)
	Memory based decisions					
Exp. 3: 3 cues	0 (0%)	4 (20%)	1 (5%)	13 (65%)	0 (0%)	2 (10%)
Exp. 4a: weak TL	0 (0%)	2 (10%)	2 (10%)	11 (55%)	3 (15%)	2 (10%)
Exp. 4b: medium TL	0 (0%)	4 (20%)	1 (5%)	9 (45%)	4 (20%)	2 (10%)
Exp. 4c: severe TL	0 (0%)	9 (45%)	0 (0%)	4 (20%)	4 (20%)	3 (15%)

TL: time limits

each participant by the number of cues. The first part was an exact replication of Experiment 1. In the second part, individuals completed more complex decision tasks in which information from six cues was provided. The three additional cues were a famous art exhibition, an important airport, and a large cathedral. In the first part, the results of Experiment 1 could be replicated (Table 19.3). In the more complex second part, a slight but insignificant reduction of the portion of CMS users was observed when compared to Part 1. Nevertheless, with a portion of 51%, CMS was still the predominant decision strategy. Decision times were again impressively low in both phases (M_{low} = 2.16 s, SD_{low} = 1.42 s; M_{high} = 2.36 s, SD_{high} = 1.43 s) and in general followed the predictions of CMS.

Both experiments showed that individuals predominantly used CMS in decision situations with openly presented information. Simplifying strategies as well as complex-rational strategies seemed to play only a minor role. Complexity of decision tasks manipulated by the number of cues did not have a significant influence on strategy selection. The results clearly indicate that individuals were able to integrate information in a weighted compensatory way. Considering the high computational demands, decision times were impressively low, and a deliberate computation of WADD can be ruled out. Simplifying fast and frugal heuristics cannot account for the choice patterns. Thus, intuitive decision strategies seemed to account best for the findings. The high correspondence of decision times with the predictions of CMS provided converging evidence that CMS and no other intuitive decision strategy was used.

DECISION STRATEGIES IN MEMORY-BASED DECISIONS

Strategy selection might be influenced by the way in which relevant information is accessible. Differences could be expected for decision tasks in which information is openly presented compared to those in which information has to be retrieved from memory (Hastie & Park, 1986). Gigerenzer et al. (1999) argued that simplifying fast and frugal heuristics might be used in memory-based decisions in particular. Bröder and Schiffer (2003b) indeed demonstrated a significantly increased prevalence rate of fast and frugal heuristics when information had to be retrieved from memory compared to its presentation on screen. Granting the fact that CMS is based on processes that have been derived from models of perception, it could be questioned whether the reported dominance of CMS generalizes to memory-based decisions. Glöckner and Hodges (2006) conducted three experiments that explored this question. Two of these experiments I report next (for convenience, continuous numbering of experiments, which differs from numbering in the original paper, is used in this chapter).

To study memory-based probabilistic inferences, the general research paradigm was slightly modified. In an initial learning phase, individuals learned cue information about the cities by heart (e.g., Wiesbaden is a state capital). In the decision phase, only the names of the cities were presented, and participants had to decide which city has more inhabitants. Thus, individuals had to retrieve cue information as well as cue validities from memory. Decision tasks again represented different versions of the six cue patterns of Table 19.2.

In Experiment 3 ($N = 20$), undergraduate students of the University of Oregon successfully learned information about German cities. Afterward, they were instructed to make good decisions and to proceed as quickly as possible. Thereby, a distribution of decision strategies was observed that was similar to that in the experiments with openly presented information. Of the participants, 65% used CMS, and only 20% used TTB (Table 19.3). The decision times again followed the predictions of CMS and were on average relatively low ($M = 5.75$ s, $SD = 2.45$ s).

In Experiment 4 ($N = 60$), the time limit for completing the memory-based decision task was manipulated between participants. A down-counting time bar was used to impose severe (3 s), medium (6 s), and weak (12 s) time limits. It was found that the manipulation of time limits had a significant effect on strategy selection. Under severe time limits, the majority of participants used TTB, whereas under medium and weak time limits, CMS was dominantly used (Table 19.3). These results are surprising because it is often assumed that due to their automatic computational mechanisms, intuitive strategies might be applied almost without time consumption (e.g., Kahneman & Frederick, 2002). The reasons for these findings could not be conclusively assessed. However, some data indicated that the observed strategy change was due not to the lack of computational capacity but was at least partially caused by stress tunneling in information processing that was evoked by the severe time limit (Easterbrook, 1959; Zakay, 1993).

In general, the results show that in certain memory-based decisions, the intuitive decision strategy CMS is also predominantly used. Under time pressure instruction and weak to medium time limits, the distribution of decision strategies converges with the distribution observed for decisions from given information. However, severe time limits lead to a significantly increased usage of a TTB strategy. The results are partially in conflict with the findings of Bröder and Schiffer (2003b) who detected a generally higher portion of TTB users. One reason for this difference might be that with a criminal story, different material was used that might have caused higher cue dispersion. Further experiments (Glöckner, 2006) have indicated that differences in cue dispersion might substantially influence strategy selection in memory-based decisions with high cue dispersion leading to the increased application of TTB. In summary, the data indicate that fast and frugal heuristics are not the predominantly used decision strategies in memory-based decisions and thus stand in conflict with assumptions from Gigerenzer et al. (1999).

MODIFICATION OF CUE VALIDITIES WITHIN THE DECISION PROCESS

One of the basic tenets of complex-rational as well as simplifying models is that pieces of information that are used in the decision process are fixed parameters. It is usually assumed that this fixed information is merely used to calculate choices by different algorithms. In contrast, Holyoak and Simon (1999) argued that the decision process is a constructivist process in which incoming information itself is modified. In line with this argumentation, the application of CMS implies that information, and especially cue validities, are modified in the decision process. D. Simon, Krawczyk, and Holyoak (2004) provided empirical evidence for the modification of incoming information in outcome-based decisions. Glöckner et al. (2006) examined whether changes in cue validities can also be found in probabilistic inferences. I summarize the respective experiments next.

In the first experiment by Glöckner et al. (2006), students had to decide whether to book a holiday in Place A or B based on four well-known sources of weather forecast (cues). First, participants were asked to judge the subjective validity of these cues on continuous horizontal scoroll-bar with the textual anchors *do not trust at all* to *trust absolutely*. After some filler tasks, participants were asked to make a decision concerning the place for a holiday. One cue predicted rain for Place A and sunshine for Place B, whereas all other cues made exactly the opposite predictions. After the decision, subjective cue validities were measured again. As predicted, the majority of the participants decided according to the predictions of the majority of cues and chose Place A. More interestingly, it was found that cue validities significantly changed in the decision process according to the predictions of CMS. The validity of the cues that belonged to the majority of cues was increased, and the validity of the single cue that pointed against the other cues was decreased. Thus, the results provided evidence that information was changed in the decision process. However, the data could not rule out that the changes of cue validities are caused by processes of postdecisional dissonance reduction (Festinger, 1964), which set in after the decision was made.

Another experiment (Glöckner et al., 2006) was carried out using mainly the same procedure as in the first experiment (Glöckner et al., 2006). The important modification was that participants did not make any explicit decisions about the place for a holiday but were asked merely to reflect on which place they would prefer on the basis of the information provided. According to CMS, automatic consistency-maximizing processes should set in when the decision situation is perceived. As expected, the results of the first experiment could be replicated. Thus, postdecisional dissonance reduction could be ruled out as an alternative explanation. The findings of both experiments clearly support the hypothesis that cue validities were being changed in the decision process. The direction of these changes was in line with the predictions of CMS. Against the fundamental assumptions of simplifying and complex-rational strategies, information was obviously modified in the decision process.

GENERAL DISCUSSION

In the reported experiments (Glöckner, 2006; Glöckner & Hodges, 2006; Glöckner et al., 2006), it was found that the intuitive decision strategy CMS was frequently used in decisions that were based on probabilistic inferences with simple dichotomous cue values. Simplifying fast and frugal heuristics seemed to play a much less important role than has been repeatedly claimed by their proponents (Gigerenzer, 2004; Gigerenzer et al., 1999). Nevertheless, simplifying strategies accounted for a smaller but still substantial portion of individual decision behavior. Regarding the explored decisions from given information and memory-based decisions, the question raised in the heading of this chapter can be affirmed: Intuition beats the fast and frugal heuristic concerning prevalence rates. Furthermore, it was consistently found that very few individuals applied complex-rational strategies such as a serial WADD strategy.

The results provide important insights about the scope and prevalence rate of fast and frugal heuristics. Although these simplifying strategies could lead to relatively accurate decisions, they are only used by a few individuals. This raises the question of why evolutionary processes have not led to a predominant use of these successful strategies as argued by Gigerenzer et al. (1999). Critical reviewing of the respective argumentation and the results of the simulations lead to a different conclusion: Evolution might have been just one step ahead of scientific endeavor. Czerlinski et al. (1999) found that fast and frugal heuristics lead to similarly accurate choices as WADD strategies. Based on this finding, it was argued that these heuristics would be preferred because they are much faster to apply and need much less information (frugality) than a complex WADD strategy. Considering the ability of participants to quickly use intuitive strategies that approximate a WADD strategy, this argumentation has to be partially revised. Intuitive strategies seem to be easy to use but nevertheless lead to good compensatory choices. Obviously, evolution has built in powerful tools for automatic information integration, which makes simplification partially obsolete. Not surprisingly, these tools are used not only in humans' higher cognition but also by other animals. Künzler and Bakker (2001), for instance, showed that swordtails use complex compensatory strategies in mating as well.

At first glance, the dominant usage of CMS seems to conflict with earlier studies in which only simplifying heuristics and WADD strategies had been detected (e.g., Payne et al., 1988). As discussed elsewhere (Glöckner & Betsch, 2006), a closer look at the classification procedures used reveals that CMS users might have been simply misclassified[3] or that the method used to measure the decision strategy could have hampered the application of CMS. Thus, in further studies, methods for strategy classification should be chosen very carefully, keeping in mind intuitive strategies.

On a more general level, the studies I summarized in this chapter highlight the importance of intuitive strategies in decision making. The results allow for a methodologically sound statement about the proportion of persons who use intuitive strategies compared with persons who use complex-rational or simplifying strategies, which have not been derived from methodologically problematic self-reports (e.g., Agor, 1986; cf. Nisbett & Wilson, 1977). Furthermore, the results indicate that two cornerstones of rational and simplifying approaches have to be questioned. First, in contrast to the basic assumption of bounded rationality (H. A. Simon, 1955, 1982), individuals seem to be endowed with the computational capacity to use complex information integration strategies quickly. Second, information that is used in the decision process is not fixed but is modified during decision making.

With CMS, a decision strategy was proposed and empirically supported that is based on automatic processes of perception, bringing classical ideas of Gestalt psychology back to decision making. However, this work should be understood only as a first step in empirically exploring intuitive decision strategies. CMS and other intuitive strategies should be subject to further research. Therefore, a more differentiated understanding of intuition will be necessary. I suggest a general classification of intuitive decision strategies by the underlying automatic processes. Considering the variety of automatic cognitive processes, there is a fascinating and relatively unexplored field of research ahead.

---

[3] It should be mentioned that several authors intentionally did not make propositions about whether the process underlying WADD is serial or automatic. Bröder and Schiffer (2003b) went one step further and explicitly analyzed predictions of image theory (Beach & Mitchell, 1996), which postulates automatic processes of information processing.

REFERENCES

Agor, W. (1986). *The logic of intuitive decision making*. Westport, CT: Greenwood Press.

Baron, J. (2000). *Thinking and deciding* (3rd ed.). Cambridge, England: Cambridge University Press.

Beach, L. R., & Mitchell, T. R. (1996). Image theory, the unifying perspective. In L. R. Beach (Ed.), *Decision making in the workplace: A unified perspective* (pp. 1–20). Hillsdale, NJ: Lawrence Erlbaum Associates, Inc.

Betsch, T. (2005). Preference theory: An affect based approach to recurrent decision making. In T. Betsch & S. Haberstroh (Eds.), *The Routines of decision making* (pp. 39–66). Mahwah, NJ: Lawrence Erlbaum Associates, Inc.

Brandstätter, E., Gigerenzer, G., & Hertwig, R. (2006). The priority heuristic: Making choices without trade-offs. *Psychological Review, 113*, 409–432.

Bröder, A. (2000). Assessing the empirical validity of the "take-the-best" heuristic as a model of human probabilistic inference. *Journal of Experimental Psychology: Learning, Memory, and Cognition, 26*, 1332–1346.

Bröder, A. (2003). Decision making with the "adaptive toolbox": Influence of environmental structure, intelligence, and working memory load. *Journal of Experimental Psychology: Learning, Memory, and Cognition, 29,* 611–625.

Bröder, A., & Schiffer, S. (2003a). Bayesian strategy assessment in multi-attributive decision making. *Journal of Behavioral Decision Making, 16,* 193–213.

Bröder, A., & Schiffer, S. (2003b). Take the best versus simultaneous feature matching: Probabilistic inferences from memory and effects of representation format. *Journal of Experimental Psychology: General, 132,* 277–293.

Brunswik, E. (1955). Representative design and the probability theory in a functional psychology. *Psychological Review, 62,* 193–217.

Busemeyer, J. R., & Townsend, J. T. (1993). Decision field theory: A dynamic cognitive approach to decision making in an uncertain environment. *Psychological Review, 100,* 432–459.

Cartwright, D. (1941). Decision-time in relation to the differentiation of the phenomenal field. *Psychological Review, 48,* 425–442.

Cartwright, D., & Festinger, L. (1943). A quantitative theory of decision. *Psychological Review, 50,* 595–621.

Czerlinski, J., Gigerenzer, G., & Goldstein, D. G. (1999). How good are simple heuristics? In G. Gigerenzer, P. M. Todd, & the ABC Research Group, *Simple heuristics that make us smart* (pp. 97–118). New York: Oxford University Press.

Damasio, A. R. (1994). *Descartes' error: Emotion, reason, and the human brain.* New York: Avon Books.

Dougherty, M. R. P., Gettys, C. F., & Ogden, E. E. (1999). MINERVA-DM: A memory process model for judgments of likelihood. *Psychological Review, 106,* 180–209.

Easterbrook, J. A. (1959). The effect of emotion on cue utilization and the organization of behavior. *Psychological Review, 66,* 187–201.

Edwards, W. (1954). The theory of decision making. *Psychological Bulletin, 51,* 380–417.

Festinger, L. (1964). *Conflict, decision, and dissonance.* Stanford, CA: Stanford University Press.

Gigerenzer, G. (2004). Fast and frugal heuristics: The tools of bounded rationality. In D. Koehler & N. Harvey (Eds.), *Handbook of judgment and decision making* (pp. 62–88). Oxford, England: Blackwell.

Gigerenzer, G., & Goldstein, D. G. (1996). Reasoning the fast and frugal way: Models of bounded rationality. *Psychological Review, 103,* 650–669.

Gigerenzer, G., Todd, P. M., & the ABC Research Group. (1999). *Simple heuristics that make us smart.* New York: Oxford University Press.

Glöckner, A. (2006). *Automatische Prozesse bei Entscheidungen* [Automatic processes in decision making]. Hamburg: Kovac.

Glöckner, A., & Betsch, T. (2006). *Evidence for multiple-reason decision making under time limits.* Manuscript submitted for publication.

Glöckner, A., Betsch, T., & Schindler, N. (2006). *Construction of probabilistic inferences by constraint satisfaction.* Manuscript submitted for publication.

Glöckner, A., & Hodges, S. D. (2006). *Strategy selection in memory based decisions: Simplifying fast and frugal heuristics versus weighted compensatory strategies based on automatic information integration.* Manuscript submitted for publication.

Goldstein, D. G., & Gigerenzer, G. (1999). The recognition heuristic: How ignorance makes us smart. In G. Gigerenzer, P. M. Todd, & the ABC Research Group, *Simple heuristics that make us smart* (pp. 37–58). New York: Oxford University Press.

Haidt, J. (2001). The emotional dog and its rational tail: A social intuitionist approach to moral judgment. *Psychological Review, 108,* 814–834.

Hammond, K. R., Hamm, R. M., Grassia, J., & Pearson, T. (1987). Direct comparison of the relative efficiency on intuitive and analytical cognition. *IEEE Transactions on Systems, Man and Cybernetics, 17,* 753–770.

Hastie, R., & Park, B. (1986). The relationship between memory and judgment depends on whether the judgment task is memory-based or on-line. *Psychological Review, 93,* 258–268.

Holyoak, K. J., & Simon, D. (1999). Bidirectional reasoning in decision making by constraint satisfaction. *Journal of Experimental Psychology: General, 128,* 3–31.

Kahneman, D., & Frederick, S. (2002). Representativeness revisited: Attribute substitution in intuitive judgment. In T. Gilovich, D. Griffin, & D. Kahneman (Eds.), *Heuristics and biases: The psychology of intuitive judgment* (pp. 49–81). New York: Cambridge University Press.

Kahneman, D., & Tversky, A. (1979). Prospect theory: An analysis of decision under risk. *Econometrica, 47,* 263–292.

Köhler, W. (1947). *Gestalt psychology: An introduction to new concepts in modern psychology.* New York: Liveright.

Künzler, R., & Bakker, T. C. M. (2001). Female preferences for single and combined traits in computer animated stickleback males. *Behavioral Ecology, 12,* 681–685.

McClelland, J. L., & Rumelhart, D. E. (1981). An interactive model of context effects in letter perception: Part 1. An account of basic findings. *Psychological Review, 88,* 375–407.

Montgomery, H., & Svenson, O. (1983). A think-aloud study of dominance structuring in decision making. In R. Tietz (Ed.), *Aspiration levels in bargaining and economic decision making* (pp. 366–383). Berlin: Springer.

Newell, B. R., Weston, N. J., & Shanks, D. R. (2003). Empirical test of fast-and-frugal heuristic: not everyone "takes-the-best." *Organizational Behavior and Human Decision Processes, 91,* 82–96.

Nisbett, R. E., & Wilson, T. D. (1977). Telling more than we can know: Verbal protocols on mental processes. *Psychological Review, 84,* 231–259.

Payne, J. W., Bettman, J. R., & Johnson, E. J. (1988). Adaptive strategy selection in decision making. *Journal of Experimental Psychology: Learning, Memory, & Cognition, 14,* 534–552.

Read, S. J., & Miller, L. C. (1998). On the dynamic construction of meaning: An interactive activation and competition model of social perception. In S. J. Read & L. C. Miller (Eds.), *Connectionist models of social reasoning and social behavior* (pp. 27–70). Mahwah, NJ: Lawrence Erlbaum Associates, Inc.

Read, S. J., Vanman, E. J., & Miller, L. C. (1997). Connectionism, parallel constraint satisfaction and gestalt principles: (Re)introducting cognitive dynamics to social psychology. *Personality and Social Psychology Review, 1,* 26–53.

Simon, D., Krawczyk, D. C., & Holyoak, K. J. (2004). Construction of preferences by constraint satisfaction. *Psychological Science, 15,* 331–336.

Simon, H. A. (1955). A behavioral model of rational choice. *The Quarterly Journal of Economics, 69,* 99–118.

Simon, H. A. (1982). *Models of bounded rationality.* Cambridge, MA: MIT Press.

Slovic, P., Finucane, M., Peters, E., & McGregor, D. G. (2002). The affect heuristic. In T. Gilovich, D. Griffin, & D. Kahneman (Eds.), *Heuristics and biases: The psychology of intuitive judgment* (pp. 397–420). New York: Cambridge University Press.

Thagard, P., & Millgram, E. (1995). Inference to the best plan: A coherence theory of decision. In A. Ram & D. B. Leake (Eds.), *Goal-driven learning* (pp. 439–454). Cambridge, MA: MIT Press.

Todd, P. M., & Gigerenzer, G. (2000). Précis of simple heuristics that make us smart. *Behavioral and Brain Sciences, 23,* 727–780.

von Neumann, J., & Morgenstern, O. (1944). *Theory of games and economic behavior.* Princeton, NJ: Princeton University Press.

Zakay, M. P. (1993). The impact of time perception processes on decision making under time stress. In O. Svenson & A. J. Maule (Eds.), *Time pressure and stress in human judgement and decision making* (pp. 59–72). New York: Plenum.

APPENDIX

The following sigmoid activation function proposed by Read and Miller (1998) was used for the general PCS network:

$$input_i(t) = \sum_{j=1 \to n} w_{ij} a_j(t)$$

$$a_i(t+1) = a_i(t)(1-decay) + \begin{cases} input_i(t)(a_i(t) - floor) & \text{if } input_i(t) < 0 \\ input_i(t)(ceiling - a_i(t)) & \text{if } input_i(t) \geq 0 \end{cases}$$

i	index of the node
t	index of the actual iteration
$a_i(t)$	activation of the ith node at iteration t (range: –1 to +1)
decay	constant decay parameter
floor	lower bound for activation of nodes (set to –1)
ceiling	upper bound for activation of nodes (set to +1)
$Input_i(t)$	incoming activation for node i at iteration t
w_{ij}	strength of the link between node i and j (range: –1 to +1)
$a_j(t)$	activation of node j at iteration t

The iterative algorithm simulates spreading activation in the network. The algorithm maximizes consistency and after a certain number of iterations leads to a balanced state in which activations stop changing.

Index

A

Aarts, H., 47
Abernathy, C.M., 23–24, 29, 33, 35, 56
Abu-Lughod, L., 225
Acquisition of cultural capital, 93–98
Activation
  behavioral, reflective-impulsive model, 45
  conceptual, reflective-impulsive model, 44–45
Agor, W., 322
Ainslie, G., 196
Aizenstein, H.J., 77, 79
Ajzen, I., 137
Alba, J.W., 270
Ambady, N., 100, 150, 167
Ames, D.R., 191–192, 197, 202, 205
Anderson
  J.R., 56, 121, 136
  N.H., 9, 58, 108–109
Andersson, P., 258
Assets of intuition, 249–326
Ault, J.M.J., 225
Automatic online implicit attitude formation, voting behavior and, 107–118
Availability heuristic, judgments of probability/frequency, 10–11
Axelrod, R., 158

B

Baddeley, A., 284–285
Badgaiyan, R.D., 75–76
Bagozzi, R.P., 174, 184
Baillargeon, R., 93
Banaji, M.R., 112
Bar-Hillel, M., 136
Bargh, J.A., 4, 31
Barnett, S.M., 125
Baron, J., 210–211, 220, 224, 226, 251, 310
Base rate neglect, 135–148
  base-rate sensitivity, concurrent, 136–137
  Bayesian reasoning, with mere-presentation effect, 143–144
  conversational maxims, 146
  intuitive cognition, 136–137
  mere presentation
    classic base-rate neglect demonstration, 140–143
    impact of, 138
    in perceptual identification, 138–140
    psychology of mere-presentation effect, 145
  visual cognition, 136–137
Bastick, T., 212, 214, 252–253
Baumeister, R.F., 164, 223
Bayesian reasoning, with mere-presentation effect, 143–144
Beach, L.R., 311, 322
Bechara, A., 5, 45, 82–83
Behavioral activation, reflective-impulsive model, 45
Bellah, R.M., 226
Bem, D.J., 45
Benefits of intuition, 251–266
Bentham, J., 176
Bergerbest, D., 76
Berns, G.S., 79
Berreby, D., 225
Berry, D.C., 76, 94
Betch, T., 108
Betsch
  C., 7, 149–150, 206, 231, 233–237, 239–242, 267
  T., 10, 13–16, 18, 42, 73, 82, 96–97, 108–109, 115, 119, 149, 173, 232–233, 241–242, 251, 257, 267–269, 272–273, 276–278, 284, 288, 292, 295, 309, 311–313
Beyth-Marom, R., 143
Bianco, A.T., 239
Biederman, I., 137
Birnbaum, M.H., 142
Blackburn, S., 216
Blair
  E., 267–268
  I.V., 47
Bless, H., 41, 155
Bloom, P., 215
Bornstein, R.F., 97, 305
Bougie, R., 176, 184
Bowers, K.S., 92
Bregman, E., 95
Brewer, M.B., 43
Bröder, A., 9, 59, 311, 315, 319, 322
Brooks, J.O., 276

Brown
  D.E., 218
  N.R., 267–268, 273, 278
Bruner, J., 42, 138
Brunswik, E., 310
Buchel, C., 74
Buckner, R.L., 75
Busemeyer, J.R., 312
Buss, D.M., 97

C

Cabanac, M., 176
Cacioppo, J.T., 48
Campbell, D.T., 217
Cantinotti, N., 258
Cartwright, D., 312
Categories of research on intuition, 213
Cavada, C., 83
Ceci, S.J., 125
Chaiken, S., 40, 46, 119, 149, 224, 298
Chajut, E., 157
Characteristics, processing judgment/decision making strategies, 7
Chartrand, T.L., 45
Chase, W.G., 95
Chen, S., 32
Church, R.M., 270–271
CMS. *See* Consistency-maximizing strategy
Cognitive-experiential self-theory, 23–38
  attribute list, intuition, 24
  experiential processing
    intuition as subset, advantages, 34
    intuition attributes, 29–33
  systems of, 26
  theory of personality, 24–29
Cohen, L.J., 137
Complex-rational decision strategies, heuristics, intuition, 310
Conceptual activation, reflective-impulsive model, 44–45
Concurrent base-rate sensitivity, 136–137
Connolly, T., 240
Consistency-maximizing strategy, heuristics, intuition, 310–322
  predictions, 314–315
Cooksey, R.W., 58
Cooper
  R.P., 59
  W.H., 284
Csikszentmihalyi, M., 99
Cue selection, reflective-impulsive model, 46
Cultural capital acquisition, 93–98

Curt, C.L., 275
Czerlinski, J., 311, 321

D

Damasio, A., 26, 32, 82–83, 224, 232, 309, 312
Daselaar, S.N., 77
Davidson, R.J., 83
Davis, D.G.S., 108
Davitz, J.R., 175
de Waal, F., 218
Decision making, 11–13
Deffenbacher, K.A., 161
Deficits of intuition, 249–326
Definition of intuition, 3, 91–93
Delgado, M.R., 79
Demb, J.B., 75
Denes-Raj, V., 25, 27, 29–30, 32
Denrell, J., 159
Deprivation, reflective-impulsive model, 47–48
DeSteno, D., 178
Detection of change, 157–158
Deutsch, R., 49, 224, 232, 256, 297
Devine, P.G., 41, 46
Dickinson, A., 47
Dijksterhuis, A., 45, 160, 285
Distinguishing characteristics, intuition, 5–8
Donovan, S., 33–34
Dougherty, M.R.P., 268, 273, 309, 312
Doyon, J., 77
Dreyfus, H.L., 56
Durkheim, E., 217, 226
Dynamic change regulation, environmental-learning decision problems, 163–166

E

Eddy, D.M., 15
Edwards
  K., 30, 101
  W., 310
Einhorn, H.J., 94, 98
Eisenberg, P., 137
Eldridge, L.L., 79
Elman, J.L., 153
Emotion, 173–190
  affect, nature of, 174
  emotion, decision making and, 176–177
  goal-based accounts, 179–181
    testing, 183–186
  information-based accounts, 178–179
    evaluation, 181–183
  nature of, 174–176
  specificity, 177–181
Emotion and intuition, 171–248

Empirical evidence, power of intuition, 11–17
Environment structure, in learning intuition, 98–101
Environmental-learning, 158–166
  distance, 161–163
  dynamic change regulation, decision problems, 163–166
  lower response criterion, 160
  sample size, 159–163
    valence, distance, triadic relation, 164
  valence, 159–161, 163
Epley, N., 260
Epstein, S., 4–5, 7, 28–34, 39–42, 56, 91, 135, 149, 212, 214, 232–233, 235, 251, 256, 297
Erev, I., 138
Ericsson, K.A., 56, 95, 202
Eslinger, P.J., 83
Esterbrook, J.A., 309
Estimation, choice, distinguished, 156–157
Existential implications, moral intuition, 222–224
Experiential processing
  intuition as subset, advantages, 34
  intuition attributes, 29–33
External cues, reflective-impulsive model, 43–44
Eyal, T., 165

F

Familiarity in intuitive judgments, 296–297
  as basis for intuition, 304–305
  dual-processing models, 297–298
  experimental investigations, 301–304
  reasons analysis, 298–300
    simple heuristics disruption, 300–301
  use, disruption of, 295–308
Fazio, R.H., 44, 109, 112, 236, 240, 257
Feedback, in learning intuition, 98–101
Feeling-is-for-doing approach, 173–190. *See also* Emotion; Motivation
Feelings, reflective-impulsive model, 45
Ferguson, M.J., 47–48
Fessler, D.M.T., 180–181, 185
Feuchtwanger, L., 3
Fiedler, K., 16–17, 48, 100, 112, 114, 145, 153–156, 159–162, 258, 271, 283–286, 292
Finucane, M.L., 173
Fischhoff, B., 141
Fishbein, M., 9
Fiske, A.P., 218, 220

Fletcher, P., 80
Förster, J., 47–48, 239
Foss, D., 137
Frabble, D.E.S., 101
Frank, R.H., 181
Frederick, S., 10
Fredrickson, B.L., 9
Freeman, W.T., 136
Frensch, P.A., 74
Frequency estimation, intuitive/deliberate strategies, 267–282
  empirical evidence, 274–277
  exemplars, availability of, 274–276
  strategy-application model, 269–274
    information, encoding of, 270–272
    retrieval, 272–274
  valence, stimuli, 276–277
Freud, S., 174
Frijda, N.H., 174–175, 182, 184
Friston, K.J., 74
Frost, R., 137
Functional neuroimaging, 73–74

G

Gallistel, C.R., 16, 268, 271
Garcia, J., 96
Geertz, C.J., 216, 219
Gender differences, in learning intuition, 100–101
Gibbon, J., 270
Gigerenzer, G., 8–9, 15–16, 18, 33, 122, 136–138, 146, 210, 224, 252, 295, 297, 309–311, 319–321
Gilbert, D.T., 49, 162, 240, 295, 298, 305
Gilovich, T., 5, 8, 16, 135, 149, 296, 298
Gladwell, M., 191, 252
Glöckner, A., 7, 12–13, 242, 252, 309–317, 319–321
Glöeckner, A., 122
Gold, B.T., 76
Goldberg, E., 191
Goldstein
  D.G., 221, 295, 301, 311
  W.M., 191, 197
Golec, P., 99
Gollwitzer, P.M., 41
Gould, S.J., 135
Graf, P., 74
Graham, T., 101
Grainger, J., 137
Green, P.E., 59
Greenwald, A.G., 4, 40, 108–109, 112–115, 232, 236, 256, 272

Grice, H.P., 138
Griffin
  D., 155
  L.A., 125–126
Griffiths, T.L., 136

H

Habermas, J., 195
Haberstroh, S., 16–17, 268–269, 273, 275–278
Haidt, J., 210, 218–222, 224–226, 251, 309
Halberstadt, J.B., 124, 253, 258, 299–300 305
Hall, J.A., 101
Hammond, K.R., 4, 7, 23–24, 29, 32–33, 42, 56, 58, 121, 191, 232–233, 252–253, 262, 312
Hansen, J., 200
Harman, G., 216
Harrison, A.A., 97
Hart, J.T., 5
Haruno, M., 79
Hasher, L., 16, 94, 268–270, 273
Hastie, R., 55, 107, 251, 283, 319
Hazeltine, E., 77–78
Hertwig, R., 18, 156
Heuristics, intuition, 309–326
  classification method, 315–316
  complex-rational decision strategies, 310
  computational algorithm, 314
  consistency-maximizing strategy, 310–322
    predictions, 314–315
  cue patterns, 317
  cue validity modification, within decision process, 320–321
  decision strategy simplification, 310–311
  information integration, 311
  information usage, 311
  intuitive decision strategies, 311–315
  memory-based decisions, decision strategies in, 318–320
  methodological issues, 315–317
  openly presented information, decisions from, 317–318
  parallel constraint satisfaction model, 312–313
  research paradigm, 316–317
  weighted additive strategies, 310–311, 314–318, 321–322
Higgins, E.T., 44–45, 239–240
Hilgard, E.R., 195
Hilton, D.J., 138
Hintzman, D.L., 271
Hodges, B.H., 164
Hoffmann, J., 126

Hogarth, R., 4–5, 7, 34, 39, 42, 48, 73, 91–92, 96, 99–100, 102, 121, 125, 131, 149, 191, 232, 242, 251–252, 256, 258, 262, 269, 284
Holbrook, M.B., 96
Holyoak, K.J., 7, 312, 320
Howes, D., 137
Hsee, C.K., 233, 235, 238, 241–242
Hugenberg, K., 44
Hull, C.L., 108
Hume, D., 224
Hurlburt, R.T., 99

I

IAT. *See* Implicit Association Test
IFG. *See* Inferior frontal gyrus
Imaging. *See* Functional neuroimaging
Implicit Association Test, 109, 112–115
Implicit learning, neuroscience in, 76–81
Implicit memory, neuroscience in, 74–76
Individual differences approach, decision making preferences, 231–248
  assessment, 233–235
  feelings, reliance on, 237–238
  implicit knowledge, reliance on, 235–237
Inferior frontal gyrus, neuroimaging, 81
Inputs into reflection, reflective-impulsive model, 42–46
  cue selection, 46
  external cues, 43–44
  internal cues, 44–46
    behavioral activation, 45
    conceptual activation, 44–45
    feelings, 45
    internal cues, heuristics, and intuition, 45–46
Internal cues
  heuristics, and intuition, reflective-impulsive model, 45–46
  reflective-impulsive model, 44–46
Isen, A., 173, 180

J

Jackson, R.C., 126
Jacoby, L.L., 45, 305
James, W., 6, 215
Janis, I.L., 295
Jevons, W.S., 176
Johnson
  E.J., 11, 59, 178, 180
  J., 122–124
Jones, E.E., 162

INDEX

Judd, C.M., 162
Judgments of probability/frequency, availability heuristic, 10–11
Jung, C., 212
Jung-Beeman, M., 92

K

Kahneman, D., 5, 8–11, 13, 15, 18, 39, 42, 44, 49, 56, 121, 135–138, 146, 222, 251, 274, 278, 309–311, 319
Kapur, S., 76
Kardes, F.R., 251
Kareev, Y., 152–153, 156, 285
Karpinski, A., 236
Kawakami, K., 44
Keane, M.M., 75
Kee, F., 58
Keller, J., 239
Keltner, D., 179
Ketelaar, T., 173, 181, 183
Khatri, N., 82
Kikyo, H., 81
Kirkpatrick, L.A., 25, 29
Klayman, J., 162
Klein, G., 95, 122–123, 131, 194
Kleinginna, P.R., 174
Knill, D.C., 136
Knopman, D., 78
Knutson, B., 79
Koehler, J.J., 120, 136, 140, 211
Köhler, W., 312
Körding, K., 136
Koriat, A., 81
Kringelbach, M.L., 83
Kruglanski, A.W., 42, 46, 161, 199, 234, 258
Kunda, Z., 224
Kunst-Wilson, W.R., 108, 305

L

Laforce, R., Jr., 78
Lang P.J., 48
Langan-Fox, J., 234
Larrick, R.P., 195
Larsen, R.J., 176
Learning and intuition, 89–170
Learning intuition, 91–106
   acquisition of intuitions, 101–103
   conceptual framework, 98–100
   cultural capital acquisition, 93–98
   environment structure, 98–101
   expertise, 94–95
   feedback, 98–101
   gender differences, 100–101

   implicit learning, 94
   preferences, 96–98
   preparedness, 95–96
   roles of intuition, 92–93
Lee, A.Y., 276
Left hemisphere, neuroimaging, 72
Lerner, J.S., 178–182, 184, 194
Levenson, T., 30
Levy, N., 215
Lewandowsky, S., 275
Lewicki, P., 94, 292
Lexicographic strategies, decision making, 8–9
Liberman, N., 162, 165
Lieberman, M.D., 39, 41–43, 48, 80, 121, 232, 256
Linville, P.W., 162–163, 196
LoBue, V., 219
Locksley, A., 143
Lodge, M., 107–108, 115
Loewenstein, G., 41–42, 45, 173, 194, 232, 237
Logan, G.D., 44
Luwel, K., 267

M

Maio, G.R., 234
Maison, D., 112
March, J.G., 195
Marcus, G.F., 93
Maril, A., 81
Markus, H.R., 196
Masters, R.S.W., 125
Mayo, R., 49
McCauley, C., 143
McClelland
   D.C., 47
   J.L., 44, 47, 312
McCord, W.M., 220
McDowell, J., 216
McGregor, D.G., 309
McMackin, J., 253, 262
McMorris, T., 123, 125
McPherson, S.L., 125
Mellers, B.A., 174, 176–177, 195
Memory-based decisions, decision strategies in, heuristics, 318–320
Mere presentation
   classic base-rate neglect demonstration, 140–143
   impact of, 138
   in perceptual identification, 138–140
Miller, N.E., 164
Mineka, S., 219
Miyamoto, Y., 162

Moderators of impulses, reflective-impulsive model, 46–48
  deprivation, 47–48
  motivational orientation, 48
  reflection, 47
Monahan, J.L., 291
Montgomery, H., 309
Moors, A., 47
Moral intuition, 209–230
  categories of research on intuition, 213
  differentiation, 220–225
  existential implications, 222–224
  moral facts, 214–217
  in morally diverse society, 225–226
  research taxonomy, 212–214
  social consensus, 221–222
  species of, 217–220
Morling, B., 25
Morris, J.P., 115
Motivation, 173–190
  affect, nature of, 174
  emotion
    decision making and, 176–177
    nature of, 174–176
  emotion specificity, approaches, 177–181
  goal-based accounts, 179–181
    testing, 183–186
  information-based accounts, 178–179
    evaluation, 181–183
Motivational foci, decision modes, 191–208
  functional taxonomy, decision modes, 192–195
  studies, 197–205
Motivational orientation, reflective-impulsive model, 48
Mouselab, 12
Murray, H.A., 195
Mussweiler, T., 260
Myers
  D.G., 29, 73
  I.B., 234

N

Nature, nurture, contrasted, in learning intuition, 93–94
Nature of intuition, 1–88
Nauta, W.J., 83
Neglect of intuition in research, 3–22
Nelissen, R.M.A., 174, 181, 183, 186
Neumann, R., 48
Neuroimaging, 73–74
Neuroscience, 71–87
  FOK prediction, 81–82
  functional neuroimaging, 73–74

implicit learning, 76–81
implicit memory, 74–76
Newell, B.R., 311
Niedenthal, P.M., 45
Nisbett, R.E., 102, 137, 299, 322
Nissen, M.J., 77
Norris, P., 27–28, 33
Nowak, M., 158

O

Objective criterion, spontaneous, deliberate judgments, studies compared, 254–255
Öhman, A., 96
Online implicit attitude formation, voting behavior and, 107–118
Orasanu, J., 120, 127
Osgood, E.E., 174

P

Pacini, R., 28, 30, 33, 233
Parallel constraint satisfaction model, heuristics, intuition, 312–313
Park, B., 162
Parrott, W.G., 176
Payne
  B.K., 45
  J.W., 8–9, 12, 32, 192, 233, 267–268, 309, 315, 321
PCS. See Parallel constraint satisfaction model
Peak-and-end heuristic, valence judgments, 9
Peeters, G., 161
Peigneux, P., 78, 80
Perrig, W.J., 5, 124
Petty, R.E., 32, 43, 109
Pfeifer, B., 238
Pham, M.T., 182
Piaget, J., 145
Pinker, S., 96
Pizarro, D., 225
Plessner, H., 32, 112, 122, 124, 191, 210, 232, 242, 256, 258–261, 269
Poses, R.M., 60
Post, E.L., 59
Power of intuition, empirical evidence, 11–17
Pratto, F., 161
Preferences, in learning intuition, 96–98
Prinz, J., 219
Probability/frequency, judgments of, 15–17
Processing judgment/decision making strategies, characteristics, 7
Psychology of mere-presentation effect, 145

R

Raab, M., 125–126, 131
Raghunathan, R., 180–181, 183–184
Rauch, S.L., 78
Read, S.J., 18, 312, 314
Reber
  A.S., 34, 76–77, 94, 125, 232, 235–236, 241
  P.J., 78
Reder, L.M., 267
Reeder, G.D., 161
Reflection
  intuition, contrasted, 256–258
  reflective-impulsive model, 47
Reflective-impulsive model, 39–54
  judgment/decision making variants, 39–54
    behavioral activation, 45
    conceptual activation, 44–45
    cue selection, 46
    deprivation, 47–48
    external cues, 43–44
    feelings, 45
    inputs into reflection, 42–46
    internal cues, 44–46
      heuristics, and intuition, 45–46
    judgmental paths, 41–42
    moderators of impulses, 46–48
    motivational orientation, 48
    reflection, 47
    schematic description, 40
    validity, 48
Research, 316–317
  intuition
    categories, 213
    neglect of, 3–22
    taxonomy, 212–214
  judgment/decision making, neglect of intuition, 3–22
Rettinger, D.A., 197
Richerson, P.J., 217
Richetin, J., 237
Right hemisphere, neuroimaging, 72
RIM. *See* Reflective-impulsive model, judgment/decision making variants
Ritov, I., 221
Rizzolatti, G., 45
Roles of intuition, 92–93
Rose, M., 79
Roseman, I.J., 175, 181, 184
Ross, L., 162
Rossetti, Y., 125
Roth, M., 45
Rothman, A.J., 45
Rottenstreich, Y., 286
Rozin, P., 180
Rugg, M.D., 74
Russell, J., 45, 174

S

Sample-size intuition, 149–170
  change, affecting, 157–158
  detection of change, 157–158
  environmental-learning, 158–166
    distance, 161–163
    dynamic change regulation, decision problems, 163–166
    lower response criterion, 160
    sample size, 159–163
      valence, distance, triadic relation, 164
    valence, 159–161, 163
  estimation, choice, distinguished, 156–157
  sample size, 151–152
  statistical model, assets of intuition, 152–158
  statistical model of intuition, evidence, 155–156
  two-person dilemma game, 158
Sampling theory, intuitive judgment application, 283–294
Sanfey, A.G., 60
Schacter, D.L., 74
Schendan, H.E., 78
Scherer, K.R., 175
Scheuer, E., 28
Schmidt, R.A., 40
Schneider, W., 40
Schnyer, D.M., 81–82
Schoenbaum, G., 83
Schönpflug, W., 121
Schooler, L.J., 99
Schultz, W., 79
Schunk, D., 233, 238, 240–242
Schwartz, S.H., 218
Schwarz, N., 45, 178, 180, 232, 257, 274, 284, 305
Scott, S.G., 149
Sedlmeier, P., 17, 94, 268, 271, 292
Seger, C., 76–77, 94
Self-theory, cognitive-experiential, 23–38
  attribute list, intuition, 24
  experiential processing
    intuition as subset, advantages, 34
    intuition attributes, 29–33
  systems of, 26
  theory of personality, 24–29
Seligman, M.E.P., 95–96, 219
Semin, G.R., 162
Shah, J.Y., 239

Shanks, D.R., 77
Shiffrin, R.M., 119
Shultz, T.R., 94
Shweder, R., 218
Siegler, R.S., 267
Simak, J., 287
Simon
  B., 163
  D., 7, 320
  H.A., 5, 8, 12, 18, 42, 59, 95, 138, 149, 196, 296, 301, 310
Simoncelli, E.P., 136
Simons, D.J., 137–138
Simonsohn, U., 67
Skosnik, P.D., 80
Skowronski, J.J., 164
Sloman, S.A., 39–40, 119, 122, 146, 232, 297
Slovic, P., 5, 97, 178, 232, 237, 305, 309, 312
Smeeton, N.J., 123
Smith
  A., 176
  C.A., 181
  E.R., 18, 40, 44, 46, 107
  J., 78
  M., 216
Social consensus, in moral intuition, 221–222
Society, moral diversity of, moral intuition, 225–226
Solomon, R.C., 174, 177
Spelke, E., 93
Sperber, D., 145, 219
Spontaneous, deliberative judgments/decisions, distinguished, 252–255
Sports, implicit learning in, 119–134
  intuitive
    deliberate processes
      decision protocol, 122
      in sports, 123–124
    deliberate processing, sports, 121–124
    learning styles, implicit, explicit, 124–127
      in decision protocol, 125–126
      in sports, 126–127
    protocol, 120–121
    synthesis, learning, processing styles, 127–130
Squire, L.R., 75
Staats, A.W., 108
Stadler, M.A., 77, 119
Stanovich, K.E., 56, 91, 135, 146, 256, 298
Statistical modeling, application to intuitive judgments, 56–58
Stewart, T.R., 58
Stimulus presentation, implicit attitude formation experiments, 14
Strack, F., 40, 47, 119

Strategy-application model, frequency estimation, 269–274
  information, encoding of, 270–272
  retrieval, 272–274
Sun, R., 125
Sunstein, C.R., 210–211, 220, 222–224, 226
Svenson, O., 268
Swets, J., 160
Systems of cognitive-experiential self-theory, 26

T

Tajfel, H., 225
Taxonomy, decision modes, 192–195
Taylor, S.E., 161, 164
Tetlock, P.E., 195
Thagard, P., 7, 312
Thaler, R.H., 196
Theory of personality, cognitive-experiential self-theory, 24–29
Thiel, C.M., 75, 80
Thomas, L., 98
Thorndyke, E.L., 124, 159
Tiedens, L.Z., 177
Todd, P.M., 310
Tooby, J., 219
Trope, Y., 164
Tucker, L.R., 58
Turner, R., 73
Tversky, A., 10–11, 16–17, 120, 136, 138, 140, 146, 260, 267–269, 273–275, 278
Two-person dilemma game, 158

U

Unconscious multiple intuitive judgment strategies, descriptive modeling, 55–70
Underwood, B.J., 270
Unkelbach, C., 6, 17, 30, 48, 100, 258, 287–292

V

Valence
  environmental-learning, 159–161, 163–164
  sample size, distance, environmental-learning, 164
Valence judgments, 13–15
  peak-and-end heuristic, 9
Validity, reflective-impulsive model, 48
Van Boven, L., 286
Vanman, E.J., 45
Vickers, J.N., 124
Visual cognition, 136–137
Volz, K.G., 79, 82

Von Neumann, J., 295, 310
Voting behavior, intuitive, 107–118

W

WADD. *See* Weighted additive strategies
Wallace, H.A., 58
Wallbott, H.G., 175
Walther, E., 240, 257
Wason, P.C., 222
Watkins, M.J., 270
Watson
 D., 162
 J.B., 95
Weber
 E.H., 271
 E.U., 191, 205
Weighted additive strategies, heuristics, intuition, 310–311, 314–318, 321–322
Wentura, D., 161
Werheid, K., 78
Westwater, H., 78
Whalen, J., 270–271
Wheatley, T., 222
Wiggins, D., 211, 216
Willingham, D.B., 78–79
Wilson
 D.S., 217
 T.D., 33, 46, 108, 112, 124, 223, 236, 240, 252, 256, 260, 298–299
Witt, K., 78
Wittgenstein, L., 288
Wojciszke, B., 161
Wundt, W., 5, 13
Wyer, R.S., 284

Y

Yanko, J., 25, 27
Yechiam, E., 145

Z

Zajonc, R.B., 5, 13, 96–97, 232, 237, 269, 276–277, 291, 305
Zakay, M.P., 319
Zeelenberg, M., 5, 149, 175–178, 180–181, 183–184, 194